About This Book

Why is this topic important?

Experts estimate that about 85 percent of Fortune 1,000 companies have a significant e-learning initiative under-way. On a similar note, ASTD and other professional organizations predict that e-learning will account for as much as 30 percent of training in the near future. This massive adoption and move to e-learning is not without grow-ing pains. The bulk of e-learning programs follow a predictable design. The challenge is to move beyond the novice strategies of linear page-turners, online workbooks, or drill-and-practice sessions. Training professionals need a portfolio of instructional strategies on which to draw to make e-learning more efficient and effective. This book is intended to help training professionals develop that portfolio.

What can you achieve with this book?

After reading this book, you should be able to do the following:

- Enhance the effectiveness of an existing e-learning program by applying one more of the ideas discussed in this book
- Plan new e-learning programs for asynchronous learning or the live virtual classroom that make use of blended and informal learning techniques, simulations, and m-learning
- Enhance the openings and closings of your e-learning programs, develop more effective and engaging interactivity, enhance the presentation of learning material, and design screens with more visual impact
- Explain your design choices by describing the logic underlying them

How is this book organized?

This book is broken into four parts, plus a conclusion. Part 1, Foundations, provides a framework for thinking about the design of e-learning, presenting the core philosophy underlying this book, a problem-based approach to design, and more in-depth background on its origins in learning philosophies and theories. Part 2, Portfolio of Design and Curriculum Strategies, explores design issues and issues that affect a series of related learning programs (a curricu-lum). Chapters in this part of the book address issues such as storytelling as a design technique, blended learning, and informal learning. Part 3, Portfolio of High-Level Design Strategies, explores some general approaches to de-signing learning programs and covers topics such as simulations, e-mentoring and e-coaching, m-learning, and live virtual classrooms. Part 4, Portfolio of Detailed Design Strategies, examines challenges in designing specific parts of e-learning programs and covers topics such as introductions and closings, exposition techniques, interaction, and visual communication techniques. The last part of this book, Closing, ties up some loose ends by suggesting unusual sources of design ideas for e-learning programs and how designers can keep up with trends that often seem to emerge at the speed of sound.

About Pfeiffer

Pfeiffer serves the professional development and hands-on resource needs of training and human resource practitioners and gives them products to do their jobs better. We deliver proven ideas and solutions from experts in HR development and HR management, and we offer effective and customizable tools to improve workplace performance. From novice to seasoned professional, Pfeiffer is the source you can trust to make yourself and your organization more successful.

Essential Knowledge Pfeiffer produces insightful, practical, and comprehensive materials on topics that matter the most to training and HR professionals. Our Essential Knowledge resources translate the expertise of seasoned professionals into practical, how-to guidance on critical workplace issues and problems. These resources are supported by case studies, worksheets, and job aids and are frequently supplemented with CD-ROMs, websites, and other means of making the content easier to read, understand, and use.

Essential Tools Pfeiffer's Essential Tools resources save time and expense by offering proven, ready-to-use materials—including exercises, activities, games, instruments, and assessments—for use during a training or team-learning event. These resources are frequently offered in looseleaf or CD-ROM format to facilitate copying and customization of the material.

Pfeiffer also recognizes the remarkable power of new technologies in expanding the reach and effectiveness of training. While e-hype has often created whizbang solutions in search of a problem, we are dedicated to bringing convenience and enhancements to proven training solutions. All our e-tools comply with rigorous functionality standards. The most appropriate technology wrapped around essential content yields the perfect solution for today's on-the-go trainers and human resource professionals.

Pfeiffer
www.pfeiffer.com

Essential resources for training and HR professionals

Advanced Web-Based Training Strategies

MARGARET DRISCOLL
SAUL CARLINER

ADVANCED
Web-
BASED TRAINING STRATEGIES

Unlocking Instructionally
Sound Online Learning

Pfeiffer
A Wiley Imprint
www.pfeiffer.com

Published by Pfeiffer
An Imprint of Wiley
989 Market Street, San Francisco, CA 94103-1741
www.pfeiffer.com

For additional copies/bulk purchases of this book in the U.S. please contact 800-274-4434.

Pfeiffer books and products are available through most bookstores. To contact Pfeiffer directly call our
Customer Care Department within the U.S. at 800-274-4434 or outside the U.S. at 317-572-3985;
fax to 317-572-4002; or visit www.pfeiffer.com.

Pfeiffer also publishes its books in a variety of electronic formats. Some content that appears in print may
not be available in electronic books.

Readers should be aware that Internet websites offered as citations and/or sources for further information
may have changed or disappeared between the time this was written and when it is read.

Figure 9.3 is copyright © 2004 IBM Corporation. Used with perimission of IBM Corporation. IBM and Lotus
are trademarks of the IBM Corporation, in the United States, and other countries, or both.

ISBN: 0-7879-6979-6

Library of Congress Cataloging-in-Publication Data
 Driscoll, Margaret, date
 Advanced web-based training strategies : Unlocking instructionally sound online learning / Margaret
Driscoll and Saul Carliner.
     p. cm.
 Includes bibliographical references and index.
 ISBN 0-7879-6979-6 (alk. paper)
 1. Employees—Training of—Computer-assisted instruction. 2. Instructional systems—Design.
3. Employees—Training of—Computer network resources. 4. Distance education—Computer-assisted
instruction. 5. Web-based instruction. 6. Educational technology. I. Carliner, Saul. II.
Title.
 HF5549.5.T7D73 2005
 658.3'124'02854678—dc22

                                                                              2004025825

Acquiring Editor: Matt Davis   Editor: Rebecca Taff
Director of Development: Kathleen Dolan Davies   Manufacturing Supervisor: Becky Carreno
Developmental Editor: Susan Rachmeler   Editorial Assistant: Laura Reizman
Production Editor: Nina Kreiden   Illustrations: Lotus Art

Printed in the United States of America
Printing 10 9 8 7 6 5 4 3 2 1

Contents

Figures and Tables

Figures

Tables

Acknowledgments

Like any book, this one represents a collaboration among many people. First, we would like to thank Kathleen Dolan Davies, the director of development at Pfeiffer, for her openness to the idea of this project and patience with us as we developed it; Matt Davis, our acquisitions editor, who shares our strong belief that this book is needed; Susan Rachmeler, our most patient development editor, for her constructive feedback on our book and for helping to blend two different writing styles into one; David Horne, our speedy, "can do" production editor; and the reviewers who provided us with useful feedback on draft versions of this material.

We would like to thank Patrick Devey, who provided substantial assistance with the "In Practice" sections, as well as the following instructional designers who generously shared their time and examples with us:

- Rod Ammon
- Carter Andrews
- Mark T. Brookshire
- Spencer Clements
- Wendy Colby
- Janice Cooper
- Dominick Egan
- Bethene Gregg
- Mitch Grossberg
- Shakeel Hirji
- Jennifer Hofmann
- Kit Horton
- William Horton
- Melinda Jackson
- Melinda James
- Donna Kalka
- Paul Kellermann
- Tao Le
- Patrick LeGranche,
- Neil Lieberman
- James McGuire
- Carol B. Muller
- Nancy Napolilli
- Jeanette Murry
- Lisa Neal
- Bob Panoff
- Tony Pettit
- Ken Reed
- Howard A. Schwid
- Ellen Slaby
- Colin Smith
- Gary Sova
- Mark Starcevich
- Janet Stevens
- M.D. Roblyer
- Russell S. Thomas
- Johanna Westbrook
- Andy Yip

Next, we would like to thank our various friends and colleagues who were pestered to provide feedback on ideas, including Clark Aldrich, Gregory Brower, Patrick Lambe, David Posner, and Patti Shank.

Last, we would like to thank our families for their support during the time we developed this book.

Introduction

Getting the Most from This Resource

I know that 'page turners' don't produce much learning, but I don't know what else I can do with my e-learning program.

I know I have to grab learners' attention at the beginning of an e-learning course, but I'm stumped for compelling ways to do it.

I have to write a quiz and have no idea what to do.

Many course designers and developers feel that they're not realizing the full potential of e-learning, but don't know how to take their work to the next level. Some tell us that they're stuck in their office and don't have a chance to see some of the great e-learning out there. Other great e-learning is proprietary and not shown to the larger community of course designers and developers. Still others simply don't have time to hunt down good examples and learn what's great about them.

This book is for designers like you. This is a design book that's intended to help you develop your instincts. Part Ebert and Roper, part Martha Stewart (before the conviction), all knowledgeably developed, we act as a critical screen for you and provide you with the most current ideas and practical considerations for implementing them.

We pick up where the primers on instructional design for e-learning leave off. We assume that you are already experienced with instructional systems design, so we don't provide a cookbook-like approach and tell you exactly how to handle every situation. Besides, no one could possibly anticipate every situation that arises.

Rather, we assume that you are dealing with specific challenges that are unique to your organization and that no cookbook could anticipate. So we provide you with an approach to thinking that should stimulate your creative juices and build your confidence in addressing whatever challenges your work presents to you.

In the process, we try to build your portfolio (repertoire) of techniques for teaching online. As graphic designers keep their work in portfolios, and as financial managers manage portfolios of stocks, we instructional designers manage portfolios of instructional techniques, portfolios with examples of effective instruction (and a few klunkers, too), and portfolios of our own work. Some educators call this a *repertoire* of techniques or "bag of tricks" (Joyce & Weil, 1986), adding that an instructional designer is only as good as the resources in this bag.

Through this book, we hope to build your personal portfolios of instructional techniques and great examples to call on when designing e-learning. We do that by providing you with a framework for organizing the key concepts of e-learning into one of these areas: foundations (ways of thinking about—or approaching—e-learning projects), design and curriculum (design issues that affect a series of related learning programs), high-level design issues (issues that affect an entire e-learning program), and detailed design issues (issues that affect an individual screen or a particular section of a course). We also provide you with two types of portfolios that you can consult as you approach your work: a portfolio of *techniques* you can use and a portfolio of *examples* that you can consult, which illustrate the effective implementation of each concept presented. The techniques and examples in the portfolios represent a broad spectrum of practice—including a broad spectrum of schedules, production budgets, industries, learners, and instructional goals.

Specifically, we explore foundational issues like the limitations of the hype regarding e-learning and e-learning design and different approaches to learning and their place in the design of e-learning programs. We also explore design and curriculum issues such as using storytelling as a design technique and the use of blended and informal learning. We explore high-level design issues like the use of m-learning, e-coaching and mentoring, and live virtual classrooms. In addition, we explore detailed design issues, such as effective ways of opening and closing courses and units; how to "expose" specific types of content, such as definitions, procedures, and examples; how to effectively use interactivity; the instructional use of simulations; and how to present content visually.

For each type of challenge addressed, we do the following:

- Define the challenge in its broadest context, which might differ from common assumptions (for example, we see storytelling as both a design and presentation technique, while most designers only think of it as a presentation technique).

- Provide a background on the challenge from a number of different perspectives: its role in instructional design, the benefits and limitations associated with the issue, and a portfolio of techniques for applying the technique in practice. These discussions are based in research and theory on learning, tempered by the realities of practice.

- Provide several examples taken from real practice, including one in-depth example and several shorter examples. Whenever possible, we provide the name of the organization that sponsored the e-course, but in some cases, organizations are sharing their proprietary courses so that we can share the ideas with you.
- Prepare you to continue your journey in learning about e-learning. At the end of each chapter, we do the following:
  - Give you an opportunity to apply the concepts presented through Reflection and Application exercises.
  - Point you to recommended readings by providing a manageable-sized list of references and explanation of why they're useful to you (not a dump of every site we ever saw).

At the end of the book, we provide appendices with some broader resources, including information about professional organizations of possible interest to you and a list of recommended "best sites" from leading experts in e-learning.

Who Should Read This Book

- Experienced e-learning designers and developers who have developed at least two e-courses and already are familiar with the instructional systems design process for e-learning. (If you have not mastered that content yet, we recommend that you read either Bill Horton's *Designing Web-Based Training: How To Teach Anyone Anything Anywhere Anytime* or one of our books, *Web-Based Training: Using Technology to Design Adult Learning Experiences* by Margaret Driscoll and *Designing e-Learning* by Saul Carliner.
- Experienced curriculum planners who are looking to expand the use of e-learning in their organizations, and who are also familiar with the instructional systems design process for e-learning.
- University students who are taking advanced courses in e-learning design, web design, multimedia development, instructional design, or technical communication.

How This Book Is Organized

This book has five parts, each exploring the design of e-learning programs from a different vantage point. Among the five parts are fourteen chapters, each of which builds your portfolio of e-learning design techniques in a specific area. Figure 0.1 illustrates the overall organization of the book. A more detailed explanation follows.

Figure 0.1. How This Book Is Organized

Foundations	Design and Curriculum Strategies	High-Level Design Strategies	Detailed Design Strategies	Closing	Appendixes
Chapter 1 Using a Problem-Based Approach	**Chapter 3** Storytelling and Contextually Based Approaches	**Chapter 6** Simulations	**Chapter 10** Introductions and Closings	**Chapter 14** Seeking Ideas Outside the Norm	**A** Rubric for Assessing Interaction
Chapter 2 Philosophies and Theories	**Chapter 4** Blended Learning	**Chapter 7** e-Mentoring and e-Coaching	**Chapter 11** Exposition Techniques		**B** Websites
	Chapter 5 Informal Learning	**Chapter 8** m-Learning	**Chapter 12** Interaction		**C** Professional Organizations
		Chapter 9 Live Virtual Classroom	**Chapter 13** Visual Communication Techniques		

Part 1, Foundations, provides a framework of thinking about the design of e-learning. Specifically, the chapters in this section explore the following.

Chapter 1, Using a Problem-Based Approach to Designing e-Learning, explains our approach to design. We see each instructional design assignment as a unique problem to be solved. We explain that previous experience and research can inform choices for addressing the unique problem, but no cookbook-like approach can provide guaranteed success. As a result, we conclude that designers must take a problem-solving approach, which is characterized by critical thinking about, and creative solutions to, instructional design.

Chapter 2, Philosophies and Theories Guiding the Design of e-Learning, continues the discussion of critical thinking about the design of e-learning by providing a background on key theories and beliefs guiding instruction—including theories and beliefs that are contradictory, but guide learning anyway. Specifically, it explores the issues and controversies of why society educates people and how people learn. We discuss the incompleteness of this body of literature and how it ultimately requires that instructional designers clarify their own values and beliefs around these issues—because these values and beliefs are ultimately embedded in the instructional strategies and techniques we use in our work. In other words, using a game-like approach means much more than creating an interactive game; it represents a belief system about the way people learn. In clarifying your values and beliefs, you may find that game-based instruction is incompatible with your values and beliefs around learning.

Part 2, Portfolio of Design and Curriculum Strategies, explores design issues and issues that affect a series of related learning programs (a curriculum). The chapters in this section address new approaches to the design process and design strategies for linking individual e-learning programs together. Specifically, the chapters in this section explore the following.

Chapter 3, Storytelling and Contextually Based Approaches to Needs Assessment, Design, and Formative Evaluation, presents a powerful technique to use in these activities. Instructors traditionally incorporate stories into their classroom and e-courses, but few realize that storytelling is a powerful tool for getting information needed to effectively analyze an instructional problem and to state design requirements in a way that an entire design team can effectively relate to and address in design so that the resulting e-learning program is both relevant to, and usable by, the intended users. Note that this chapter does not discuss how to use storytelling as a teaching technique. Several other sources address this issue competently; we do not feel that we can add anything meaningful to that discussion.

Chapter 4, Blended Learning as a Curriculum Design Strategy, explores ways to mix e-learning, classroom learning, and other learning strategies into a unified whole. This chapter approaches blended learning as a curriculum design strategy, rather than a course design strategy. Using this approach, this chapter explores a general, performance-based curriculum design strategy that takes learners from no knowledge about a topic up through expertise and provides a framework for choosing the appropriate medium (such as e-learning or classroom learning) in which to present different parts of the curriculum.

Chapter 5, Informal Learning, explores how to develop performance among learners using materials other than tutorials and e-courses. This chapter introduces the concept of informal learning and explains how it complements and supplements formal courses. Then it provides a number of strategies for designing informal learning materials and identifies a number of different types of informal learning materials that you can develop.

Part 3, Portfolio of High-Level Design Strategies, explores general approaches to designing a specific learning program. The chapters in this section focus on technologies that can be used in e-learning as well as general approaches to designing individual learning programs. Specifically, the chapters in this section explore the following.

Chapter 6, Simulations, explores nine strategies for integrating simulations into e-learning programs. This chapter presents a variety of types of simulations, including attitudinal simulations, case studies, games, symbolic (invisible) simulations, physical simulations, role plays, procedural simulations, software simulation, and virtual reality. Through a portfolio of examples, this chapter makes you aware of the range of types of learning objectives that can be addressed by simulations, development issues (such as cost) that affect the design of simulations, and the levels of engagement possible in simulations.

Chapter 7, e-Mentoring and e-Coaching, differentiates between mentoring and coaching, explores how to provide personal attention to learners despite the distance that the computer creates in the learning process, and how to use the computer to extend these strategies to an e-learning environment.

Chapter 8, m-Learning, explores a nascent technology for teaching online. First, this chapter differentiates among the three uses of mobile learning: as a desktop replacement, as performance support, and for collaborative learning in context. Then it explores ancillary learning tools in m-learning that support classroom activities, such as student response units and record-keeping devices.

Chapter 9, Live Virtual Classroom, provides a portfolio of approaches for teaching synchronously online (when learners and instructors are both online at the same time). This is called the *live virtual classroom* and is an increasingly popular approach to e-learning as companies and employees alike try to curb training-related travel. Specifically, this chapter helps instructional designers move beyond the all too common strategy of preparing an online lecture with PowerPoint slides by presenting a range of strategies for encouraging interactions and group learning.

Part 4, Portfolio of Detailed Design Strategies, examines challenges in designing specific parts of e-learning programs. Some of these challenges center on the presentation of content, like introductions and closings. Other challenges center on engaging learners, like designing for interactivity. Specifically, the chapters in this section explore the following.

Chapter 10, Introductions and Closings, considers ways to open and close e-learning programs and units. It explores the several purposes of openings and suggests ways to address each. It also explores the several purposes of closings and offers suggestions on how to handle those sections, too.

Chapter 11, Exposition Techniques for Writing e-Learning Content, considers exposition, a term from the field of composition theory that refers to the way that authors "expose" or write specific content. Relying on research from instructional technology and the related fields of educational psychology and technical communication, this chapter specifically explores the educational and business value of the traditional lecture. Although our positive opinion of lectures probably seems out of step, the empirical evidence is clear—the lecture has a valuable role to play in learning. This chapter also presents ways to engagingly adapt the traditional lecture for both virtual classrooms and asynchronous e-learning to effectively present specific types of declarative content, including definitions, procedures, and explanations.

Chapter 12, Interaction, examines the holy grail of e-learning—how to engage learners. Although clients and designers alike advocate for interactivity in e-learning programs, few offer practical suggestions on how to engage learners and do so "on-topic." This chapter does so. It provides two schemes for approaching interactions. First is Moore's model of interaction, which draws distinctions among three types of interaction: learner-content interaction, learner-instructor interaction, and learner-learner interaction. The second scheme is Jonassen's, which suggests that learners use computers three ways: learning *though* computers, learning *from* computers, and learning *with* computers.

Chapter 13, Visual Communication Techniques, considers ways to enhance the impact of e-learning programs by presenting content visually rather than verbally. That 83 percent of all learning occurs visually (Stolovitch, 2004) challenges instructional designers to present content visually. Furthermore, because the computer screen uses the same technology as television, the computer—like television—communicates most effectively through visuals. The chapter first explains the educational and cognitive value of visuals, then presents strategies for presenting specific types of content visually rather than with text. It closes with some technical considerations for presenting visuals.

Part V, Closing, ends the book with one chapter:

Chapter 14, Seeking Ideas Outside the Norm, ties up some loose ends by suggesting unusual sources of design ideas for e-learning programs and how designers can keep up with trends that often seem to emerge faster than the speed of sound.

Several appendices supplement the text. Some provide additional background; others prepare you to continue your journey in learning about e-learning. These appendices include

- Appendix A, Rubric for Assessing Interactive Qualities of Distance Learning Courses, provides a tool you can use to assess the interactivity of your own courses.

- Appendix B, Websites for Training Professionals, which provides an annotated list of the top sites about e-learning, a list culled from an informal survey we conducted of thought leaders in the field.

- Appendix C, Professional Organizations, which presents a list of professional organizations that you can consult to share information about e-learning with like-minded people.

Website

In addition to this book, we have prepared a website with related materials intended to extend this learning experience. The website contains bonus chapters, additional examples, resources, and other useful material that did not fit into the book. The *Advanced Web-Based Training Strategies* website can be found at www.advancedwbt.com.

Part I

Foundations

Design is more than a process; that process, and the resulting product, represent a framework of thinking. Before we address specific issues in the design of e-learning programs, we start this book by taking a look at the frameworks of thinking about learning that guide the development of effective e-learning programs. Specifically, the chapters in this section explore the following issues.

Chapter 1, Using a Problem-Based Approach to Designing e-Learning, explains our approach to design. We see each instructional design assignment as a unique problem to be solved. Therefore, each solution is unique. We explain that previous experience and research can inform the choices for addressing a unique problem but no cookbook-like approach can promise guaranteed success because no two instructional challenges are identical. As a result, we conclude that designers must take a problem-solving approach, which is characterized by critical thinking about, and creative solutions to, instructional design problems.

Chapter 2, Philosophies and Theories Guiding the Design of e-Learning, continues the discussion of critical thinking about the design of e-learning by providing a background on key theories and beliefs guiding instruction, including theories and beliefs that are contradictory, but guide learning anyway. Specifically, in this chapter we explore the issues and controversies of why society and organizations educate people and how people learn. We discuss the incompleteness of this body of literature and how that ultimately requires instructional designers to clarify their own values and beliefs around these issues because these values and beliefs are ultimately embedded in the instructional strategies and techniques chosen. In other words, using a case-study approach means much more than presenting a case; it represents a belief system about the way people learn. In clarifying your values and beliefs, you may find that case-based instruction is incompatible and, as a result, may choose a different strategy. But you can only do so after considering the range of value and belief systems surrounding learning.

Chapter 1

Using a Problem-Based Approach to Designing e-Learning

Some argue that a science of design is possible and represents an important goal. Cross, reporting on a number of studies in design, argues that design is quite different from science. While scientists focus on the problem, on discovering the rule that is operating, designers focus on the solution, on achieving the desired result.

Rowland, 1993, p. 81

In This Chapter

This chapter introduces our general approach to design, a problem-based approach. In doing so, this chapter explores some of the myths surrounding e-learning and the role and nature of design in the process of addressing real-world challenges with e-learning. Specifically, this chapter considers the following questions:

- Why won't simple solutions solve fundamental design problems with e-courses and e-curricula?

- What is the *design* of e-learning?

- What is the problem-solving approach to design described in this book?

◆ ◆ ◆

In early 2001, the executives at a large corporation decided to move its highly regarded management training online. Even though the training department had no experience with e-learning, executives hoped to duplicate the success that the corporation found in the classroom online, while significantly slashing training delivery costs.

Without a choice, the training department took up the challenge of transferring the curriculum. Adopting the concept of *blended learning,* in which different courses in a curriculum are delivered by different media (thus *blending* the delivery method), instructional designers moved some of the material into self-paced web-based training units (called *asynchronous learning,* because the instructor and learner are separated by both time and geography) and the rest into a *live virtual classroom* (a classroom session conducted online, with an audio connection, PowerPoint® slides, and the ability to interact with the instructor, called *synchronous learning* because learners and the instructor are both online at the same time).

Because the management training curriculum had been taught extensively for years, the instructional designers knew that they had effective content that was properly tailored to the needs of the intended learners. So the designers focused their efforts on converting the materials. Content that required interaction with an instructor was placed in the live virtual classroom. Content that stood alone was placed in a web-based training format. Once designers determined that material would be presented online, designers followed procedures for converting the material that had been suggested in basic books on designing e-learning. In total, course designers converted five days of classroom training.

Because they felt that the content was well-tested, the designers did not conduct early pilot tests with prospective learners of the first units of the program that they finished developing to make sure that their approach would be successful. They conducted the pilot test only after the entire course had been converted. Unfortunately, the course received mixed reviews from participants in that pilot. Management looked at the comments, specifically focusing on the issue that the logistics of the blended course were confusing to learners and administrators. Concerned that the blended curriculum would fail, management terminated the project rather than see it through to completion.

This conversion is like so many early efforts by organizations to move content online: full of high hopes, only to be dashed by the realities of production and implementation. In fact, studies suggest that 62 percent of learning technology initiatives fail to meet expectations (Van Buren & Sloman, 2003). In this case, like so many others, management entered the project with a realistic business goal—reducing training expenses. Course designers entered the project with extensive experience with the content and the design process. Learners entered the course with every interest in learning. But the course failed because of a simple fact: designing e-learning is different than designing classroom and workbook-based learning.

Although helpful, previous experience with the design process itself does not guarantee that the designers reach a successful end. That requires consideration of a number of issues that apparently were not addressed by the sources consulted by the designers of this failed online curriculum.

e-Learning is easy to get started with, but succeeding is another story. And the statistics bear this out. Adoption rates for e-learning are much slower than originally forecast. For example, although one prediction made in the year 2000 suggested that 53 percent of all corporate learning would be online by 2003, actual adoption rates suggest that, by 2005, e-learning represents at most 30 percent of all corporate learning (Sugrue, 2004). Although some proponents of e-learning have claimed that it offers a superior learning experience, satisfaction levels are disappointing. In a survey conducted by DDI in 2002 (reported by Van Buren & Sloman, 2003), corporations in several countries were asked to rate the effectiveness of e-learning in their organizations. On a scale of 1 to 10 (with 10 being high), the average rating of effectiveness was 3.9. And a number of people just think most e-courses don't work. For example, one major food manufacturer had to customize 75 percent of the off-the-shelf e-courses it purchased because the content didn't work with its staff. So much for the plug-and-play value of e-learning (Van Buren & Sloman, 2003).

Lest you believe that the case for e-learning is hopeless because e-learning has not been adopted at predicted rates and is not generating exceptional levels of satisfaction, consider these other signs. For the past five years, training directors have repeatedly reported that e-learning is at least moderately successful in meeting their needs (Carliner, Groshens, Chapman, & Gery, 2004). Barron (2002) reports that e-learning has shown success in contexts such as certification and training on information technology.

In other words, e-learning is a relatively new approach to instruction, and instructional designers are just starting to find ways to make it work in their organizations. Although it has not achieved the hype predicted for it during the e-learning-is-the-next-killer-app years of the late 1990s and early 2000s, it is also not a dismal failure. It is, like most instructional design challenges, a complex challenge that involves identifying and addressing a variety of issues. e-Learning succeeds when designers understand the educational, economic, and technical challenges they face and the ways to best use the computer to address these challenges.

Why the Simple Solutions Won't Solve Fundamental Design Problems with e-Curricula and e-Courses

Addressing this complexity requires an equally complex approach to design. In fact, the more complexity that designers encounter, the larger and more varied the number of solutions they bring to a situation. This body of solutions is called a *portfolio* of techniques and represents a "bag of tricks" that instructional designers can call on when faced with an e-learning problem.

The Solutions to Effective Teaching Online

Unfortunately, that's not the message that the industry press offers us. In an economy and industry that emphasizes "next big thing," "experts" offer easy and all-encompassing solutions to complex problems of learning and instructional design. These solutions have served as one of the biggest impediments to instructional designers developing a rich portfolio for designing e-learning. Before we can explore the development of such a portfolio, we have to consider the easy and all-encompassing design solutions for e-learning that have been offered and why they are neither easy nor all-encompassing.

For starters, consider these claims:

- e-learning is more effective than classroom learning.

- Games are the only way to teach online because the today's youngsters seem to be excited by games (Prensky, 2002).

- Simulations are the best way to teach online and all learning should be interactive and engaging (Aldrich, 2003).

- Enterprise learning is the answer because it's much cheaper and more efficient to manage all learning from a central source (Gold, 2003).

- e-Learning must be personalized because different people have different learning styles and computers can tailor the learning experience to individual needs.

- Learning comes in mix-and-match pieces that can be recombined at the moment of need to create a course that addresses a learner's unique content needs (Longmire, 2004).

- Finally, some people believe that we just haven't measured enough to prove that e-learning is effective.

The Problems with the Solutions

But think about this practically. Are the strategies that make a great algebra class the same ones that make a great physical education class? Civics? Cooking? Private investigator licensing? These subjects share nothing in common, so why should they be forced to share a pedagogy in common?

Perhaps, then, e-learning is not a noun to describe the learning experience, but an adjective that merely identifies the medium of instruction. The nouns are "mathematics," "manufacturing training," "new hire orientation," and "rocks for jocks" (that is, geology for nonscientists). The courses each have unique material, unique sets of learners, unique development and implementation budgets, and unique development schedules and are offered by different types of learning institutions—some offering courses for academic credit, some offering them to maintain an existing job, some just for fun.

For designers to take their e-learning to the next level, they have to move past these "I've got the universal solution" approaches because they simply aren't universal. Consider the responses to each of the universal solutions presented in the previous section:

- The effectiveness of e-learning compared to the classroom: The research suggests that e-learning is merely *as effective* as classroom-based learning—no more, no less. These comparison studies also assume that the material in both formats has been professionally designed (Russell, ongoing).

- The limitations of game-based learning: Although youngsters do enjoy their computer games, most of them recognize that learning and computer games are not the same activity and have different expectations for the two.

- The limitations of simulation learning: Simulations are useful for teaching many types of content (Sugrue, 2004), but not all content. For example, one need not simulate the experience of swimming. It can be taught by letting learners actually swim (an off-line experience).

- The limitations of enterprise learning: Although enterprise-wide learning is a great strategy, there are few courses that both the receptionist and the CEO need to be enrolled in. Furthermore, because many organizations like to empower their operating units, resulting differences in operations may result in differences in training that render enterprise training inappropriate.

- The limitations of learning styles: Although learning styles are a popular theory, few studies show that learning styles really contribute to actual learning achievement (Sugrue, 2004). So addressing them in the design of courses is a time-consuming effort that pays few dividends. Even if learning styles were proven to be effective, the difference between effectively presenting content for verbal and visual learning styles involves more than presenting visuals first or second, which is the dominant approach to such design. Rather, developing courses to reach different styles requires that the courses be re-developed completely for each learning style. A course for visual learners would rely almost exclusively on pictures and other visuals, while a course for verbal learners would rely almost exclusively on text.

- The limitations of reusable learning content: Although some learning materials can indeed be reused, the use of reusable learning content—called *reusable learning objects*—in most corporate environments—especially those in organizations with fewer than 50,000 workers—has not worked. As one director of a major consulting firm that decided to implement learning objects admitted, "It was a disaster." Even in private, most learning objects experts admit that much of the concept does not yet work in practice, saying that efforts to design learning objects focus more on standards for using them with particular types of software than the instructors who will actually need to use them.

- The need for more measurement: Although some people claim that e-learning produces a high return on investment, empirical studies conclude that e-learning has failed to generate the productivity gains it has promised. In fact, one of the fundamental justifications for computerizing learning has been the promise of increased productivity of educators. Computers have led to such productivity gains in other fields. For example, by letting customers order products online, companies have achieved significant reductions in inventory costs and improvements in delivery times. e-Learning has not delivered such benefits. For example, some proprietary studies say that the only savings that have been realized from e-learning have been travel-related. In addition, many instructors who teach online courses find that they take more work than their classroom equivalents (National Education Association, 2000).

In other words, rather than looking for a single silver bullet to effective e-learning, instructional designers might look inward—at the specific performance problem or content to be presented—for suggestions on ways to effectively teach online.

The Right Way?

When looking at these specific design challenges, another approach that's prevalent within the world of instructional design is to look for the "right way" to do things. The "right way" often refers to research-based solutions to challenges. When addressing problems like these, designers consider what might be more effective: teaching a lower-level psychomotor skill with visuals alone or teaching one with visuals and sound.

The answers make a number of assumptions:

- That indeed a researcher has conducted research on this specific problem. Despite the claims of many authors and speakers (for instance, Wallace [2004] claims that training and the related field of human performance technology are "research-based disciplines"), in many instances, there is no research.

- In those situations for which research has been performed, the research also needs to be relevant to the case at hand. In some cases, the research was performed with a group of learners who share nothing in common with yours. For example, most of the science of multimedia is based on research with U.S.-based college students. Most of these students are in their late teens and early twenties and have not held full-time professional employment (Clark & Mayer, 2002). Most trainers work in environments that employ people who are considerably older and who have held professional employment for an extended period of time. Both the physical capabilities and learning strategies employed by the research group and the group of actual learners substantially differ. In the research groups mentioned earlier, most of the participants speak and write English as their first language, but much training goes to people who use English as a second or third language. A substantial body of research suggests that second-language learners have different strategies than first-language learners.

- In addition to differences among learners, many of these studies controlled the learning situation so extensively that the content under study substantially differs in reality from the problem about which the designer has an interest. For example, some studies suggest that off-topic learning games distract interest. But the studies only looked at brief learning segments (less than 4 minutes). In most actual learning programs, these activities often exceed 15 or 30 minutes. Therefore, the studies may not provide complete insights into the situation (Thalheimer, 2004).

- But perhaps the most significant omission of this "scientific" research is that hardly any of it states the practical considerations facing the designers of the learning experiences. Most corporate instructional designers have limited budgets with which to develop their courses, but few studies state either the budgets or development schedules used to create the courses that were covered in the study. Most academic instructors have even less design and development time than their corporate counterparts. For example, university instructors are advised to allot just one hour of preparation for each hour of classroom instruction. Admittedly, this metric assumes that the instructor is already conversant in the subject matter. Instructors are supposed to spend their time, instead, on their academic research. So although a learning strategy suggested by the research might seem appropriate to a given situation, the designer might not have the actual resources to implement it and thus must choose a different alternative. In many instances, the alternative seems less than optimal at the time the decision was made but, in the end, may prove just as effective educationally as the original strategy.

Similarly, many instructional designers turn to e-learning not because it is the best choice for a given situation, but because it is a requirement of the assignment. So e-learning will be chosen regardless of its likely effectiveness. The instructional designer doesn't choose the medium in an instance like this; the instructional designer chooses strategies that make the medium work to its best advantage.

The *Design* of e-Learning

On the one hand, we've probably offended a lot of people by now by sacrificing their sacred cow. But the truth is, if these solutions were so effective, they would be working now and e-learning would be in a different state than it is.

But we think that the problem with e-learning ultimately arises from the definition of design.

Most books on designing e-learning define what learning means to the author. But the authors aren't really writing about learning. They're writing about the design process, and few explain their beliefs about design. Those beliefs about design guide the discussion of designing e-learning. So we believe that, to understand the approach in this book, we must explain how we view design.

What Is Design?

We see design as:

> A disciplined inquiry engaged in for the purpose of creating some new thing of practical utility. It involves exploring an ill-defined situation, finding as well as solving a problem(s), and specifying ways to effect change. Design is carried out in numerous fields and will vary depending on the designer and on the type of thing that is designed. Designing requires a balance of reason and intuition, an impetus to act, and an ability to reflect on actions taken [Rowland, 1993, p. 80].

In other words, we see design as a problem-solving discipline. Problem solving implies two things: first, that an effort must be made to define the problem and, second, that the solution is intended to address the problem identified. The more thoroughly the problem is identified, the more likely that the solution will address it.

What Are the Basic Beliefs About Design?

Underlying this definition are the following beliefs:

- No two problems are the same. That is, each time someone designs a course, he or she faces a unique set of circumstances. Admittedly, sometimes many characteristics will be the same (similar learners, similar organizations). But, if nothing else, the point in time at which the training is designed is always different.

- One of the key purposes of defining the problem is identifying the constraints underlying the situation. Many of these constraints limit the solutions designers can consider. Although some courses are presented online because that seems to make the most sense for the particular learning material, many more courses are presented online because a sponsor or some other stakeholder required it. Designers did not consider classroom learning because it was not an available option.

- Rarely does a single, perfect solution exist to a given problem. Rather, several possible solutions exist, and one of the jobs of the designer is making a tradeoff among educational, economic, and technical issues to devise a solution that is likely to address the learning objectives and the needs of the sponsors and the learners, within the schedule, budget, and technology constraints imposed on the project.

The Limitations of a Scientific Approach to Design

Reaching a solution is part science, part instinct, part art. In studies of designers, most exhibit a strong idealism (Carliner, 1995). They want their courses (or whatever they're designing) to have a positive impact on the people who use them. They want their work to be the most effective that it can be.

But many designers are also realists, and the best enter design projects with a strong awareness of practical limitations. This is where instinct comes in; a good designer has an instinct for what will work in a given situation and what can be done with a given schedule, budget, and technology infrastructure. That instinct is honed with experience. The stronger the base of experience, the more situations that the designer can draw on for inspiration (Christensen & Osguthorpe, 2004). That's why new designers rely so strongly on research. Because they lack experience, research allows them to substitute the experience of others to help guide their instincts (Christensen & Osguthorpe, 2004; Clark, 2003).

When using studies that are performed with similar students and in similar situations, the studies can provide a greater sense of comfort that a given solution (or partial solution) is likely to be effective. What new designers have to realize, however, is that the more different the situation that they face is from the one described in the research study, the less they can rely on that study to predict the likelihood of their own success. Experimental studies, which are the ones most often cited to suggest the effectiveness of certain approaches, are intended to demonstrate a predictable relationship. But the situation cannot be predicted with the same level of confidence if the characteristics that are key to those relationships differ.

Advocates of the scientific approach also note that following the instructional systems design process results in more effective instruction (Clark & Mayer, 2002). Unfortunately, little evidence supports that claim. Although scores of instructional design models exist, only one has been actually been tested in practice, according to Gustafson and Branch (2002), who have tracked and documented all of the instructional design models for the past several decades.

Rather than *de*scribe actual instructional design practice as observed in organizations, these models *pre*scribe how instructional designers should approach the design task. The steps listed in these formal processes say more about the things that instructional designers value about instructional design than they do about the tasks that instructional designers actually perform. For example, a typical instructional design process like Dick, Carey, and Carey's (2000) has five steps for needs assessment and related activities and only one step each for instructional design and development. This would suggest that the bulk of instructional designers' time is spent on assessment. Empirical evidence suggests otherwise. Surveys of instructional design practice conducted through the years suggest that few instructional designers perform more than a cursory needs assessment (Guerra, 2003; Wedman & Tessmer, 1993; Zemke & Lee, 1987, to name a few). Research also suggests that only a limited amount of evaluation actually occurs (Van Buren & Erskine, 2002, reported in Arthur, Bennett, Edens, & Bell, 2003). Instead, the bulk of instructional designers' efforts are spent on instructional design and development. Perhaps the reason that most models describe needs assessment in such detail is that they represent the process as their authors would like for it to be performed. Many of the same studies also suggest that instructional designers believe that they should be spending more time on needs assessment.

In other words, the scientific approach suggests that instructional design is a methodological process that makes extensive use of analysis and evaluation and that relies on research-based solutions when, in fact, instructional design is more of a design and development process that relies on a limited amount of analysis and that improvises solutions that balance educational, economic, and technical challenges.

Limitations of the Philosophical Approach to Design

Because much of the scientific basis for instructional design falls apart under close scrutiny, some designers choose to take a totally intuitive approach. They often base design decisions on their philosophy of learning. Two well-known philosophies of learning are

1. *Behaviorism,* which states that learning is a change in behavior and that the only behaviors that matter are those that can be observed and measured. The behaviorist approach is evident in much corporate technical training and technical colleges because it focuses on teaching observable and measurable skills. Much of the instruction is focused on helping learners build the capacity to perform these skills (behaviors) without unnecessary assistance

2. *Constructivism,* which states that learning "is an active process in which learners construct new ideas or concepts based on their current [and] past knowledge" (Bruner, 2002). The constructivist approach is evident in many academic courses and management education programs because it focuses on the acquisition of concepts and their situational application. In the constructivist approach, much instruction is focused on helping learners develop their critical thinking skills.

Because these designers are primarily guided by philosophy, much as Cubist, Impressionist, and De Stijl artists (among others) were guided by philosophy, we classify this approach to design as the *philosophical* approach.

One of the issues with the philosophical approach is that its practitioners promote it almost religiously, even when the philosophy is clearly limited.

Because many behaviorist designers insist on following rules, they dogmatically follow rigid templates to designing courses, whether or not these make sense or apply all that well. For example, an instructional designer for a computer installation course insisted on including interaction every three screens in a web-based training program because he had read that guideline in a textbook on instructional design. He insisted on retaining that guideline, even when someone pointed out that the guideline was developed for computer-based training in the 1980s, before graphical user interfaces were available and before simulations, graphics, and pop-up windows could make a course interactive without asking questions, thus outdating this guideline.

This inappropriate application would not be lost on a constructivist designer, who focuses primarily on thinking skills. Such designers often fall into the trap of designing courses that promote thinking, but fail to determine what they really want learners to think about. Consider, for example, the academic e-course in which the instructor led a lively discussion online about computer security with students. The instructor was proud because he had helped learners discover the principles of the topic. Unfortunately, after the lesson, learners wondered why they had spent an entire virtual session on computer security when the topic of their course was research methods.

In some instances, advocates of instructional philosophies like behaviorism and constructivism are not aware of their names, much less the epistemological foundations of these philosophies (*epistemological* refers to the belief system underlying the philosophy, including fundamental beliefs about what knowledge is).

In our experience, neither of these philosophies is inherently better than the other. Both are only effective when they are judiciously applied. For example, a behaviorist approach can be useful in teaching installation skills because there really is a preferred way of performing this task. Designers would not want learners "discovering" the procedure through trial and error. Although some learners might discover the correct procedure, others would not or would discover a procedure that is only partially correct. The time needed to discover such a procedure would also be much longer than if designers merely told it to learners.

Similarly, a constructivist approach is effective for teaching learners about the application of principles and policies. For example, although an organization may have a clear policy on approving time off for workers, the challenge to managers is in the application. In some departments, such as a product development or corporate communication department, nearly all of the staff can take off on a holiday without jeopardizing the company. In other departments, some staff must always be working to avoid jeopardizing the company, such as the security and help desk departments. Constructivist learning helps sensitize managers to these differences.

Furthermore, although behaviorism and constructivism are the best-known learning philosophies, others exist, such as humanism and liberal education, to name a few. (We discuss these further in the next chapter.)

In addition, most experienced instructional designers see the philosophies as laid out on a continuum and, within a given course, may choose learning activities that exhibit qualities of both philosophies, because the activities seem appropriate to the content being taught at the moment. Figure 1.1 shows a simple continuum of some of these philosophies. The next chapter explores them in detail.

Figure 1.1. Continuum of Educational Philosophies

Behaviorism	Cognitivism	Constructivism
Instructor-supplied knowledge		Student-discovered knowledge

The Problem-Solving Approach to Design

Although the philosophies are often presented as distinct from one another, many courses actually reflect several philosophies. The reason that many experienced instructional designers can integrate several philosophies into a single course is that most instructional designers are guided more by practical considerations than by philosophical ones. Enriched by many instructional design projects, these designers see each project in its own light, and use the philosophies as a means of illuminating one part of that project. Instead of a philosophy governing their entire approach to a course, these designers rely on something else. From their portfolios of instructional design techniques that they have used on previous projects, these instructional designers choose a design technique that has successfully worked on a similar project and either apply it as is or adapt it to address the needs of the situation.

Such instructional designers first define the problem they've been assigned to address, then suggest a solution. Research suggests that most instructional designers perform minimal needs assessments (Rossett and Czech, 1996). In fact, they rarely approach design as a linear process. Instead, these designers perform several design tasks at once, especially when designing e-learning programs.

Some approach design as an iterative process, in which designers first perform simple background research on the instructional problem, the learning context, and the intended learners, then quickly develop a prototype of the e-course. Then designers show the sample designs to representative learners and obtain their feedback. As a result of the feedback, designers deepen their understanding of the learners and the learning situation and revise the prototype course (Stone & Villachica, 2004). Designers repeat this process until the design is acceptable to the intended learners. This iterative approach combines the needs assessment and design phases. This is one example of the pragmatic, problem-solving approach to design.

The problem-solving approach is an informed one. For each project, instructional designers must research the background of the learning content, learning context, and intended learners before suggesting a solution. But problem-solving designers do so in an abbreviated way that takes advantage of the instinct developed with experience. For example, a designer performing her fourteenth project for the same company is not as likely to conduct a full audience analysis as is one working on her second. She already knows a lot about these learners and can quickly find the information she does not have.

Furthermore, although the problem-solving approach has a less dogged adherence to the research, it does not ignore it. It accepts research for what it is—a source of ideas that also provides insights to the likely success of an idea. But the problem-solving designer also recognizes that the only way to assure success of a given approach is to test it with the intended learners of the actual course.

The Problem-Solving Approach to Design Described in This Book

If design is a problem-solving discipline, then the best way to learn about design is by exploring the problems that arise during the design process, not by exploring the process itself (Dabbagh, Jonassen, Yueh, & Samouilova, 2000).

By exploring design problems, instructional designers can first consider how they might solve a problem, then explore that choice again under a microscope of sorts. They can consider the learning content, learning context, intended learners, and constraints that affected that decision. They can consider the principles that guided them in making that decision, and how those principles might or might not work in similar situations—and dissimilar ones. Then designers can consider how they would actually handle dissimilar situations, thus broadening their design experience.

This book prepares such designers. Our problem-solving approach assumes that you already have been exposed to the instructional design process in general and have considered it in the context of e-learning. Although you may have each worked with different formal instructional design models, they are all essentially the same and cover the same types of issues (Gustafson & Branch, 2002).

In this book we do not assume that you have much experience with some of the more fundamental philosophies and theories that guide decision making in instructional design, especially for e-learning. So Chapter 2 begins with an overview of some guiding concepts in learning.

Learn More About It

Clark, R.C., & Mayer, R.E. (2002). *e-Learning and the science of instruction: Proven guidelines for consumers and designers of multimedia learning.* San Francisco: Pfeiffer.

For a different perspective, consider this book. It presents a scientific approach to design, citing the studies and suggesting how the findings apply to the design of e-learning. Although some of the research transfers, we believe that several of the claims are broader than the research actually suggests.

Gagne, R.M., Briggs, R.L., & Wager, W.W.W. (1992). *Principles of instructional design.* San Diego, CA: Harcourt Brace College Division.

Gagne and company have written what many consider to be a classic in instructional design. This book delivers just what the name promises—the principles of instructional design—and that includes an explanation of the process for learning, a taxonomy of the domains of learning, and processes for designing instruction.

Prensky, M. (2002). *Digital game-based learning.* New York: McGraw-Hill.

For a different perspective, consider this book. It explains why a game-like approach to learning is essential in the digital era. Although we like games, we think that the book applies the concept too broadly.

Reigeluth, C. (Ed). (1999). *Instructional-design theories and models: A new paradigm of instructional theory.* Mahwah, NJ: Lawrence Erlbaum Assoc.

This book is for advanced practitioners who want to explore a wide range of instructional theories and models. The book provides a discussion of the similarities and differences among the theories that range from multiple intelligences to open learning environments.

Shank, R.C. (2001). *Designing world-class e-learning: How IBM, GE, Harvard Business School, and Columbia University are succeeding at e-learning.* New York: McGraw-Hill.

This book presents an idealized version of e-learning and has played a significant role in shaping ideas in corporations and universities about what makes effective e-learning.

Website of Interest

www.nosignificantdifference.org

Compiled by Thomas Russell, this site explores most of the research on distance and e-learning spanning the past eighty years and concludes that the medium of instruction makes no significant difference (hence, the name) in the quality of instruction when instructional design is equally good in both media.

Chapter 2

Philosophies and Theories Guiding the Design of e-Learning

There is nothing so practical as a good theory.

Kurt Lewin, 1951, p. 169

In This Chapter

To provide you with a foundation on which to assess the appropriateness of the techniques described in this book to your specific e-learning design challenges, this chapter introduces you to various theories and philosophies of learning, as well as their controversies. In this chapter we will

- Describe the philosophies of education
- Explore the five leading theories of learning
- Describe the relationship among research, philosophy, and theory
- Explain how these philosophies and theories influence a problem-solving approach to design

◆ ◆ ◆

When instructional designers first learn about different theories of instruction such as *constructivism*, they're anxious to use them in their work, whether or not the theories are even appropriately applied. And in some cases, instructional designers are not even aware that a specific approach to instructional design actually embodies a particular line of thought. To apply these approaches in your e-learning then, requires an understanding of what learning is, the different approaches to learning, the roles of the student and instructor embodied in those approaches (they're not always the same), and the circumstances under which these approaches work well—and the ones in which they don't.

This area of consideration is generally called *learning theory* because it considers the theories, philosophies, and schools of thought underlying learning. The practical outcome of these different theories, philosophies, and schools of thought are a variety of teaching approaches, some of which are familiar to you by both terminology and experience, and some may be familiar only by experience. Because problem-based design advocates that you choose the most appropriate approach to instruction for a given problem, it assumes that you not only have a large portfolio of teaching techniques, but also understand the rationale for each. So before we try to help you build your portfolio of techniques for teaching online, we must first introduce you to learning theory so you have the rationale for considering different types of teaching techniques. This chapter introduces you to philosophies and learning theories. In it, we ask you to think about knowledge and learning and explore the different approaches to designing instruction. By the way, not everyone agrees with every approach, so we'll also introduce you to the controversies in the field of instructional design. By the end, we'll introduce you to a large number of general approaches to teaching. These approaches lay the foundation for the strategies presented in subsequent chapters.

Why Instructional Designers Should Study Philosophies of Education

Perhaps you have designed or attended a training course on how to use a new piece of software. It is likely that the first part of the course was designed to explain why using the software is helpful to the learner; then the course described a procedure, such as entering information. Next, the learner saw a demonstration of how to enter information, then was given a chance to practice on his or her own. Then the course summarized the procedure for the learner, and the learner took a self-test to assess whether or not he or she could really perform the task. The sample Viewlet™ from Qarbon in Figure 2.1, which shows learners how to add a contact to Microsoft Outlook, takes this approach.

Change the subject, and you still have the same structure for a training course. That's the way all training courses are designed. Right?

Not really. First, there are a large variety of approaches to designing training courses. But more fundamentally, the approach just described makes a number of assump-

Figure 2.1. Example of Software Training

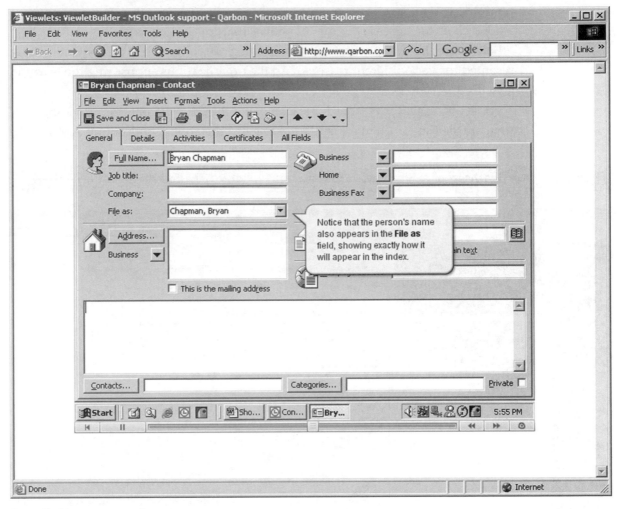

Source: Qarbon.com. www.qarbon.com

tions about what learning is, the roles that students and instructors play in a course, the way to best teach the content and, most fundamentally, what education really is.

Different approaches embody different thoughts. The structured approach just described, and frequently used in technical training, differs substantially from one in which learners are thrown right into a situation and have to figure out the concepts on their own. An example of this is Anesoft's Bioterrorism Simulator, which helps physicians, nurses, and other health care providers improve their response to biological and chemical attacks. Learners are asked to treat "simulated patients" and, in the process, must make a diagnosis and administer the most appropriate treatment. To help learners as they encounter this simulation, the course provides an online help system. In addition, an automated record-keeping system provides a detailed chart for the case. Figure 2.2 shows a sample screen from this course.

Both strategies are appropriate for presenting the content, but the content is being presented for very different reasons, and the organizations sponsoring the learning do so for different societal goals.

These differences in reasons for teaching and the societal goals for providing education are the fundamental issues underlying an educational philosophy. A *philosophy*

Figure 2.2. An Example of a Simulation Course on Bioterrorism for Medical Personnel

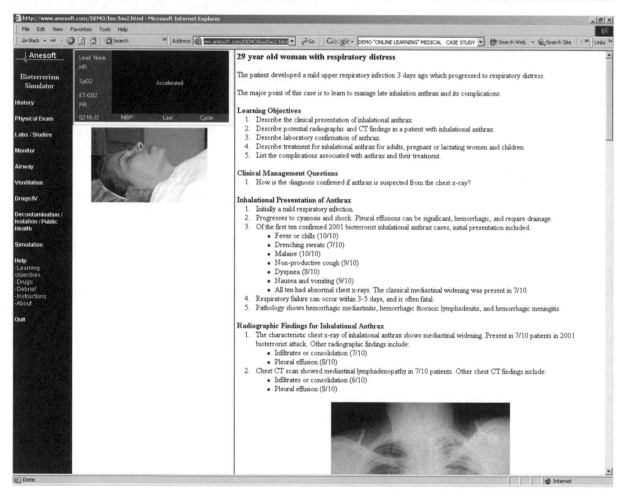

Source: Anesoft.com. www.anesoft.com/DEMO/bio/bio.html

is a set of beliefs regarding the purpose of education. It delineates these beliefs or rationale for why society wants to educate people. In most academic institutions, the philosophy is explicitly stated. In fact, most professors are expected to state their philosophy of education in their teaching portfolios. In contrast, most business organizations do not explicitly state their philosophies of education. Most probably haven't even thought about it formally, but they have one all the same. This unstated philosophy unconsciously guides most choices regarding training, from the preferred method of teaching to the outcomes expected and the bottom-line benefit to the organization (or even that a tangible bottom-line benefit (usually financial) should be expected). Although the philosophy can be seen in the choice of teaching techniques, these techniques represent only a manifestation of a philosophy, not the philosophy itself.

Understanding these philosophies is important because they underlie decisions about who gets educated, what kind of learning experiences the sponsors will pay for, on whose time learning should occur, who is qualified to teach, how sponsors measure results, and dozens of similar issues.

A second reason for taking the time to understand the basics of educational philosophy and learning theory is that understanding them helps you design effective learning programs. Once you understand the range of goals that an educational program should fulfill, you can consider which philosophy or philosophies best match the goals of your program, reflect on the roles for learners and facilitators, and then choose strategies associated with each.

What Are Examples of Philosophy of Adult Education?

A number of philosophies of education exist, and they vary based on K–12, higher education, and work place learning. Because we assume that most readers of this book are preparing learning programs for adults and university-age learners, we focus our discussion on philosophies of adult learning. In the following sections, we specifically discuss five major philosophies underlying adult education. These include (1) liberal adult education (a popular philosophy underlying education in colleges and universities); three philosophies that dominate corporate training, including (2) progressive adult education; (3) behaviorism; and (4) humanistic adult education; and the lesser known, but equally influential philosophy, (5) radical adult education. Although this discussion focuses on philosophies underlying adult learning programs, similar philosophies underlie primary, secondary, and higher education, so although our discussion focuses on adults, the lessons transfer to other learning environments.

The discussion of each philosophy addresses these questions:

- What is the purpose of education?
- What is the role of the learner?
- What is the role of the instructor?
- What are related concepts and key words?

Additionally, in these discussions, you'll also see how the different philosophies express the value of learning and how they place value on it.

A Philosophy Rooted in an Academic Model: Liberal Adult Education

Liberal adult education is probably the most widely understood and employed philosophy of learning in the Western world, although it is not common in corporate training. People who believe in liberal education value the education of minds in general over training people for specific jobs or careers in particular. Often called *liberal arts*, programs developed from this perspective focus on developing learners who have a basic knowledge about the world in which they live and hone the learner's ability to analyze and synthesize a situation to make decisions. As you might expect, examples of e-learning designed with a liberal adult education philosophy are common in academic settings.

Philosophies of Learning Common to the Workplace

Although many learning professionals may not be able to name certain philosophies of education, they would be able to recognize their characteristics and the differences each suggests for the roles played by learners and facilitators, the presentation of information, and the assessment techniques. The following sections present three of the philosophies that underlie most corporate training. We illustrate them by showing how the topic "food safety" would be taught in each. As we will discuss later, few programs purely embody one strategy, but the examples for the following three philosophies have clear leanings.

Progressive Adult Education

Progressive adult education is the raison d'etre for training in many organizations. This philosophy emphasizes vocational and utilitarian training that betters the individual, society, and the organization. Training programs based on progressive beliefs are, first, learner-centric (that is, course design emphasizes the success of the learner in achieving the goal rather than the transmission of the content to the learner) and, second, problem focused (that is, courses are designed around solving problems).

Because an assumption underlying this philosophy is that learners are self-directed (that is, learners take initiative for learning and responsibility for successfully completing it, such as contacting instructors on their own to ask questions), the role of the instructor becomes one of planner, instigator, and arranger of the conditions for learning. The utilitarian and pragmatic nature of this philosophy has extended its use to other agencies that transmit skills and knowledge such as churches, government agencies, and social movements. A great example of this is Risk Focused Inspections published by the State of Alaska, Division of Environmental Health. This course is anchored in a progressive philosophy that emphasizes practical knowledge of food safety and sanitation and the problem-solving skills needed to conduct a risk focused food inspection. As the screen shown in Figure 2.3 illustrates, the program

Figure 2.3. State of Alaska: Food Safety and Sanitation, an Example of Progressive Adult Education

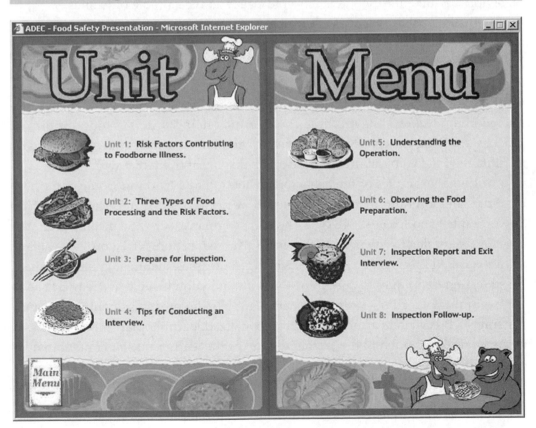

Source: State of Alaska ADEC/EH Food Safety & Sanitation. www.state.ak.us/dec/old_dec/deh/sanitat/risktrain.htm

is well organized and guides the learner through the experience. You can find examples of other equally pragmatic courses at government sites such as the U.S. Small Business Administration (www.sba.gov) and U.S. Centers for Disease Prevention and Control (www.cdc.gov).

Behaviorist Adult Education

Behaviorist adult education has inspired many of the current practices in e-learning, from the design of courses using the mastery model, such as the software course described earlier in this chapter, to such advanced practices as learning objects linked to behavioral objectives, personalization of content based on gap analysis, and competency modeling. In its most extreme form, behaviorist education is simply training that teaches learners rote behaviors through drill and practice. This philosophy has been adopted by corporate training because it is grounded in psychological principles that efficiently produce overt, observable, and measurable outcomes, which are popular in corporate environments that are also focused on measurable results. Behaviorist adult education lends itself to clear and measurable outcomes.

To illustrate behaviorism as a learning philosophy, we turn to a different course about food safety, Farm Food Safety Analysis from TEAGASC (shown in Figure 2.4). The program reviews overall principles of analyzing food hazards, and teaches learners to master the Hazard Analysis and Control Principles (HACCP) approach to identifying hazards. More specifically, this program focuses on mastery of concepts related to food safety. The multiple-choice exam offers learners an opportunity to practice applying the concepts and provides good feedback. The assessment takes advantage of the Web's ability to let learners display and interact with images.

Additional examples of the behaviorism abound in e-learning. Some of the best examples are programs that teach learners how to use desktop applications such as PowerPoint™ and Excel™. NETg, a Thomson company (www.netg.com), offers an excellent example of evidence of behaviorist adult education. NETg provides an application called Precision Learning™, which is a preassessment using performance-based testing techniques to determine the skills and knowledge that a learner has at the beginning of a course. After learners complete the preassessment, the system generates a Precision Learning Track, a personalized learning plan and sequence of modules recommended to the learner that helps the learner master content that he or she did not demonstrate mastery of during the preassessment.

Humanistic Adult Education

Humanistic adult education is concerned with the development of the whole person, with emphasis on the emotional and affective dimensions of the learner. Programs

Figure 2.4. Farm Food Safety and Hazard Analysis, an Example of a Course Representing the Behaviorist Philosophy

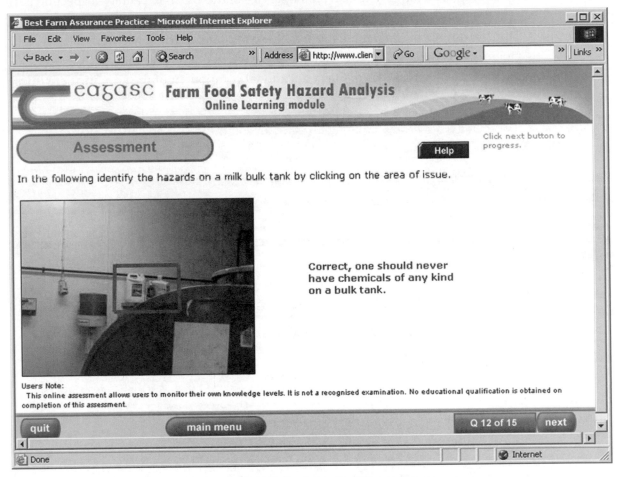

Source: TEAGASC. www.client.teagasc.ie/food_assurance/haccp/Assessment/Page12Assessment.asp

with a humanistic design are generally targeted to learners who are highly motivated and self-directed. In fact, this high motivation and self-direction are hallmarks of humanistic programs, in which learners assume full responsibility for learning. In such programs, instructors act as guides, organizers of learning, and helpers. That is, rather than dictate the learning program, instructors in humanistic adult education programs help learners decide their own learning paths and rely heavily on communication and collaboration tools.

To illustrate the philosophy of humanistic adult education, we turn to yet another example drawn from the topic of food safety. This time, we look at the Interactive Knowledge Exchange (IKE), an online service of the U.S. Food Safety Inspection Service (FSIS) Technical Service Center. Figure 2.5 shows a sample screen from the IKE. This learning program relies on e-mail to send out scenarios twice a month to Field Operations employees. These scenarios are authentic problems that are ambiguous—like those in the real world. One educational component of the scenarios are ques-

Figure 2.5. Interactive Knowledge Exchange (IKE), an Example of a Program Designed with a Humanistic Philosophy

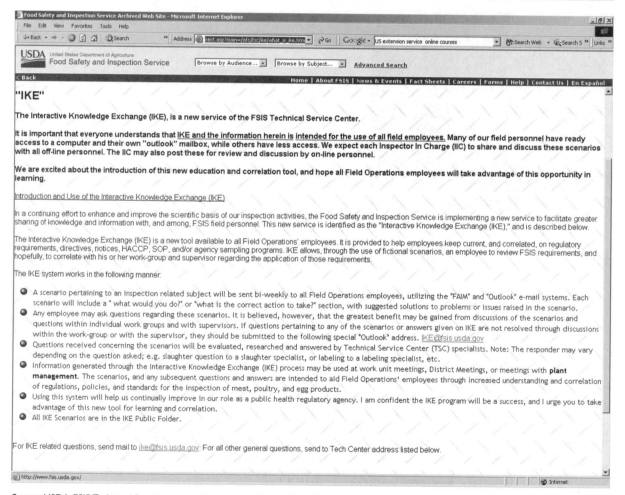

Source: USDA FSIS Technical Services. www.fsis.usda.gov/Frame/FrameRedirect.asp?main=/ofo/tsc/ike/what_is_ike.htm

tions like "What would you do?" and "What is the correct action?" These questions are intended to drive discussion and learning in the field. The goal of this program is to increase employee understanding of how to apply regulations, policies, and standards for the inspection of meat, poultry, and egg products by presenting them with realistic scenarios in which aspects of these regulations, policies, and standards must be addressed. Help from experts working in the headquarters is available to learners but to succeed in achieving its goal, the program relies on motivated learners who initiate a dialogue with work groups at the regional and plant levels. The questions and answers generated by the program are archived for future students to review.

A Lesser-Known Philosophy: Radical Adult Education

In addition to the liberal adult education (which is popular in colleges and universities) and the three philosophies of education that dominate corporate training (progressive, behaviorist, and humanistic adult education), there is a fifth dominant philosophy in adult education, radical adult education.

Radical adult education is not as well known as the other four philosophies discussed in this section, but is prevalent throughout e-learning designed for adults. Radical adult education is the belief that social, political, and economic changes can be brought about through education. Examples of radical adult education include programs designed to raise consciousness, teach critical thinking and reflection, and spur political action or change. One example is Living Sustainably on the Earth (http://environment.jbpub.com/home.cfm), which encourages sustainable living practices. Another example is the gang violence prevention program, Coming Soon to a School Near You: A Project on Youth Gangs (http://mail.nvnet.org/~cooper_j/YouthGangWQSite/), shown in Figure 2.6. Coming Soon to a School Near You is an award-winning WebQuest designed for high school students. WebQuest is an online teaching strategy developed by Bernie Dodge that uses inquiry-oriented activities in which learners interact with information gleaned primarily from other sites on the Internet (hence the name WebQuest because learners embark on a quest for information on the Internet). Although not technically designed for adults, the strategies used provide a clear example of radical adult education. Notice how images and questions are used to raise awareness. The questions in this program promote critical thinking and reflection, ultimately to help learners decide whether to stay out of or join a gang. The goal of the program is to influence students to make a thoughtful choice that has a social and economic impact.

Figure 2.6. Coming Soon to a School Near You, an Example of a Program Designed Under the Radical Adult Education Philosophy

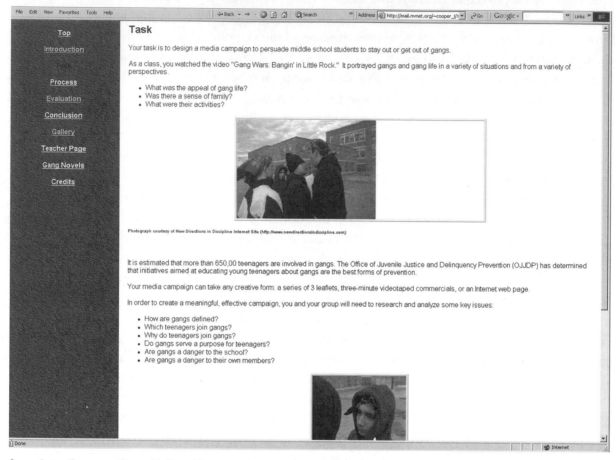

Source: Janice Cooper and James McGuire, Northern Valley Regional High School at Old Tappan.
http://mail.nvnet.org/~cooper_j/YouthGangWQSite/

Learning Philosophies and You

Table 2.1 summarizes the five philosophies just presented.

As you review these philosophies and reflect on your own beliefs, you might conclude that your beliefs fall into more than one category. That's fine. In most cases, philosophies are not mutually exclusive. A person's beliefs often span two or more philosophies.

But to help you identify what your philosophy might be, consider taking Lorain Zinn's (1983) Philosophy of Adult Education Inventory (PAEI), a tool for assessing

Table 2.1. A Summary of Adult Learning Philosophies

	Liberal Art Education	Behaviorist Adult Education	Progressive Adult Education	Humanistic Adult Education	Radical Adult Education
Purpose of Learning	To develop intellectual powers of the mind; to make a person literate in the broadest sense intellectually, morally, spiritually, and aesthetically.	To bring about behavior that will ensure survival of human species, societies, and individuals; to promote behavioral change.	To transmit culture and societal structure; to promote social change, to give learners practical knowledge and problem-solving skills.	To enhance personal growth and development; to facilitate self-actualization.	To bring about, through education, radical social, political, and economic changes in society.
The Role of the Learner	"Renaissance person"; cultured; always a learner; seeks knowledge rather than just information, conceptual, theoretical understanding.	Learner takes an active role in learning, practicing new behavior, and receiving feedback; strong environmental influence.	Learners' needs, interests, and experiences are key elements in learning; people have unlimited potential to be developed through education.	Learner is highly motivated and self-directed; assumes responsibility for learning.	Equality with teacher in learning process; personal autonomy; people create history and culture by combining reflection with action.
The Role of the Teacher	The "Expert"; transmitter of knowledge; authoritative; clearly directs learning process.	Manager, controller, predicts and directs the learning outcomes.	Organizer, guides learning through experiences that are educational; stimulates, instigates, and validates learning process.	Facilitator, helper, partner, promotes but does not direct learning.	Coordinator, suggests but does not determine direction for learning; equality between teacher and learner.
Related Concepts and Key Words	Liberal learning; learning for its own sake; rational; intellectual education; general education, traditional knowledge; classical humanism.	Stimulus-response; behavior modification; competency based; mastery learning; behavioral objectives; trial and error; skill training; feedback; reinforcement.	Problem solving, experience-based education; democracy; lifelong learning; pragmatic knowledge; needs assessment; and social responsibility.	Experiential learning; freedom; individuality; self-directness; interactive; openness; cooperation; authenticity; ambiguity; feelings.	Consciousness-raising; praxis; non-compulsory learning; autonomy; critical thinking; social action; de-institutionalization; literacy training.

Descriptions summarized from J. Elias and S. Merriam (1980), *Philosophical Foundations of Adult Education*. Malabar, FL: Robert E. Krieger Publishing Company.

your philosophical orientations toward learning. We recommend that you take the PAEI to better understand your values. The results of the inventory may surprise you. You may also want to ask your peers to take it and discuss the results. Several online sites offer access to this assessment; to find copies of the PAEI online, search for PAEI and Zinn. Figure 2.7 shows an example of this assessment.

As you consider your philosophy and those of your peers, you are likely to discover that none of you is a purist—that is, an advocate for a single belief. In fact, most instructional designers are not purists. They integrate bits and pieces from each

Figure 2.7. Online Version of Philosophy of Adult Education Inventory (PAEI)

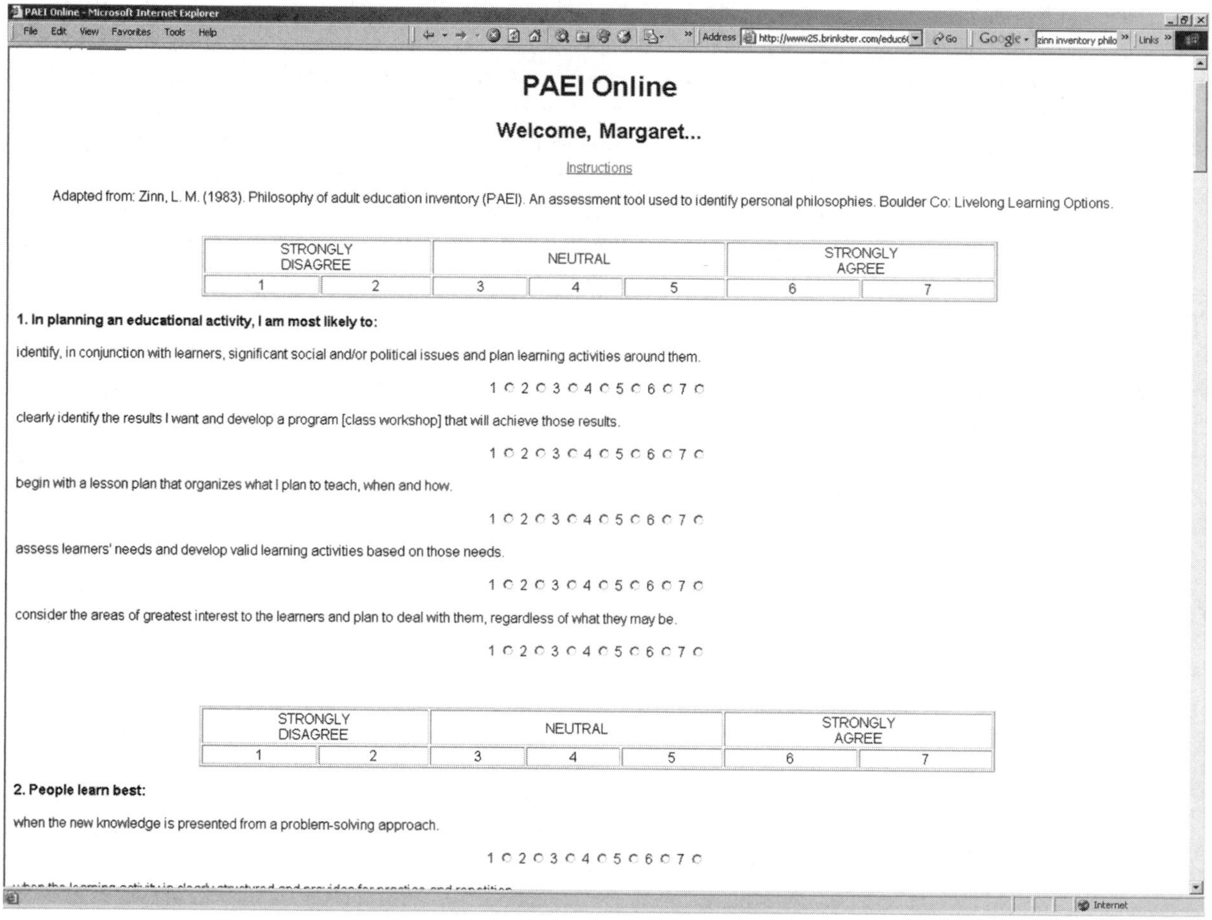
PAEI Online - Microsoft Internet Explorer

File Edit View Favorites Tools Help

Address http://www25.brinkster.com/educ6

PAEI Online

Welcome, Margaret...

Instructions

Adapted from: Zinn, L. M. (1983). Philosophy of adult education inventory (PAEI). An assessment tool used to identify personal philosophies. Boulder Co: Livelong Learning Options.

STRONGLY DISAGREE		NEUTRAL			STRONGLY AGREE	
1	2	3	4	5	6	7

1. In planning an educational activity, I am most likely to:

identify, in conjunction with learners, significant social and/or political issues and plan learning activities around them.

1 ○ 2 ○ 3 ○ 4 ○ 5 ○ 6 ○ 7 ○

clearly identify the results I want and develop a program [class workshop] that will achieve those results.

1 ○ 2 ○ 3 ○ 4 ○ 5 ○ 6 ○ 7 ○

begin with a lesson plan that organizes what I plan to teach, when and how.

1 ○ 2 ○ 3 ○ 4 ○ 5 ○ 6 ○ 7 ○

assess learners' needs and develop valid learning activities based on those needs.

1 ○ 2 ○ 3 ○ 4 ○ 5 ○ 6 ○ 7 ○

consider the areas of greatest interest to the learners and plan to deal with them, regardless of what they may be.

1 ○ 2 ○ 3 ○ 4 ○ 5 ○ 6 ○ 7 ○

STRONGLY DISAGREE		NEUTRAL			STRONGLY AGREE	
1	2	3	4	5	6	7

2. People learn best:

when the new knowledge is presented from a problem-solving approach.

1 ○ 2 ○ 3 ○ 4 ○ 5 ○ 6 ○ 7 ○

Internet

Source: Paul Kellermann. http://www25.brinkster.com/educ605/paei_online.asp

of these belief systems—especially those of us who work in the pragmatic world of workplace learning.

But in some cases, you may experience a situation in which two instructional designers have polarized views about the appropriate way of handling a particular instructional challenge. One may strongly advocate for a structured approach to learning, much like the software lesson described at the beginning of this chapter, while another may strongly advocate for an unstructured approach, like that of Coming to a School Near You. In fact, you may have found yourself in one of these situations. These impasses may be approached by the two individuals involved as a clash of right and wrong, but they are actually clashes in values. The real clash is not about structured or unstructured approaches to teaching but the fundamental beliefs about the way individuals learn.

Why Instructional Designers Should Study Theories of Learning

Ultimately, articulating your philosophy of education helps you describe how you feel about learning, but philosophies don't provide guidelines for creating learning programs.

That's where learning theories come in. Learning theories explain predictable relationships. In the field of learning, theories usually describe a relationship between communicating content and the outcomes of learning (often indicating a link between the presentation of learning material in a particular type of situation and how effectively learners will master the content).

More specifically, a theory of learning provides a general explanation for observations made over time, explaining and predicting behavior of learners in response to particular presentations of content in specific learning situations. In addition to explaining such a relationship, a theory embodies a series of beliefs and, therefore, cannot be proven beyond a reasonable doubt. In practical terms, that means someone can find a hole in your favorite theory and it's likely to be a real one. That doesn't mean the theory is a bad one; the theory just needs to be modified to explain that situation in which it did not work.

One other thing about theories: Theories are to education what fashion is to clothing. Theories become popular among educators and, at their height, everyone "wears" them. Of course, like fashionable clothing, the theories can be accessorized (that is, adapted differently), and knockoffs exist (situations in which theories are applied but not necessarily as appropriately or as well as prescribed in the original). Like fashion, too, theories go out of style.

Hundreds of theories exist to explain how people learn. Within each theoretical domain, dozens of specific sub-theories explain how to implement a given theory. But some theories hold up more strongly over time than others.

Three schools of theories dominate the discussion of learning theory: *behaviorism, cognitivism,* and *constructivism.* These do not align with the philosophies of adult learning, even though they have similar names. Each school of theory embodies an approach to learning, thoughts about the extent to which lessons should be structured, and approaches to evaluating the outcomes of learning. Each school of theory is also associated with a number of theorists. In addition, the framework of human performance improvement (also called human performance technology) guides the development of learning materials in workplace settings and is presented here.

Behaviorism grew out of a movement in psychology and philosophy that emphasizes outward observable behavior. The mind is believed to be a black box that can only be understood through visible and outwardly manifested behaviors. This movement dismisses perceptions, thoughts, images, and feelings because they are internally experienced and therefore subjective and cannot be measured. As a result, thoughts, images, and feelings cannot lead to objective science.

Behaviorism also has a long association with instructional technology. Theories of behaviorism and philosophies of behaviorism offer the best alignment of philosophy and theory. Many of the strategies used in self-paced courses today are based on principles of behaviorism that hark back to its founders, Skinner (1961) and Watson (1913). The following instructional techniques have their roots in behaviorism:

- *Shaping* is a technique used to achieve a *terminal behavior* (an end state or main objective) by reinforcing small steps or approximations of them on the path to achieving the terminal behavior. In the case of shaping, successive responses that are increasingly similar to the desired end result are reinforced, and they increase. A good example of this can be found in the drawing lessons provided on About.com (http://drawsketch.about.com/library/bl-step-dog.htm). In this example, learners master sketching animals by following a series of steps. Other examples are exercises that become progressively more difficult as they move learners from novice behavior to mastery of the skill. Another example is The Math Zone (http://www.woodlands-junior.kent.sch.uk/maths/timestable/), which offers practice in multiplication. It has progressively difficult drills with scores and time limits that shape multiplication behaviors.

- *Opertant conditioning* is a technique used to reinforce a proper response or correct answer by providing a reinforcement or stimulus. Examples of positive reinforcements are checkmarks, a pleasant tone, or a word of encouragement. The sounding of a buzzer or a clock running out of time are examples of negative reinforcements. For examples of positive and negative reinforcements, visit Sheppard Software (http://www.sheppardsoftware.com/web_games.htm). Sheppard's educational game, Locate the State, uses visual and audio reinforcements.

- *Programmed instruction* techniques include content arranged in small chunks and organized in a sequence advancing from simple to complex. The learner progresses to more complex material by responding correctly to the earlier, simpler material, receiving feedback, and responding to it. The low-tech PowerPoint 2000 lesson from the Land Grant Training Alliance (http://www.lgta.org/ppt2000)is an excellent example of programmed instruction. It presents material in a simple to complex sequence and, throughout, provides exercises with feedback that enables learners to move at their own pace.

Cognitivism evolved out of the increasing dissatisfaction with a behaviorism that refused to acknowledge perceptions, thoughts, and images—the processes that go on in learners heads. Cognitivists choose to describe how learners process, store, and retrieve information using terms and analogy that are highly influenced by computer information processing models introduced in the 1960s. Evidence of this can be seen in the naming of concepts such as the "Three-Stage Information Processing Model" (Atkinson & Shiffrin, 1968) used to describe the process of moving information from short-term to long-term memory.

Like behaviorism, cognitivism views the nature of knowledge as objective. That is, the goal of instruction remains to communicate or transfer knowledge to learners in the most efficient, effective way possible. Examples of cognitivist techniques that facilitate effective transfer of knowledge are advance organizers (previews at the beginnings of lessons to help learners begin organizing the new content and integrating it into their existing knowledge bases), mnemonic devices (memory aids), metaphors (tools for helping learners link new content with known content), chunking content into meaningful parts, and the careful organization of instructional materials from simple to complex. Many of the instructional strategies used in the examples in this book use tactics that have their roots in the work of cognitivist theorists such as Jerome Bruner and David Ausubel. The following are instructional techniques that have their roots in cognitivism:

- New information is organized in a meaningful way to make learning efficient. Look for programs that use advance organizers, analogies, hierarchical relationships and matrices to make it easier for learners to remember and retrieve information. The BBC site for teaching German (http://www.bbc.co.uk/ languages/german/index.shtml) is an excellent example of organizing information in a meaningful way. Notice how the lessons differ in the German for Work, German for Travel, and Quick Phrases in German.

- New information is linked to existing knowledge. As you sample programs in the strategy section, take note of who the learners are and what their background might be and ask yourself what assumptions the instructional designers make about learners' previous knowledge. A good example of how learning might be linked to past knowledge and used to motivate is the Annenbergy/CPB Learner.org program Amusement Park Physics (http://www.learner.org/exhibits/parkphysics/coaster.html). This site builds on grade school children's experience of roller coasters. Using interactive graphics, learners develop an understanding of concepts such as velocity, time, and force.

- Programs guide and support learners in processing information. One technique for doing so is dual processing, which uses multiple channels to get information to the learner, such as text and visuals. A good example of a learning program that uses dual processing is Eatturkey.com (http:// www.eatturkey.com/foodsrv/celebrty/main.htm). This site features thirty virtual chefs who use visuals, text, and audio to teach learners how to cook with a turkey. Other techniques for guiding and supporting learners include progressively increasing the difficulty of tasks, using diverse problems, as well as the more explicit approach of devices such as pop-up menus and help screens that guide and support learners. These techniques help learners create mental connections; making these connections is a key component in cognitive theory.

Constructivism is based on the premise that learners can create their own understanding of the world by reflecting on current and past experiences. Learning takes place as a result of learners actively gathering and organizing or reorganizing information. Unlike behaviorism, in which learners are passive, blank slates into which teachers inject information, in constructivism, learners actively build or construct knowledge as they strive to make sense of their world. The role of the instructor is to encourage learners to discover principles, engage learners in dialog, and make information accessible to learners.

Supporters of constructivism see the growing capabilities of computer-based training, e-learning, and the Internet as an opportunity for developing constructivist environments. These environments would differ greatly from the behaviorist environment. Jonassen (1994) delineates the characteristics that characterize constructivist learning environments:

1. Provide multiple representations of reality.

2. Avoid oversimplification by showing the complexity of the real world through multiple representations.

3. Emphasize knowledge construction instead of knowledge reproduction.

4. Emphasize *authentic tasks* (real-world tasks) in a meaningful context rather than abstract instruction out of context.

5. Provide learning environments such as real-world settings or case-based learning instead of predetermined sequences of instruction.

6. Encourage thoughtful reflection on experience.

7. "Enable context- and content-dependent knowledge construction."

Constructivist learning environments support the collaborative construction of knowledge through social negotiation, not competition among learners.

Table 2.2 summarizes the differences among the three schools of learning theory by examining the nature of the learning, the type of learning for which each is best suited, and a sample of the tactical methods related to a given theoretical school.

Human performance technology is a framework that strives to apply what is known about human and organizational behavior, including learning, to solve workplace problems. This framework looks beyond the narrow confines of learning and cognition to explain why workers fail to transfer learning. Broader explanations are explored, such as environment, motivation, and resources. Solutions often incorporate elements of behaviorism and cognitivism. HPI is often presented as a theory but is more aptly described as a methodology. For example, learners cannot use new software skills if the software hasn't been installed on their computers—a resources issue. In other instances, learners do not perform tasks because they lack the motivation. In other words, prospective learners do know what to do; they just don't feel like doing it. Sometimes, the problem exists with the individual, but more frequently the problem results from something in the unit or organization (Rummler & Brache, 1995). In instances when resources and motivation are lacking, no amount of training will solve the problem. Only solutions that address the lack of resources or motivation will work. In a practical sense, most problems have elements of all three—lack of skills and knowledge, resources, and motivation—and any solution should address all three. Human performance improvement, which supposes that instructional designers can ultimately engineer human behavior, is becoming the dominant theory guiding workplace learning.

In the view of human performance improvement, learners are supposed to achieve a well-defined result, which is related to a particular job task. Learning occurs within the context of the job, ideally within job tasks. The instructor is a guide of sorts, who helps learners achieve the desired performance, often commenting on the extent to which learners achieve the desired performance. But learning is only prescribed when learners lack skills and knowledge; for performance problems resulting from a lack of resources or motivation, learning is not an appropriate solution. Other characteristics of human performance improvement include the following:

- Performance improvement focuses on outcomes or end results, rather than means, like training.

- Performance improvement takes a systems view. Addressing a problem involves looking at the system in which the problem exists and recognizing all of the environmental issues that created it. It also uses a systematic approach to identifying and resolving performance problems, much as instructional systems design (ISD) takes a systematic approach to identifying and resolving learning problems.

- Performance improvement specialists first focus on defining problems; they do not suggest a solution until the problem is fully analyzed and defined.

- Performance improvement specialists constantly evaluate their work, both in formation and after it is released in the field, to assess its effectiveness and then use the feedback to adjust solutions so that they can be more effective (ISPI, 2004; Stolovitch & Keeps, 2004).

Typical approaches to learning usually involve self-instruction or materials embedded into a job task. These include job aids (brief tips that remind people how to perform a task), performance support (electronic tools that assist people in performing a task, usually one that is performed online), on-the-job training, and wizards (software that performs tasks with minimal intervention by users, so that people achieve the intended results with minimal work). An example of an electronic job aid is MapQuest (www.mapquest.com), which provides directions and a map that helps users travel between two points. The Install Shield that appears whenever users install software on Windows-compatible systems is an example of a wizard. To see an example of electronic on-the-job coaching, look at the cash register screen the next time you check out of a department store. The screen prompts the sales associate to perform various tasks, including inserting a check (if the customer pays by check) or verifying that the signature on a credit card matches the signature on the receipt.

An e-learning program that exemplifies the performance improvement approach (more specifically, performance support) is Quicken's website (www.quicken.com). It helps users assess financial situations and, if users assess themselves as ready for a given task, provides links to perform it. For example, in the loans section a user can assess various options for a home loan to determine which best meets their needs, as well as the user's likelihood of being approved for a loan. If the user feels ready, the site also links users to sources of online mortgages. In this case, users are able to achieve goals within the context of the task they are performing.

The Relationship Among Research, Philosophy, and Theory

In the last chapter, we made some broad claims about the quality of research in instructional design.

Like education, research is rooted in these philosophies. In fact, the different philosophies generate different purposes of research. The dominant paradigm of research is to prove a theory. This is called *quantitative research* (sometimes called *positivist research*). More specifically, quantitative research is intended to prove that a causal relationship exists between two characteristics of the learning environment—for

Table 2.2. Comparison of Three Schools of Learning Theories

	Behaviorism	Cognitivism	Constructivism
How is learning described?	A change in the probability of a particular behavior occurring in a particular situation.	A change in knowledge is stored in memory.	A change in meaning constructed from experience.
What is the role of the instructor?	Provide a highly structured environment in which to practice behaviors.	Structure and organize information to make the processing more efficient and effective.	Guide and provide materials from which learners can construct knowledge.
What is the role of the learner and the nature of knowledge?	The learner is passive, an empty vessel to be filled with knowledge that exists independent of the learner.	The learner is active in processing the information but the knowledge is still independent of the learner.	Learners are active participants who construct their own knowledge.
How does transfer happen?	Learning happens when a correct response is demonstrated following the presentation of a specific environmental stimulus. Emphasis is on observable and measurable behaviors.	Learning happens when the learner encodes and stores information in memory in a meaningful way.	Learning happens when the learner builds a personal interpretation of the world based on his or her experiences and interactions.
What types of learning are best explained?	Best for teaching behaviors that can be observed or demonstrated.	Problem solving, deep processing: exploring, organizing, and synthesizing content.	Higher order thinking skills such as analysis, synthesis, and evaluation.
What principles are relevant to instructional designers?	Reinforcement, Shaping, Stimulus/ Response.	Events of instruction, types of learning, Bloom's taxonomy, learning hierarchies.	Collaborative learning, learner-centered instruction, scaffolding, metacognition, problem-solving.

Table 2.2. Comparison of Three Schools of Learning Theories, Cont'd

	Behaviorism	**Cognitivism**	**Constructivism**
How should instruction be structured?	Programmed instruction; teacher-centered instruction; direct instruction.	Organize and modularize new information; link new information to existing knowledge; use techniques to guide and support students' attention, encoding, and retrieval.	Provide multiple representations of reality; Present authentic tasks; Foster reflective practice; Support collaborative construction.
Theorists	Skinner, Watson, Thorndike, Pavlov,	Bruner, Ausubel. Gagne, Bloom, Guilford	Knowles, Mezirow, Vygotsky, Gardner
Examples of Strategies	• Instructional cues to elicit correct response • Practice paired with target stimuli • Reinforcement for correct responses • Building fluency (get responses closer and closer to correct response) • Multiple opportunities/trials (drill and practice) • Discrimination (recalling facts) • Generalization (defining and illustrating concepts) • Associations (applying explanations) • Chaining (automatically performing a specified procedure)	• Information Processing Model Explanations • Demonstrations • Illustrative examples • Gestalt Theory • Matched non-examples • Corrective feedback • Outlining • Mnemonics • Dual-Coding Theory • Chunking Information • Repetition • Concept Mapping • Advanced Organizers • Analogies • Summaries • Keller's ARCS Model of Motivation • Interactivity • Synthesis • Schema Theory • Metaphor • Generative Learning • Organizational strategies • Elaboration Theory • Links to prior knowledge	• Modeling • Collaborative Learning • Coaching • Scaffolding • Fading • Problem-Based Learning • Authentic Learning • REALs • Anchored Instruction • Cognitive Flexibility Hypertexts • Object • Transformative learning

example, use of multimedia and comprehension or the use of humor and learning achievement.

In contrast to quantitative research is *qualitative research,* an increasingly popular paradigm that is intended to *generate* a theory. Rather than starting with a hypothesis, this research *ends* with a hypothesis. Rather than test an assumed relationship between two characteristics in the learning environment, qualitative research seeks to identify all of the characteristics in a learning environment and closes by describing predictable relationships that researchers have observed.

One other major difference among the two approaches to research is the nature of the results. The purpose of quantitative research is to generate conclusions that can be broadly applied, or generalized. Qualitative studies are intended to generate conclusions about one specific context that might provide insights into others. This insight is called *transfer* because the concepts transfer from one to another, though not necessarily in their entirety.

Both types of research inform learning theories. Research is intended to scientifically observe learning and reach some conclusions about how it happens. Scientific means that the observations are systematic (not just isolated incidents, but observations at several points in time), and careful efforts have been taken to prevent rigging, or biasing, the results. The resulting conclusions are intended to support a theory and are embodied in theory. The more research that supports a given theory, the stronger that theory becomes.

One of the problems with research, however, is that the conclusions often do not explain as much as some would like to believe. For example, although quantitative research is intended to generate *generalizable* insights (insights that can be applied broadly to a number of situations), the insights only actually apply to situations that are similar to the ones researched. So if someone conducts research on a group of college students, the results only apply to other college students with the same age, gender, socioeconomic, and cultural demographics. But we often see instructional designers apply the results of experimental research more broadly than this—and that's why we take exception with such research. We do not necessarily have difficulty with the research itself, just with the extent to which its conclusions are applied.

Similarly, the conclusions from a qualitative study only apply to the environment studied. The conclusions have insights that might be applicable to other environments, but they may not be. But some qualitative researchers attempt to generalize their results—that is, rather than characterize them as appropriate to the situation studied, they report that the results apply to all learning situations. This situation is no different from over-generalizing the results of a quantitative study, and that's an issue we have with qualitative research.

We don't want to dissuade you from valuing research; we want to caution you how to read it *properly*.

Research is used to support theory. We don't want to dissuade you from adopting theories, either. We just want to caution you to recognize their limits. Rather than become a solitary devotee of one theory or of one type of research, we suggest, instead, that you take a universal approach to theory and research. That is, use all of it to inform your decisions, noting that, in any given learning situation, one set of research and theory may be more helpful than others. In other situations, research may not be helpful because the research performed in a particular area of interest was performed with a very different population of learners or very different type of learning environment (such as an academic one, and you're working in a corporate environment).

How These Philosophies and Theories Influence a Problem-Based Approach to Design

This approach of choosing theory and research that has the best fit with the learning challenge you're facing is consistent with a problem-based approach to design.

A problem-based approach to design is not a design theory or philosophy. Rather, it is merely a pragmatic framework that focuses the design effort on the learning challenge to be addressed. It focuses attention first on defining the problem as thoroughly as the designer believes is necessary, then devising a solution that addresses the key issues raised by the problem. In theory, instructional systems design (ISD) works the same way, but the processes of ISD have become so elaborate that the fundamental issues seem to have been lost in its application. Furthermore, many believe that its effectiveness comes from following the process. But merely following a process does not ensure effective instruction. Ultimately, what makes instruction effective is whether or not the instructional program achieves the goals established for it. Because ISD has become so thoroughly identified with the process and because some of its most vocal advocates have advocated for process over solution, from a pragmatic standpoint, ISD is no longer a problem-solving approach. The process has taken on a life of its own and, within the field of instructional design, many experienced instructional designers disregard it (Zemke & Rossett, 2002).

The problem-centered approach to design does not lose this focus on problem solving. It is holistic. Rather than advocating for one theory or concept over another, such as constructivism over behaviorism, a problem-solving approach says that the appropriate theory or concept is one that helps the designer best address the problem identified.

Similarly, rather than advocating for one medium of instruction over another, such as online over classroom, a problem-solving approach advocates for the medium that will most effectively and efficiently deliver the instructional message, given the goals of the learning program, the schedule and budget available for developing the program, and the technology available to designers and developers for developing and viewing the learning program. It admittedly draws much of its inspiration from human performance improvement. Learning only solves a problem if the intended learners lack the skills and knowledge to perform a task. In instances when resources and motivation are lacking, no amount of training will solve the problem.

Addressing resource and motivational issues is beyond the scope of this book, but the idea of a solution-free approach to design is not. When designers decide that they will use a constructivist approach to learning before researching the skills to be taught and the learning environment, they have not taken a problem-based approach. They have taken a solution-based approach. Similarly, when designers assume that a course must be presented online before researching the needs underlying that course, they have taken a solution-based approach to design.

But wait! This book is about design for e-learning. One might logically conclude that this book takes a solution-based approach to design. It does not. Although this book explores e-learning as a solution to learning problems, it does not advocate that e-learning is always the solution. But if it is, then this book will have ideas for you. And many of the ideas are also appropriate for the classroom or workbooks. When that's the case, we let you know that.

Similarly, we have already noted that we take a holistic view toward learning philosophies and theories. We agree with Mergel (1998) that each philosophy and theory has its place in the community of solutions to learning challenges.

Similarly, we recognize the value of following a consistent process when designing, because a well-structured process ensures that the right questions are asked at the right time in the design effort. But we agree with Robinson, who notes:

> I am not at all of the school of thinking that says that the wonder and
> the spark of an intuitive solution doesn't matter in this world, or that
> all design is going to become rational. The best of things always have

a huge streak of play in them, and there are always gaps. What project planning, research design, and design planning do is set up situations so that those problems that need a more intuitive approach are much more clear; they allow people to apply personal experience, intuition, and personal points of view to the right kinds of problems. In many ways, I think the discipline that gets brought to these more complex programs can open up a lot of opportunity for people for those things to have a most profound impact [Robinson, 2000].

In other words, as a tool for structuring problem solving, we think that a process is helpful. But when the process overtakes the problem, it ceases to serve its function. In fact, we have observed that experienced instructional designers ultimately follow a personalized version of the ISD process, one shaped through their own experience that evolves with each project.

In terms of philosophies and theories, we not only see a place for a variety of theories, but more fundamentally, we see instructional design theories and concepts much like processes—tools to assist designers in defining problems and framing solutions. They are not templates around which all solutions must be crafted.

In addition to these design theories and concepts, we also recognize that instructional designers must address financial and schedule issues and work within distinct organizational cultures. Most design theories and concepts ignore these issues but practicing instructional designers cannot. A designer cannot implement a constructivist simulation online if he or she doesn't have the budget to build it, or if the sponsor doesn't see how learners can measurably demonstrate their success with the learning goals.

In other words, a problem-centered approach is a pragmatic approach to design. It borrows from concepts and theories that, in the purest form, do not seem compatible. It recognizes that every project has its constraints, and that "pure" applications of design theories and concepts rarely work as purely in practice as they do in the pages of books describing them.

Because a problem-centered approach to design is rooted in the real world, it also recognizes that several solutions might address the same problem. In many cases, one solution is not necessarily better than the other, but one may address all of the challenges and constraints more fully than others. For example, a web-based and classroom-based approach may work equally well for a training course, but a lack of travel funds will make the online solution more effective.

Conclusion

This chapter is placed early the book because understanding the range of philosophies and theories of education is essential to your practice. Chapters in Parts II, III, and IV present different strategies that tangibly represent the philosophies and theories presented here. As you visit the URLs presented in this chapter to explore examples of the philosophies in action, consider the following issues:

- A philosophy of education is a set of beliefs regarding the purpose of education. It delineates these beliefs or rationale for why society wants to educate people and the beliefs about the nature of knowledge.

- Five leading theories of learning include liberal adult education, progressive adult education, behaviorism, humanistic adult education, and radical adult education.

- Four schools of theory in learning include behaviorism, cognitivism, constructivism, and human performance improvement.

- Most instructional designers employ a combination of philosophies and theories in their work.

- As learning philosophies and theories describe the beliefs and values on which instruction is based, similar theories and values underlie the conduct of research. As a result, you need to consider the beliefs guiding a research study as you decide how it applies to your situation.

Being able to articulate your beliefs about how people learn is key to growing your portfolio of solutions and applying problem-based design. If the only philosophy you knew were behaviorism, then your training would quickly focus on a narrow group of strategies that dealt with reinforcement, shaping, and stimulus/response. Understanding a range of theories gives you a larger toolbox for creating solutions. As you look at the examples in this book, consider the designer's assumptions about how people learn.

Learn More About It

Anderson, T., & Elloumi, F. (Eds.) (2004). *Theory and practice of online learning.* Athabasca, Canada: Athabasca University Press. This book is also available online at http://cde.athabascau.ca/online_book/.

Students and educators can view, download, and print this book at no cost. It covers a wide range of subjects from an academic perspective, but readers from corporate and government organizations will find some information of value.

Driscoll, M.P. (1994). *Psychology of learning for instruction*. Needham, MA: Allyn & Bacon.

This is a must-have for instructional designers seeking to develop a personal theory of learning. This book provides the foundation for understanding behaviorism, cognitivism, and constructivism.

Duffy, T., & Jonassen, D. (1992). *Constructivism and the technology of instruction: A conversation*. Mahwah, NJ: Lawrence Erlbaum Associates.

This book examines the design of instructional materials from a constructivist perspective. It asks readers to examine their assumptions about how people learn and to consider constructivism and situating cognitive experiences in authentic activities. Readers with strong objectivist beliefs will find this book provocative.

Elias, J., & Merriam, S. (1980). *Philosophical foundations of adult education*. Malabar, FL: Robert E. Krieger.

This book provides an excellent overview of the philosophies of adult education for practitioners who want to survey the field. The book provides clear explanations of the difference among the philosophies and provides a historic context for understanding what gave rise to each.

Gagne, R.M. (1985). *The conditions of learning and theory of instruction* (4th ed.). New York: Holt, Rinehart and Winston.

This book is one of the seminal works on cognitivism for instructional designers. Among its many well-known contributions are the nine events of instruction model, which is referred to several times in this book. You might also detect the behaviorist roots of cognitivism.

Merrill, M.D., & Twitchell, D.G. (Eds.). (1994). *Instructional design theory*. Englewood Cliffs, NJ: Educational Technology Publications.

Merrill, who recently retired from his professorship at Utah State University, is probably the best-known advocate of behaviorism in instructional design in our time. His book explores specific applications of behaviorism in instructional design.

Stolovitch, H., & Keeps, J. (1999). *Handbook of human performance technology* (2nd ed.) San Francisco: Jossey-Bass.

This book is the bible of the human performance improvement movement, defining the concept, exploring the various components of this systematic approach, and suggesting applications in various types of work environments.

Websites of Interest

www.funderstanding.com/about_learning.cfm

This well-organized site offers a good starting point for learning more about theories of learning. Start here with twelve different theories on how people learn.

http://coe.sdsu.edu/ect. The Encyclopedia of Educational Technology

This site is a product of San Diego State University Department of Educational Technology. It is a rich resource of theories, theorists, concepts, and tactics related to cognition and learning.

http://tip.psychology.org. Explorations in Learning & Instruction: The Theory into Practice Database

A more in-depth look at the theory can be found at the Theory into Practice Database (TIP). TIP is a tool intended to make learning and instructional theory more accessible to educators. The database contains brief summaries of fifty major theories of learning and instruction. These theories can also be accessed by learning domains and concepts.

REFLECTION AND APPLICATION

Pick the last three courses that you have designed or taught. Identify the theories and concepts of design embedded in those designs. Then identify the philosophies of learning embedded in those theories and concepts. Do you notice that one theory or concept dominates your designs? If so, why do you think that you rely on this theory or this concept dominates? If not, how are the theories embodied in your work consistent with one another? Different?

Find two learning strategies that you have never used in Table 2.2. Do the following:

- Learn more about those strategies by visiting sites on the Internet that discuss them. (You can start with some of the sites listed in the Websites of Interest section.)

- Identify examples of courses designed around these strategies and the underlying concepts.

- Consider whether you would use this strategy in your designs. If yes, how would you use them? What would you have to change about your approach to design to incorporate these? If not, why not?

Part II

Portfolio of Design and Curriculum Strategies

This section of the book explores design issues and issues that affect entire curricula of e-learning programs (that is, series of related e-learning courses). The chapters in this section address a number of approaches crucial to problem-based design that emphasize the creative nature of instructional design, the holistic approach of effective design, and the performance improvement paradigm that underlies most learning today, especially corporate learning.

Specifically, the chapters in this section explore the following.

Chapter 3, Storytelling and Contextually Based Approaches to Needs Assessment, Design, and Formative Evaluation, presents a powerful technique for performing these design activities. Instructors traditionally incorporate stories into their classroom and e-courses, but few realize that storytelling is a powerful tool for unearthing the needs underlying a learning program and stating the design requirements in a way that an entire design team can relate to and that ensures that the resulting e-learning program is both relevant to, and usable by, the intended users. (Note that this chapter does not discuss how to use storytelling as a teaching technique. Several other sources address this issue competently; we do not feel that we can add anything meaningful to that discussion.)

Chapter 4, Blended Learning as a Curriculum Design Strategy, explores ways to mix e-learning, classroom learning, and other learning strategies in a unified whole. Rather than as a course design strategy, this chapter approaches blended learning as a curriculum design strategy. Using this approach, this chapter explores a general, performance-based curriculum design strategy that takes learners from no knowledge about a topic up through expertise and provides a framework for choosing the appropriate medium (such as e-learning or classroom learning) in which to present different parts of the curriculum.

Chapter 5, Informal Learning, explores how to develop performance among learners through online materials other than tutorials and e-courses. This chapter introduces the concept of informal learning and explains how it complements and supplements formal learning programs. Then it provides a number of strategies for designing informal learning programs and identifies a number of different types of informal learning materials that you can develop.

Chapter 3

Storytelling and Contextually Based Approaches to Needs Assessment, Design, and Formative Evaluation

Storytelling predates the written word, people have been telling stories for as long as we have had speech. Even after the invention of writing only a minority had access to the written word. . . . Even now we think in narrative and tell anecdotes, urban myths and personal stories almost without realising it.

The Society for Storytelling, 2004

In This Chapter

In this chapter, we will

- Define the terms storytelling and contextually based design techniques
- Explain how storytelling and contextually based design techniques can serve as powerful tools for needs assessment, design, and formative evaluation of e-learning projects
- Describe the challenges for using storytelling and contextually based design
- Describe a portfolio of storytelling and contextually based techniques
- Describe an in-depth example of storytelling as a design technique

Note to Readers: Although this chapter explores the use of storytelling, it only considers it as a needs assessment, design, and formative evaluation technique. This chapter does not explore storytelling as a teaching technique. If you are interested in using storytelling as a teaching technique, see the chapters on simulations, exposition techniques, and interaction. In addition, many fine books address this subject.

◆ ◆ ◆

A problem-solving designer begins the task of designing an e-learning program with a desire and a practical need to understand the whole context in which learning occurs. That's the purpose of a needs assessment. Most instructional design books give extensive coverage to this topic (such as the popular instructional design texts by Dick, Carey, and Carey [2000] and Smith and Ragan [2000]), but basically approach the process as one of information gathering. As a result, although the information it yields may be complete, it is also usually sterile and may not help designers connect with learners in a meaningful way.

Similarly, when approaching the task of designing the learning materials, a problem-based designer wants to deftly link the learning to the context in which the learner works. Yet the typical instructional design text focuses attention on choosing and adapting existing materials (Dick, Carey, & Carey, 2000) or on choosing an instructional strategy (Smith & Ragan, 2000). Such approaches also leave instructional designers with a void because these approaches address only the instructional content and neither help designers address practical issues in the learning environment that affect learners' motivations nor connect with learners in a meaningful way. But instructional "design is about making information personal" (Moldenhauser, 2002/2003, p. 230). So, to fill these voids, many experienced designers add contextually based techniques to their portfolio of needs assessment, design, and formative evaluation techniques, such as adaptations of storytelling. These techniques are adapted from ones used to design software, in which designers from backgrounds in theater, literature, and music have turned to stories as a way of meaningfully linking users to design software that helps make these meaningful connections. This chapter explores these storytelling techniques as they apply to the design of e-learning programs. In it we try to expand your concept of storytelling from a teaching technique (which is not discussed in this chapter) so you also see its value as a needs assessment, design, and formative evaluation technique. After defining storytelling and contextually based design, we explore the rationale for using these techniques in needs assessment, design, and formative evaluation and provide a portfolio of techniques you might employ in your own work.

What Are Storytelling and Contextually Based Design Techniques?

Storytelling is the recounting of events. More than a mere repetition of facts or a moment-by-moment accounting of an event, storytelling provides a perspective on the events. Each story consists of a story *teller* (the vantage from which the story is told), *characters* (people who participate in the incident, as described by the story teller), *plot* (a description of one or more related incidents, usually in detail), and *commentary* from the story teller (that gives readers the story teller's view about the events and helps readers interpret the incidents).

In classroom learning, storytelling is a commonly used teaching technique. Instructors verbally illustrate concepts by telling stories about the ways that people have applied the concepts in real life. In some cases, the stories come from the instructor's own experience. In other cases, the stories are ones that the instructor has read in the literature or heard about from colleagues. Learners enjoy these stories because they make abstract concepts concrete. They also enjoy stories because they're entertaining. Stories liven up a classroom lecture. In fact, some of the most popular classroom trainers are master storytellers. Indeed, many creative training techniques workshops teach corporate trainers how to integrate stories into their teaching.

But, as discussed at the beginning of this chapter, storytelling also has a significant role to play in needs assessment, design, and formative evaluation. In needs assessment, storytelling techniques prove useful in eliciting content from experts in ways that might not be possible with other techniques. For example, a technique called *day in the life* helps instructional designers understand how learners apply content by following their use of the content over a period of time, such as a day. In design, stories can be used to describe the content and learners in a three-dimensional way. For example, one design technique is to develop *personas* of intended users of the learning program (also called *archetypes* [Cooper, 1999] or *character sketches*). Because instructional designers rarely have the opportunity to meet with potential learners before piloting a learning program (and in many instances, not until the learning program is formally launched), the more three-dimensional description of learners provided by a persona significantly increases designers' understanding of learners and their use of the material. In formative evaluation, storytelling techniques can be used to provide authentic testing situations, such as test scenarios.

Closely related to the concept of storytelling as a needs assessment, design, and formative evaluation technique is the broader concept of *contextually based design,* a process by which someone becomes familiar with the entire situation in which people use a product (in this case, learning) and designs the product so that it fits nicely within that environment, as well as with the users' motivations at the time he or she uses the product.

The Benefits of Storytelling and Contextually Based Design Techniques

In addition to those already stated, storytelling and contextually based design provide a variety of benefits as both design and teaching techniques. As a design technique, storytelling provides these benefits:

- *More complete information.* Consider the two versions of the description of a new product in Figures 3.1 and 3.2. The version in Figure 3.1 takes a factual approach, providing lists of tasks that the software performs and demographics of the intended users. The version in Figure 3.2 takes a contextually based approach and adapts storytelling techniques. It includes brief "stories" about the ways that people might use the software and character sketches of three intended users. Certainly the amount of detail in the version using storytelling techniques is more complete. More than the quantity of information, however, the nature of the content differs substantially in the second version. By describing real users and their actual uses of the software, the second version suggests that people use the application in ways that differ from the way that product designers intended it.

Figure 3.1. First Version of Source Material About an Application, Using a Factual Approach

Purpose of the Application: learning management system

Key tasks:
- Enrollment in classroom and e-courses
  - Electronic enrollment and wait-listing in training courses
  - Automatic generation of confirmation letters
  - Automatic generation of reminder letters
- Reporting of aggregate learning results
  - Report on enrollments by course or student
  - Provide completions reports

Figure 3.1. First Version of Source Material About an Application, Using a Factual Approach, Cont'd

- Tracking of learner progress
  - Track starts and completions
  - Track "stalled" students—ones who enroll but never complete
- Interfacing with related systems, such as HR or Information Systems
  - Provide completions to the employee education record
  - Related bookkeeping
  - Online payment for services
  - Automatic generation of bills
  - Posting of payments to registrations

Users:
- Administrative
- Two years of post-college
- Predominantly female
- Currently serve as administrators doing similar tasks as those listed above manually and with separate applications

Figure 3.2. Second Version of Source Material About an Application, Adapting Storytelling Techniques

Purpose of the Application: A learning management system, which serves as an electronic registrar for a company's training operation, performing many of the same tasks as a university registrar but in a corporate context and with corporate training courses.

Scenarios of Use: The system performs four main tasks:
- Enrollment in classroom and e-courses
- Reporting of aggregate learning results
- Tracking of learner progress
- Interfacing with related systems, such as HR Information Systems

Here are some scenarios in these tasks might be performed.

Preparing a Compliance Report: Leslie is a manager of medical records specialists for a large urban hospital that has installed the learning management system. All of the records specialists are certified, but must receive at least twenty hours of training

> **Figure 3.2. Second Version of Source Material About an Application,
> Adapting Storytelling Techniques, Cont'd**

annually to retain their certification. Every fifth year, the specialists must receive a new certification. Because her hospital is in the process of being re-accredited by the Southern Regional Hospital Association, her manager has asked her to make sure that all employees' certifications are up-to-date. So Leslie uses the learning management system to check on the status of each of her employees. She wants to make sure that each has received twenty hours of training in the past twelve months and that all certifications are no more than five years old.

Planning Personal Training Needs: William is a junior engineer working for an aerospace manufacturer that has installed the learning management system. William's manager has told him that he needs to complete the required training curriculum for new engineers within the next twelve months. Although William's manager told him which courses to take, William has misplaced the list. He's supposed to enroll in the courses by tomorrow. So he goes online with the learning management system to first find out which courses he's supposed to take, then enroll in them.

Generating the Gee-Whiz Report: Andrew manages the management training department for a medium-sized national retailer, and his company has installed the learning management system. As Andrew gets ready to prepare his quarterly report, he wants to collect some "gee-whiz" statistics from the learning management system to inform his management about the number of people his staff has trained in the past quarter and the results of that learning (which is assessed by tracking the results of tests administered).

Preparing Classrooms for the Coming Week: Odell is an administrator at the training center for a company that has installed the learning management system. As part of her weekly routine, every Friday, Odell prepares the classrooms for the coming week. From the learning management system, she prints a list of all classes scheduled in the coming week. Next, for each class, she prints a roster of all people enrolled. She also prints a setup list and sets up the classroom according to the instructions in the setup lists. Last, she checks to make sure that each learner has paid his or her tuition for the class. For students who have enrolled but not yet paid, she instructs the learning management system to send a reminder note that tuition must be paid in full before learners can attend class.

Figure 3.2. Second Version of Source Material About an Application, Adapting Storytelling Techniques, Cont'd

Users: According to the Marketing Department, the typical user is administrative, two years of post-college, likely to be female (67 percent of users), and currently serve as administrators doing similar tasks as those listed above manually and with separate applications.

Here are descriptions of three typical users:

Leslie is a manager of medical records specialists. As a former medical records specialist and as someone who continues to keep her certification active, she is familiar with the systems used to keep medical records and has been looking forward to the installation of the learning management system. She estimates that each September, she spends 30 percent of her time making sure that her employees have the correct number of training hours for the year (or are scheduled to receive them). This is especially aggravating because year-end reports are also due in September (her organization's financial year ends September 30) and, as the mother of three young children, September is also the first month of the school year (with all of its attendant problems). She would welcome a system that automatically generates the reports that she needs.

Odell is an example of an expert user. Odell uses the learning management system to manage a training center. From it, she prints class rosters and setup lists, assigns courses to individual classrooms, makes sure that each learner paid his or her tuition, and produces training-related correspondence that is automatically generated by the system. Odell has been managing her education center for ten years, mostly through manual procedures supported by many specialized pieces of software. Although the new system promises to simplify Odell's work, adjusting to the new system is another story. The new system uses a Windows interface; Odell has only used mainframe applications, although she helps her high-school-age daughter with her homework on a Windows system. Odell is also concerned that moving many of the tasks to the system will result in her ultimately losing her job. As a single mother, Odell cannot afford to lose her job.

Andrew is the embattled manager of a training department in a medium-sized corporation. He was moved into the job when, as sales manager, he failed to meet quota two years in a row. Andrew's career had a promising start; he was a sales star for his

Figure 3.2. Second Version of Source Material About an Application, Adapting Storytelling Techniques, Cont'd

first five years. The longer he worked in sales, the less his management expected him to conform to policies and procedures. That changed when Andrew was promoted to sales manager, a role in which he was expected to enforce the policies and procedures he previously eschewed. That task was made all the more difficult by his limited software skills. But rather than seek assistance, Andrew was afraid he would look incompetent if he were to ask for computer training, so he has tried to fake it. Many Web applications are simple enough that he can do so, but he has been less effective with Office and specialized applications, like learning management systems. Realizing that Andrew was not an effective sales manager, upper management moved him to this training position. But Andrew now finds himself being asked to demonstrate that the investment in training is really effective. The sales representative for the learning management system told Andrew that he could use the reports for such a demonstration, but Andrew has to figure out how to do so.

- *Emotional connection with learners.* One of the challenges of designing e-learning, especially asynchronous e-learning, is the anonymity of the experience. Not only are learners separated from the instructor by time and geography, but in many instances, course designers do not have the opportunity to meet the learners at all. In classroom courses, face-to-face interaction provides instructors with an opportunity to better tailor the content to learners' needs. In response to misguided looks and direct questions from students, instructors can mention things in the current class and tweak the content for future class sessions. That's not possible with asynchronous e-learning and difficult to do with synchronous (that is, live virtual) courses. Furthermore, changing an e-course, especially an asynchronous e-course, is costly. As a result, the more that instructional designers can find out about learners before designing a learning program, the better designers can meet the needs of learners. For example, course designers who are not aware of Leslie's needs might easily overlook content about preparing compliance reports in the design of the learning program, leaving Leslie and learners like her to figure this out on their own (if Leslie even could). But with this information, a designer might include a special section of the learning program for generating compliance reports and might even stress the ease of generating reports under tight deadlines, like those imposed by government agencies.

- *More authentic evaluations.* By using storytelling and contextually based techniques for evaluating online learning programs, instructional designers evaluate materials in contexts that are closer to actual learning environments and receive feedback that is more likely to reflect concerns of real learners in real-life conditions. The resulting changes help designers tailor the learning materials to the realities of their learning situations.

Challenges in Using Storytelling and Contextually Based Design

Using storytelling techniques for research, design, and presentation of content poses a variety of challenges to the course designer. Among the most significant are

- Contrast with the engineering approach

- Lack of standards

- Credibility

The next several sections explore each of these challenges in more detail.

Contrast with the Engineering Approach

As discussed earlier in this book, two approaches dominate education, behaviorist and constructivist. Although both are scientific in the sense that they are based on empirical inquiry (that is, research based on actual observation of phenomena) and require extensive rigor (in other words, merely observing something is not sufficient—the phenomenon must be observed several times and from a variety of perspectives), the more traditional approach in education—the behaviorist—is more consistent with the engineering approach followed in many organizations, especially certain corporations and government agencies. The engineering approach makes extensive use of hypothesis testing and statistical data.

Storytelling is more representative of the other scientific tradition that dominates education—constructivism. In fact, the interviews and analysis of documents (called *artifacts*) used to elicit background stories for learning programs are the same research methods usually preferred by constructivists.

Because the engineering approach dominates many organizations in which learning professionals work, in some of them, the use of a storytelling and contextually based design may create discomfort. In some of these instances, sponsors are not familiar with the scientific rigor in the methods of research and may feel that they are inappropriate as an approach to needs assessment, design, and formative evaluation. One of the challenges to instructional designers who consider using storytelling and contextually based design techniques is the issue of whether such approaches will be accepted within the culture of the organization for whom designers are working.

Lack of Standards

Although a variety of storytelling and contextually based design techniques exist for training needs assessment, design of learning programs, and formative evaluation, no standards exist. That is, no standard format exists for conducting day-in-the-life research or for presenting personas and scenarios. At the most, some organizations have formats for presenting such content.

Nor are standards expected. Contextually based design is about choosing what is appropriate in a given situation, not force-fitting design to meet a standard. As a result, instructional designers must feel comfortable developing and refining their own approaches.

Credibility

The greatest challenge in storytelling is credibility. That is, are the stories credible and believable to the people who are using them?

In terms of needs assessment, credibility usually refers to the credibility of the data emerging from the assessment. The data must be complete and accurate. In practical terms, the question is, Did the instructional designer consider all key views regarding the data? Does the reporting reflect those varieties of views? Did the instructional designer consider situations that contradict the data collected and, if so, are those contradictions represented? For example, does the needs assessment merely represent the views of learners or does it also include that of managers?

In terms of design, credibility refers to the believability of the personas and scenarios created. How accurately do these represent the real world of learners? Do they represent the full spectrum of learners? If not, has the designer explained why these other personas and scenarios are not presented? For example, suppose the designer prepares a persona of a typical user for an upcoming learning program about a new system. Does the persona represent the user as blindly embracing the new system or does it acknowledge doubts that users will likely have?

A Portfolio of Storytelling and Contextually Based Design Techniques

Course designers can specifically use storytelling techniques in three different situations:

- In needs assessment
- In the design plans
- In formative evaluation of designs

The next three sections explore each of these approaches in detail.

Storytelling and Contextually Based Design Techniques for Needs Assessment

In needs assessment, storytelling and contextually based design provide a way for describing not only the tasks that the intended learners must master, but the context in which people will perform them and their likely feelings about the situation. Three storytelling techniques let you uncover the content to be taught:

- A day in the life
- Cognitive task analysis
- Oral history

A Day in the Life

Coming from the field of human-computer interaction (HCI), a day in the life is a research technique in which a course designer follows a "performer" (someone who regularly performs the task to be taught) for a period of time. The technique gets its name because most people conduct the research over the course of a day. In some instances, however, the research must be conducted over a different time frame (Wilson, 2001).

Using this technique, the course designer acts like a fly on the wall, observing and recording everything that the performer does, as well as the environment in which the performer interacts. The course designer can record the activities in a hand-written journal but often videotapes the performer.

In some instances, the performer being followed is an expert performer, and the goal of the learning program is teaching others to perform like this expert. In other instances, the performer being followed is a weak performer, and the goal of the research is to understand what makes weak performance so that the learning program can directly address the problem. In ideal situations, instructional designers look at both expert and weak performers and figure out how their learning program fills the "gap" between the two.

In addition to observing the behavior and environment in which it occurs, instructional designers also interview the performer. The interviews occur throughout the day, at times when they would not intrude on the work being observed. Through the interviews, instructional designers gain insight into decisions that the performer makes and other behaviors that might not be visible or might not be clear from observing. Instructional designers also gain insight into challenges that the performer faces and motivations underlying the performer's work.

Finally, instructional designers include their thoughts about the situation when conducting day-in-the-life research. These thoughts might include questions that can be answered later (especially in the interviews), impressions, and issues that designers might need to address in a learning program.

Cognitive Task Analysis

A cognitive task analysis is a technique used to elicit information about how to perform a task from an expert. The task is usually a thinking—or cognitive—one, in which most of the tasks are not observable to the eye. Rather, they are only observable if the performer were to write down each task.

A cognitive task analysis is a two-part process. In the first part, an instructional designer asks the expert how to perform a task. The task is usually approached in a broad way, such as "How do you make an airline reservation?" The expert explains, and the instructional designer records the process in a step-by-step fashion.

But many experts do not fully explain the processes in which they have expertise. In some cases, the omission is purposeful. Some experts believe that they have unique knowledge and fear that this uniqueness will be lost if they explain how to perform the task in which they are expert. So these experts purposefully omit information. (One example is a baker who shares a cookie recipe but purposely leaves out an ingredient so the cookies won't taste the same if others make them.)

More often, however, the omission is accidental. Most experts unconsciously perform much of their work, performing tasks without even thinking about them. For example, many U.S.-based travel agents would automatically try to route domestic travelers to Chicago to Midway airport. They would not consider O'Hare, but if asked, could explain that flights to Midway are usually less expensive than those to O'Hare, and Midway is closer to the urban center than O'Hare.

So to find out how experts *really* perform a task, an instructional designer would ask a second time. But instead of asking, "How do you make a reservation?" instructional designers would pose the task as a real-world problem—the beginning of a story, sort of. "So suppose I come to you and ask you to make reservations for a trip between Pittsburgh and Chicago, what would you do? I would need to leave on Thursday the 25th and return on Monday the 29th, and want to stay at a hotel near Michigan Avenue, but not pay more than $125 a night before taxes." The experts would finish the story, explaining exactly what they would do.

If needed, instructional designers would pose similar problems to gain additional perspective.

Instructional designers then compare the two versions of the task—the original and the one told in a story format—to see what was included in the second version that was left out of the first. This gives designers not only a more complete version of the task but helps them figure out which parts of the task learners might eventually perform without thinking.

Oral History

Oral history is a technique used in other branches of the social sciences such as history and anthropology to capture pivotal events in the past from the people who lived through them. The recounting of events is usually told as a story. The *informants* (people who lived through the events) usually experienced the events from one perspective, and the account that they tell usually represents this perspective. For example, a writer assigned to develop a book about the fiftieth anniversary of a military base interviewed all of the general managers who were still living, as well employees who had worked at the base for at least thirty years. Each informant provided a different perspective. Some focused on the changing politics of the military, others on the changing look of the base, and still others on the changes in military technology. Only through the entire set of interviews did a more complete history of the base emerge.

Oral histories have become increasingly popular as a means of researching topics of corporate interest, such as corporate history, management decision making, and design processes. For example, when preparing a section on corporate culture for a new employee orientation course, an instructional designer interviewed several long-time company employees to get a sense of the values that have been emphasized over the years and to find tangible evidence of those values in action.

This first-person, "I was there," perspective adds a sense of authenticity and completeness to the content, but usually lacks perspective. In some instances, people fill in missing facts with second-hand information. In other instances, key facts may be missing altogether. To address this incompleteness, instructional designers collect as many people's perspectives on the situation as possible. The additional perspectives provide for a more complete—if not fully complete—story. In other instances, instructional designers augment the oral histories with news accounts from the time.

Storytelling and Contextually Based Design Techniques for Design

In design, storytelling and contextually based design techniques help instructional designers present the content to be covered in a learning program in a way that complements the learning objectives. Whereas the objectives present the "whats" and "hows," these other techniques provide the "whos," "whys," and "whens." Specific techniques include scenarios of use and personas. These techniques are adapted from the field of human-computer interaction (also called *usability*), which explores ways to make software and hardware as easy to use as possible by linking them to human processes. To get to this ease of use, human factors engineers have developed techniques that help software interface designers better understand the real-world situations faced by their users and empathize with users' challenges.

Scenarios of Use

A scenario of use describes the task to be taught in one or more contexts of actual use. As shown previously in Figure 3.2, these scenarios of use describe both the tasks to be performed, the situation driving people to perform the task and the likely feelings of people at the time they perform the task. For example, all of the scenarios in Figure 3.2 describe situations in which people use a learning management system. Note how Odell's use as someone who is making arrangements for various training classes substantially differs from Andrew's, who needs to provide management reports.

Course designers can create two types of scenarios of use. One type of scenario pertains to the content to be taught. To create such a scenario of use, course designers start with objectives, because these describe the tasks to be performed. Then course designers describe scenes underlying the task: what was happening that would prompt learners to start performing the task; in which work environment do performers actually conduct the work; and what pressures, interruptions, and other constraints learners encounter when performing the task in the real world. Designers would prepare several scenarios, ideally encompassing at least two to three typical situations that each key audience faces.

These scenarios provide the "hooks" onto which a designer can better relate content to learners. For example, scenarios about a learning program on consumer travel would describe the stiff competition that travel agents face from online travel sites. Acknowledging that, a course designer can include material on ways that travel agents provide consumer services that are not available online. Consider the example in Figure 3.3. Instructional designers would also use such scenarios to create realistic examples and exercises within a course.

Figure 3.3. Partial Example of a Scenario for a Course for Travel Agents on Handling Objections to Using a Travel Agent

Michael is a travel agent for an older agency that is going through tough times. Business has dropped considerably with the rise of Internet sites. Occasionally, Michael calls past customers to find out how he can assist with their travel needs only to discover that these customers are using the Internet to make their own travel arrangements.

When Michael asks them why they do so, he typically hears one of three responses. The first is from customers who are self-employed. When they are traveling on their own, they want to make sure that they're getting the lowest price and often visit several travel sites before making reservations to make sure that they are, indeed, getting the lowest price. These customers also echo the second most common response: When making reservations for business clients, they say that their clients will only reimburse for the lowest price tickets. The last typical response is from leisure travelers, who are not only price conscious, but often decide "on the spot" to take a trip, and that usually happens in the evening, after the travel agent has closed for the day.

At moments like this, Michael imagines that he has a "reason buster," a secret weapon he can use to target these objections and explain how the travel agent can actually keep costs low, while simplifying the process of making travel reservations. From his own work with online travel systems, Michael is aware that finding the best web fare is time-consuming. Consumers do not have access to all of the available fares, and many will check two, three, or even four or more sites to see if they are getting the best fare. This takes time, and the money saved by going to a web-based service is likely to be spent in time spent searching for the best price.

A second type of scenario created by designers of e-learning programs is one about the use of these programs. Rather than starting with learning objectives, designers would consider what prompted a learner to initiate an e-course. This is especially important for people designing elective asynchronous courses (that is, courses that learners are not required to take). Designers can choose formats and approaches that would be appropriate in the scenarios facing their intended learners at the time they take a course. Scenarios are also useful to designers of synchronous learning programs. By considering the entire context of learning, course designers can provide complete support for the learning experience and are likely to encounter far fewer unanticipated problems when the learning programs are taught.

Personas

Personas are descriptions of people who use the learning program. Personas are character sketches about real users of the learning program (or, if real people are not available, fictional people who are similar to real users). Instructional designers use these as a means of visualizing real learners when designing an e-learning program. Rather than writing to someone who has 15.32 years of education, is 67 percent male, and has been at a company for 3.45 years, designers write to "Thom," "Freda," and "Gena."

Cooper (1999) recommends that designers prepare personas for each primary audience. Some courses have several primary audiences. In those instances, instructional designers prepare personas for each group of users, rather than a single set of personas that addresses all learners. For example, suppose that a product training course had primary audiences of marketing representatives and customers. Instructional designers would prepare two sets of personas: one of the marketing representatives, another of the customers. Similarly, suppose a time management course is intended for professionals, administrative staff, and managers. Instructional designers would prepare three sets of personas: one for professionals, one for administrative staff, and one for managers.

For each group of personas, instructional designers prepare three separate personas. The first is a low-maintenance learner, one who does not need much attention. The second is a high-maintenance learner, one who needs more than his or her share of attention. The last is one who best typifies the "average" learner (Cooper, 1999). By covering these three learners, Cooper suggests that designers will have covered 90 percent of their audience.

For example, for the product training course for marketing representatives and customers, the instructional designer would prepare six personas altogether: three about the marketing representatives, three about the customers. Similarly, for the time management course mentioned earlier, instructional designers would prepare nine personas: three about the professionals, three about the administrative staff, and three about the managers.

Figure 3.4 shows examples of personas for a new employee orientation for a coffee house. This course has one set of primary learners.

Figure 3.4. Examples of Personas for a Course That Orients New Employees of a Coffee House

General Demographics

This learning product has only one primary audience: new employees. They range in age from seventeen (the company does not hire people who have not yet entered their senior year of high school) to age seventy. (Older employees are welcome, but as of now, none have applied for the job.) Most share a love of coffee and prefer to work for a local chain rather than a national chain of coffee houses.

Character Sketches

Thom is a second-year art student at the Art College of the East Village. He hopes to become a graphic artist with a web-development firm. Although he has student loans to pay college tuition, he needs to work twenty to thirty hours weekly to earn spending money, money for books, and the room and board his parents charge him (he lives at home). Because he has a strained relationship with his parents, he's a night person, and has afternoon classes, Thom hopes to work in the coffee house during evening hours. He does not have a car, and relies on public transportation to get to work.

Thom has previous food service experience, having worked for Wendy's after school and summers during his high school years. He primarily worked in the kitchen and did not have experience working the cash register. In fact, Thom does not consider himself to be gifted using electronics, nor does he like math. Ultimately he hopes to become a barista, but Jesse and Janet only hire experienced counter help from their stores for those coveted positions.

Freda is a fifty-year-old widow with two grown children. Because she only has a high school diploma and has not worked outside the home since 1987, when her oldest child was born, she has little work experience. When her husband passed away a year ago, she found herself at loose ends at home, and also found that his life insurance

**Figure 3.4. Examples of Personas for a Course That
Orients New Employees of a Coffee House, Cont'd**

policy did not completely fill the gap in his lost income. She has decided to work. Through friends, she learned that Something's Brewing is looking for people who might eventually become store managers. Before she had her children, Freda was an assistant manager for a private restaurant and thinks that's what she would eventually like to do. She likes the fact that Janet is supportive of her returning to work and is willing to train her. Freda understands that her first position at Something's Brewing will be at the counter. Because Freda has not worked in nearly twenty years, she is a bit concerned about keeping to a regular work schedule and using all of the high-tech equipment in the store. But she knows she has great people skills (Freda organizes and hosts the quarterly pancake breakfasts at her church).

Gena is a twenty-five-year-old college sophomore at State U. Her major is undeclared. This is her second stint at college; she flunked out of a private college in the middle of her junior year because she had difficulty managing time. Although Gena does not admit it, she also was active on the club circuit and found that it interfered with her studying. Her parents cut off her allowance after she was kicked out of college, and Gena went to work in a succession of jobs. At first, Gena was a poor employee, lasting only two or three weeks in a job. But then she got a job at the cosmetics counter at the local department store, where she blossomed. Gena had hoped to continue in that job, but was told that she would need a college diploma to be considered for a promotion. She applied to State U. and was accepted. She moved to town to start school. Although Gena's parents will cover the tuition and rent, they expect her to earn her own spending money and money for food. Because her department store does not have a branch in town, Gena needs a new job. Unfortunately, the department stores that are in town do not need assistance in the cosmetics department, so Gena thought she would explore employment in another line of work. The coffee shop seemed like something different—after all, that's where Jennifer Anniston got her start on *Friends,* so she thought she'd try her luck at Something's Brewing.

Storytelling and Contextually Based Design Techniques for Formative Evaluation

In formative evaluation, storytelling and contextually based design provide a way for providing authentic evaluations within the context of use. This authentic evaluations are called *usability tests.*

A usability test is a special type of formative evaluation in which people who are representative of the intended learners take the learning program for a "test drive" (Duin, 1993). The test drive usually occurs under conditions that resemble ones that the learner might encounter in the real world. In some instances, evaluators set up a special test room to look like the office or learning center where learners would take the learning program. In other instances, evaluators actually conduct the evaluation in test participants' workplaces or homes. Evaluators choose test participants whose demographics closely resemble those of the intended learners.

As test participants use the materials, independent observers record responses and make the development team aware of the issues that arose during the review. By observing test participants, evaluators see first-hand the strengths and weaknesses of the learning program under real-world conditions. Before proceeding with the design, designers would reinforce the strengths and address the weaknesses. To ensure their independence, evaluators who conduct usability tests are usually not involved in the design or development of the learning program.

Usability tests are essential for asynchronous learning programs, because learners must be able to use them without assistance. But without a usability test in advance, that might not be feasible. Studies have shown that usability tests identify numerous roadblocks that other reviews cannot find. In fact, a study compared the number of problems found in a draft by usability experts with those actually encountered by users. The "best" expert could only find 48 percent of the roadblocks that users found (Boren & Ramey, 2000). This means that the only way to effectively identify roadblocks is through a usability test. Another benefit of conducting a usability test on a prototype is that the design and development team might differ in its proposed approach to covering the content. The test assesses whether the approach presented in the prototype will work.

The heart of a usability test is the scenario used in it. Figure 3.5 shows an example of a usability test scenario. It shows the scenario from two perspectives: that of the test participant and that of the evaluator. Note the differences among the two; the scenario for evaluators includes instructions on how to conduct the evaluation, while the version for participants provides instructions for completing the scenario.

Figure 3.5a. Participant's Version of a Usability Test Scenario

Task

You are a new employee working for the Something's Brewing Coffee Company. It is your first day of work and, after the store manager has introduced herself, completed some paperwork (like tax forms and payroll information), given you a tour of the store, and introduced you to your co-workers, she asks you to take an introductory course about your job as a store associate on a computer in the back room of the store. The manager sits you down at the computer, hands you a CD with the course materials, and says that she'll be back in an hour to check on you.

Using the CD and computer, begin the course and start taking it. Follow on-screen directions, where provided. If you have questions, you can contact the manager by leaving the back room and going into the "storeroom."

Figure 3.5b. Evaluator's Version of a Usability Test Scenario

Part 1: Get Background Information

Participant: _____

Date: _____

Background:

Estimated Age Range (mention that we are tracking the following information for reporting purposes):

☐ 21–25   ☐ 41–45
☐ 26–30   ☐ 46–50
☐ 31–35   ☐ 51–55
☐ 36–40   ☐ 56 or older

Highest Level of Education Completed:

☐ High school   ☐ Some undergraduate
☐ Bachelor's   ☐ Ph.D., M.D., J.D.
☐ Master's

Previous Work Experience (especially retail): _____

Previous e-Learning Experience: _____

Part 2: Observe Learning

Time Started: _____   **Time Completed:** _____

Errors (total number): _____

Figure 3.5b. Evaluator's Version of a Usability Test Scenario, Cont'd

Main task: Take the new employee orientation course for Something's Brewing

Supporting Tasks

Time	Actions	Comments

Debrief the Experience

1. On a scale of 1 (horrible) to 5 (extremely useful), how useful was this course? Why?

2. What content was the easiest to learn? Most difficult?

3. What was the most effective aspect of the course?

4. What specific changes would you make?

In Practice: Storytelling in e-Learning: The World Bank's Money Matters Program

General Description of the Project

Title: Money Matters

Publisher: International Bank for Reconstruction and Development

Producer: World Bank Group, Washington, D.C.

Brief Description: This program explains how to manage personal financial issues to World Bank employees in developing nations, particularly administrative staff, rather than financial staff. The program was developed to inform World Bank employees in these nations about banking and financial planning benefits provided to them, but that are not typically available in developing nations (for example, mutual funds are not typically available in most developing nations). The entire program consists of a classroom course and three online courses. The three online courses include: (1) Personal Budgeting, (2) Savings and Investment, and (3) Retirement and Life After the Bank. Each course has five units. Learners take one unit per week. Note that a learner may take only one or two of the three courses. Also, the courses are not scheduled one after the other (for example, the second course may not begin on week six).

Through these courses, employees learn how to set a personal budget, how stocks and bonds work, and how to budget for retirement—and have a rewarding retirement. The program arose because employees (especially administrative and nonfinancial employees) would be asked to make investment choices about their World Bank pension program, but did not have the financial literacy to make effective choices. This program was intended to bridge that gap. As a side benefit, learners can use the knowledge and skills gained in this program in their work at the World Bank.

Associated with these online courses are templates and forms that learners can download and use as performance support tools in their own financial planning.

The online courses were originally designed to support and enhance the core material of a classroom course. The classroom course taught the financial concepts needed to grasp the retirement plan, but learners wanted more in-depth information about financial products and their implications to personal finances. These issues were addressed in the e-learning courses of the Money Matters program. Because of budget constraints, the classroom course is used less and less and the e-learning pieces have essentially replaced it.

Two of the courses are available in English and French (the language used by many West African learners in this program).

Although the courses themselves make extensive use of storytelling, the use of storytelling started much earlier, as a tool for designing this course. To help them better relate to the needs of their learners, designers developed personas and used them to generate the structure and learning strategy used in the courses. In fact, though designers intended to use them only for design purposes, the personas eventually became a central part of one of the courses.

Intended Audiences

- *Primary*—Nonfinancial staff of the World Bank, who work in developing countries and would not be able to attend classroom course.

- *Secondary*—Staff at the Washington, D.C., headquarters of the World Bank. They hear about this course through word of mouth.

Size of the Audience: Several hundred. Learners go through the courses in cohorts of twenty to fifty, the maximum number of learners that can be supported. Each course is facilitated by a subject-matter expert (SME) who has been trained in this skill. Before learners begin a course, they must commit to participating in the discussion. To ensure that they do participate, the instructor phones and sends regular e-mail messages to people to encourage participation and when she notices that a learner has not participated.

The course is now being adapted by the WB Institute, a training institute within the World Bank, for use by partner organizations, as well as by the Aga Kahn Foundation so the training can be delivered to refugee women. (World Bank-specific information is being removed from this version.)

About the Learning Goals

Overall Goal of the Project: Traditional learning

Primary Learning Objectives: Figures 3.6 and 3.7 provide examples of the objectives.

Figure 3.6. Objectives from the Savings and Investment Course of Money Matters Program

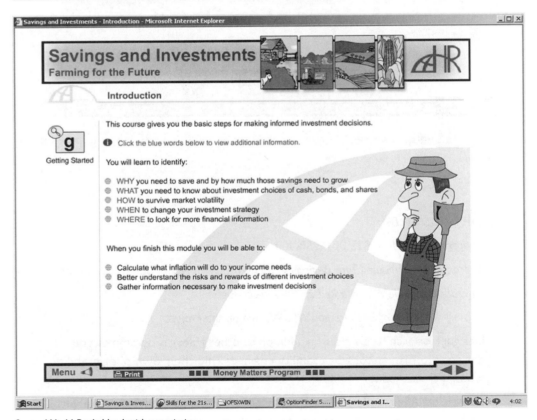

Source: World Bank. Used with permission.

Figure 3.7. Objectives from the Budgeting Course of Money Matters Program

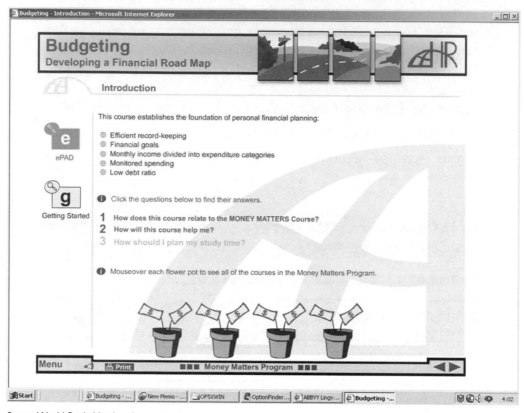

Source: World Bank. Used with permission.

The Numbers

Approximate Budget: **$25,001-$50,000**

Approximate Schedule (from Beginning to End of the Project): **Four to six months**

Number of People Who Worked on the Project: **Eight**

Primary Job Skills of Each Person Who Worked on the Project:

Designer or architect, writer (in addition to other roles), programmer, graphic designer, human factors or usability engineer (did their own pilot usability type), technical editor

Other Issues Affecting the Project: The challenge was in taking such a dry subject, while working with a subject-matter expert who's so close to the content, and make it fun, address it with imagination. Dominick Egan and Jeanette Murry, the two primary designers, went through a very creative period when the two of them shared an office. They plastered their wall with Post-it® Notes and posters, drew and scheduled, came up with ideas, brainstormed, and wrote dialog (the story underlying the course). In the process, they started imaging a relationship between a mentor and mentee around personal finance, created characters, and scripted it out as a story, which would run through various learning objectives. This helped them better understand the learner but remained a teaching device. The designers feel that this scriptwriting approach, with imagined characters, gives a human touch to the material and makes it accessible to learners. It was also one of the aspects of the course that was best received by pilot group.

Technology Infrastructure

Delivery Medium: Intranet or extranet
Media Used Within the Learning Program: Text, graphics, animation, photographs
Delivery Platform: PC running Windows 2000® (then the World Bank standard)

Authoring Environment

- Flash® (Flash action script too, animation, and interactivity)
- Dreamweaver®
- Graphics software: Illustrator®, PhotoShop®
- Course management software: WebCT®

Results of the Course

- *Student evaluations:* The overwhelming majority of learners rate the course as excellent. (Overall evaluation is 4.5 on a scale of 5.) That's because, in addition to the training, the facilitator requests, and later establishes, a personal relationship with each learner. Most of the learners are women, and they identify with her and the issues that the facilitator raises in the course, thus creating an intellectual bond between the learners and the facilitator. She calls learners on the telephone. Learners tell their friends about their positive learning experience, adding that their friends "have to take this course with Carrie" (the facilitator).
- *Learning time:* People might take only one of the three courses, each of which involves thirty hours of instruction. In addition, learners spend lots of time in threaded discussions between sessions. (Participation in

these threaded discussions is 100 percent because contributions to
them are required.)

- *Test results:* Life is the test. At the end of the course, learners should
  have a personal budget, and many learners comment that this, alone,
  is helpful to them. For many, setting a personal budget is an eye-
  opening experience.

Conclusion

Although trainers primarily rely on storytelling as a teaching technique, instructional
designers can make effective use of various storytelling and contextual design techniques to get more comprehensive information about the design problem, to generate more meaningful designs, and to provide more authentic formative evaluations.
By transforming design from a sterile, linear process to a contextually based challenge, designers can more completely encapsulate the problem and, therefore, develop more effective and rewarding solutions.

To reach this conclusion, this chapter explored the following points:

- Storytelling is the recounting of events. More than a mere repetition of facts
  or a moment-by-moment accounting of an event, storytelling provides a
  perspective on the events. Each story consists of a story teller, characters,
  plot, and commentary.

- Contextually based design is a process in which someone becomes familiar
  with the entire situation in which people use a product (in this case, learning) and designs the product so that it fits nicely within that environment,
  as well as with the users' motivations at the time they use the product.

- Designers should consider using storytelling and contextually based design
  techniques in needs assessment, describing design plans, and formative
  evaluation. The benefits include more complete information, because the
  story provides contextual and motivational information, and an emotional
  connection with learners.

- The challenges of using storytelling include

  - Its contrast with the engineering approach, with an emphasis on rich
    qualitative data rather than quantitative data

  - Lack of standards for using various techniques

  - Creating credible stories

- Storytelling and contextually based design techniques include
  - For needs assessment, a day in the life, cognitive task analysis, and oral histories
  - For design, scenarios of use, and personas
  - For formative evaluation, usability test scenarios

Learn More About It

Carroll, J. (2000). *Making use: Scenario-based design for human-computer interaction.* Cambridge, MA: MIT Press.

Explains how to use storytelling resources as a design device.

Wacker, M., & Silverman, L. (2003). *Stories trainers tell: 55 ready-to-use stories to make training stick.* San Francisco: Pfeiffer.

For those of you who are interested in using storytelling as a teaching technique, this resource guide helps get you started with this teaching technique.

Websites of Interest

http://advance.aiga.org/resources/storytelling.html. American Institute for Graphic Arts resources on storytelling

Serves as a portal, of sorts, to resources on the Internet that explain how to use storytelling as a design tool.

www.storycenter.org. Digital Storytelling Center

A nonprofit project development, training, and research organization dedicated to assisting people in using digital media to tell meaningful stories from their lives.

REFLECTION AND APPLICATION

To reflect on the material presented in this chapter and apply it in a real e-learning situation, consider how you would respond to the following challenges. (Each of these challenges is intentionally left vague. If you are unsure about a piece of information, make an assumption about it and list the assumption.)

- You work in a start-up organization. Because its pace of business is fast and its markets extremely competitive, your company never documents its procedures. But as it expands, the venture capitalists are concerned that experts in various areas may leave the company and their replacements will have no material from which to learn their jobs; and they are equally concerned that many jobs currently performed by one or two people will need to be performed by several people as the company grows. This is especially true in the area of sales. The company currently has one sales representative, who has a unique gift for qualifying and selling to clients. The company wants you to develop a training course for new marketing representatives that teaches them how to qualify and sell to customers. How would you go about learning about this subject, especially as it relates to this organization?

- You are designing an e-course to train users of new financial management software. You have a copy of the functional specifications for the product, from which you prepared the learning objectives for the course. You also have demographics of the intended users of the product and a statement about the environments for which the software was designed. But this information all seems dry to you, and you feel that you have no material onto which you can "hook" the instruction. What can you do to make the content more personal, so you can develop a more relevant learning program?

- You have designed an e-learning program to provide training on manufacturing safety procedures. After you sent the first draft of the materials for review, one of the manufacturing managers raised loud concerns about using e-learning to teach this material. He claims that his employees have little computer experience and he does not feel that they will master the content. What can you do to assess whether the manager's concerns are true and, at the same time, assess the ease with which users can take the course?

Chapter 4

Blended Learning as a Curriculum Design Strategy

Blended learning can be a powerful strategy for businesses who want to build employees' skills. It can also be a recipe for disaster.

Brodsky, 2003

In This Chapter

In this chapter, we will

- Define the term "blended learning"
- Describe the curricular and emotional benefits of blended learning
- Describe the guiding principles underlying the design of blended curricula (ones that blend different types of learning strategies and media)
- Describe a portfolio of strategies for designing blended curricula
- Describe an in-depth example of a blended curriculum

Angela is designing a course to train customers of her company on ways to program telecommunications systems, which route telephone calls and Internet connections. To successfully program the system, users must not only know the system and its specialized programming instructions, but must also know the concepts underlying telecommunications. Although Angela's product is a new one, many of the users have experience with similar products and familiarity with telecommunications concepts.

In addition, Angela's company is under pressure from customers to reduce the length of training classes because their companies have slashed travel budgets. Because some of the training requires access to specialized equipment, all customers must travel to the company's training centers in Dallas, Chicago, or Toronto to receive training.

As Angela approached the challenge, she quickly realized that she could shorten the training for customers who have experience with similar systems by letting them skip the material covering the fundamentals of telecommunications. The more Angela looked at the fundamentals, however, the more she realized that because the material is factual and basic, it was ideally suited to presentation online. Although the programming could be simulated online, Angela's company did not have the budget to create the simulations.

As a result, Angela decided to split the material into two parts: an asynchronous, online part that teaches the basics of telecommunications and a classroom course, in which learners learn how to operate and program the system.

Placing some of the material in an online format and others in a classroom format is called *blended learning.* Although many people think of blended learning like this as a *course* design strategy, it is actually a *curriculum* design strategy. That is, blended learning looks at more than a single course; it looks at a series of courses and learning events that work together to achieve a larger learning objective. This chapter explores blended learning. In it, we first define the term blended learning. Then we describe some of the guiding principles underlying curriculum design in general, and designing blended learning in particular. Next, we present a portfolio of strategies for designing curricula with blended learning. The chapter closes with an in-depth example of a curriculum designed for blended learning.

What Is Blended Learning?

Blended learning integrates—or blends—learning programs in different formats to achieve a common goal. Most often, blended learning programs integrate classroom and online programs. For example, a blended learning program might present prerequisite material through an asynchronous web-based program, then teach newer content of the curriculum in a classroom, as in the example earlier in this chapter.

But blended learning can also integrate materials in other formats. For example, a blended learning program might begin by presenting prerequisite material in an asynchronous online format, then present the next set of content through a virtual classroom. Rossett, Douglis, and Frazee (2003) observe that anything can be blended in blended learning, whether it be classroom and e-learning, two or more types of e-learning, or two or more types of off-line learning. They suggest that blended learning programs blend material presented from the traditional classroom, live virtual classroom, and asynchronous instruction (Rossett, Douglis, & Frazee, 2003).

Benefits That Blended Learning Offers

Blended learning has become popular among instructional designers for a variety of reasons, some curricular, some personal.

Curricular Benefits of Blended Learning

Writing in a report for Brandon-Hall.com, Marsh (2001) suggests the benefit of blended learning is that it takes the best from self-paced, instructor-led, distance, and classroom delivery to improve instruction. The report states that blended learning has the advantage of being able to overcome the fact that "most e-learning is boring, requiring greater discipline on the part of the student."

More specifically, blended learning offers these curricular benefits:

- Blended learning lets designers split off prerequisite material from the rest of a course. In classroom-only courses, learners must sit through this material, even if they have mastered it. By separating it and using the computer, designers can test learners in advance. Those who can demonstrate mastery of the prerequisite content can skip the online part and go directly to the classroom section. Those who are not familiar with the content can learn it at their leisure, without other learners nearby who already know the material and are visibly expressing their frustration with the novice learners. The computer has infinite patience with these novices. See the section, In Practice, at the end of this chapter for an in-depth case study of a project like this.

- Blended learning lets instructional designers separate rote content focusing on lower-order thinking skills, which can be easily taught online, from critical thinking skills, which many instructors feel more comfortable addressing in the classroom. (These skills *can* be taught online, but many instructors and students are more comfortable addressing them in a classroom.) For example, some companies have overhauled their management training programs to use an approach like this. The programs begin with online modules about management policies and procedures. These online materials include online lessons, use of online guides—such as policies and procedures guides—and study groups, comprised of other managers who are at relatively the same point in their positions. Once students demonstrate mastery of the basic policies and procedures, they continue with a classroom course, in which learners practice complex management situations, such as establishing performance plans, giving performance appraisals, and addressing performance challenges. The classroom segment uses role plays, case studies, and other discovery learning procedures that explore higher-order thinking about these policies and procedures in real-life management situations. Learners can have more meaningful conversations about these topics because they have developed a familiarity with basic management policies and procedures and have had time to integrate what they know into their thinking. Figure 4.1 shows the general flow for a curriculum such as this.

Figure 4.1. Sample Flow of a Basic Management Training Curriculum That Uses Blended Learning

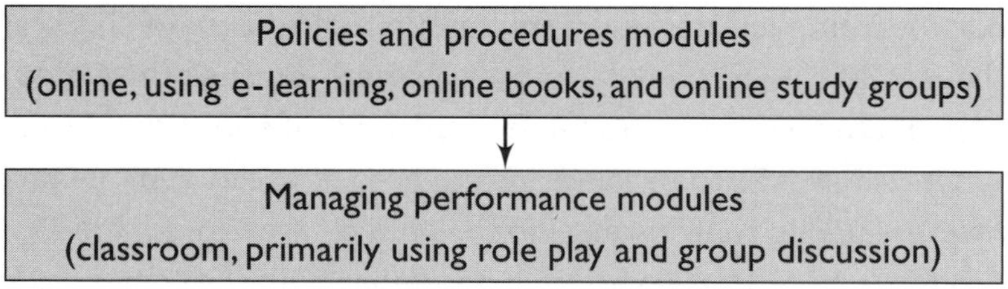

Policies and procedures modules
(online, using e-learning, online books, and online study groups)

Managing performance modules
(classroom, primarily using role play and group discussion)

- Blended learning lets designers tailor learning content to the unique needs of different audience segments. In some instances, designers have a basic core of content that all target learners need, but different segments of that group apply that content differently. In an ideal situation, different learners would learn just the material they need. In a classroom, however, an instructor must teach everyone the unique material meant for just a few. For example, when teaching about a learning management system (LMS), everyone may need to learn about the purpose of the LMS and how to become a registered user. But LMS administrators also need to learn how to add courses and manage users' accounts; training managers need to learn how to print and use reports from the system; instructional designers need to learn how to manage curricula through the LMS; and end users need to learn how to manage their learning plans. A blended curriculum might include a quick, live introduction to the LMS, followed by computer-based modules that teach the different audiences how to use the system in the appropriate way. Figure 4.2 shows the flow of a blended curriculum that uses e-learning to tailor the learning content.

Figure 4.2. Using Blended Learning to Tailor Content

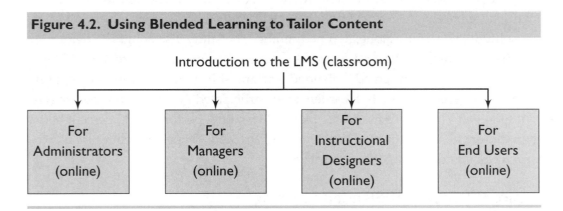

- Blended learning can help reduce total training time and minimize time away from the job for training. Although many enterprises are committed to workplace learning, they face the practical reality of tight budgets and need for workers to quickly acquire new skills and knowledge. As a result, many training managers face pressure to minimize the time spent on training, both actual class time and time away from the workplace. Because of class-related travel, time away from the workplace can be as long (or longer) than the actual class (especially for a shorter classroom course taught in an inconvenient city). But some subjects are sufficiently complex that much of them must be covered in a classroom. However, some elements can still be taught online. Some instructors blend classroom and live virtual classroom (also called synchronous instruction), running some class sessions online, which lets workers take the courses at their workplace. Furthermore, these online sessions can be scheduled at slow times, to minimize absence from work during high activity times.

Training and performance improvement professionals strongly believe that blended learning provides for a more effective learning experience. For example, a 2003 study by The eLearning Guild, found that the top three reasons for using blended learning were

- More effective than classroom alone (76.0 percent)

- Higher learner value and impact; the effectiveness greater than for non-blended approaches (73.6 percent)

- Learners like it (68.6 percent)

These findings are consistent with those reported in a study by Thomson (2002). The Thomson study sought to determine whether there was a significant performance difference on real-world tasks among learners who received a blended learning solution, e-learning alone, and no training. The study also sought to determine whether there are significant differences in time to performance on real-world tasks among learners who received a blended learning solution, e-learning alone, or no training. The study found that learners who participated in a blended program (one that followed Thomson's model for blended learning) performed 30 percent better than those who only took an e-learning program, and 159 percent better than those who received no training (the control group).

Personal Benefits of Blended Learning

In addition to these curricular benefits, blended learning offers a unique personal benefit to instructional designers—namely comfort. When e-learning hit the Internet in the late 1990s (to be technically precise, e-learning first emerged in the late 1960s but was called computer-based training until the Internet boom), many of its strongest proponents suggested that classroom learning was going to decline or disappear altogether. To experienced classroom instructors and designers of classroom instruction, these e-learning advocates were essentially saying that they had become obsolete. Some of these people became resistant to e-learning, even though signs indicated that, after nearly three decades of "experimental" status, e-learning would finally become a significant part of corporate training and higher education.

Blended learning offered a comfortable middle ground. On the one hand, it acknowledged that e-learning would play a significantly larger role in corporate learning and higher education programs. On the other hand, blended learning left a significant and meaningful role for classroom learning. Rather than addressing feelings of being displaced by computers, instructors could focus on meaningful ways to blend the learning experience, appropriately integrating computers where they make sense and providing classroom experiences when they felt computers could not appropriately teach the content.

Guiding Principles Underlying the Design of a Blended Curriculum

When designing a curriculum for blended learning, instructional designers should consider:

- The role of blending in the overall learning strategy
- The purpose of a curriculum in general
- The competency and skills to be developed through the particular curriculum featuring blended learning

The next three sections explore these issues.

The Role of Blending in the Overall Learning Strategy

A *strategy* is a formal, published document that outlines the role of learning in the organization and how the organization will deliver that learning. The strategy provides a general roadmap for the type of learning programs that the organization supports—and which ones it does not support—as well as the way that organization plans to integrate learning technologies into its overall approach to learning. A strategy should first clearly state why the organization supports learning and how learning supports the organization in achieving its broader goals. Then it states (a) who the intended learners are, (b) why they are participating in learning programs, (c) how learning will be provided, (d) how learning will be supported, (e) why the organization is using learning technologies to support this effort, (f) how efforts to move content online will be supported, (g) how success will be measured, and (h) a list of resources committed to this endeavor. This approach to developing a strategy is essentially the same in business, government, and academic organizations. Ultimately, the strategy represents a commitment to learning in general, and learning technology and blended learning in particular.

Some organizations, however, see blended learning as a quick way to break into e-learning, but have no strategy in place. On the one hand, the research suggests that this group is in the majority. In a survey of larger corporations, only 25 percent had a strategy for e-learning (Van Buren & Sloman, 2003). But on the other hand, the results of such blended learning efforts could be disappointing. Sixty-two percent of learning technology initiatives fail to meet expectations (Van Buren & Sloman, 2003).

The Purpose of a Curriculum

As mentioned earlier, most people think of blended learning as a course strategy, when it is actually a curriculum strategy. The word curriculum comes from a Latin word that means to run a course or racetrack and indicates a specific direction and distance. Curriculum design is the practice of designing a roadmap for taking a learner from knowing nothing about the content to reaching a designated level of competence with it.

As part of this effort, instructional designers must consider what they feel is the purpose of training and education. For example, for a corporate training curriculum, it might be asking a seemingly obvious question, like "Why do we train new employees?" Although the ostensible answer is that an organization does so in order that new employees can effectively perform a job, other purposes exist, such as integrating new employees into the corporate culture and building loyalty among them. Similarly, for an academic curriculum, some might respond that the purpose of education is "preparing learners to become productive members of society"; others might respond, "preparing learners for employment"; and still others might respond, "to help the learner develop critical thinking skills in the subject area." Notice how these purposes are not necessarily mutually exclusive.

This, in turn, helps designers figure out which content will be emphasized strongly and which will receive less emphasis. For example, an instructional designer of a civics curriculum in a school who believes that the purpose of education is to create productive members of society might focus on topics of attitudes toward elections and the meaning of referendum questions, while an instructional designer of a civics curriculum who believes that the purpose of education is to prepare learners for employment might focus on voting procedures and employment opportunities in the political sphere.

The Competencies and Skills to Be Developed

With the values around education clarified, designers can consider the content to be addressed. As a starting point, some instructional designers begin by identifying the competencies and skills to be taught. This is where most corporate instructional designers begin. At this point, instructional designers would consider the following:

- *What is the main competency that learners should develop while completing this curriculum?* This isn't a simple skill, like inserting a needle or solving a quadratic equation. Rather, this competency refers to something much more broad, such as "designing bridges that stand up" (civil engineering), "caring for patients" (nursing), and "performing in a drama" (theatre). Specifically, a competency is the quality of being fit physically and intellectually for a task. Bowie (1996) calls this main competency *job one.* Job one often gets lost in the minutia of planning specific aspects of the curriculum.

- *What skills must learners master to successfully achieve this competency?* These skills would be the main foci of designing a curriculum. For example, if the main competency is preparing customer support representatives to resolve problems with equipment or software (depending on the type of support provided), the main skills taught would include troubleshooting failures, diagnosing problems, and resolving them. Typically, a curriculum focuses on a limited number of main skills, and each main skill becomes the focus of a unique learning program (or part of a unique program). For example, the customer support curriculum might have separate programs on troubleshooting, diagnosing, and resolving problems.

Note, too, that in this discussion, the term "skill" also encompasses the term "knowledge." The supporting knowledge needed to perform a main skill is ultimately expressed as a cognitive task—that is, a task that is performed internally rather than visibly, but whose results can be seen externally. For example, adding is a cognitive task because people generally perform it in their heads, but others can see the results of the addition. Similarly, matching prospective customers with the appropriate models of a product is a cognitive task. On the one hand, it requires that learners do something (match people and products), but it is performed internally. What makes these cognitive skills different from tasks like "understand" and "know" (which you have probably already learned are inappropriate for use in instructional objectives) is that if someone were to perform the skill while talking aloud, his or her cognitive process and the criteria for successful performance would be clear enough that different observers would likely reach the same conclusions. With knowing and understanding, different observers might reach different conclusions and have no externally verifiable criteria from which they can assess the differences in conclusions.

- *What supporting skills must learners master to achieve the main ones?* For example, to diagnose problems with software, learners must be able to distinguish between hardware and software problems, re-create problems (if needed and possible), and follow diagnostic procedures to isolate a specific problem. Because a complex task has many supporting skills, curriculum designers often identify several layers of supporting skills.

- *What skills must learners have mastered before they can enter the curriculum?* These are called *entry skills.* One of the challenges of teaching advanced topics is making sure that learners have the prerequisite skills and knowledge. For example, before learners can train to become computer support representatives, they must be able to describe the inner workings of a computer. But how can designers verify that these people can do so? Therefore, designers must also specify criteria for assessing the skill. In this instance, learners can explain how computers process information and how the different parts of the computer participate in that process.

Notice that in all of these examples, competencies and skills were expressed in observable and measurable terms, just like learning objectives. Although some competencies and skills are admittedly difficult to express in such a way, by making the extra effort to do so, instructional designers help to clarify the learning content to be covered in the curriculum. Explaining the inner workings of a computer differs from mapping out the processing of information and results in different information being taught.

Note, too, that instructional designers working like this approach curriculum planning from an output point of view: that is, they start by focusing on the end result, the *output* of the curriculum. Other approaches exist, and would approach the content differently. This identification of skills becomes a starting point for figuring out how to blend the content.

A Portfolio of Strategies for Creating a Blended Curriculum

Once the competencies and skills to be developed through a curriculum are identified, designers figure out how the individual pieces of the curriculum will be presented and how to pull the pieces into a cohesive whole. This is the heart of blending.

The next sections explore how to do this. The first group of sections explores models of blending. The next group of sections explores issues associated with blending the programs in the curriculum.

Different Approaches to Figuring Out What Material Goes in Which Format and Medium

As many people believe that blended learning is a course design strategy when it is actually a curriculum design strategy, so many people think that a decision about which material to put in a given medium is a decision about media when it is essentially a decision about the content.

After instructional designers have figured out what competencies and skills to cover in the curriculum, they next get a general idea of which formats and media to use to teach particular skills. A *format* refers to the type of learning program. Although instructional designers tend to assume that the only type of learning program is a course, the truth is, a variety of formats exist, such as demonstrations, cue cards, tutorials, tips of the day, and wizards. The next chapter on informal learning identifies a number of formats available, and the type of content for which each would be most appropriate.

Only after choosing a format should designers choose a *medium of communication*. In some cases, the format suggests the medium. For example, cue cards (in which users work through an online task one step at a time) are, by nature, online. In other cases, the designer actually has a choice of media. For example, material taught in a classroom can be taught in a traditional or live virtual classroom.

Two approaches are popular for choosing a medium: one based on the complexity of the content and the other by the nature of the subject matter. The next two sections explore these approaches individually, and a short section after that explains what happens next.

Choosing a Format Based on the Complexity of the Content

After identifying the content to be taught in a curriculum, many instructional designers then classify the content to figure out how to blend it. One popular classification scheme is Bloom's taxonomy. This scheme identifies the complexity associated with particular skills based on the action verb in the statement of the skill. Then based on the level of the majority of skills in a particular segment of the curriculum, designers determine the format and medium best suited to teach it. Table 4.1 shows Bloom's taxonomy, the action verbs associated with different levels of the hierarchy, and the formats that instructional designers often use to present content at those different levels of the hierarchy.

Table 4.1. Bloom's Taxonomy, a Hierarchy of Learning Objectives

	Domain	Action Verbs Typically Used with Learning Objectives in This Domain	Preferred Format
Lower-Order Skills	*Knowledge:* Remembering previously learned material.	Defines; describes; enumerates; identifies; labels; lists; matches; names; reads; records; reproduces; selects; states; views.	Drill and practice, often online or another self-study format, although it can be addressed in a classroom.
	Comprehension: "Grasp the meaning of material."	Classifies; cites; converts; describes; discusses; estimates; explains; generalizes; gives examples; makes sense out of; paraphrases; restates (in own words); summarizes; traces; understands.	Presentation followed by practice; often online or another self-study format, although it can be addressed in a classroom
	Application: "Use material learned in new and concrete situations" such as by solving problems.	Acts; administers; articulates; assesses; charts; collects; computes; constructs; contributes; controls; determines; develops; discovers; establishes; extends; implements; includes; informs; instructs; operationalizes; participates; predicts; prepares; preserves; produces; projects; provides; relates; reports; shows; solves; teaches; transfers; uses; utilizes.	Presentation followed by demonstration, then practice; often online or another self-study format, although it can be addressed in a classroom.
Higher-Order Skills	*Analysis:* "Break down material into its component parts," especially abstract concepts.	Breaks down; correlates; diagrams; differentiates; discriminates; distinguishes; focuses; illustrates; infers; limits; outlines; points out; prioritizes; recognizes; separates; subdivides.	Case study and other problem-solving approaches followed by discussion and debriefing; often classroom based or handled in a live virtual classroom.

Table 4.1. Bloom's Taxonomy, a Hierarchy of Learning Objectives, Cont'd		
Domain	**Action Verbs Typically Used with Learning Objectives in this Domain**	**Preferred Format**
Synthesis: Put parts together in novel ways to create a new whole.	Adapts; anticipates; categorizes; collaborates; combines; communicates; compares; compiles; composes; contrasts; creates; designs; devises; expresses; facilitates; formulates; generates; incorporates; individualizes; initiates; integrates; intervenes; models; modifies; negotiates; plans; progresses; rearranges; reconstructs; reinforces; reorganizes; revises; structures; substitutes; validates	Case study and other problem-solving approaches followed by discussion and debriefing; often classroom-based or handled in a live virtual classroom.
Evaluation: Assess material, to determine whether it is likely to achieve its given purpose (if given one choice) and determine which of several choices is most suitable to address a given challenge.	Appraises; compares and contrasts; concludes; criticizes; critiques; decides; defends; interprets; judges; justifies; reframes; supports.	Complex problem solving formats, such as case studies, role plays, and similar formats, often classroom based or handled in a live virtual classroom.

Adapted from the Corrosion Doctors, www.corrosion-doctors.org/Training/Bloom.htm.

The idea of matching the format of the content to the nature of the skills is also at the heart of a second model, proposed by the Masie Center (see Table 4.2). Similar to the model based on Bloom's taxonomy, this one suggests different formats and media to consider for different types of material.

Table 4.2. The Masie Model of Blended Learning		
	Technology-Based Techniques	**Non-Technology-Based Techniques**
Announcement	LMS e-mail push	flyer mail phone
Overview session	e-mail Webinar	traditional classroom
Self-paced learning	Web-based tutorial e-books EPSS simulations	articles books job aids on-the-job training
Query resolution	e-mail FAQ instant messenger	face-to-face meeting
Demonstration	Web meeting simulations	traditional classroom
Practice	simulation	workbook assignment
Feedback	e-mail	face-to-face meeting print report
Closing session	e-mail Webinar	traditional classroom
Certification	Web-based test	print test

Notice that, in this model, some of the instruction happens off-line and some of the learning happens informally (that is, outside of a traditional course). As mentioned earlier, Chapter 5 addresses informal learning.

Choosing a Format Based on the Subject Matter

Another common way of determining how to blend material in a curriculum is based on the type of content. Typically, the type of content refers to the subject matter of the learning material. In academic institutions, content is usually divided up according to subjects, such as anthropology, English, education, engineering, fine arts, history, mathematics, natural sciences, and sociology. In academic subjects, some topics seem more likely to be placed online in part or in full than others. The most popular online programs include computer science and information technology, education (many different sub-disciplines), and business. Continuing medical education has worked well online, although basic medical education (as in preparation for the M.D. degree) has not.

Training organizations divide up content differently. Some common ways of dividing up content include the following (note that some of these schemes overlap with one another):

- *Hard and soft skills.* Hard skills generally refers to technical skills, usually applicable in a specific context. Soft skills refers to abstract content that has broad applicability, such as negotiating skills, time management, and career planning. Hard skills are often easier to define than soft skills, and the learning material is often more concrete.

- *End-user training.* This usually refers to training end users of software applications or specialized hardware. Such training focuses on helping learners use the product, but provides little guidance on how to customize the software or hardware or how to troubleshoot problems with it, other than the most common ways of doing so.

- *Product training.* This refers to training that introduces an audience to a product. Three types of product training typically exist. Customer training teaches customers how to use a product and, if the product is complex enough, teaches customer administrators issues associated with managing the use of the product (such as teaching administrators of large computer networks how to manage those networks). Sales training teaches marketing representatives about the product and how to differentiate it from others on the market and identify and qualify prospects for the product. Service training teaches service representatives how to handle complex installations, customize the product, and troubleshoot complex problems.

- *Compliance training.* This refers to training resulting from a government or industry requirement, or from a corporate directive. This type of training usually addresses occupational safety and health issues, but may also address banking and healthcare regulations, and quality training (like ISO 9000).

- *Management training.* This refers to training that provides managers with basic supervisory, budgeting, and project management skills, as well as special management topics, such as preventing harassment and implementing new management policies.

- *Leadership development.* This refers to programs that are intended to prepare high-potential candidates for executive positions. This type of training occurs in community organizations as well as in corporations and government agencies.

- *Interpersonal skills.* These refer to programs that explain how to interact with other people, such as sales, counseling, management, and telephone skills.

- *Basic skills training.* This refers to training that addresses a deficiency in skills that workers are otherwise assumed to have, such as basic literacy and numeracy skills.

- *Professional continuing education.* This refers to programs that continue the development of people within their chosen professions. In some instances, the body that licenses professionals requires that training, such as required continuing education for medical doctors. In other instances, the education is required so that professionals maintain their employability, such as continuing education for programmers and Web developers.

Generally, hard skills, end-user training, and compliance training seem to have the most success online.

Linking the Pieces Together

When choosing a format, instructional designers figure out how to split the skills among individual learning programs or parts of the curriculum. After doing so, instructional designers consider how the individual pieces work together and initially plan the roadmap.

More than the format of the material, the links between the different pieces of the curriculum need to be clear. Which material should learners take first? Second? Where do learners have choices about their progress? The act of preparing a roadmap (visual representations of curricula and the paths learners would take through them) helps instructional designers think about these links.

Although each curriculum follows a unique path, the next several figures show some common pathways through blended curricula, each tied to one of the curricular benefits described earlier in the chapter.

One common roadmap separates prerequisite content from the main content. In it, learners first take prerequisite material in a self-study format (and, in many cases, have an opportunity to take a test to place out of the material), then move into a traditional or virtual classroom for the main content. Figure 4.3 shows the roadmap for such a curriculum.

Figure 4.3. A Roadmap for a Curriculum with Prerequisite Material

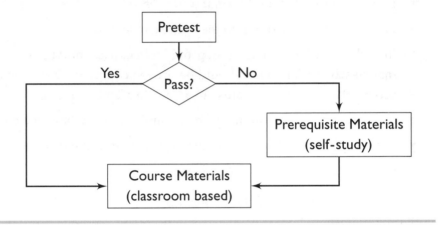

Other curricula have learners start working with a common set of content, then continue with specialized content suited to their area of interest. Figure 4.4 shows an example of a roadmap for such a curriculum.

Figure 4.4. A Roadmap for a Curriculum Tailored to Different Groups

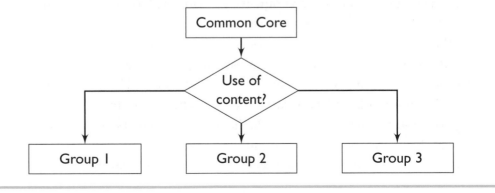

Completing the Curriculum Design

At this point, the choices of formats and media are preliminary, and the relationships among parts of the curriculum are preliminary. Designers then explain the curriculum plan that does the following:

- Considers the practicality of the proposed plan.

- Includes a related plan to make sure learners complete the self-study parts of the curriculum.

- Explains why a blended format was chosen.

- Provides a clear roadmap to the entire curriculum.

- In each part of the curriculum, provides backward and forward signposts that clearly explain what should have been completed before starting a program and what programs are available after completion.

- Includes a plan for validating understanding throughout the curriculum.

- Provides consistent support to learners throughout the curriculum.

The next several sections explore these issues in detail.

Consider the Practicality of the Proposed Plan

Until now, educational needs have driven most of the decisions about design. That is, choice about the format of content and the medium of communication have resulted from the nature of the content being taught.

Before committing to these choices, instructional designers need to consider their practicality. Issues affecting the practicality of design choices include:

- *Time available for development.* Self-study materials generally take more time to develop than ones intended for a traditional or live virtual classroom. Generally, the average time needed to develop one hour of asynchronous e-learning is just under 225 hours (Chapman, 2002) (note that this time is an average; it assumes an experienced development team and minimal media other than the computer, graphics, and programming; extensive use of video could more than double this estimate). In contrast, a typical hour of classroom training requires about forty hours of development time, and a typical hour of live virtual classroom takes about sixty to eighty hours. (Note that these estimates include the time of all members of the development team and assume that although the team has experience developing content, it does not have experience with the subject matter and conducts a full needs assessment.) For projects on tight schedules, content that a designer might have initially wanted to prepare in an asynchronous online format might be presented in a classroom because of the lack of sufficient time to develop it.

- *Funds available for development.* Even if sufficient development time is available, sufficient funds must also be available for the chosen format.

- *Compatibility of the technology and learning environment to the chosen medium.* To take asynchronous online learning programs or programs in a live virtual classroom, learners must have access to computers connected to the Internet. In addition, for programs with sound, learners must have access to a location where they can play the sound without disturbing others. If not, practical issues force designers to move content originally intended to be presented online to another format.

In addition, although blended learning involves e-learning, the organization sponsoring the blended learning curriculum might not realize a substantial cost savings on its efforts. Although the length of a classroom course may be reduced by moving some of the content online, learners may still have to travel to attend the classroom segments of the curriculum. Although lodging costs are reduced because the classroom sessions are shorter, the largest course expense is travel, and that is usually not reduced as a result of blending courses.

Include a Related Plan to Make Sure Learners Complete the Self-Study Parts of the Curriculum

Although learners and trainers say they like blended learning, one of the practical realities is that learners often do not complete the self-study programs in the curriculum. If the self-study materials are essential to having a highly productive classroom session, instructional designers must provide incentives to ensure learners complete the prerequisite materials.

If the learners are internal or academic students, instructional designers have a variety of incentives at their disposal, such as reports to management for workers and grades for academic learners.

But when learners are customers, such as in the case of customer education and continuing education, instructional designers need to find more positive ways of encouraging learners to take the self-study parts. In addition, instructional designers must also have realistic expectations about learners' likelihood of completing prerequisite material. For example, one organization used blended learning for a customer training course. Management had set a goal of 95 percent completion of an asynchronous online pre-course before the classroom course. When surveyed at the beginning of the classroom course only 65 percent had completed it. Of the other 35 percent, 13 percent said that they could not have completed the asynchronous course—their work did not afford them time to do so. In other words, 100 percent completion is not a realistic target.

Designers may find that they need to provide incentives for completing the entire curriculum. The incentives used for completing the entire curriculum are often similar to those used to encourage learners to complete prerequisite material. For example, external incentives such as academic credit, certification, and qualifications for a job promotion also encourage learners to complete a blended curriculum.

Explain Why a Blended Format Was Chosen

Although learners are likely to support a blended approach, the fact that different parts of the curriculum come in different formats could be disconcerting to them.

In the curriculum plan, include plans to make learners aware that the learning program is blended and explain why. Plan to do so through print and online catalogs and similar materials that promote learning programs. For example, if many learners are expected to already know some of the prerequisite material, state that, "Because learners are coming from so many different backgrounds, the program starts with a self-study program that lets learners all work up to an equal level of skill before starting the classroom part of the course."

Or if the program is a blend of asynchronous and live virtual classrooms, state that "To minimize travel costs, we have moved this program online. But to provide you with variety in the learning experience, some segments of the material are self-paced, while others are taught in a live virtual classroom."

Provide Learners with a Clear Roadmap to the Entire Curriculum

One of the major concerns to learners is knowing where to begin the curriculum and where they can go. One of the most effective tools in helping learners figure their way through a curriculum is a curriculum roadmap. An effective curriculum roadmap shows learners the recommended order for covering the material.

An effective roadmap also tells learners the format of the individual parts of the curriculum. For example, consider the curriculum on training for instructional designers shown in Figure 4.5. This roadmap differs from the ones presented earlier in this chapter in that it is intended for presentation to learners; it provides additional signposts not necessary in a roadmap intended for other instructional designers.

Figure 4.5. Sample of a Curriculum Roadmap Intended for Use by Learners

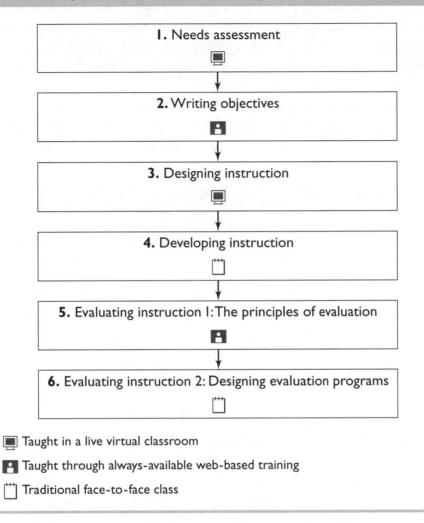

1. Needs assessment

2. Writing objectives

3. Designing instruction

4. Developing instruction

5. Evaluating instruction 1: The principles of evaluation

6. Evaluating instruction 2: Designing evaluation programs

Taught in a live virtual classroom

Taught through always-available web-based training

Traditional face-to-face class

Notice that the sample roadmap not only gives the titles of the programs in the curriculum, but also states the format (such as web-based training or traditional face-to-face class) and suggests an order in which learners should take the courses. Although, in theory, adult learners like to have the flexibility of taking courses and units of courses in their own order, in practice, when adult learners are dealing with a new curriculum area, most prefer to have a recommended path through the content and often follow it as recommended.

In Each Part of the Curriculum, Provide Backward and Forward Signposts

In addition to the roadmap, plan to provide "signposts" in each part of the curriculum that link individual learning materials to those that come before and afterward.

At the beginning of materials, show a copy of the roadmap and highlight the material taught in the current section. Figure 4.6 shows how the earlier roadmap would be highlighted.

In addition, at the beginning of one part of a curriculum, tell learners what they should already know before starting it. Although these are often stated as titles of units that learners should have taken or a list of topics that learners should be

Figure 4.6. Sample of a Curriculum Roadmap Presented Within a Course

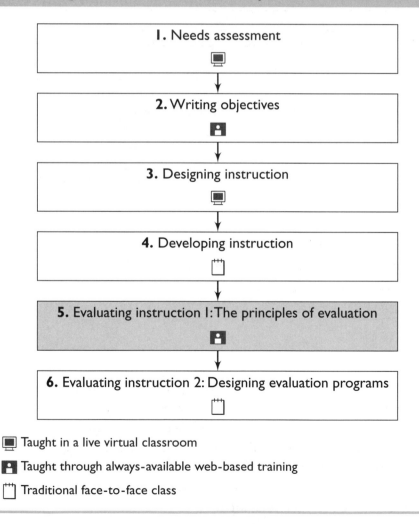

1. Needs assessment

2. Writing objectives

3. Designing instruction

4. Developing instruction

5. Evaluating instruction 1: The principles of evaluation

6. Evaluating instruction 2: Designing evaluation programs

▣ Taught in a live virtual classroom

▉ Taught through always-available web-based training

▯ Traditional face-to-face class

familiar with, this material is ideally stated in terms of skills that learners should have mastered. When the content is presented in terms of skills, learners are not just informed of the topics they need to learn, but they also have a tool for assessing whether or not they have mastered the content. For example, in a course on evaluation, the prerequisite skills might be

- Analyze the needs underlying a unit of instruction.

- Develop objectives for a unit of instruction.

- Design a unit of instruction.

- Develop the learning materials according to the designs.

This list of skills is more useful to learners than "You should have taken the modules on analysis, design, development, and implementation."

At the end of a unit, tell learners two things:

- Which competencies they should develop to continue their learning. These should be stated similarly to those stated in the list of prerequisite skills, but should list skills not yet learned.

- Which parts of the curriculum help learners develop those competencies.

Include a Plan to Validate Understanding Throughout the Curriculum

As learners progress from one part of the curriculum to the next, it is essential that their skills be assessed. Content in a later part of the curriculum often builds on content presented in an earlier part. If learners have not mastered the earlier content, the later content is likely to confuse them (and, of course, they're not likely to master it).

Assessing learning at the end of each phase of a curriculum allows learners to validate that they're ready to progress to the next. If the curriculum does not include a formal test, use informal assessments to help learners ensure that they progress only when they're ready.

If learners have not mastered one part of the curriculum, rather than recommending that they move to the next part, suggest that learners repeat the current part. Use the incorrect answers to a criterion-referenced test at the end of the unit to direct learners to remediation of interest. See the website accompanying this book for guidance on providing remediation to learners.

Provide Consistent Support Throughout the Curriculum

Although the different content is presented in different formats throughout the curriculum—web-based, live virtual classroom, traditional classroom, video, and others—some things need to remain constant throughout. One of the most significant is the support available to learners.

Regardless of whether learners are taking a course in a live virtual class or web-based format, access to tutoring services and technical support should come from the same place—the same telephone numbers and e-mail addresses. Ideally, learners would deal with the same people for support to ensure some level of consistency in taking the blended curriculum.

A single face of support provides continuity in the program, and continuity is believed to be positively linked with achievement.

In Practice: A Blended Curriculum at Hearing Master

General Description of the Project

Title: Implementation Training

Publisher and Producer:

Brief Description: Hearing Master is a startup company that produces custom-fitted hearing protectors. Sonomax must certify the skills of the people who make the custom hearing protectors (people whose job is called *implementer*) before they are allowed to work with clients. Because the process for making these hearing protectors is unique and requires that trainers observe learners, the material about custom fitting hearing protectors must be taught in a classroom. But among the other topics emphasized in the certification training is basic audiology concepts. Some learners already have a background in audiology, others do not. To make sure that people with audiology backgrounds do not need to waste their time repeating content they already know, the company decided to teach that content online. To make sure that only those who need to take it do so, the course begins with a pretest that assesses how much learners already know about the topic. If learners pass the pretest, they can proceed directly to other training. Learners who do not pass the pretest take the material about audiology, which is presented online, then proceed to take the classroom component. After successfully completing that, learners begin a period of monitored work, in which their work is observed. After completing that phase, learners are certified as implementers. After certification, implementers receive a variety of updates. Furthermore, they must periodically renew their certification.

Intended Audience: Prospective implementers of Hearing Master products, who have backgrounds in occupational safety and health and working with hearing issues.

Size of Audience: Several hundred implementers across North America, Europe, and Japan.

About the Learning Goals

Goals of the Project: Traditional learning. To certify learners as implementers of Hearing Master custom-fitted hearing protectors.

Primary Learning Objectives: Given a customer environment and an individual worker in that environment, prepare a pair of custom-fitted hearing protectors for that worker.

Learning Issues Underlying the Project

- Learners come from a variety of backgrounds.
- This blended certification curriculum replaces an existing classroom-only certification.
- Certification requirements also include the following: showing proof of insurance (implementers work for other companies and, therefore, must have their own liability protection); implementers are monitored while conducting their first several fittings before they are fully certified.
- This is both the company's and employees' first experience developing material for e-learning.

The Numbers

Budget Range: $25,000-$50,000 for five hours of instruction. Includes a 1-year lease fee for a learning management system that manages the implementation.

Schedule (from Beginning to End of Project): 120 days.

Approximate Number of People Who Worked on the Project: Five

Skills Used in Project: Instructional design, programming, graphic design

Other Business Issues Affecting the Project: Because implementers work almost exclusively for dealers who market Hearing Master hearing protectors, Hearing Master also had to market the certification process as part of the training program. To do so, modules were added to the e-learning part of the program because the online modules were the first that learners would encounter.

Technology Infrastructure

Delivery Medium: Internet (or intranet)

Media Used Within the Learning Program: Text, graphics (Vector Art), audio (music, sound effects, narration), animations

Delivery Platform: Macromedia Flash® (standalone, or as a plug-in in a Web browser)

Authoring Environment

- Development software: Macromedia Dreamweaver® and Flash. Storyboards prepared in MS Word® and PowerPoint®.

- Delivery Platform: NetDimensions EKP Gold Learning Management System, used to track successful completion of the various components of certification, as well as provide tests, and to provide automatic reminders when implementers need to renew their certification.

Figure 4.7 shows the roadmap of the curriculum.

Figure 4.7. Roadmap of the Hearing Master Curriculum

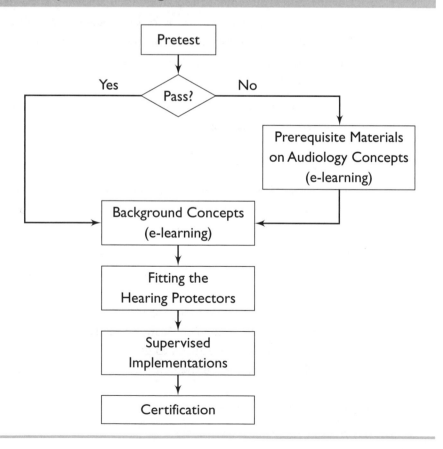

Conclusion

Blended learning is a curriculum strategy that lets instructional designers present learning content in the format and medium that seems most appropriate to the material. To reach this conclusion, this chapter explored the following points:

- Blended learning integrates—or blends—learning programs in different formats to achieve a common goal. Most commonly, blended learning programs integrate classroom and asynchronous online programs. But blended learning can also integrate materials in other formats, as well as two or more types of online learning programs.

- Blending offers both curricular and personal benefits:

    - Curricular benefits include splitting off prerequisite material from the rest of the course, separating rote content focused on lower-order thinking skills from that focused on higher-order thinking skills, tailoring the learning content to the unique needs of different audiences, and reducing total training time and minimizing the time away from the job for training.

    - Personal benefits include comfort for instructors who feel threatened by e-learning, especially those concerned about a meaningful future role for classroom learning.

- When designing a curriculum for blended learning, instructional designers should consider these guiding principles:

    - The role of blending in the overall learning strategy. A *strategy* is a formal, published document that outlines the role of learning in the organization and how the organization will deliver that learning. Rather than serving as an easy entry point into e-learning, blended learning must make a contribution to the larger strategy.

    - The purpose of a curriculum in general: designing a roadmap for taking a learner from knowing nothing about the content to reaching a designated level of competence with it.

    - The competency (main job, such as build bridges) and main and supporting skills (that is, skills needed to achieve the main competency, such as the skills needed to build bridges) to be developed through the particular curriculum featuring blended learning.

- A portfolio of strategies for designing a blended curriculum involves the following:
  - First, consider the strategy for deciding which content goes in which format and medium, such as a format based on the complexity of the content or the nature of the subject matter.
  - Link the pieces together by designing a roadmap for the curriculum. The roadmap specifies the order in which learners should go through the material.
- Before finalizing the roadmap, consider these issues:
  - Consider the practicality of the proposed plan, and whether it works within the available schedule, budget, and technology infrastructure.
  - Develop a related plan to make sure learners complete the self-study parts of the curriculum; too often, learners skip the prerequisite content unless designers add in controls and incentives to require them to do so.
  - Explain why a blended format was chosen, so that sponsors and learners understand why they're receiving the training in several smaller pieces.
  - Provide a clear roadmap to the entire curriculum, so learners have a sense of the whole range of learning available.
  - In each part of the curriculum, provide backward and forward signposts, so learners get a sense of what they have completed and what they have left to learn.
  - Validate understanding throughout the curriculum to make sure that learners are ready to move from one learning program to the next and provide remediation if learners are not ready.
  - Provide consistent support throughout the curriculum, such as tutoring.
  - Provide learners with incentives for completing the curriculum to ensure as high a success rate as possible.

Learn More About It

Barbian, J. (2002, Summer). Blended works: Here's proof! *Online Learning*, 6(6), 26–28, 30–31.

Discusses blended learning strategies and reports results of a two-year empirical study that concludes that blended learning methods boosts employee productivity over single-delivery options. Highlights include examples from a variety of companies, which included scenario-based exercises; realistic business situations; mentors; classroom instruction; CD-ROMs; and web-based courses.

Brooks, S. (2002). *Blended training: Prerequisites and purple monkeys.* Available online from www.learningcircuits.org/2002/jun2002/elearn.html. [Retrieved July 13, 2003.]

This article focuses exclusively on using blended learning as part of prework. The article delivers solid advice using a mixture of humor and sarcasm. It introduces readers to the steps needed to successfully apply blended learning in prework and also cautions about potential problems. The article is notable for its solid grounding in the real challenges faced by course designers.

Morrison, D. (2003). *The search for the holy recipe.* www.morrisonco.com/downloads/blended_learning_holy_recipe.pdf. [Retrieved July 13, 2003.]

The article examines what is required to design a blended learning course. The author stresses the need to design blended learning based on a strategy and not based on rules or recipe-like directives driven by learning style or media selection.

Thorne, K. (2003). *Blended learning: How to integrate online and traditional learning.* London: Kogan Page.

In her usual practical style, Kaye Thorne shows how the concept of blended learning can be applied most effectively in a training program. Case studies from a wide variety of organizations from Rolls Royce to small businesses illustrate her points.

Troha, F.J. (2002). Bulletproof instructional design®: A model for *blended learning.* *USDLA Journal, 16*(5).

Discusses the need for adequate planning in instructional design and describes the "bulletproof model" for the design of blended learning, a model to guide instructional design that combines elements of electronic learning with traditional instruction. Assumes that a performance analysis indicated the need for training.

REFLECTION AND APPLICATION

To reflect on the material presented in this chapter and apply it in a real e-learning situation, consider how you would respond to the following challenges. (Each of these challenges is intentionally left vague. If you are unsure about a piece of information, make an assumption about it and list the assumption.)

- You're teaching a new manager's training course for a large corporation. Before you can jump into the "meat" of the course, learners must demonstrate familiarity with the corporate policies and procedures guide. But many of the learners will have working experience with corporate policies and procedures from their previous job. You know that they will complain if they have to sit through that content. How can you make sure that all learners have the desired level of familiarity before proceeding with supervisory training and, at the same time, avoid requiring those learners who already are familiar with the policies and procedures to sit through content they are familiar with?

- You have decided to launch a product training program for your customers. Your software product is complex and requires a fair amount of conceptual knowledge about software design before administrators can implement it. The instructor for the implementation class has decided that all of the prerequisite concepts must be taught online; he will not cover them in the classroom. So learners are expected to take a precourse before attending the classroom. But the learners are paying customers, not your employees. How can you motivate these learners to complete the prerequisites, without offending them?

- In the upcoming semester, you are teaching an online course about sociology and American health care at a local university. Class sessions will be held through a live virtual classroom. You are also providing web-based materials and a discussion board through Blackboard® (the software product for class management). Is this a blended course? Why or why not?

Chapter 5

Informal Learning

Some people, without expectation of credits, degrees, job promotions, salary increases, or recognition, invest their resources to a significant degree so that they may become knowledgeable—even expert—in a given discipline. . . . [These] individuals . . . indicated they were seeking connections between disciplines or a higher truth.

Graham, 1991, p. ii

In This Chapter

In this chapter, we will

- Define the term informal learning
- Explore why informal learning is a useful approach to online curricula
- Describe the guiding principles underlying informal learning
- Provide a portfolio of strategies for informal learning
- Describe an in-depth example of informal learning

Consider this. Micah manages the database of technical support questions for a software publisher. The database contains every question logged by the technical support staff, as well as the responses provided. When customers call with questions, technical support representatives check this database. But Micah believes that this database has the potential to teach technical support representatives, customers, and system designers how to use their systems more effectively. So he designs a special web page that lets users answer "big" questions about the software by linking them to answers about more specific questions. Interested readers can read until they feel that they can comfortably perform the tasks described.

Or consider this. Aisha is a technical writer for a large software company who decides that, for her next job, she wants to become a technical trainer who leads virtual classes on the Web. Although she can find programs that prepare people to be trainers, Aisha cannot find any program that specifically prepares her for becoming a trainer in a virtual classroom. So she decides to create her own curriculum. She uses e-mail to contact experts in virtual classroom training, and she asks them to identify the skills she should develop. Then she pieces together a combination of readings, courses, and experiences that will prepare her for the job. She estimates that the transition should take about eight months.

Both of these situations describe examples of *informal learning*. In some ways, informal learning is the ultimate form of blended learning (the topic of the last chapter) because it involves learning from a number of resources—both formal and informal, and in a variety of media and formats. Because it involves a variety of materials working together to achieve a common goal, informal learning—like blended learning—is a curriculum development strategy. This chapter explores informal learning. We first define the term and contrast it with the terms formal and self-directed learning. Then we explain why informal learning is a useful approach to online curricula. Next we describe principles guiding the development of informal learning. Then we provide a portfolio of strategies for informal learning. We close the chapter with an in-depth example of informal learning.

What Is Informal Learning and Why Is It a Useful Approach to Online Curricula?

Informal learning is

> a type of education or training program in which learners define what they want to learn and learning is considered successful when learners feel that they are able to master their intended objectives (whether or not the course designers believe that the learners have or have not demonstrated mastery) [Carliner, 2004].

Some experts believe that as much as 70 percent of all adult learning is informal (Cross, cited in Lowry, 2002).

Informal learning contrasts with *formal learning,* in which instructional designers "identify the intended outcomes long before the course begins and learners are only considered to have successfully completed the learning program when they demonstrate successful mastery of these outcomes" (Carliner, 2004). Most guides for developing e-learning focus almost exclusively on developing material for formal learning (such as Alessi & Trollip, 2000; Carliner 2002a; Driscoll, 2002; and Horton, 2000).

We feel that, for e-learning to live up to its promise of providing any time, anywhere learning, it must encompass informal learning. In fact, certain types of e-learning for the workplace are essentially informal, especially knowledge management and performance support (also called *workflow-based training*).

Informal learning is closely tied to the concept of self-directed learning, which is defined as "a process in which individuals take the initiative, with or without the help of others," to diagnose their learning needs, formulate learning goals, identify resources for learning, select and implement learning strategies, and evaluate learning outcomes (Knowles, 1975, cited in Lowry, 2002). Informal learning and self-directed learning are compatible concepts. For the purpose of this book, the primary difference is that informal learning refers to the materials prepared by a designer, and self-directed learning refers to the design of a plan of learning by a student.

Many people confuse informal learning with asynchronous courses that are available on demand, such as a course on MS Excel® that learners can take anywhere they have access to the Internet. Although such courses are available almost whenever learners need them, the courses themselves are still formal. The objectives are furnished by the instructional designers, as are assessments at the end of the course. If the courses are employer-sponsored, learners' performance on these courses is often tracked and reported.

For something to be informal learning, it cannot have externally prescribed objectives. It rarely has formal tests either. Rather, the content stands on its own, and designers do their best to make specific pieces of content easy to find. For example, the U.S.-based medical website WebMD site provides information on a variety of health-related matters, including diseases, chronic conditions, and wellness. Figure 5.1 shows another example of a "center," in which Craig Marion introduces the topic of human-computer interaction, then links readers to related readings. Users find the topic of interest to them and continue reading until they feel they have read all that they need to. The site also provides links to more in-depth content on the Web should users feel that they need more information than is provided at the site.

Figure 5.1. Introductory Screen on Human-Computer Interaction

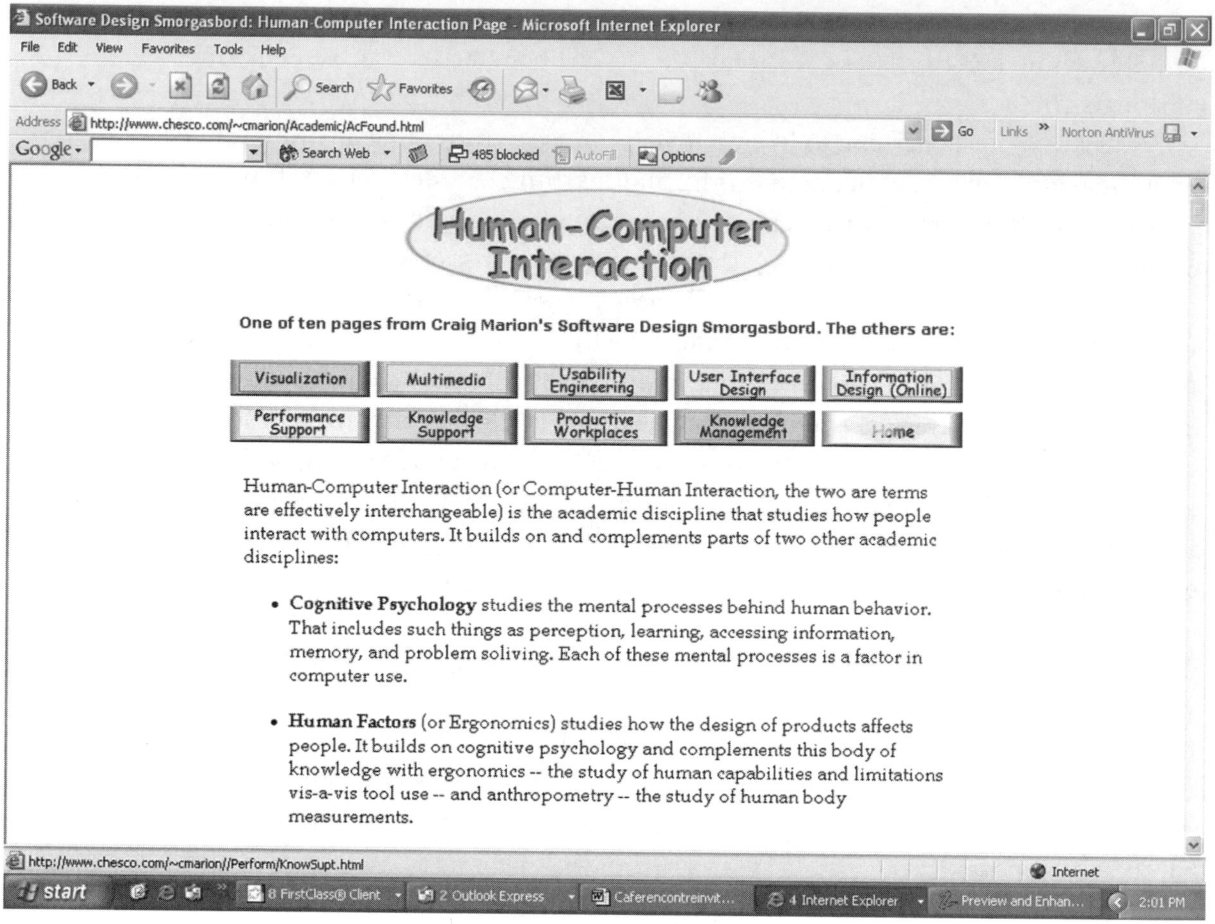

Source: Craig Marion's Design Smorgasbord, http://www.chesco.com/~marion/Design/UIDesign.html. Used with permission.

Similarly, *Computerworld,* the trade newspaper for the computer industry, has a number of Quick Studies, which provide background information about a hot topic in the information technology industry. A learner who needs a crash course on a topic like network sniffers or netiquette can find a briefing at this site. If the learner wants more in-depth content, the Quick Studies provide links to articles from the *Computerworld* archives. Figure 5.2 shows an example of a Quick Study on benchmarking.

Figure 5.2. Example of a Quick Study on Benchmarking from *Computerworld*

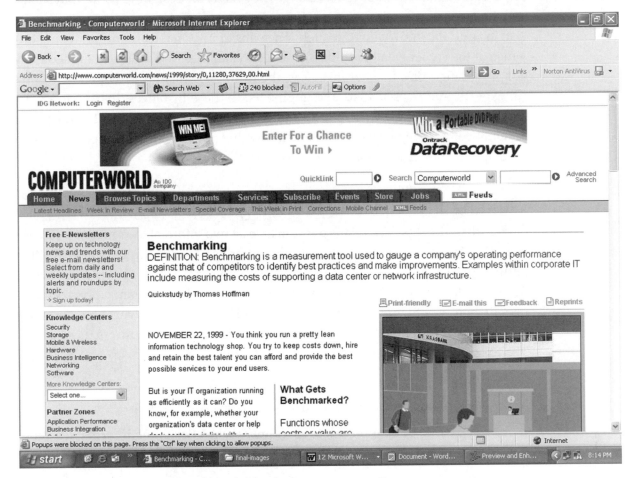

Source: *Computerworld.* www.computerworld.com/quickstudy

Although neither the WebMD nor Computerworld example was designed specifically to build skills (the most technical definition of learning), both provide a learning experience because users can acquire information and act on it.

Although learners are at the center of informal learning programs, instructional designers play a key role in the learning process. When designing curricula for informal learning, instructional designers serve as guides, helping learners choose the types of experiences that will benefit their objectives and link those experiences together in a meaningful way. In some instances, instructional designers prepare original materials for informal learning. They focus on designing content in such a way that users can easily find it in when a moment of need arises. Designers also design around the known limited attention spans of informal learners, show the relevance of the content, and provide meaningful examples that users can immediately adapt in their work. In other instances, the learning content is provided by technical experts, such as scientists and engineers. In these instances, instructional designers prepare forms or templates through which experts can easily enter their material yet can prepare the material in a way that novice learners can grasp the material as effortlessly as possible.

Guiding Principles Underlying Informal Learning

One study found that Canadians perform at least two informal learning projects each year. That's not surprising; the theory of andragogy (adult learning) suggests that adults are self-motivated learners and are willing to learn things on their own if needed. Informal learning, therefore, is a powerful tool that organizations can harness to their benefit. But what are the specific principles that instructional designers should follow to ensure that their informal learning programs address these needs? The following sections explore these guiding principles:

- Reconsider your value system

- Reconsider the role of the instructional objective

- Reconsider your approach to assessment when designing informal learning materials

- Design for the short attention spans of informal learners

- Design informal learning as an interpersonal experience

- Design content that builds skills, not merely informs

Reconsider Your Value System

One of the challenges of designing informal learning is that each learner comes to it with his or her own goals and decides for himself or herself when the goals have been successfully achieved. In other words, learners set the instructional objectives, not you, the instructional designer. This runs counter to the teaching of most instructional design texts, which prescribe that designers prepare instructional objectives before preparing the content, because these objectives indicate what the content should be.

In addition to setting their own learning objectives, learners also determine for themselves when they have successfully completed the material. As a result, some learners might only read a paragraph and feel that they've learned enough. That means that formal evaluations like tests on which instructional designers typically invest a considerable amount of effort—and that we believe to be the only way to assess learning—are also inappropriate for informal learning.

This does not mean that you do not set objectives or write assessments. It just means that both you and your learners need to approach them from a different frame of mind. The next two sections specifically explore the different ways of considering objectives and evaluations for informal learning programs.

Reconsider the Role of the Instructional Objective

Although instructional designers must always remember that learners set the objectives in informal learning programs, the practical reality is that most learners come to the content with similar or identical needs. One of the jobs of the instructional designer is to anticipate those needs and design for them.

The traditional instructional objective serves as a tool for doing so. While objectives for formal learning programs serve as a yardstick against which to measure the success of their efforts and define what designers intend to teach and become the instrument for writing assessments, in informal learning, these learning objectives serve a substantially different role. Certainly objectives describe what designers intend to cover in the material. But the objectives also serve as a tool for setting expectations on the part of learners. By defining up-front what learners can expect to achieve as a result of using the content, designers can help learners determine whether the material will help them achieve their personal goals.

In informal learning, instructional objectives also provide these additional benefits:

- *Focus content under development.* The objectives state what the content covers—implying that material not mentioned in the objectives is not covered. By sticking to the material stated in the objectives, instructional designers ensure that extraneous material is left out and does not confuse learners. For example, when preparing a procedure for end users on diagnosing computer problems, a subject-matter expert might try to add material about how the computer processes information. Although interesting, such material is distracting to the task at hand—figuring out what's wrong with the computer. Admittedly, a curious user might be interested in how the computer processes information, but not when the computer is broken and the user is unable to finish important work.

- *Manage projects.* In addition to setting the expectations of learners, objectives set the expectations of sponsors. Material stated in the objectives is covered; other material is not. If, during the development of a learning program, a subject-matter expert chooses to add content not covered by the objectives, the instructional designer has some leverage to gain additional time or funding because the additional content is outside of the agreed-on scope of the project. For example, suppose that, in the middle of developing material on setting performance plans, someone from Human Resources asks to add material on interim coaching of employees. Although the material is useful, developing that content would take an additional two weeks and, more significantly, the course objectives do not cover that material. The instructional designer could go back to the sponsor and ask for an additional two weeks for the assignment and funding to cover the additional labor because the additional material represents a change in scope and was not estimated into the original plans for the project. The objective would then be changed.

- *Provide entry points to the content for learners.* Because designers use them to divide up content and place it in a hierarchy of main (terminal) and supporting (enabling) objectives, learning objectives also provide entry points to the content. Learners can look at the hierarchy of content and determine where they would like to begin their informal learning.

- *Provide criteria for assessing learning.* In formal learning, the criterion-referenced assessments (that is, ones in which each test question directly emerges from an objective) provide a means for learners to determine whether or not they have achieved the objectives. Instructional designers can provide such assessments in informal learning programs, too. The difference in informal learning is that the assessments are optional—learners do not need to take them if they choose not to. The next section explores assessment in more depth.

Reconsider Your Approach to Assessment When Designing Informal Learning Materials

Informal learning presents a variety of problems for assessment. Because learners set their own objectives and decide for themselves when they have completed an informal learning program, the philosophy of formal testing conflicts with informal learning. Not surprisingly, hardly any informal learning has tests associated with it. At best, some informal learning opportunities provide self-assessments to learners, but the scores are not recorded or transmitted to others.

As a result, learning that must certify knowledge—such as technical training, training on policies and procedures, and certification training—makes bad candidates for informal learning.

But assessment problems are not limited to learning. Assessing a learning program at all of the other levels of the Kirkpatrick (1998) model also poses a problem. Because learners usually have limited interaction with informal learning content, they often do not feel the need to complete a satisfaction survey if one is offered. Furthermore, because learners do not formally register to take the content (they might register to use a site, but their use of the site often extends beyond the topic of their informal learning), identifying who is learning what and assessing transfer of that learning is nearly impossible. When you cannot assess transfer of the learning, assessing impact is similarly difficult. In corporate environments that thrive on accountability, these issues pose serious problems.

Although you cannot formally assess learning nor conduct a traditional four-level evaluation, as suggested by the Kirkpatrick model, you can still evaluate some aspects of informal learning programs:

- *The number of people who use it.* This can be counted by tracking the statistics of usage on individual web pages. Although this number is not a perfect measure (for example, it also includes all of the people in your organization who visit the page), it does provide some indication of whether people are using the content.

- *Satisfaction.* Although you should not expect response rates that approach those of the classroom, it is possible to survey users of informal learning programs about their satisfaction with it. But recognize that most people who complete the survey do so because they have strong positive or negative feelings about the learning program, which may not represent the average learner's response.

- *Learning and behavior.* Although you cannot test learners formally, some designers have found ingenious ways of informally assessing knowledge. For example, consider the assessments of prior learning about topics like dengue fever at the Hong Kong Health Department's Men's Health site (http://www.hkmenshealth.com/eng/calculator/index.asp). In addition to informal assessments, you can conduct interviews and observations with learners and their supervisors and co-workers to find out how they have made use of the content in the informal learning programs. Although this approach may not provide statistical evidence of learning, the overwhelming quantity of content that interviews and observations provide should yield convincing evidence.

Design for the Short Attention Spans of Informal Learners

One of the significant limitations of informal learning is that attention spans are short and dropout rates are high. Some of this has to do with the general behavior of adult learners. According to Knowles (1980), while adult learners are generally goal-oriented and self-directed, they also have other things in their lives that interrupt learning. This is especially true when the learning happens in the workplace or at home, both of which are fraught with interruptions. Some of this has to do with the behavior of users online. They tend to have short attention spans and "surf" around when connected to the Internet. As a result, learners start topics and don't finish, not because they reached a point of completion but because they were distracted by something else. For example, suppose a person heard someone mention *derivative investments* at a business lunch. Not wanting to look foolish, the person did not ask the speaker to define the term, so when he returned to his office he immediately searched for information. He found a brief tutorial on the topic at a financial services website, and as soon as he finished with the definition he went back to work. He achieved his personal learning objective, defining the term *derivative investment*, and did not need to continue studying.

Design Informal Learning as an Interpersonal Experience

Contrary to the opinions of many, informal learning is not solitary learning. To be effective, many informal learning programs should be approached as social activities. For learners using informal learning as part of a career planning strategy, access to more experienced advisors is essential. Although learners might have an idea of how they would like for their careers to develop, they do not have the ability to assess the likelihood of succeeding on their chosen path, nor should they expect to find all of the resources needed to determine how to most effectively develop their careers. Chapter 7 explores mentoring of e-learners in more detail.

Design Content That Builds Skills, not Merely Informs

When designing materials for informal learning, instructional designers can easily confuse informational materials with ones intended for learning. In many instances, informal learning materials double as informational materials, such as online help and online guided tours (also called demonstrations).

The primary difference is that *informational materials* familiarize readers with a topic, but there is not necessarily an expectation for them to act on the material presented. *Learning materials* are intended to help users develop psychomotor, cognitive, or affective skills—that is, do something with the content and continue doing it long after the learning session.

As a result, preparing an online demonstration alone rarely serves as training because it does not build skills. But used in combination with a user's guide and either on-the-job work or informal practice, this demonstration can become part of an informal learning program. For example, to learn how to take a high-quality photograph a learner might first look through the guided tour of the top ten tips for great pictures at the Kodak website (http://www.kodak.com/eknec/PageQuerier.jhtml?pq-path=317&pq-locale=en_US), then read the in-depth material on the site and purchase photography books to develop these techniques.

A Portfolio of Strategies for Informal Learning

With the guiding principles of design for informal learning in mind—reconsidering the role of instructional objectives and the approach to assessment, making informal learning accessible and quick, and designing for short attention spans—we will now consider some of the specific strategies for designing informal learning programs. These strategies include:

- Take a two-tiered approach to design
- Design the curriculum as a performance improvement campaign with built-in consistency and redundancy
- Consider informal learning either as a stand-alone program or a supplement to formal programs

- Creatively package content
- Ensure easy navigation to the learning content

Take a Two-Tiered Approach to Design

Many instructional design texts suggest taking a two-tiered approach to designing individual courses. The two tiers include:

- A *high-level design,* which presents the overall strategy for designing a curriculum. It explains how the content will be divided among specific learning programs and the general strategy for approaching content in each of those programs. A high-level design is much like the site plan for a new construction project. It states the different components of the curriculum, shows how they interrelate with one another, and states the main (terminal) objectives that each covers.

- A *detailed design,* which provides in-depth plans for each of the learning programs identified in the high-level design. In e-learning, a detailed strategy often includes storyboards for each screen in the program, showing exactly which content will be covered on a screen, and the graphics, audio cues, and programming accompanying that screen. See the website accompanying this book for a sample of storyboards for an e-learning program. A detailed design is much like the blueprints for a construction project.

The two-tiered approach is essential to designing a curriculum for informal learning. Although learners are not likely to go through each component of the curriculum, designers can provide a number of resources—some redundant—that are likely to provide learners with the type of content and support that they seek at a given point in the development of their skills and competencies.

For example, people who are new to a topic often need to be convinced of its worth before exploring it. Similarly, in addition to the basics of "how do you do this," novices often want answers to specific, common questions or to develop a broad understanding of the content. Sometimes, novices also require reminders about how to perform specific tasks. Intermediate users often want to find a faster way of completing a task or to break beyond the basic ways of handling specific work online. Experienced users often seek answers to questions that are not covered in formal courses. When preparing a high-level design, instructional designers consider the different needs at different phases of performance. Table 5.1 explores in depth four general phases in the development of learners' skills.

Table 5.1. The Four General Phases in the Development of Learners' Skills	
Phase in the Performance Development Process	**Description**
Advance Notice	Learners benefit from material that builds motivation to learn the concept or technical subject. Informal learning products whose objectives are primarily affective (motivational) work best. These include brief demonstrations (guided tours), preview articles in newsletters, and "advertisements" of the concept. If some learners might have previous experience, self-assessments help learners determine the extent of their prior knowledge and build their confidence in transferring skills.
Getting Started	This is the time when learners are trying out a skill or concept for the first time. Motivation to learn is high, but so is apprehension. Formal learning products that are focused on developing first-day performance (that is, getting people to perform something useful on the first day and that shield users from unnecessary choice) are most useful. Informal learning products—some of which might be introduced in the formal class—serve as reminders back on the job.
Feeling Arrogant	These are intermediate users who have mastered the basic skills and now want to improve their efficiency and effectiveness. Some affectionately refer to learners at this level as "arrogant" because they often become a bit overconfident in their skill at this phase, unaware of the extent of what they do not know. A combination of formal and informal learning products helps learners at this phase. Short tutorials introduce learners to what they can do; help and other informal types of products provide instructions.
Feeling Humble	These are advanced users who are ready to tackle content that might not even be documented yet. Some affectionately refer to learners at this level as "humble" because, although they are extremely proficient with the basic and intermediate skills, they are usually aware of the limits of their knowledge. Informal learning products that let learners interact with other experts help learners most at this level.

Source: Adapted from S. Carliner (2002), *Designing e-Learning.* Alexandria, VA: ASTD Press.

Design the Curriculum as a Performance Improvement Campaign with Built-in Consistency and Redundancy

When choosing strategies to address these different needs, instructional designers must also consider how to reach learners in the most logical, efficient manner. That is, instructional designers must consider what learners might be doing at the moment they sense a need for the content. Then instructional designers need to think about where learners are likely to look for that content, so that learners are likely to find the content of interest when they seek it.

For example, if learners are wondering how to perform a specific task, they are probably performing something already and might look up the instructions in an online user's guide or online help screen. In contrast, to learn new ideas, learners might check sources external to the situation at hand, such as a newsletter or website.

Because these similar questions may arise at different times and in different situations, a curriculum of informal learning usually includes several separate learning programs. This is called a *campaign,* because, in the way that the pieces of an advertising campaign (Web, television and newspaper advertisements, billboards, and other promotions) work together to present a message, so the pieces of a performance campaign work together to build skills in a broad topic area.

Some of the issues to consider when preparing the high-level plan for a curriculum include:

- *Consistency.* Although the different informal learning programs in a curriculum are separate from one another, they should look like they come from the same place. This means ensuring consistency on a number of different levels, including:

  - *Visual consistency.* That is, the individual informal learning programs need to look like they came from the same place. Using the same type families, layout grids, and color schemes helps to promote visual consistency.

  - *Intellectual consistency.* That is, content presented in one learning program should not contradict that in another (unless the contradiction is explicitly stated and the reason for it is explained).

  - *Editorial consistency.* Although the learning programs are separate from one another, they should express similar ideas in similar ways. Terminology presents a special challenge for instructional designers, because it needs to be consistent across the different learning programs (which may be developed by different people and, therefore, raises the possibility of inconsistency). For example, in the early days of computers, the screen went by several different names—work station, monitor, terminal, and CRT display. While representing some technical difference to the authors, the terms meant the same thing to users and, rather than conveying distinct technical meanings, the terms only confused users.

- *Purposeful overlap and redundancy.* In many instances, instructional designers cannot expect informal learners to have read prerequisite material or to have seen other sources. (They often don't do so for formal learning and are even less likely to do so for informal learning.) In such instances, instructional designers must include information in all relevant places. But because the content is essentially the same, it should read essentially the same.

One way to do so is to repeat the content verbatim. Such situations are one of the instances that people had in mind when developing the concept of *reusable content.* Why write the material again when it is essentially the same? Note, however, that although the content is identical, the formatting of it might not be, or the context may differ.

Here's an example of this concept at work. Suppose that a learner is wondering how to change margins with a desktop publishing program. The designer decides to provide the information through informal learning. The designer makes the content available through a user's guide (which is available online as a PDF file), online help, and as a Frequently Asked Question. Although the material is identical in all three situations, it must be formatted distinctly in each. In the user's guide, the material is designed for printing and might include screen shots with examples. In online help, the material is presented in a separate window, often without screen shots as samples. As a Frequently Asked Question, the material is formatted much like that in the online help, but as a web page.

Consider Informal Learning as Either a Stand-Alone Program or a Supplement to Formal Programs

In a curriculum, informal learning programs can either stand on their own as a series of related programs, or they can be designed to work in conjunction with formal learning programs. The following sections explore both uses.

Informal Learning as a Stand-Alone Program

In some instances, designers create entire curricula from a series of related informal learning programs.

Two e-learning contexts specifically support informal learning:

- *Knowledge management.* This represents an effort by organizations to manage knowledge in the same way they manage other assets, like inventory and real estate. At the least, managing knowledge involves recording all of the "known" or explicit knowledge in their organizations, cataloging it, and making it available to all members of the community. *Explicit* knowledge refers to material as mundane as names and addresses in a telephone directory and as complex as the various versions of plans for a new product. At the most, knowledge management involves generating and recording the knowledge that is in people's heads, also known as tacit knowledge. *Tacit* knowledge might include different peoples' perspectives on a strategic direction for the organization and the alternative approaches for solving technology problems. The Internet Movie Database (www.imdb.com) is an example of a knowledge management system designed for the general public. The Online Writing Center at Purdue University (http://owl.english.purdue.edu/) is a knowledge management system that provides extensive online resources on academic writing, as well as information on in-person services available to students.

- *Performance support.* Performance support provides workers with the informational and educational resources needed to perform their jobs online and within the flow of the work. Popularized by Gloria Gery in the early 1990s, the concept is sometimes called *workflow-based training* (Adkins, 2003). Quicken®, the popular personal accounting software that walks users through each financial activity, is an example of a performance support system.

Informal Learning as Supplement to Formal Learning

In other instances, designers use informal learning as a supplement to formal courses and create a curriculum that blends the two. For example, many university professors supplement their classroom courses with websites. In addition to resources that support formal learning, such as syllabi, course schedules, and assignments, these websites might also include links to external websites, professional associations, alternative commentaries, and similar resources that allow highly motivated students to continue their learning. For example, consider the list of resources from Saul's course on human performance technology shown in Figure 5.3.

Figure 5.3. List of Resources from a Website Supporting a Course on Human Performance Technology

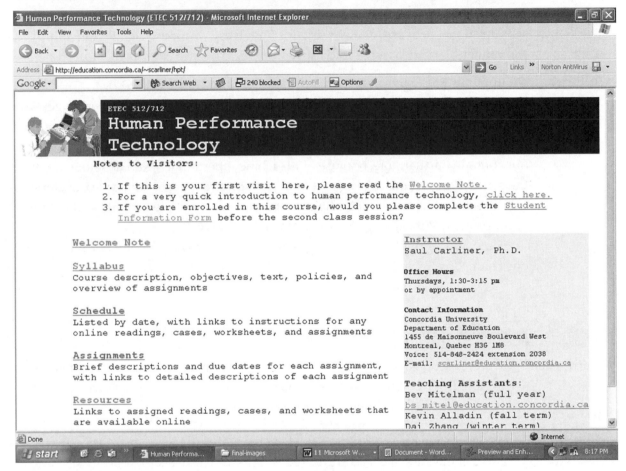

Source: Saul Carliner. http://education.concordia.ca/~scarliner/hpt/resources

Similar approaches can be taken with online, asynchronous training courses. For example, at the end of a course on how to use a new heart monitor, one provider sends informal e-mail messages to learners at intervals after the training to remind learners about the proper use and care of the devices.

Such after-course, on-the-job reminders of content are called job aids because they're intended to aid participants in remembering key learning points on the job (Rossett & Gautier-Downes, 1991).

Creatively Package Content

Because informal learning does not rely on formal courses to deliver content, it challenges instructional designers to find ways to ingeniously and effectively place content in front of learners. This is called *packaging* the content, because, like a package sent through a delivery service, this effort involves "wrapping" content in approved "containers" and delivering it to learners.

Change the Package

Because most instructional designers are used to one primary type of package—the course—and just a few ways of delivering it—classroom, synchronously online, and asynchronously online—we often have difficulty identifying alternate packages for our content. Furthermore, because our teaching repertoire is often developed within the context of teaching courses and that's what we're most comfortable developing, we often have difficulty expanding our repertoire to include formats that are most appropriate to "packaging" informal learning content.

Some additional "packages" that course designers might consider include the ones named in Table 5.2.

Table 5.2. Alternative Packages for Learning Content	
Advertisements	Promotions of various aspects of a product or service. Often appear inside the front or back covers of a publication or on the screens displayed by an application when users start or install it.
Blogs (also called weblogs)	An online column of sorts, in which the author (blogger) provides ongoing commentary and links to related websites on a particular topic of interest. Publication frequency varies, but may be as frequently as daily and as infrequently as whenever the blogger has time to contribute. In a few instances, a blog might have several contributors.
Columns	Ongoing feature articles from experts whom learners come to respect. Although similar to a newspaper columnist, columnists contributing to informal learning usually provide how-to information in their columns, rather than opinions (as many news columnists do). Learners seek out the advice of these experts in their given areas. Columns might be posted semi-weekly, weekly, bi-weekly, monthly, or quarterly.

Table 5.2. Alternative Packages for Learning Content, Cont'd	
Coaches and Advisors	Online tools that assist users with cognitive (intellectual) tasks. Examples of coaches include: • Online assistants that prompt customer support representatives whose traditional job has been taking address changes to identify marketing opportunities • Online assistants that tell customer service representatives at credit card companies whether or not they can extend a customer's credit limit • Online tools that help workers choose a personalized curriculum of training courses
Cue Cards	Instructions that tell learners how to perform a task and that are displayed by the system one step at a time. These visually resemble a flash or cue cards, from which they receive their name.
e-Mail Reminders	Provide a follow-up reminder to learners about a topic presented in another context. For example, following a formal course on clean room procedures, learners might receive a few reminder messages by e-mail with checklists they should go through before entering a particle-free manufacturing area. Or an intermediate learner who finds a couple of useful tips in a newsletter might sign up to receive free tips later on.
e-Newsletters and Webzines	Contain a collection of articles and provide ongoing communication with a target group. For example, a product newsletter provides ongoing contact with the customers who have already purchased a product. An employee newsletter provides ongoing contact with the employees in a department or within an entire organization (Price & Price, 2002).
Frequently Asked Questions	A list of questions that help users answer an immediate question. The questions often emerge from logs of feedback from users. Because the logs indicate that users frequently ask certain questions, designers place those questions online so users can quickly receive an answer without having to call for help. In some instances (especially for content that is so new that people have not yet used it), content designers and developers generate the list of questions based on ones they anticipate users having.

Table 5.2. Alternative Packages for Learning Content, Cont'd

Gaming/Simulations	Learning experiences that replicate the central characteristics of complex situations (that's the simulation) and that let users experience the consequences of decisions made in that situation (the gaming aspect). Examples of gaming/simulations include: • Aircraft and nuclear simulators, which recreate disaster situations that can be used to train pilots and operators • Training courses in interpersonal relations, such as sales and management
Guided Tours (also called demos)	An online movie or slide show that provides users with a "tour" of a product. The tour may be "narrated" or may be self-running. Often, demos provide users with an opportunity to try certain aspects of a product.
Help (online user assistance)	A special type of user's guide for software that is available to users online as they use software applications (Mobley & DeLoach, 2003).
Job Aids and Quick References	A communication product intended to give users a brief refresher about a topic. Examples include a summary list presented online or a cheat sheet presented online (Rossett & Gautier-Downes, 1991).
References	Encyclopedic listings of all major topics on designated subjects. A telephone directory is a reference. So is the *Physician's Desk Reference,* as are the programming references provided with software. Programming references list all of the commands that programmers can use to create their own applications using that software.
Tips of the Day	A tip about a product or subject that is not required for everyday use, but the knowledge of which could increase the productivity of the user.
Tutorials	A lesson, or series of lessons, intended to develop a skill that users can immediately use. The lessons are taken asynchronously; that is, all of the learning content is available online. Learners can take lessons at their convenience (Driscoll, 2002).
Virtual Classes	A lesson, or series of lessons, intended to develop a skill that users can immediately use. The lessons are taken synchronously. That is, the learners interact online with an instructor who is online at the same time. A recording of the learning session might be available for later use.

Table 5.2. Alternative Packages for Learning Content, Cont'd	
Wizards	Online "agents" that automatically perform complex tasks for learners, only prompting learners when they must make a decision. When learners are prompted to make decisions, the system should have a default (presumed) choice to offer (Wickham, 2001).

Source: Adapted from S. Carliner (2002), *Designing e-Learning.* Alexandria, VA: ASTD Press.

Consider the Packaging

One of the ways to build comfort working with a new type of "package," or form of learning content, is by becoming aware of the conventions associated with it. Different types of packages are actually different *genres* of materials. You may be familiar with the term genre from literature and film. Just as film has different genres, such as comedies and dramas, so learning materials have different genres, such as tutorials and references. One characteristic of genres is that each has specific *conventions*—the expectations that learners bring to that type of learning product (Kostelnick & Roberts, 1998). These conventions help audiences receive messages and respond meaningfully (Allen, 2000), thus improving the productivity of reading and using content. For example, a convention in Frequently Asked Questions is the display of a series of questions and answers. A convention in printed references is an alphabetical ordering of topics.

In addition to choosing a genre when designing informal learning materials, designers must also consider the conventions of that genre. By considering the conventions and designing around them, designers take advantage of learners' existing knowledge and help them to use the materials more efficiently. Specifically, designers should consider the following issues to make sure that they correctly design materials for the chosen genre:

- *The way that learners will find or be presented with information.* Different types of learners are likely to bring different expectations about the way that they will be led to content of interest to them. For example, people are likely to expect to go directly to information of interest in a reference through use of searches and an alphabetical listing of entries, but to be led through the information in a tutorial one screen at a time. These conventions also extend to the manner in which users navigate through the content. They are more likely to rely on search strategies in reference material and more likely to use buttons moving them forward and backward in a tutorial.

- *Types of information available.* Within different types of learning products, learners expect to find different types of content. For example, people expect to find screen shots to illustrate procedures in a user's guide, but just the basic instructions in online help.

- *Format of the information.* Within different types of learning products, learners expect different presentation strategies that are tailored to both the nature of the content and users' needs and motivations. For example, people are likely to expect step-by-step procedures in a user's guide, but just a general overview of a procedure in a newsletter article.

- *Writing style.* Within different contexts, users are likely to expect communicators to address not only their need for content, but their roles in accessing it and motivation to use it. For example, people are likely to expect a direct writing style in references and a more supportive and persuasive style in tutorials.

- *Screen design.* As a result of conditioning by similar sites, learners are likely to expect that certain types of online content will follow a certain type of presentation. For example, tutorial screens usually fit the physical screen and do not require users to scroll. In contrast, news-like articles typically extend beyond "the fold" (the length of the screen) and begin with a mini table of contents, linking readers to different sections of the article.

- *Organization.* Within different contexts, learners are likely to expect not only a different organization of the content, but also differing levels of control. For example, tutorials follow a well-defined structure and often recommend a path that users should follow. Tutorials typically begin with objectives and follow with an introduction of the material, exercises, summary, and an assessment. In contrast, references provide a search structure or follow an alphabetic organization. Learners expect parallel structures among entries within the reference, especially if the structures address the same type of content (for example, learners would expect the sections on individual commands in programming languages to have identical section headings).

- *Quantity of content.* Within different contexts, learners are likely to expect different quantities of information. For example, a novice learner checking a tutorial might expect to learn only one way to cut and paste text, while a user checking a reference manual might expect to see all available methods described.

One tool for ensuring that content in various formats meets the expectations of learners is the use of *templates.* Templates are forms that standardize the format of content in particular situations. For example, suppose that you are designing a help system to promote formal learning. You might have a particular format for each topic, and prepare a template to ensure that every topic follows a consistent structure and has a consistent appearance. For example, Figure 5.4 shows a template for a course calendar used in an academic course.

Figure 5.4. Template for a Course Calendar

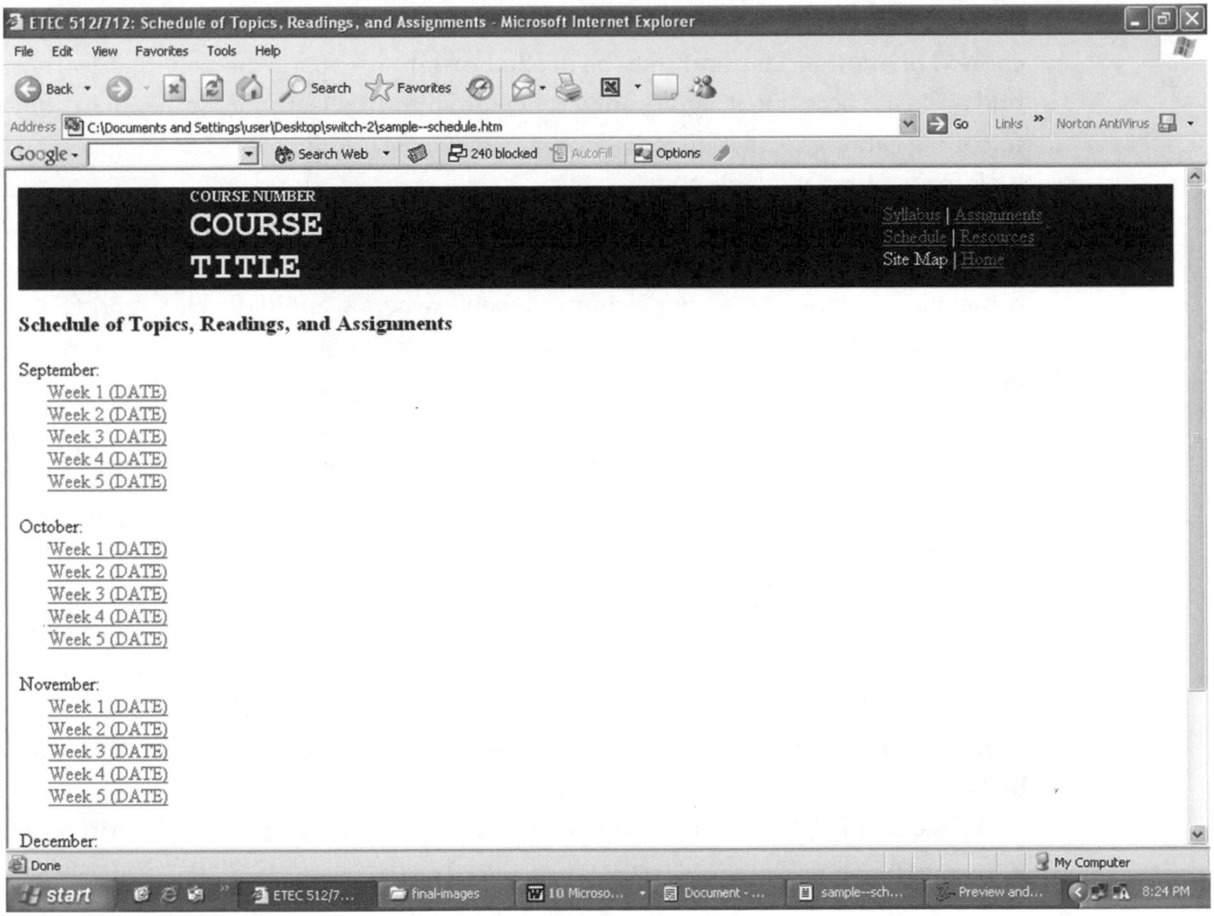

In addition to considering the expectations of learners, designers must also consider programming, technical, and usability issues when considering the form (genre) of given learning materials in some instances. For example, when preparing wizards, designers try to shield users from the complexity of tasks. Designers must program the system to perform tasks for users—and make sure that the system performs them efficiently. Although the system performs most of the work in a wizard, in some instances, the system must prompt users for information on how to complete the task. In those instances, designers must present users with a limited number of well-selected choices and, when possible, a logical default choice.

Ensure Easy Navigation to the Learning Content

The last consideration in designing informal learning is ensuring easy navigation to the learning content of interest. Because informal learning often happens within the context of another task and may be needed instantaneously, the way that learners find and gain access to it significantly differs from formal learning. Rather than going to course catalogs and registering for courses, informal learners sense a need and look for the first available source.

Because some informal learning is needed within a particular work context, the ideal way of helping learners navigate to it is by building the learning within that context in an obvious way. For example, when learners want to develop reports with Quicken, they click on Reports on the menu bar. Or when learners need to learn the official airport code for a city, they can click on the Airport Code options just below the entry field in most online travel services.

Sometimes, designers cannot make the learning so obvious. In those instances, they can use the Help menu to make learning options clearer. For example, some Help menus have had options like "What is?" and "How do I?" to help direct learners to either explanations or procedures.

In other instances, learners want to find specific pieces of information. In such instances, "search" provides a useful option. For example, suppose that a learner wants to find out how to change line spacing on a PowerPoint® slide. Because the number of procedures for PowerPoint is large, a learner could speed up the search by typing the words into a search field.

While helpful, however, studies show that users find the intended information with search in less than 50 percent of their searches (Spool, 1997, 2001). One reason is terminology; learners have one term for a concept while the designers of the content have another. For example, line spacing is called "leading" in publishing circles, but "line spacing" in PowerPoint. Designers can address that problem by including synonyms in indexes.

But sometimes, learners simply don't know what they're looking for. In such instances, a hierarchy of menus is helpful. Many designers are concerned that using menus to direct learners to a particular piece of information might require that designers violate the "three clicks rule." The "three clicks rule" says that users should have to click no more than three times to get to content of interest. But the truth is, no one knows where the three clicks rule comes from, and other studies suggest that if users feel that their search is fruitful, they'll stick with it until they reach content of interest.

In Practice: An Example of Informal Learning from Microsoft

One excellent example of informal learning is the material for Microsoft Office® users, available at the Microsoft website (www.microsoft.com). Microsoft promotes informal learning on a variety of topics; most of the learning seems especially geared toward intermediate users (ones who are "feeling arrogant"). More significantly, Microsoft provides informal learning through a variety of types of content:

- Demonstrations, which show how to use material

- Articles, which provide how-to information

- Self-assessments, which are designed to be fun—but also help learners determine how much they really know about a topic; learners are then directed to relevant materials

- Templates, which help learners efficiently and effectively prepare material in various Office applications

Consider these examples. To begin the informal learning experience, learners first visit Office Online (shown in Figure 5.5), the central location for materials about Office applications, which include Access®, Excel®, FrontPage®, Outlook®, PowerPoint®, and Word®.

Figure 5.5. Microsoft Office Online, the Beginning of an Informal Learning Experience for Intermediate Users

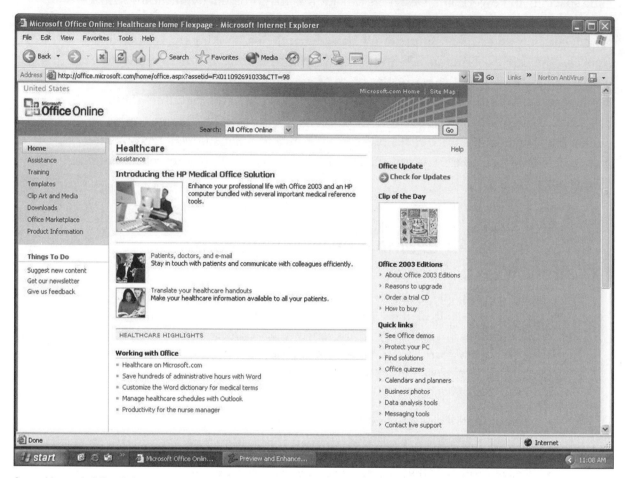

Source: Microsoft Office Online. www.microsoft.com/office. Screen shot reprinted by permission from Microsoft Corporation.

To figure out how to build their skills, learners might first choose to take a self-assessment. Figure 5.6 shows the list of self-assessments and Figure 5.7 shows a sample self-assessment for an aspect of PowerPoint.

Figure 5.6. List of Self-Assessments Available at Microsoft Office Online

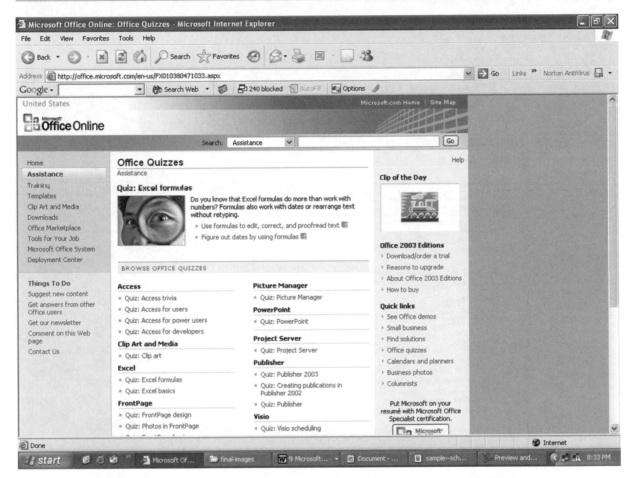

Source: Microsoft Office Online. www.microsoft.com/office. Screen shot reprinted by permission from Microsoft Corporation.

Figure 5.7. A Self-Assessment on PowerPoint

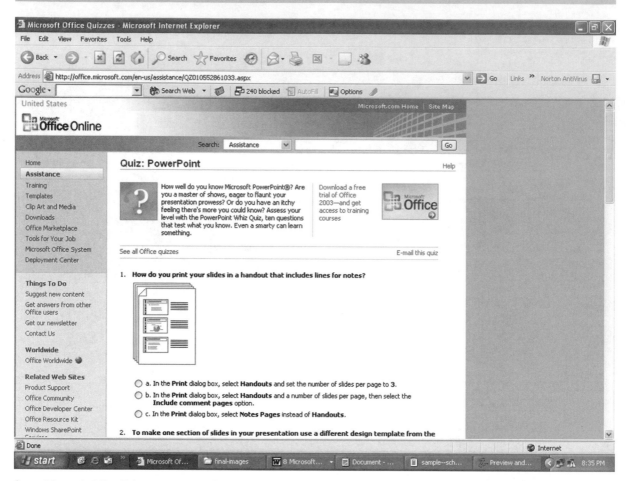

Source: Microsoft Office Online. www.microsoft.com/office. Screen shot reprinted by permission from Microsoft Corporation.

Next, learners choose among the various options. One possibility is a demonstration, so learners can see how to perform various tasks (often called "show me" help). Figure 5.8 shows the menu of possible demonstrations and Figure 5.9 shows a sample demo of a task in Outlook.

Figure 5.8. List of Demos Available from Microsoft Office Online

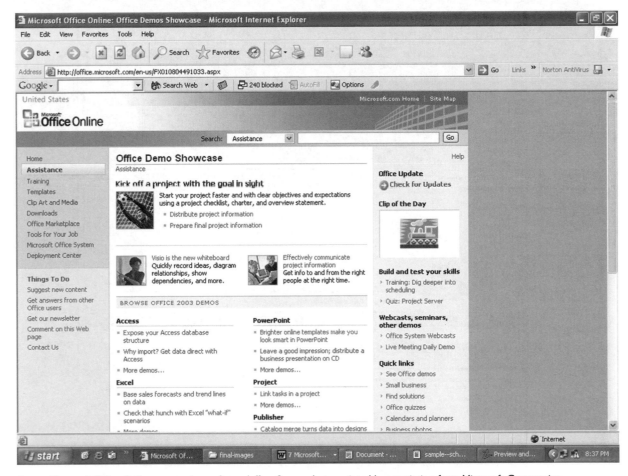

Source: Microsoft Office Online. www.microsoft.com/office. Screen shot reprinted by permission from Microsoft Corporation.

Figure 5.9. Sample Demo of a Task in Outlook

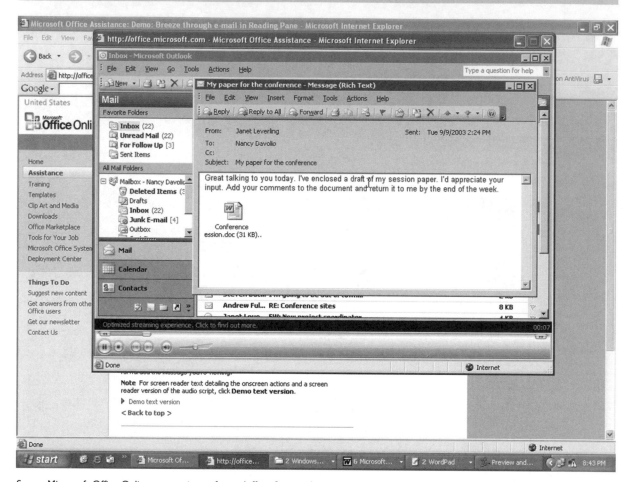

Source: Microsoft Office Online. www.microsoft.com/office. Screen shot reprinted by permission from Microsoft Corporation.

Some learners come to respect the advice of a particular expert and regularly read the material they post. This expert is called a *columnist,* much like columnists in newspapers. Figure 5.10 shows a list of columns available at Office Online, and Figure 5.11 shows an example of a column from the Crabby Office Lady.

Figure 5.10. List of Columnists Who Contribute to Microsoft Office Online

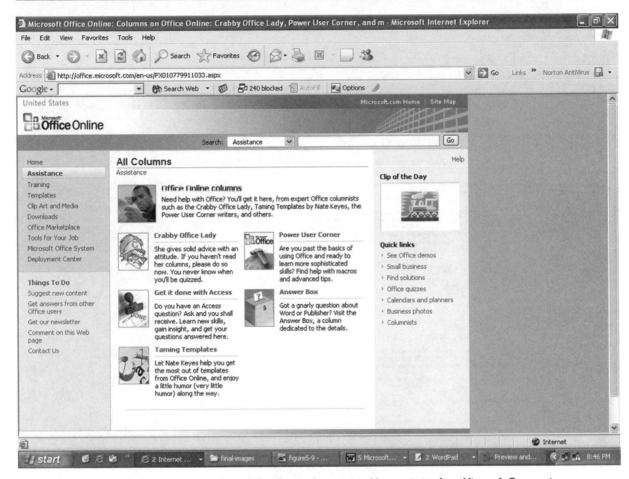

Source: Microsoft Office Online. www.microsoft.com/office. Screen shot reprinted by permission from Microsoft Corporation.

Figure 5.11. A Column About Word from the Crabby Office Lady

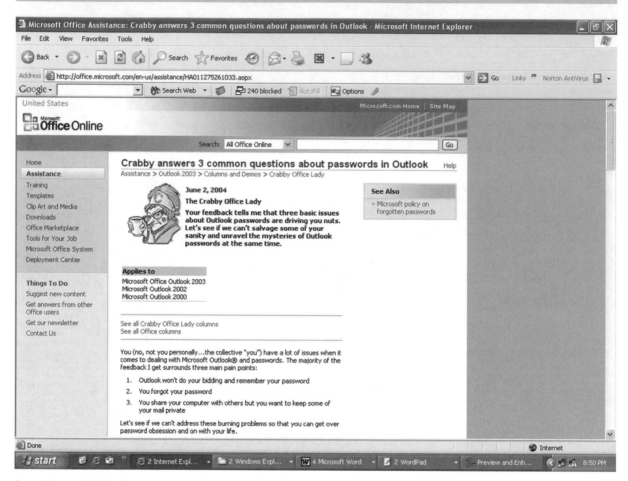

Source: Microsoft Office Online. www.microsoft.com/office. Screen shot reprinted by permission from Microsoft Corporation.

Conclusion

Informal learning helps designers realize the any time, anywhere aspect of e-learning, by encouraging them to break free from the traditional tutorial and providing learners with just the content they are likely to need at a given point in their use of a particular product or concept, and provide that content in a medium and format that's suited to that need. To reach this conclusion, this chapter explored the following points:

- *Informal learning* is a type of education or training program in which learners define what they want to learn, and learning is considered successful when learners feel that they are able to master their intended objectives (whether or not the course designers believe that the learners have demonstrated mastery). It contrasts with *formal* learning, in which instructional designers set the objectives and assess whether learners have successfully achieved the objectives. Informal learning also contrasts with *self-directed* learning, in which learners also define their own learning needs, but do so using materials that were not originally intended for learning.

- Principles guiding the design and development of informal learning programs include the following:

  - Reconsider your value system, in which instruction is based on objectives that the instructional designer provides and is only successful when learners complete a formal test of those objectives. Although objectives and evaluations play a role in informal learning, the learner is the one who ultimately sets objectives and assesses completion.

  - Reconsider the role of the instructional objective. Rather than telling learners what they must learn, objectives help set learners' expectations, help designers focus and segment content, manage projects, and provide appropriate entry points for learners.

  - Reconsider your approach to assessment when designing informal learning materials. Rather than serving as a tool for the instructional designer, assessments become tools to help learners determine for themselves how well they have mastered content. In addition, because it was designed for formal learning, Kirkpatrick's four-level approach to evaluating learning must be adapted for use with informal learning.

  - Design for the short attention spans of informal learners, and prepare for learners to start but not finish these programs. Consequently, avoid using informal learning for material for which learners must complete all content and demonstrate mastery of it.

  - Design informal learning as an interpersonal experience. Design into it activities that involve consultations with other learners and experts.

  - Design content that builds skills, not merely informs. In other words, informal learning must help learners do, not just know how to do.

- Consider these strategies for designing informal learning programs:
  - Design the curriculum as a performance improvement campaign with built-in consistency and redundancy. A campaign involves preparing a series of related learning programs that, together, achieve the performance goal. Consistency means that the materials have visual consistency (look alike), intellectual consistency (ideas in one place do not contradict those in another), and editorial consistency (use terminology and approach other editorial issues in a like way). Because learners are not expected to use all materials—and other learners might forget material they previously read—some of the material must be repeated (redundant).
  - Consider informal learning as either a stand-alone program or a supplement to formal programs.
  - Creatively package content, using formats other than the tutorial and online help, such as cue cards, e-newsletters, and wizards. After choosing a form, consider the conventions for structuring and designing content in that form: (1) the way that learners will find or be presented with information; (2) types of information available; (3) format of the information; (4) writing style; (5) screen design; (6) organization; and (7) quantity of content.
  - Ensure easy navigation to the learning content. Place links to the materials in places where learners are likely to look for them, use good terms for indexing the content, and provide a clear hierarchy of menus for those learners who would prefer to be led through the material rather than search through it.

Learn More About It

Gery, G. (1991). *Electronic performance support systems.* Tolland, MA: Gery Performance Guild.

The seminal work introducing the concept of electronic performance support systems.

Price, J., & Price, L. (2002). *Hot text: Web writing that works.* Indianapolis, In: New Riders Press.

In addition to general guidance in writing material for presentation online, the last part of this book explains how to write content in various forms (genres). Many of the genres presented in the book are ones that facilitate informal learning.

Rossett, A., & Gautier-Downes, J. (1991). *A handbook of job aids.* San Francisco: Pfeiffer.

Although the authors do not explain how to produce online job aids, this book provides in-depth explanations of how to design seven types of job aids. The guidelines transfer to the design of job aids and similar types of informal learning materials online.

Stolovitch, H., & Keeps, E. (1999). *Handbook of human performance improvement.* San Francisco: Jossey-Bass.

This book first explores the concept of human performance improvement (technology) in general, then explores a variety of approaches that build performance without formal training. Most of these approaches, called *interventions,* involve informal learning.

Websites of Interest

www.brint.com/km/

A portal leading to a number of online resources about knowledge management. The founders of the site even prepare a book by combining readings available elsewhere on the Internet.

www-distance.syr.edu/sdlhome.html. Self-Directed Learning web page.

A page that seems to have started as a resource for a course, but has become a source for self-directed learners about self-directed learning.

www.epsscentral.com. EPSS Central.

Contains a variety of resources about electronic performance support systems, including an archive of articles published on the topic. Also directs visitors to sites with resources on related topics.

REFLECTION AND APPLICATION

To reflect on the material presented in this chapter, and apply it in a real e-learning situation, consider how you would respond to the following challenges. (Each of these challenges is intentionally left vague. If you are unsure about a piece of information, make an assumption about it and list the assumption.)

- Your company is launching a new program for electronically filing purchase requests. Because you are the trainer for the program, you have observed usability tests with prospective users. One of the things that you noticed is that most users can electronically file their requests for the first time without any assistance. (That is, the prompts that are already on the screen are sufficient.) Do you need product training for this application? If yes, why? What will the training cover? If no, why not? Would you provide other support instead? If so, what?

- You have been talking to the thought leader on e-learning in your company. He is extremely proud of the company's third web-based training course. "It's really electronic performance support," he claims, adding that "users keep going back to this course after taking it just to check a fact or verify a procedure." But is this really electronic performance support? Why or why not?

- You process all of the comment forms in your organization. You've received two interesting notes. One comments on a discrepancy between the online course and the online user's guide. One tells users to cut and paste by using the icons on the button bar at the top of the screen. The other tells users to cut and paste using keyboard shortcuts, like Ctl+X and Ctl+V. Although both are correct, the customer thinks that this discrepancy in your documentation is a problem. Is it? Why or why not? Another learner complains because the procedure for placing text in bold type is the same in the user's guide as in the online help. The writer says, "How cheap can you get? Couldn't you afford a second writer?" But is this repetition a bad thing? Why or why not?

Part III

Portfolio of High-Level Design Strategies

This section looks at four broad strategies for approaching the design of material that will be delivered online. They are called *high-level design strategies* because they focus on issues that affect the theme and approach of the entire learning program, rather than the presentation of specific content or specific types of content. Design that focuses on the presentation of specific content or specific types of content is called *detailed design.* The next section describes strategies for detailed design.

Each of the approaches described in this section can serve as a primary approach to the design or be used in combination with one another. These strategies differ from the curriculum strategies described in the previous section, because they affect only a single e-learning program; curriculum strategies affect several related programs. When high-level design strategies are used, they become the heart of the design for the program.

The first two chapters in this section address different approaches to teaching.

Chapter 6, Simulations, describes how to use simulations in teaching. Simulations create authentic learning experiences that engage learners, supply authentic practice, encourage critical reflection, and provide feedback. Instructional designers who choose to use simulation have a number of strategies from which to choose.

Chapter 7, e-Mentoring and e-Coaching, describes how to teach online within the context of a real job or task, rather than by creating a safe environment for practice and experimentation.

The last two chapters in this section show instructional designers how to move beyond simply mimicking the traditional classroom and how to expand their thinking about the collaborative, just-in-time, and context-based learning opportunities.

Chapter 8, m-Learning, explores ways to move learning off of a bulky computer and onto more portable devices, while working within the constraints of these systems.

Chapter 9, Live Virtual Classroom, suggests ways to effectively teach synchronously online.

Chapter 6

Simulations

Simulations offer society the opportunity to play out strategic moves to see the outcome before actually committing oneself to a real-life plan. They can, for instance, empower biologists to explore the growth of cells, network managers to analyze the flow of information, city planners to play through complex growth and pollution scenarios, school children to experience the fragility of food webs, and more.

Ioannidou & Repenning, 1999

In This Chapter

In this chapter, we will

- Define the term simulation
- Discuss the factors that have been obstacles to the adoption of simulations as an instructional strategy
- Describe the benefits and limitations of simulations
- Describe nine types of simulations to add to your portfolio of simulation techniques and explain how these types of simulations differ
- Provide a portfolio of examples of simulations

Simulations are described as "the most cutting-edge e-learning technique" (Lipschutz, 2004). They offer a radical departure from the highly criticized page-turns, drill-and-practice programs, and workbooks online. Simulation-based programs promise to engage learners by making them active participants in real-world problem solving and allowing them to engage in role plays, providing a safe environment for exploration. These promises have captured the attention of the instructional designers and their clients. Simulations must be evaluated in the context of the problem-based design. Simulations are not a silver bullet, but they should be an important part of your portfolio.

This chapter explores a wide range of simulations that include attitudinal simulations; case studies; games; symbolic (invisible) simulations; physical simulations; role plays; procedural simulations; software simulation; and virtual reality. These strategies are grouped together because they require active participation in order for learners to gain news skills and knowledge. The active and hands-on nature of these strategies results in understanding based on experience.

What Is Simulation?

Simulations are models or representations of devices, equipment, principles, processes, and situations that enable learners to experience and learn about these things in a safe and supported environment.

Online learning simulations are models of real systems that enable learners to conduct experiments for the purpose either of understanding the behavior of systems or for evaluating various strategies. The degree to which simulations model or represent real-world phenomena, physical objects, and interpersonal events varies greatly. Budget, time, and technology also dictate the scope of simulations.

Using technology-based simulations, learners have the opportunity to experiment and to try a variety of strategies in ways that are often not practical or financially feasible in traditional classroom-based simulations.

Why Use Simulation?

The question "Why use simulation?" is worth considering. As Billhardt (2004), writing for *Chief Learning Officer* magazine, points out, simulations have not gained widespread adoption in corporate training. He cites "the largest roadblock to widespread adoption of online simulations as uncertainty over how to develop, use, and incorporate simulations successfully into exiting training environments."

As you look at the portfolio of examples in this chapter, you will see four reason why instructional designers choose simulations. Simulation strategies are essential problem-based design tools when you must gain attention, create a reflective opportunity, provide authentic practice, or teach software applications.

Consider simulations when you must develop training on a topic that is "old news," such as time management or corporate policies. Simulations can also breathe new life into subjects that are theoretical or complex. Consider simulations for teaching topics such as cardiovascular health or stock market concepts. Involving the learner in a story or asking him or her to play a role gains attention.

Think about simulations when it is not enough to simply know the right answer. Instructional designers asked to deliver programs for teaching high-order thinking skills such as analysis, synthesis, and evaluation should consider simulations. Simulations can provide an opportunity for reflection or a chance for learners to consider how they arrived at an answer, why the answer is right/wrong, and the outcomes of alternative answers. In many e-learning programs, learners read and respond to multiple-choice questions and rarely reflect on their answers. Simulations can be an excellent strategy to encourage reflective thinking by allowing learners to try alternative choices and observe the outcomes of their decisions. In physical simulations such as *Control the Nuclear Power Plan*, learners can experiment in a safe environment with a model of a nuclear reactor, and in a role play such as *The Doctor's Dilemma*, learners can reflect on ethical issues with no clear right or wrong answers.

Simulations can also enable instructional designers to create authentic practice. Consider the authentic practice that firefighters get from *interFIRE VR* or the kind of realistic patient assessment skills medical professionals develop using case studies such as the *KUMC Burn Patient*. Simulations with authentic practice not only engage the learner, but they may improve the skills transfer from learning to practice.

As Brenda Sugrue (2003a) argues, "The active ingredient in simulations is authentic practice with feedback to correct errors. Authentic practice can be expensive and time-consuming to produce. Good practice mimics the decision-making process, the problem-solving steps, and the application of skill and knowledge involved in the real task. Corrective feedback is equally challenging to develop. Feedback should do more than ask the learner to 'try again' or tell her the correct answer. Corrective feedback should explain why the response is wrong and why the alternative answer is right."

Think about simulations when you are asked to develop software application training. Simulations offer instructional designers a range of options from full immersion strategies of NETg and SmartForce to narrated simulations.

As you build your portfolio of problem-centered design strategies, consider simulations when you want to gain attention, create a reflective opportunity, provide authentic practice, and teach software applications.

The Benefits and Limitations of Simulations

Simulations can rescue many online learning topics. As the challenges discussed previously illustrate, there are some situations for which simulations are ideal. This section looks at the benefits and limitations of using this instructional strategy. Clearly there are lots of good reasons to use simulation, but these need to be seen in light of the real limitations. As you review the examples in the Portfolio of Simulations Strategies in the next section, consider these factors in the context of your practice. Instructional designers need to decide what tradeoffs they are willing to make in the context of the training program they are designing; there are no absolute right or wrong answers.

The Benefits

Simulations engage the learners by thrusting them into the learning experience. These kinds of interactions actively engage learners to analyze, synthesize, organize, and evaluate content and result in learners constructing their own knowledge. The following section looks at the benefits of active learning through simulations.

Allow Learners to Learn by Doing

From our own experience we know that the best way to learn how to do something is to actually do it. In our home and work life, learning by doing is a natural and practical way of learning how to do things such as bake a cake or operate a new copy machine. We could learn how to do these things by reading, listening to someone tell us how to do them, or by watching a video, but these strategies are far less effective than learning by doing. Simulations offer learners an opportunity to learn by doing in a virtual environment. Examples of learning by doing such as EMTB.com's automated external defibrillator (www.emtb.com/8e/Interactive_simulation_view .cfm?simid=11) and the CADWeb coronary artery disease programs put learning by doing into practice.

Allow Learners to Practice Tasks That Might Otherwise Be Too Expensive, Dangerous, or Impractical

Experienced instructional designers will tell you the challenge of advocating for a learning-by-doing strategy is the practicality. Some cases, such as teaching people how to deal with an angry customer, how to drive on wet roads, or how to recognize the effects of different dosages of a hypertension medication, are best done in a simulated environment. In these cases, it is either not practical to allow learners to perform every skill in a real setting, it may be too dangerous, or the equipment may not be available. The example of managing a nuclear reactor in the next section illustrates this point. In many cases it may be too expensive to allow large numbers of learners to learn by doing. In these cases simulations can provide realistic experiences not possible otherwise.

Engage Learners in Active Exploration and Learning

Gaining the learner's attention is one of the first steps in many theories of learning (Gagne, 1985; Keller, 1987; Dick, Carey, & Carey, 2000). In addition to gaining the learner's attention, program developers needs to *keep* the learner's attention. One way to gain and to maintain learners' attention is to make learners active participants by creating simulations that challenge them to solve problems and apply new knowledge. For example, after teaching the principles of supply and demand, use a simulation requiring learner to set the price and determine the number of units to optimize three outcomes maximizing profit, maximizing market share, and minimizing manufacturing costs. MIT offers an online version of *The Beer Game* to teach supply chain management. Programs like this require learners to actively explore and learn how changes in supply and demand affect profitability, market share, and the size of a manufacturing run.

Simplify Complex Concepts, Processes, and Situations

Reality is messy and complex; simulations allow educators to build artificial environments and objects that simplify reality. Using a simple model, learners can solve problems, apply procedures, and understand processes in a safe environment. This simplified world allows learners to gain confidence and build skills and mental models needed to address real problems. For example, a role-play simulation for medical professionals required to ask for organ donation can teach the essential communication skills and legal considerations. Another example of this can be seen in the Kansas University program to teach medical professionals how to treat burn patients.

Motivate Learners

Motivation is often defined as the internal or external force that accounts for the arousal and the direction and sustenance of behavior. Simulations have the ability to motivate learners by showing them how the learning is relevant and meaningful to them. An example of this can be seen in the patient education for Prozac. A simulation called SimProzac (http://agentsheets.com/Applets/simprozac/), created by a psychiatrist for his patients, motivates learners (patients) to explore the relationships among Prozac, the neurotransmitter serotonin, and neurons and how those interactions may affect them. By playing with this simulation, patients are more motivated to learn about the drug than by reading the paper-based description included with the drug.

Set the Stage for Future Learning and Provide Practice and an Opportunity for Knowledge Integration

Simulations can set the stage for future learning. When simulations are used as a pre-instructional activity, they provide motivation by linking future learning to real-world application, reveal misconceptions that would inhibit learning, provide a context or cognitive structure for receiving new material, and serve as concrete examples of complex, abstract concepts. For example, prior to attending a traditional class on controlling hypertension, doctors are required to complete three simulated cases in which they need to diagnose the problem and prescribe medication. These simulations provide the groundwork needed to prepare them for the classroom portion of the class by revealing their misconceptions about hypertension and provide a context for understanding the new information that will be presented in the classroom portion of the class.

The Limitations

Simulations, like other instructional strategies, have limitations. Learning through exploration and learning through doing put high cognitive demands on learners. Learners are expected to analyze and assimilate new information; this is more taxing than simple memorization or taking notes in a lecture. Often more of a dissuading factor is the cost and time required to create simulations. These limitations need to be weighed in light of the problem being solved and the tradeoffs evaluated.

Simulations Can Result in Inefficient and Ineffective Learning Behavior

This can happen if the learner founders through the simulation. Simulations must undergo formative evaluation to ensure they are effective and efficient. Formative evaluation will dictate when learner support and guidance are required to assist a student working through a simulation. This support and guidance are accomplished in simulations through the use of prescriptive feedback and a "help page" that supplies supplementary guidance and instruction. If you don't have time to build effective and efficient direction and feedback, simulations may not deliver.

Simulations Can Be Difficult to Design

Simulations are rule-based interactions, and it is not clear that any set of rules simple enough to incorporate into a computer program are also adequate to describe the complexities of the physical world or virtual world. Instructional designers need clarity regarding the goal of the simulation, model, or role play. It is also important to understand the assumption and biases that are part of simulations. A popular simulation program is SimCity (http://simcity.ea.com/), a program designed to allow users to build a city by making decisions regarding things such as zoning, sanitation, and public transportation and to see the results of these decisions. This is an excellent example of a program that has many assumptions about cause and effect regarding urban development and demonstrates the challenges of design.

Simulations May Oversimplify

The simplification of complex reality is an educational asset of simulations. By focusing the learner's attention on a simple set of rules, procedures, concepts, and processes, it is easier for the learner to understand these things than it would be in the complex real world. Instructional designers need to be aware that in the absence of hands-on experience, learners may confuse the simplified model with reality. When possible, learners should be given an opportunity in the curriculum to transition from (or at least compare) simulation to reality to avoid any confusion.

In Simulations for Software Applications or Soft Skills, It Can Be Difficult to Find Realistic and Meaningful Activities

This is especially true for broad applications used across a wide domain. For example, it's difficult to develop scenarios that are directly related to a specific user's job for general word processing applications. Likewise, it is difficult to develop programs for skills such as negotiations, communication, and supervision that cross industries and organizational cultures.

Simulations Are Expensive to Develop

Simulation development is typically so expensive it is usually undertaken only when poor performance in "real life" would lead to a crisis. In general, simulations should be used when the cost of alternate instructional strategies is high, the risks involved are considered too high, and demonstration of competence in a controlled risk-free environment is sought, or when it is impossible to study concepts in "real time." The expense of this strategy is offset by the benefits of having an instructional application constantly available that is repeatable, consistent, takes less time, and costs less than alternative instructional strategies such at learning on the job (potentially making costly errors) and providing one-on-one instruction.

An example of an organization that found value in using simulations is the Rotman's Change Management and Health Leadership programs at the University of Toronto. In this program, learners get to test out change management theory and practice in a scenario-based game that compresses the cause-and-effect relationship of their decision making. In Rotman's alumni magazine, Greg Warman, a senior partner at ExperiencePoint, who developed Rotman's living case study, provides some insight. Warman discusses the number of technical specialists and amount of time needed to complete a project. He observes that, "not surprisingly, the cost is high, ranging anywhere from $250,000 to $1 million" (Bradford, 2003). He also points out that these costs dictate that customizable simulations must have shelf life.

Simulations Can Be Technically Challenging to Distribute

Simulations often rely on plug-in or software applications to help them play the simulation. Other programs require that the user download a program to make the simulation, model, or role play function. Keep in mind, many organizations do not allow learners to install plug-in or other application or in other cases learners simply don't have the skills needed to install a plug-in or execute a download. Even simulations, models, and role plays that rely on Java Applets or Serverlets may encounter problems with firewalls.

A Portfolio of Simulation Strategies

Have you ever taught a class of training professionals? If you have, then you have met the toughest group of critics.

While critical reflection is good and part of our professional heritage, it needs to be tempered with insight into the context of the examples you are about to experience and with an appreciation for parts done well. As you look at the examples, remember that they have been chosen for a specific aspect that has been done well or for how they have overcome budget constraints, technology limitations, or a design challenge like no right answers or a population with poor reading skills.

The examples have been divided into nine kinds of simulations to form a rough taxonomy. It could be argued that a given simulation example could fit in more than one section. In cases where an example could be in more than one place, we have chosen what we think is that example's strength and placed it in that category.

The examples presented here feature a screen shot and web address. At the time of writing, these examples were free and could be found by following a link from the URL provided. If the links don't work, try searching using terms like simulation, simulator, online learning, web-based training, demo, free sample, and other terms.

Attitudinal Simulation

Attitude simulations teach learners *how* to deal with the attitudes and behavior of people in different situation. These simulations allow the learner to experiment with multiple approaches to solving a problem. Learners try different solutions in a safe environment and receive feedback.

The example in Figure 6.1 is an excerpt from an eight-hour "Senior Friendly" program developed by Snyder, Inc., in partnership with EDT Learning. The program helps young workers in senior care facilities learn to communicate better with seniors. The program has great production values with lots of scenario-based learning. Take the time to get to the point where you play *Teresa* (the character shown) and you make decisions about patient/family relationships. The role-play portion is well done with realistic dialog. This uses video, so moderate bandwidth is required. Great attention is paid to the dialog, and the use of a moderator keeps the program flowing. The video takes advantage of the nursing home background and rich details to establish creditability while avoiding details that would date the program.

Figure 6.1. Example of an Attitudinal Simulation

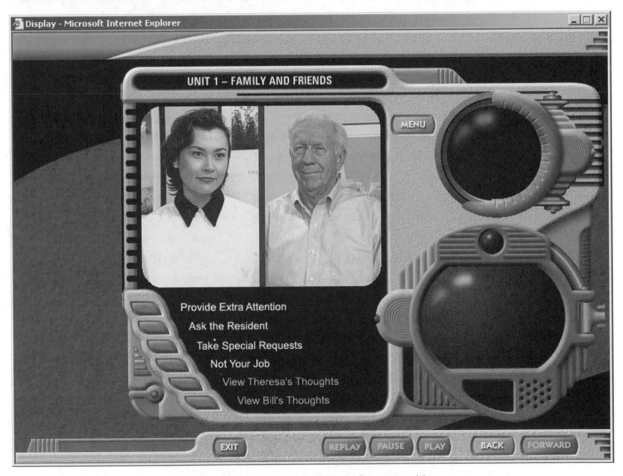

Source: iLinc Communications. http://customer.edtlearning.com/snyder/ (choose Briggs example)

Other attitudinal simulations:

- Business Etiquette: Communicating in Today's Workplace. http://www.netg.com

- Manager as Coach and Councilor. www.skillsoft.com

Case Study

Case studies offer a low-cost way of simulating or reproducing a situation in which learners can be asked to apply new skills and knowledge. Case studies can be developed from actual events or they can be created to ensure the goals of the program are realized. Using the Web, case studies can be as simple as text-based cases posted on a website or e-mailed to students, or they can be more elaborate presentations featuring streaming video and access to backup documents and data accessible online.

Case studies take advantage of adult learners' preference for learning experiences that have practical application. The cases require learners to draw on their past experience and to apply new knowledge to solve a problem. The challenge in writing a case study is to select a problem that is relevant and interesting to students given their level of experience and knowledge of the concepts being taught. Online learning offers a variety of options that range from working alone to working in groups on the analysis. Case studies can be delivered in real time using live virtual classrooms, chat, and instant messenger or asynchronously using e-mail, static HTML pages, or streaming media.

According to Harvard Business Online, "The case study method is designed to provide an 'immersion' experience, challenging students by bringing them as close as possible to the business situations of the real world" (2004). Case studies work best when the topic being studied does not have clear right or wrong answers. The topic should be conflict provoking, and the process of analysis should be as important as the final answer.

Try the example featured in Figure 6.2 to see a well-written case study without fancy graphics or slick programming. The program teaches concepts, principles, and practices related to treating burn patients. Review the objectives and then page through the program. Notice how the lesson maps to the objectives. The navigation allows learners to move back and forth between information and to link to additional reference material. The testing strategy is also worth noting; learners must request to have the quiz mailed to them—keep in mind there is no mandate for automation of testing. One of the other things to note is that the program is interdisciplinary (that is, it serves multiple medical audiences). Rather than writing a separate program for each audience, the base-level content is reused and the specific audiences are branched to discipline specific information when needed. The Department of Respiratory Care Education at the KU Medical Center is to be applauded.

Figure 6.2. Example of a Case Study Simulation

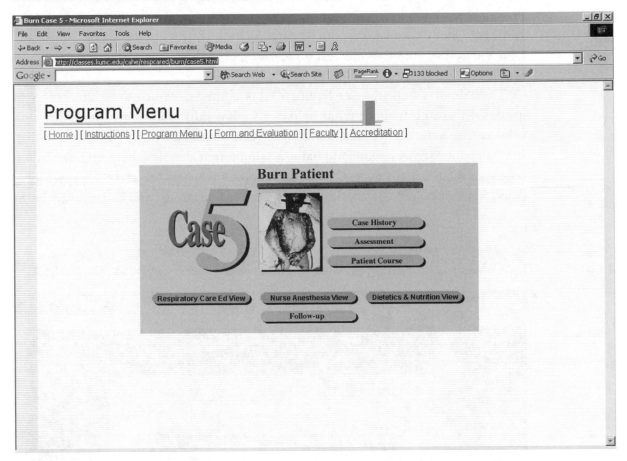

Source: University of Kansas Medical Center Respiratory Care Program. http://classes.kumc.edu/cahe/respcared/

Other examples of case studies include:

- InteractiveEval (A Social Work Case Study).
  www.socialwork.ed.ac.uk/EAL/InteractivEAL/index.html#video

- American Academy of Family Practice Case Studies.
  www.aafp.org/x22313.xml

- Case studies for an undergraduate course in pharmacology.
  http://cvu.strath.ac.uk/courseware/socialwork/fal/#

- Family and Life Span Development.
  http://cvu.strath.ac.uk/courseware/socialwork/fal/#

Game-Based Simulations

Games are an instructional strategy to which an entire chapter could be devoted. In this chapter we are looking at games as they relate to simulations. In this context the games are really simulations with scoring. As the examples in this section illustrate, games-based simulations are best for learning objectives that are right/wrong and scorable.

The Salmon Challenge (see Figure 6.3a) is a game designed to teach learners in grades 4 through 9 about what helps and what inhibits the health of Chinook salmon. The federal government placed the Chinook on the endangered species list. In this game, learners adopt and name a salmon that they will help migrate. In the course of the salmon's migration to Puget Sound, learners are asked ten questions. Good answers help the learner's salmon grow big and strong, and bad answers harm

Figure 6.3a. The Salmon Challenge

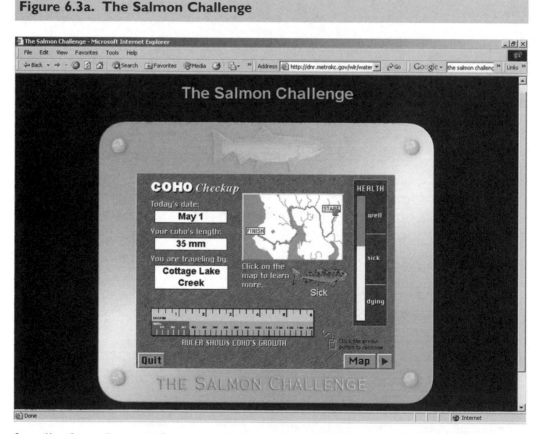

Source: King County Community Outreach and Grants. http://dnr.metrokc.gov/wlr/waterres/salmonch.htm

or kill the learner's salmon. This program uses nice reinforcement techniques for good and bad answers. The authors have gone beyond trite responses of "try again" and "correct." The support materials such as the map and the health check offer learners additional depth in learning about related issues. This is a single player game. I would recommend that you contrast this to one of the multi-player games such as *International Communication and Negotiation Simulations* (found in Role Play). It is also interesting to look at the scoring mechanisms in other educational games.

The Health Care Game (see Figure 6.3b) is a simulation based on the lives of four families who encounter a range of health events. These events force learners to seek information about how the family will identify and access the services required. Working in teams of five to six people, learners use a threaded discussion to discuss their advice and options for the family.

Figure 6.3b. The Health Care Game

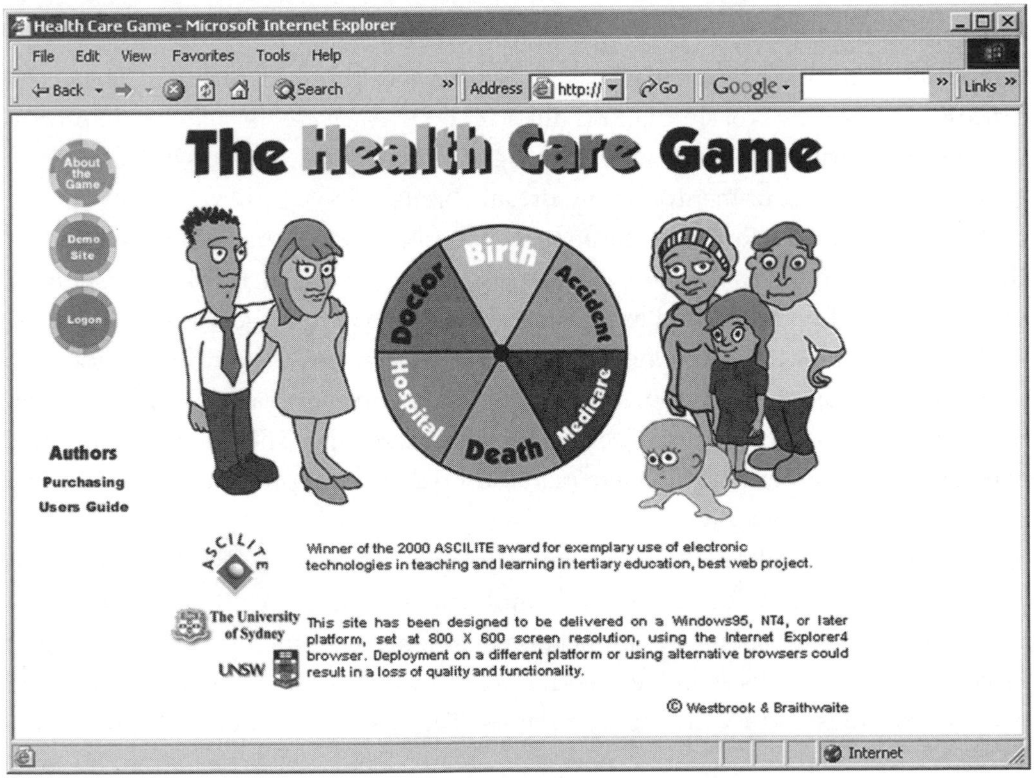

Source: Center for Health Informatics University of New South Wales. http://www.unsw.edu.au/currentStudents/nonAward/pve/csnafmedicine.html

This game demonstrates outstanding instructional design. The demo site provides readers with an opportunity to see well-designed problem-based learning and well-crafted dilemmas that bring in the complexity of economic, social, and cultural issues. What you cannot see but can read about in a paper about this game (Westbrook & Braithwaite, 2000) is the editable database. The game can be modified so that event answers may be updated and family histories can be changed. The ability to edit the game means the framework for this game can support teaching students from different health disciples, or the problems can be changed to reflect local medical, cultural, or economic conditions. Compare this game created for teams of medical students to single-player games and other workplace games.

Other examples of game-based simulations include:

- FunBrain: K-12 Games. http://www.funbrain.com/

- MIT Beer Game. http://beergame.mit.edu/

- Explore Cleveland. www.fathomi.com/elearning/case-studies.asp

Physical Simulations

Physical simulations teach learners about the workings of physical objects or processes. These kinds of simulations differ from *process (step)* simulations. In process simulators, learners interact with the program by making step-by-step decisions, choosing responses, or manipulating virtual objects.

In *physical* simulations, the learner sets variables and sits back to watch and reflect. Physical simulations give learners insights into *things,* such as combustion engines and blood pressure, that are not easily understood by observation.

Physical simulations are ones in which the learner has the ability to observe a physical object or phenomenon, such as observing a nuclear reactor working or witnessing the process of flies mating and the genetic results. These simulations may even allow the learner to slow down or speed up a physical process to gain a greater understanding of how it works.

This simulation called *CADWeb,* shown in Figure 6.4, is used for educational purposes. The model provides learners a simple model to evaluate their risk for coronary artery disease. Using this application, learners create their own test cases and discover the CAD risks associated with different variables. Notice how easy it is to change variables and try multiple scenarios. Think about how easy it is to see the impact of smoking, heredity, and obesity without a lecture!

Figure 6.4. Example of a Physical Simulation

Source: The Shodor Education Foundation, Inc. www.shodor.org/master/biomed//physio/cadweb/disclaim.htm

Other examples of physical simulations include:

- Control the Nuclear Power Plant (Demonstration). www.ida.liu.se/~her/npp/demo.html

- World Population. www.census.gov/cgi-bin/ipc/popclockw

- Circuit Simulator. www.udel.edu/present/showcase/watson/

- Electric Circuit. www.article19.com/shockwave/sg04.htm

- Models in Medicine. www.shodor.org/master/biomed//
- Eye Simulator. http://cim.ucdavis.edu/eyes/version1/eyesim.htm

Process (Step) Simulations

Process simulations focus on teaching *how* things work. They teach learners how to execute steps in a procedure and how to deal with a situation. When teaching learners how to execute steps in a process such as how to land a space shuttle or how to dissect a frog, the simulations may require the learner to manipulate virtual objects such as flight controls or knives in a dissection kit. The point of these simulations is not to use virtual objects but to master the procedure.

Experience two very different process simulations. With ETMB.com's simulation (see URL below), learn how to execute the steps needed to operate an automated external defibrillation. Contrast this to NETg's step-by-step process for teaching software, shown in Figure 6.5. Both programs are well suited for simulation because the order in which tasks are accomplished are generally fixed. Notice how each program focuses the learner on a clear, well-defined path. NETg disables buttons and features that are not relevant to the learner and keeps the focus on the process being taught. ETMB.com uses sounds and visuals that are essential to the process.

Examples of process simulations include the following:

- ETMB.com Cardiovascular Emergencies Simulation. www.emtb.com/8e/ interactive_simulation_view.cfm?simid=11
- Frog Guts. www.froguts.com/flash_content/demo/frog.html
- Windows Server 2003 Interactive Training Simulations. http://www .microsoft.com/windowsserver2003/techinfo/training/sims.mspx

Role Play

Role-play simulation is a learning strategy in which the learners assume the roles of fictional characters in a defined scenario. Role-play strategies are one of the less expensive simulation options because the program can be run in a live virtual classroom environment or via text in the form of e-mail, instant messaging, or threaded discussion. The examples that follow offer fully developed scenarios in which the learners play a role and the system uses branching and feedback to enhance the learning experience.

Figure 6.5. Example of a Teaching Software Application

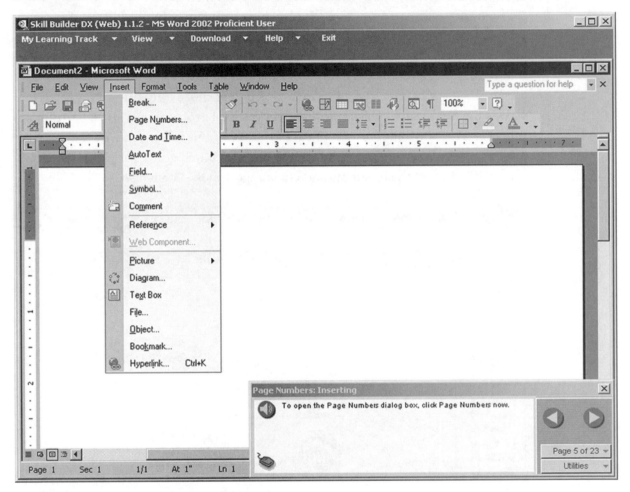

Source: Thomson/NETg. www.netg.com/DemosAndDownloads/

Role plays, when well-designed, take advantage of adult learners' life experience. The learners are able to try out different problem-solving strategies in a safe environment. Learners can be asked to do things such as take a point of view contrary to their beliefs and thus to explore a different point of view. Learners are also able to try approaches and reflect on the outcomes. The interactions can be spaced days apart to allow learners time to reflect on their interactions and to prepare for the next encounter. The challenge with web-based role play is the missing physical dimension of facial expressions, gestures, and intonation. Without these elements the transference of skills to real-world situations is lacking a dimension.

Role-play simulations are best for teaching problem-solving skills within a context. Popular training topics for role plays are business problems such as hiring, decision making, and delivering feedback and political and organizational problems that require negotiation and communication skills.

The Doctor's Dilemma (see Figure 6.6) is one of those e-learning programs that stands the test of time. This program gives medical professionals an opportunity to reflect on their own moral and ethical ideals. All of this is done in the context of the doctor-patient relationship. This program has so much going for it that I am only going to point out the top items and encourage you to see the rest.

Figure 6.6. Example of Role Play: The Doctor's Dilemma

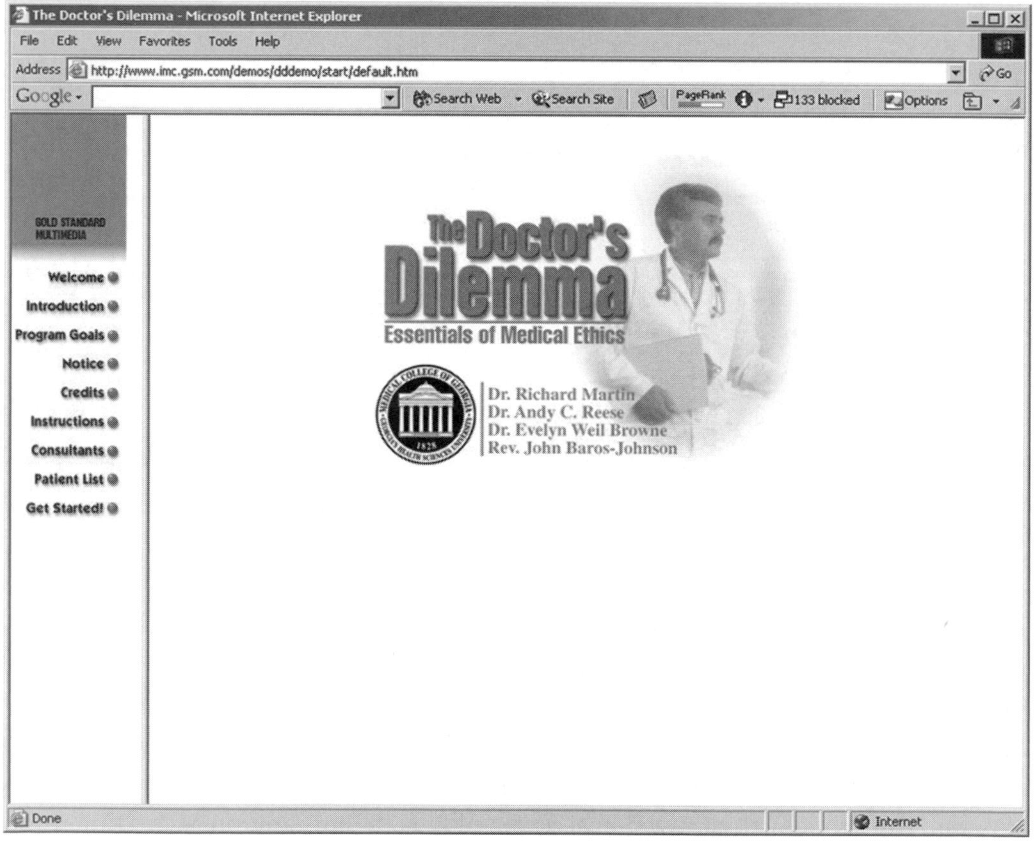

Source: Gold Standard, Inc. www.imc.gsm.com/demos/dddemo/start/default.htm

Everything about this program drives you to get into the role of doctor. The program begins with learners picking their character's gender. Then learners look at their patient schedule for the day. The dialog is well written, and the dilemmas are clear but not easy to resolve. The program uses the clever device of getting advice from different religious, legal, medical, and scientific experts in order to see other perspectives for the issues. The program also uses a very savvy technique to encourage learners to think about their decisions. In a situation in which there are no clear right or wrong answers, the learner makes a decision and then the system raises questions about the learner's decision and allows him or her to think more about that decision.

Additional examples of role plays include:

- The Bureau of Alcohol, Tobacco, Firearms and Explosives (ATF). www.atf.gov/firearms/ffrrg/ltright.htm
- WebQuest: It's Mine. www.education.tas.gov.au/itproject/webquests/copyright/index.htm
- Flight to Freedom. http://ssad.bowdoin.edu:9780/projects/ flighttofreedom/persona.shtml
- International Communication and Negotiation Simulations. www.icons.umd.edu/ICONS
- New York Emergency Room RN. http://www.nyerrn.com/simulators.htm
- Taking Control of Your Day. www.skillsoft.com
- Smoking Cessation for Pregnancy and Beyond. iml.dartmouth.edu/ education/cme/Smoking/install.html

Software Simulation

Software simulations are probably the most common kind of simulation. As the name implies, these are programs that mimic or simulate a software application. Software simulations allow learners to practice skills such as word processing or spreadsheets in a controlled environment. Unlike working in the actual application, the leaner works in a simulated environment where very little can go wrong. The simulation limits the number of interactions that are recognized so a learner cannot delete a database entry or change the applications setting. The simulation not only provides a safe environment, but it provides a clear path with abundant feedback.

Developing software simulation is becoming easier with new authoring tools, but it is still time-consuming and requires good design skills. The lessons need to be well designed to create logical groups, wise decisions regarding the level of detail, and significant amounts of formative evaluation to ensure the feedback is meaningful. In most cases, organization will purchase software simulations for things like Microsoft Office or other common applications rather than develop their own software simulations.

Software simulations are an excellent option for teaching proprietary software application for things such as expense reporting developed in-house or customized SAP or PeopleSoft self-service functions.

Sample the NETg course for Microsoft office shown in Figure 6.7. The design shows some of the hard choices that designers need to make and NETg's clear understanding of how to teach software. Try making a mistake; notice the feedback.

Figure 6.7. Software Simulation: NETg's Course on Microsoft Word 2002, Proficient User

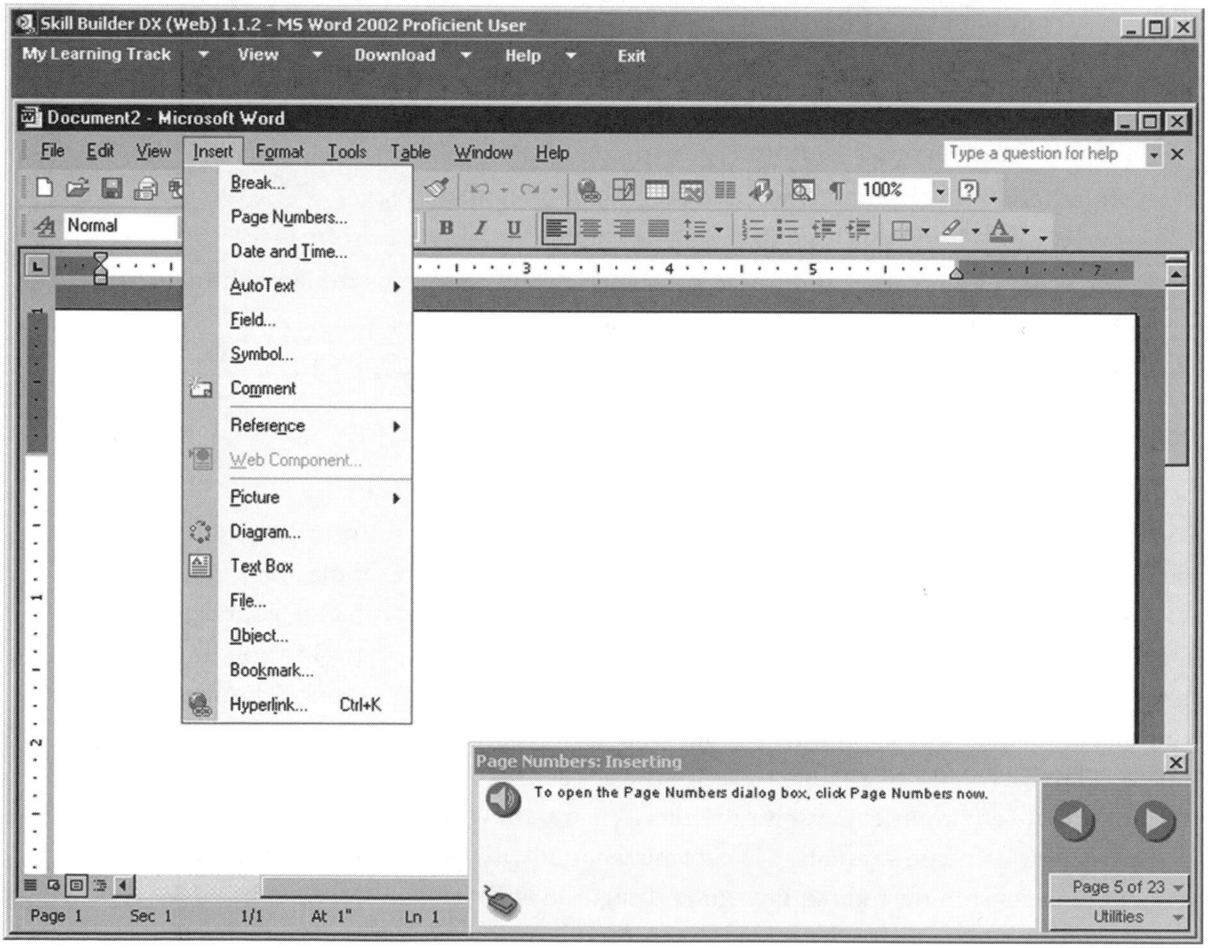

Source: Thomson/NETg. www.netg.com/DemosAndDownloads/

The delivery mode offers two options, the student can listen to the instructions or can read them. Scan the course outline and notice how the topics have been organized and the size of the objectives.

Other examples of software simulations include:

- Robodemo. See the customer examples http://www.macromedia.com/software/robodemo/customer_examples/

- Thomson/NETg: Other courses available. www.Netg.com

- SkillSoft: Microsoft Office. www.skillsoft.com

- Camtasia. www.techsmith.com/products/studio/default.asp

- Apex Web Media. http://apex.vtc.com/

Symbolic (Invisible) Simulations

Symbolic simulations teach learners about things that are not visible. Symbolic simulations provide learners with insights into how processes and principles that cannot be seen operate. Like physical simulations, these simulations allow learners to set variables, sit back and watch, and reflect on relationships. Examples of symbolic simulations can be seen in programs allowing learners to observe principles such as supply and demand, market volatility, and the spread of disease.

The challenge in developing symbolic process simulations is that one must be able to develop a model that has the right level of detail to allow learners to understand cause and effect. The model must not be too complex or it will be difficult to see cause and effect or too simplistic so that the lessons are not transferable.

Models pose additional challenges when dealing with social systems because of biases that can be built into models. An example of social systems bias can be seen in the model underpinning SimCity. While playing SimCity with his daughter, Paul Starr (1994), a professor of sociology at Princeton, pondered these biases: "What assumptions were buried in the underlying models? What was their 'hidden curriculum'? Did a conservative or a liberal determine the response to changes in tax rates in SimCity? While playing SimCity with my eleven-year-old daughter, I railed against what I thought was a built-in bias of the program against mixed-use development."

Models are best for explaining concepts that are difficult to understand because they are not visible. They are particularly good for explaining how complex situation with multiple variables work. There are a number of very good models that explain concepts related to math, physics, health, and economic theories. Consider using symbolic process simulations when you are able to create a model for the concept or principle you are trying to teach.

STOCK-TRAK is a comprehensive financial markets simulation featuring stocks, options, futures, spots, bonds, mutual funds, international stocks, and future options (see Figure 6.8). This simulation is used by tens of thousands of students and the general investing public each year. It provides an ideal method to practice investment strategies, test theories, practice day trading, learn about the various markets, and compete against your classmates, friends, and colleagues. I would recommend that you compare this symbolic simulation to the Hollywood Stock Exchange (www.hsx.com), which also teaches about the stock market but in a less direct fashion. Consider which simulation learners would find more engaging, which one would have better rates of transfer of skills and knowledge. Think about the use of a group-based simulation versus an individual simulation.

Figure 6.8. Example of a Symbolic (Invisible) Simulation

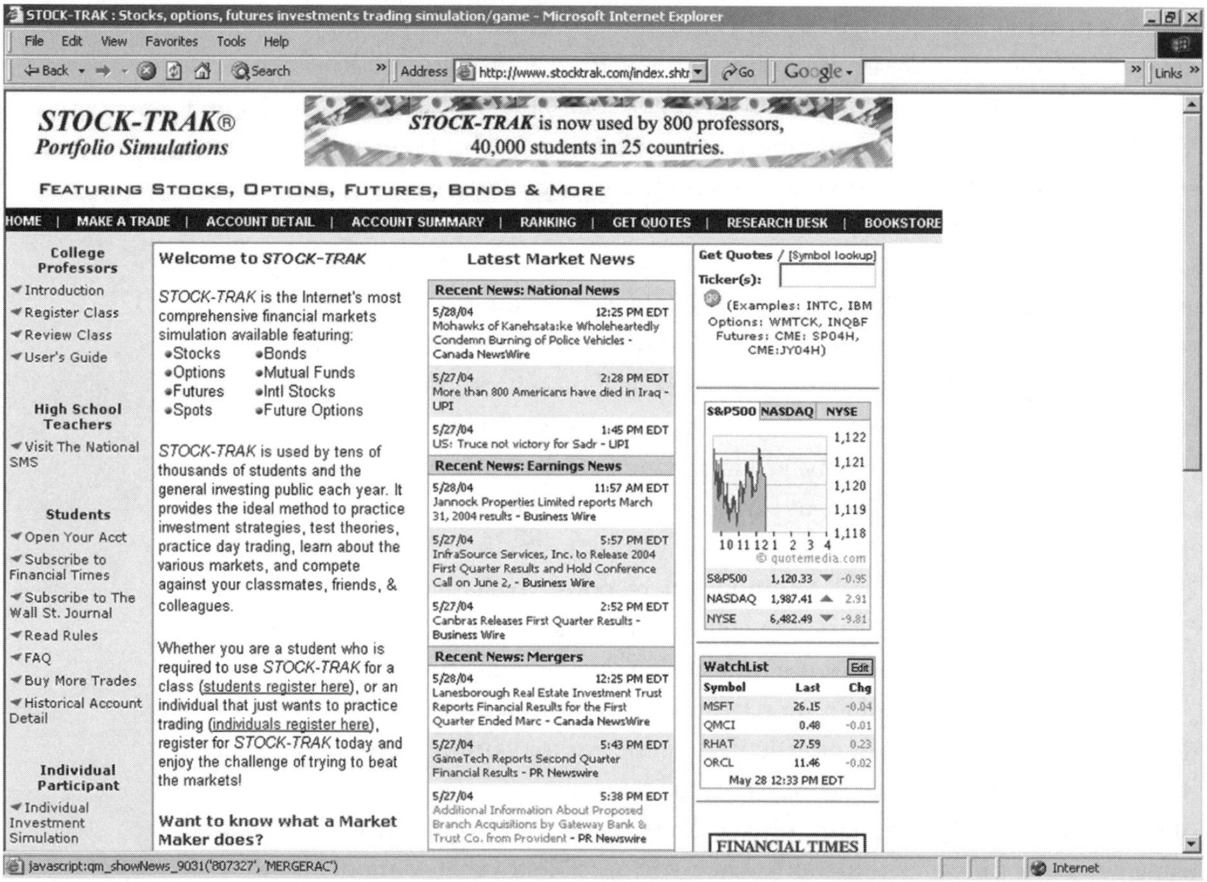

Source: STOCK-TRAK Portfolio Simulation. www.stocktrak.com/index.shtml

Examples of other symbolic (invisible) simulations include:

- Hollywood Stock Exchange. www.hsx.com/

- Modeling for K-12 Science. http://mvhs1.mbhs.edu/ncsa/hydrology.htmll

- Math and Science Meta site. www.edp.ust.hk/physics/explore/dswmedia/indexb.htm

- Explore Learning. www.explorelearning.com/index.cfm

- CyberPet. http://rspcapet.onlinemagic.com/intro.html

Virtual Reality

Virtual reality (VR) is a technology that began in military and university laboratories more than twenty years ago. Originally VR was a computer-created sensory experience that allowed a participant to believe and barely distinguish a "virtual" experience from a real one. Today virtual reality is used more broadly to refer to a range of computer-based approaches using visualization of concepts, objects, or spaces in three or more dimensions with user interaction.

The challenges when developing VR simulations for training are the cost of development and the computation power needed to run the program. As the examples in this module illustrate, they would not be described as "barely distinguishable from a real experience." The technical limitations of providing VR experience are compounded when the learning must be delivered over the Internet, making rich media and interaction difficult to deliver. It is also a challenge to develop interfaces that are intuitive and at the same time place the learning in a real experience.

Although virtual reality has evolved to have broader uses since its early days as a military tool, it still plays an important role in military training. The Army's Simulation, Training, and Instrumentation Command, known as STRICOM, spent $1 billion on VR training for Afghanistan. ABC News (2004) reported that "there are thousands of STRICOM simulators at U.S. bases around the world. The simulators vary in size and design, from small booths for pilots and tank personnel, to larger rooms with wall-sized high-resolution displays for squads of infantry. . . . At the end of the simulation, commanders play back the firefight, with the positions of the soldiers' shots appearing on the screen. The soldiers can review their performance, and learn from their mistakes."

Other popular training subjects are public safety, dangerous construction projects, high-stakes medical procedures, and aviation. What all of these topics share is a high cost of failure and a learning curve that is too steep or risky to allow on-the-job training.

The free examples of VR available on the Web would not meet most people's definition of virtual realty. In many cases the virtual reality e-learning programs are delivered on CD-ROM or the programs use a combination of the computer and peripheral equipment such as CPR mannequins that connect to a PC.

The interFIRE site shown in Figure 6.9 is worth a visit even if you don't have a high-speed connection. The VR simulation makes a commendable effort to provide a virtual reality experience of touring a house that has just had a fire. The interFIRE VR house empowers the learner to move through the remains of a burned home and

Figure 6.9. Virtual Reality: interFIRE.org VR House Fire

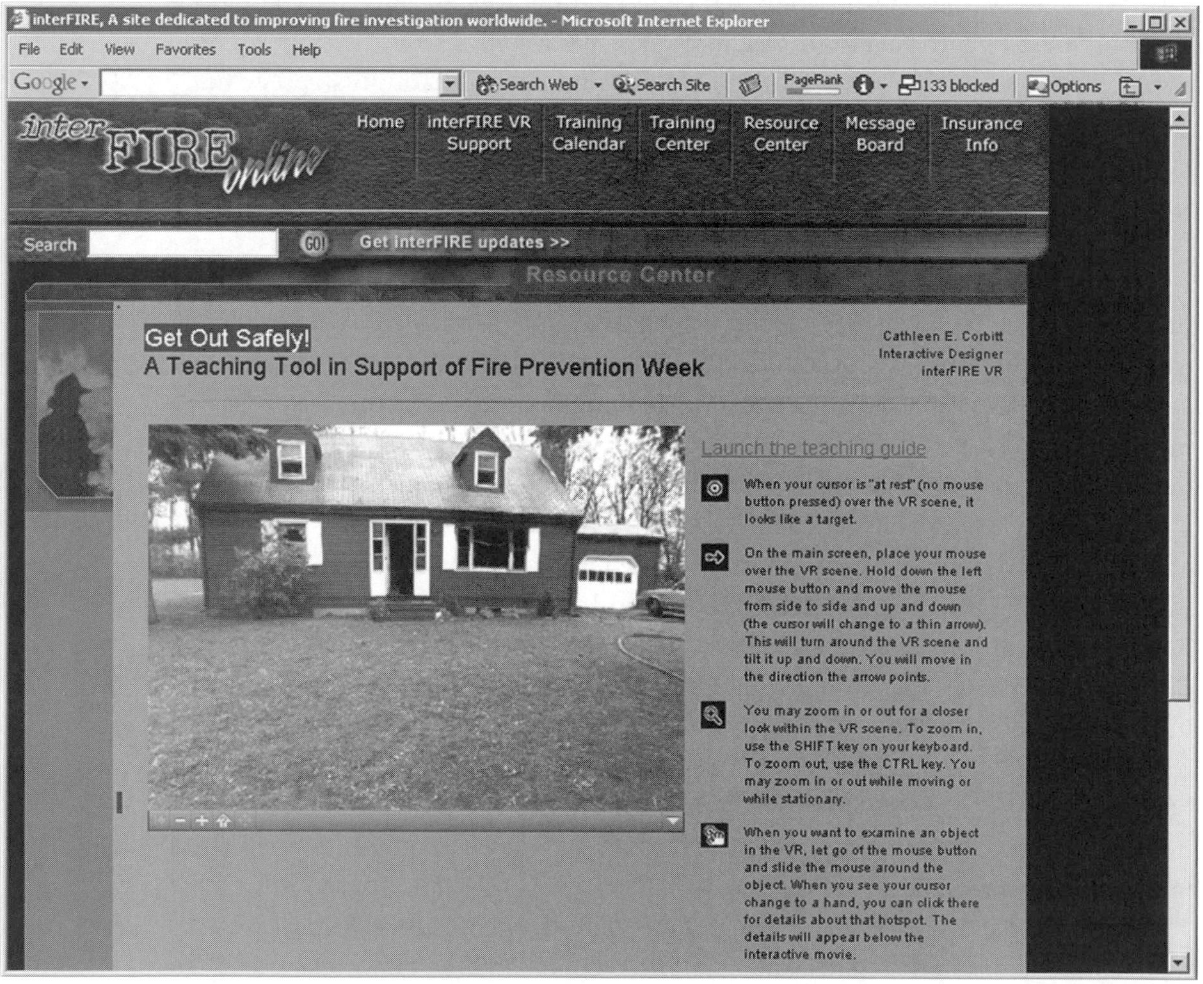

Source: Stonehouse Media, Inc. www.interfire.org/

look for evidence of arson. Take the time to experience the 360-degree movement and the ability to pick up objects. The site also does a great job getting value from the VR media asset. The same VR house that is used to teach firefighters to look for evidence of arson is also used to provide a VR tour for school children learning about fire safety.

Other examples of virtual reality include the following (note that you may need to download or order the examples):

- EMT Training. www.patient-simulation.com/demo.htm
- AIMS Research: VR Safety Training. www.nottingham.ac.uk/aims/VR-Site/HTML/SafeVR.html
- VStep: VR Safety Training. www.vstep.nl/

In Practice: Melinda Jackson: EnterTech

About the Project

This In Practice section looks at the innovative use of simulations with a non-traditional population. Melinda Jackson, project director of the Digital Media Collaboratory at the IC2 Institute at the University of Texas at Austin, shares what she learned from this project and her instructional design insights for simulations (see Figure 6.10).

Melinda Jackson was the lead instructional designer for the EnterTech program. She supervised the design, development, and piloting, and (when necessary) revision of the forty-five hours of blended learning. With this much experience, Melinda shares the lessons from this project.

Engage the SME as Soon as Possible. Melinda is an absolute believer in the value of having subject-matter experts (SMEs) brought on to the project as soon as possible. She recommends bringing them on during the creative phase if possible. SMEs are particularly important when designing workplace learning because they bring an intimate perspective into the culture, terminology, or vernacular, and the normalized practices associated with the job. Melinda discussed one unit in which she planned to teach math skills for calculating shipping costs. When the SME reviewed the unit, she suggested modifying the section because there are job aids typically associated with the task and people in that job did not need to utilize math skills in the ways presented by the instruction. Melinda emphasized that SMEs are vital to making the context of simulations real and ensuring the skills will transfer to real-world situations.

Figure 6.10. EnterTech Simulation

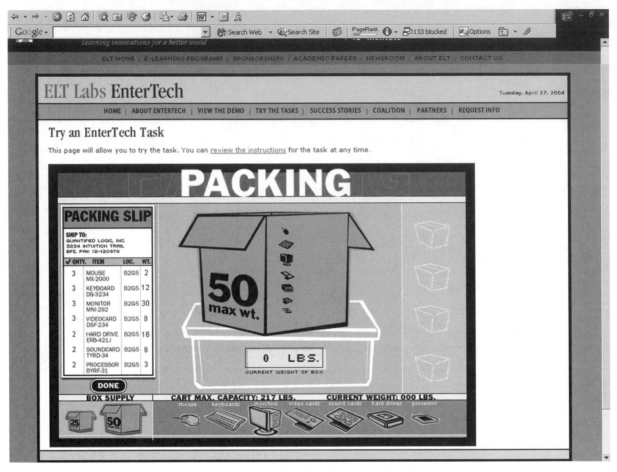

Source: Digital Media Collaboratory (DMC), The University of Texas at Austin. www.entertech.utexas.edu/about/index.html

Use Spiral Development. The EnterTech program relied on a process called "spiral development." In the process, small chunks of the program such as content, user interface, characters (avatars), exercises, and assessments are built and tested with users. Rather than building the sections in a linear fashion, testing each part of the program as it is developed, the program is developed in spiral fashion. The spiral begins with a wide circle or general approach. In the initial design, prototypes of the instructional elements from a wide range of the program (some from beginning, middle, and end) are developed. As these small pieces are developed, they are piloted with SMEs and end-users.

The feedback from these reviews leads to another round or turn of the spiral. Each turn results in greater refinement.

Spiral development done in the early phase of the project saved EnterTech a great deal of time and money. In the initial design, a decision was made to develop drawing-rendered characters using Macromedia Director™. Early character drawings were shown to the target audience. Members of the target audience were clear that they did not like the avatars. The design team learned that the audience thought of them as cartoons. Based on this feedback, a decision was made to change to photo-realistic character images. The development team found it easy to give these photo-realistic images personality quirks and to make them compelling. Learners empathized with the characters in the simulation and were able to better relate these characters to real life. Melinda's advice is "test early and often."

Plan for Remedial Material. One of the unanticipated challenges in building simulations was not simulating equipment like a dazer magnifier, a meter gauge, or a shipping form. The challenge was providing the remedial skills needed to do things like read a meter, estimate time, and calculate percentages. One of the lessons learned was that the adults in the program had been away from math concepts for a long time. Learners needed a "tune up" in their math skills before they could apply new skills. The design had to be changed; a help button was added. The help button linked to context-specific remediation materials aimed at what was being taught within the specific instructional scenario. For example, in teaching learners how to read an invoice, they received additional basic math skills such as how to calculate tax (multiplication with percentages). When remedial help required more than what could reasonably be delivered online, workbooks were added to support the learner. Melinda recommends that designers factor in the additional time for creating the remedial content that is not part of the main line of instruction, but which is necessary to ensure success of instructional goals.

Consider Blended Learning Options. EnterTech was developed as a tool for adults facing "welfare to work." The intended learners were mostly minority women who may not have finished high school, had limited work history, and had significant responsibilities for childcare and extended family obligations. Target learners also lacked resources such as transportation and childcare and access to community support system.

EnterTech focused on a blended approach, using online learning simulations, traditional classroom instruction, self-study workbooks, and collaborative learning opportunities. Each element of the blended learning was chosen to accomplish specific goals. The e-learning simulations allowed learners to practice soft skills in a safe environment and then have an opportunity to debrief those experiences with others in class. The simulations were designed to confront the learner with real entry-level job challenges such as a difficult managers, co-workers who are slackers, gossips, or snitches, and personal challenges such as a sick child, lack of transportation, and balancing family demands. The e-learning segments were kept to five to twenty minutes and featured two or three activities per unit of instruction, blocked in fifty-minute increments. The traditional classroom program segments focused on reinforcing interpersonal and team skills. Additional paper-based activities were used to reinforce the skills presented in the simulation.

Workbooks allowed learners to work at their own pace using familiar paper-and-pencil materials. The workbooks provided learners with remedial work for all of the instruction's forty-four performance objectives and provided a way to level the playing field.

Finally, collaborative learning activities were used to bring pairs or triads of learners together to discuss how to solve challenging problems. The simulations, which were initially taken as individual e-learning experiences, were revised and used again by groups of collaborative learners. The groups watched the scenarios again as a team. As a collaborative activity the group would discuss and evaluate the potential solutions. The teams would then rejoin the entire class and discuss their solutions as part of a class-wide debriefing. These collaborative learning exercises made it possible to re-use the simulated e-learning scenarios, and generated new learning by exposing the learners to alternative points of view.

Debrief All Simulations. The key to any simulation is to provide feedback. Melinda discussed the value of debriefing to ensure learners understand the rationale and consequences of their choices. Although the e-learning simulation provided feedback as part of the online material, the EnterTech program always made a point to have the class debrief at the end of the instructional time, usually allotting ten to twenty minutes for group discussion. The instructor-led debriefing was an additional opportunity to probe for understanding and to correct misunderstandings. This is particularly important in soft skills program in which the learners may not always agree with how the simulation evolved or ended.

Choose Proven Tools and Don't Let Technology Dictate. One of Melinda's enduring lessons is that good projects concentrate on the instructional design and less on high-end technology and software. Early in the project, the EnterTech team had to pick tools for development. The challenge was the conflict between the newest technology and the most appropriate technology. The team insisted on focusing on the instructional goals first and the technology second. In the end, the group compromised and chose older, proven tools. Even though there were many newer authoring tools that promised more bells and whistles, the team focused on instructional design. Melinda reminds instructional designers that in the classic Dick and Carey model, media section is one of the later steps in the process—and for good reason.

A Few Numbers

The EnterTech program was a grant-funded program. The grant was awarded from 1998 to 2001, and the program continues to be used today. The three-year grant total was for $2.1 million. Here are some of numbers that may be of interest to you:

- The initial research and design period was six months. During this phase, a core team of ten worked on early spiral development of goals, objectives, storyboards, user interface, and graphics.

- Once the program was designed, the development of the program took twelve months. During this phase, spiral development continued. The program was iteratively written and piloted, and revised.

- The team consisted of forty individuals over the period of eighteen months; these included producers, programmers, engineers, artists, instructional designers, and student interns. At any given time there were five to ten people working on the program.

- The actual development work required:

  Six months' lead time

  Twelve months' development time

  Six months' pilot time (included two months of corrections to "bugs")

  Twelve months of summative evaluation

Conclusion

Simulations are a strategy whose time has come. They offer an opportunity for you to broaden your portfolio and to offer learners engaging programs.

Using the examples in this chapter, think about how you might use simulations in a blended mode. If you don't have the budget, time, or support to develop a pure simulation-based program, consider simulation as a post-training program. Use smaller programs with a focus on authentic practice and corrective feedback to reinforce classroom lessons.

Think about the examples in this chapter and the range of production values. While everyone naturally thinks about the high-end examples, consider the less expensive options. The hallmark of good simulations is that they put the learner in the context and provide authentic practice. Authentic practice (and corrective feedback) can be accomplished with great writing—compelling case studies, realistic situations, engaging dialog, and models that walk the fine line between too simple and too complex.

When using simulations, be sure to follow through. More important than the media, programming, and graphics is the debriefing activity or feedback. Don't leave the lesson learned to chance. Be sure to pilot the programs to ensure learners are taking away the right lesson and that they can apply the lesson in real life.

Share this chapter with colleagues as you being to consider simulations.

Learn More About It

Aldrich, C. (2003). *Simulations and the future of learning: An innovative (and perhaps revolutionary) approach to e-learning.* San Francisco: Pfeiffer.

This book provides a provocative look at simulations. If you are interested in where simulations have the potential to take the industry, this book provides a well-reasoned forecast and points readers to some places where they can see the future today.

Fripp, J. (1992). *Learning through simulations: A guide to the design and use of simulations in business and education.* New York: McGraw-Hill.

This book describes the advantages and disadvantages of business simulations in relation to other learning methods and gives insight into the essential steps that must be carried out to successfully design and use them. The book will be of interest both to those new to simulations and to those wishing to improve their understanding and use of computer-based simulations.

Gredler, M. (1992). *Designing and evaluating games and simulations.* New York: City Stylus Publications.

This book is out of print, but copies can still be found via interlibrary loan. If you want the ultimate "cookbook" with grounded research and educational rational, this book is for you.

Shirts, G. (2000). *Ten secrets of successful simulations: Simulations for business.* www.stsintl.com/articles/tensecrets.html. [Retrieved April 4, 2004.]

This article is a good touchstone for developers to review before fully committing to a simulation strategy. The ten secrets also make a great checklist that might help you weigh the value of simulation in your particular situation.

REFLECTION AND APPLICATION

To reflect on the material presented in this chapter and apply it in a real e-learning situation, consider how you would respond to the following challenges. (Each of these challenges is intentionally left vague. If you are unsure about a piece of information, make an assumption about it and list the assumption.)

- The vice president of human resources in your company has scheduled a meeting with you to talk about an initiative to improve customer service. Your company is in the hospitality business and its primary customers are elderly vacationers and holiday makers. The staff, on the other hand, is eighteen- to twenty-four-year-olds with limited work experience and very little understanding of the needs or expectations of your customers. The facility operates twenty-four hours a day, seven days a week, 365 days a year. Staff turnover is almost 100 percent in a year. You are considering recommending an online learning program that uses a simulation strategy. Outline the benefits and limitations of this strategy before your meeting.

- Your IT department is rewriting the program that every employee must use to order office supplies, to request things like business cards and catering services, and to schedule maintenance on the printers. The old system served only headquarters. The new system will serve headquarters and fifteen branch offices. The help desk people have already warned the company that when the switchover happens they can't teach end-users one call at a time, so there had better be some training! What are your options? How might you deliver this training if you don't get the $30,000 budget you requested?

- A sales person from a local multimedia company has called on your boss. The sales person demonstrated a really nice health and safety simulation to use in new hire orientation. The game-based simulation was created for another company, but your boss is thinking that with some customization this would be good for your manufacturing sites. You ask a few questions and learn that the simulation requires the learner to take on the role of an Occupational Safety and Health Administration (OSHA) inspector and to issue citation as a means of applying what they learned about safety and as a way of scoring points to win the game. You are going to have a chance to see the game next week when the sales person comes back. What will you be looking for in this game-based simulation?

Chapter 7

e-Mentoring and e-Coaching

Coaches hoping to remain relevant in the networked world need to bridge the physical workplace with the online environment.

Barbian, 2002

In This Chapter

In this chapter we will

- Discuss the difference between mentoring and coaching
- Define the terms e-mentoring and e-coaching
- Explain why instructional designers are using e-mentoring and e-coaching
- Describe the benefits and limitations of e-mentoring/e-coaching
- Describe five e-mentoring/e-coaching strategies.
- Summarize guidelines for designing e-coaching and e-mentoring programs
- Provide examples of e-coaching and e-mentoring

This chapter explores two e-learning strategies that have great potential but also require a great deal of work to execute. Mentoring and coaching offer organizations an opportunity to make skilled resources available to a larger population and to provide developmental opportunities to people who may be too senior or experienced to benefit from classroom-based programs.

If there were a contest to find the most abused terms in e-learning, e-mentoring and e-coaching would win. Of course the contest would have to take into consideration that the terms are often used interchangeably and that neither term has an agreed-on meaning in the traditional training world. People have chosen to make the following terms interchangeable: e-coaching, e-facilitator, e-mentoring, e-guide, cyber coaching and a few other idiosyncratic terms. The lack of clarity in the terminology is a red flag that indicates what one can anticipate for clarity regarding instructional strategies. On the other hand, the delivery strategies for these kinds of online learning programs are a snap compared to the instructional strategies.

This chapter sorts out mentoring and coaching as *instructional strategies* and then looks at e-mentoring and e-coaching as *delivery strategies.* The debate about these terms may sound like a fussy semantic argument, but it is essential to clarify what we mean by e-coaching and e-mentoring. Optimizing the use of technology for these instructional strategies requires well-framed goals.

What Are Coaching and Mentoring?

If you have recently paged through training or human resource magazines, you probably think mentoring and coaching were discovered in the last ten years. You would be a little bit right and a little bit wrong.

In reality, the concept of mentoring dates back to Greek mythology. Mentoring gets its name from Mentor in *The Odyssey.* In this story Odysseus entrusted his son, Telemachus, to an old man named "Mentor." Mentor became Telemachus' guide, giving him prudent counsel and helping him develop into a wise ruler. Since then, wise and trusted advisors have been called "mentors." Aside from making you recall your high school classics, this side track will help delineate the difference between a mentor and a coach.

Mentoring is typically a relationship between an experienced and a less experienced person in which the mentor provides advice, guidance, support, and feedback. Mentoring programs can either be formal programs sponsored by the company or informal relationships sought out by individuals. If the company sponsors a mentoring program the goals are often to help employees learn about organizational culture, to facilitate personal and professional growth, and to foster career development. Informal relationships are frequently developed by chance or serendipity, often with the mentor choosing the mentoree.

A more recent phenomenon is the growth of *coaching.* You may have seen stories about executive coaching, career coaching, life coaching, team coaching, and just about any other adverb you care to put in front of "coaching." The field of coaching is experiencing rapid growth. *The Washington Post* (Capuzzi-Simon, 2003) reports that, "Some 20,000 full-time coaches practice worldwide, about three-quarters of them in the United States, according to the International Coach Federation (ICF), coaching's credentialing organization. More than 6,000 are members of ICF, up from 1,500 three years ago."

The idea of coaching is based on a sports analogy. Although the role of executive coach has been described as "part boss, part consultant, part therapist" (Morris, 2000), it is a good idea to stay away from strategies that verge on psychotherapy. *Fast Company* has characterized executive coaches as "not for the meek. They're for people who value unambiguous feedback. If coaches have one thing in common, it's that they are ruthlessly results-oriented. Executive coaching isn't therapy. It's product development, with you as the product" (Tristram, 1996). Like an athlete who has a great deal of talent, an executive or any worker can benefit from someone who can help motivate him or her, help build on his or her talents related to work.

Given the number of overlapping definitions that exist, a study done by Starcevich (1998) provides a concise way of delineating between the two forms of intervention. In the Starcevich model (see Table 7.1), there are six distinguishing characteristics. It is possible to find examples of coaching or mentoring that contradict this model, but for educational purposes the following discussion of the model stress a clear delineation between these two concepts.

Table 7.1. Differences Between Mentoring and Coaching

	Mentor	**Coach**
Focus	Individual	Performance
Role	Facilitator with no agenda	Specific agenda
Relationship	Self-selected	Comes with job or hired
Source of Influence	Perceived value	Position
Personal Returns	Affirmation/learning	Teamwork/performance
Arena	Life	Task-related

Source: Matt M. Starcevich, Center for Coaching and Mentoring, www.coachingandmentoring.com/Articles/mentoring.html.

Focus

The first characteristic, *focus*, is the purpose for engaging in the relationship. Mentoring focuses on developing the person. Coaching is focused on developed or improving performance, that is, cultivating work-related skills and knowledge.

Role and Relationship

In mentoring, the role is that of a facilitator—someone who guides but does not dictate the direction. The mentor and the protégé determine the goals as a collaborative activity. Mentoring is a power-free, two-way, mutually beneficial relationship. Mentors are teachers who allow the protégé to discover their own directions. The mentoring relationship offers the protégé and the mentor choice. The relationship works within an agreed-on framework of frequency of meetings, timeframes, communication methods, structure and when to bring the relationship to a close.

Coaching relationships can either be the result of a company that hires and assigns a coach to an employee or an employee can hire his or her own coach. If the coach is hired by the company, the role of the coach and the goals are defined by the company. The coach's role is to focus on reinforcing or changing skills and behaviors. The relationship between the employee and the coach is centered around the job. Unlike the mentoring relationship, with its mutually agreed-on framework, the coaching relationship is contractual or a job competency with clear terms and expectations.

Source of Influence

Interpersonal skills often determine the effectiveness of both coach and mentor. Coaches have an implied or actual level of authority by nature of their position; ultimately they can insist on compliance. Mentors generally do not have formal power over their protégés. The mentoring relationship is based on mentor/protégé rapport.

Personal Returns

In a mentoring relationship, both the mentor and the protégé benefit from the association. The experience provides a feeling of satisfaction and affirmation in being able to help another person learn and grow in his or her career. Mentors may also see mentoring as a way of giving back if they have been helped at some point in their careers. Mentors are not paid for their service. Coaches from outside the company receive compensation. If the coach is internal, the returns are in the form of more team harmony or better job performance.

Arena

Mentoring relationships are sought out by protégés. The relationship focuses on life and career issues. Because there is no defined goal the mentor/protégé dialog can result in a mentor sharing his or her network, providing advice on work/life issues, and acting as guide and confidante. The coach is focused on developing a product and getting results. The relationship is best described as directive or prescriptive.

Understanding the difference between mentoring and coaching will help you sort out the strategy that is best for your organization.

So What Are e-Coaching and e-Mentoring?

e-Coaching is coaching delivered using the Internet. Like traditional workplace coaching, e-coaching helps employees improve performance and builds work-related skills. The e-coaching environment is available 24/7; and it allows people to work asynchronously with their coaches at times that are convenient for them. e-Coaches take advantage of synchronous and asynchronous communication tools such as e-mail, instant massaging, and voice over Internet protocol (VOIP), that is, live telephone-like conversations. Coaches can also take advantage of the environment to use online diagnostics and assessment tools to help learners set goals and track their progress.

e-Mentoring is mentoring that uses the Internet to conduct, enhance, or extend the mentor-protégé relationship.

A survey of the literature suggests that the benefits of e-coaching and e-mentoring are the technologies' ability to

- Overcome geographic distance

- Reduce costs relative to travel and logistics

- Provide asynchronous interactions enabling coaching/mentoring to fit into busy schedules

The challenge for instructional designers it to create e-coaching and e-mentoring programs that are well-thought-through and meet the needs of their organization. This is to say the programs are designed with a clear goal, an understanding the organizational culture, an adequate amount of funding to launch and maintain the program, and a realistic assessment of the commitment of coaches, mentors, and protégés.

There are a number of questions designers should reflect on as they create programs. Here are some considerations:

- What learning or development problem are you solving? Is the goal to develop the learner personally and professionally? Are you addressing a clear gap in performance or work-related skills?

- How will you know the program is successful?

- What resources are available to staff the program?

- Will the mentors and coaches be volunteers? Will their participation be part of their job responsibility?

- How will you pair people as mentors and protégés? How will you align people for coaching roles?

- If the pairings fail, how will you make corrections?

- How will you prepare people for the role of coach or mentor?

- Will the program be formal or informal? Voluntary or mandatory?

- Is there a time limit? Three months? A year?

- Are the mentors and protégés comfortable with the technology? In your environment is it realistic to expect people to develop a meaningful interpersonal relationship using the Internet? Will coaching be effective using the medium?

- Will mentoring via the Internet be rewarding and satisfying to the participants?

- If coaches are external, what kinds of compensation models are acceptable? If the coaches are internal, how will you measure their success?

- Will the mentor or coach have input into their protégé's or learner's annual review?

Why Use e-Mentoring and e-Coaching?

The educational reasons for implementing e-mentoring and e-coaching programs are the same reasons that people implement traditional mentoring and coaching programs. The key differentiator is the reliance on technology to provide the communication. Although these programs are called "e," they rely on more than just Internet technology. e-Mentoring and e-coaching use telephone, fax, and videoconferencing as well as e-mail, instant messaging, chat, and threaded discussions. In many programs the "e" elements are supplemented with traditional meetings and conversations. Logistic and financial considerations are the impetus for many of these programs.

The Benefits and Limitations of e-Mentoring and e-Coaching

The Benefits

Some of the benefits of mentoring and coaching have already been addressed; this section looks at the benefits that are unique to virtual mentoring and coaching.

Organizations use e-coaching and e-mentoring for the following reasons:

- *Makes worldwide talent available locally.* National and global organizations have employees who could benefit from mentoring and coaching programs but who are geographically too far apart for traditional programs. They must be sure that mentors and protégés in different locations are connected and that there is access to expertise.

- *Optimizes learning for people with busy schedules.* The use of asynchronous communication such as e-mail, instant messaging, and threaded discussions makes it possible for mentors and protégés to communicate when it is convenient. Using technology, mentoring and coaching can fit into busy schedules at work, on the road, and from home.

- *Creates thoughtful communications.* e-Mentoring and e-coaching allow the mentor and protégé time to respond in writing. When the mentoring involves electronic communication, it creates an opportunity to clarify thinking before writing and to reflect on the communication. The mere exercise of having to put a problem or a response into writing forces a level of organization and focus that might not be present in a traditional mentoring meeting or conversations.

Record of Communication

The use of e-mail results in a record. The correspondence can be read and threads (a string of e-mail about a given topic) reviewed at the participants' leisure. The record allows participants to look for themes, reflect on advice given, and to review dialog after the mentoring period has ended.

Good Option for Time-Constrained Workers

e-Mentoring and e-coaching are good learning strategies for mid-level managers who don't have time to attend traditional training. These managers are able to gain professional development around their time schedules and access mentors whose availability may not suit the schedule of a harried mid-level manager.

Good for Senior-Level Executives

This is also a good strategy for senior-level executives who are seeking a way to improve their performance. Virtual mentoring and coaching can provide development opportunities that fit their schedules. These managers may also find e-mentoring/e-coaching programs to be a practical way to provide guidance and share expertise with less experienced managers.

Easy Accessibility

Virtual mentoring and coaching make it convenient to participate in a relationship. This mode eliminates the need to coordinate meetings that accommodate two busy schedules and require traveling to a meeting place. This format also affords greater accessibility to the mentor. It is possible for protégés to seek the advice of their mentors or coaches when it is needed because it does not require leaving what they are doing to attend a face-to-face meeting.

The Limitations

e-Mentoring and e-coaching are subject to the same limitations as traditional mentoring and coaching programs. Some of the most common problems are lack of support for the program and lack of commitment to maintain the momentum. Problems can also arise when mentors and protégés have different expectations of the program. There are significant difficulties in finding good mentors who are capable and committed. These problems are exacerbated by technology. The following limitations are specific to virtual programs.

Impersonal

Programs that do not have face-to-face components have been described as impersonal. Without the visual clues such as facial expressions or gestures and indicators such as tone of voice or rate of delivery, e-mail and other online dialogs can be impersonal. It can be difficult to get a sense of the full person over the Internet.

Interrupted Flow of Communication

Technology offers an opportunity to shift time so that we can communicate when it is convenient to us. Time shifting by its very nature means that the relationship relies on asynchronous communication such as e-mail or threaded discussion. So if the protégé asks a question it may be hours or days before he or she receives a response. The natural flow and the give-and-take of communication are interrupted by spaces of time. This breaks the natural train of thought and flow of communication.

Easy to Delay Replies

The use of e-mail and threaded discussions makes it easy to delay a reply. It is a temptation to make replying the last item to be addressed when working on one's e-mail or put off reading e-mail for days.

Less Likely to Meet Colleagues of Mentor

Traditional face-to-face programs where the mentor and protégé are co-located offer fringe benefits. In traditional programs there are opportunities to introduce the protégé to the mentor's colleagues and to see the protégé in the context of the work.

Technology Infrastructure and Participant Skills

e-Mentoring and e-coaching assume a reliable and ubiquitous infrastructure. An obstacle to virtual programs can be participants who lack access to a computer, e-mail accounts, or the skills needed to use a computer and e-mail.

A Portfolio of Strategies for e-Mentoring and e-Coaching

Three primary strategies exist for e-mentoring/e-coaching. The two most straightforward approaches are to simply move coaching and mentoring to the Internet or to blend traditional mentoring/coaching with e-mentoring/e-coaching. The third strategy is to use e-mentoring/e-coaching to support instrumental (tactical) learning, such as assigning a coach or a mentor to help someone who has just completed an online course. Arguably, supporting instrumental learning is not really mentoring or coaching but, as discussed earlier, there are no fixed definitions.

e-Mentoring and e-Coaching Straight Up

The most obvious strategy is to move the relationship from the physical world of face-to-face meetings and dialog to the virtual world of Internet-based exchanges and dialog. The challenge of implementing formal e-mentoring/e-coaching should not be underestimated. As with a traditional program, there must be clear goals and senior management buy-in to get support and help in promoting the program, and a means of program evaluation.

In best practices documented by Single and Muller (n.d.) of MentorNet, they identify the structured implementation as "the most important, and overlooked, elements of a mentoring program. Structured implementation includes the training, coaching, and community building tasks that help participants make the most of the e-mentoring experience." In addition, e-mentoring/e-coaching programs require reliable and supported infrastructure and technology such as e-mail, instant messaging, threaded discussions, and other applications.

Structured e-mentoring/e-coaching programs can be voluntary or mandatory, but in either case there must be incentives to motivate both mentor and protégés. While incentives are part of traditional programs, they deserve extra attention in virtual programs, where it is easier to lose interest because there is no physical connection. There is also the added requirement of making sure that technical frustrations do not create obstacles. If protégées or mentors are technically challenged using e-mail or they are frustrated by websites that are not reliable, these challenges will consume energy and time that should be spent on the mentoring experience.

The role of the instructional designer or program manager in implementing online mentoring and coaching is significant. Despite the ubiquitous nature of e-mail, instant messaging chat, and the use of other technology for communication, participants must be oriented. Part of running a program is preparing participants to assume their roles, to understand the goals and non-goals of the program, and to recognize boundaries. The task of matching mentors and protégés is a larger responsibly for e-mentor/e-coaching program coordinators than for traditional program coordinators. Selecting and matching virtual pairs has an added dimension of challenge because the program administrator may not know the parties. The greatest effort in these programs is related to the organizational and interpersonal issues.

Blended e-Mentoring and e-Coaching

Blended mentoring and coaching is likely to happen in traditional programs, even if it is not formally organized. Mentors and protégés skilled in using online tools will naturally gravitate to this mode of communication. There are a number of tactics for blending face-to-face and virtual mentoring/coaching. In a model recommended by the Australian Association of Professional Engineers, Scientists and Managers (n.d.) there is heavy reliance on e-mail for administering the program and as the primary contact mode for mentors and protégés, but it is assumed there will be face-to-face meetings.

e-Coaching for Instrumental Learning

One of the popular value-added services from commercial WBT course library providers is to make an e-coach (sometimes called online mentor or e-mentor) available to learners. These programs provide learners with someone to answer questions about the course content or the mechanics of the WBT program. The coaching takes place via e-mail, online chat, or application sharing.

These relationships are not "mentoring" or "coaching," as discussed above, but they do share some attributes. The relationship has very clear goals and expectations. One of the key differences is that the mentor/coach does not have an exclusive relationship with the learner. In instrumental coaching there is a generic e-mail address, instant message name, or chat room for the learner to contact. A coach is available 24/7 but may not be the same person all the time. The interactions have more of the flavor of JIT assistance than a personal relationship.

Metacognitive e-Coaching

There is yet another form of e-coaching that does not conform to the definition of traditional coaching—metacognitive e-coaching. This strategy is to provide the learner with coaching or support for learning how to learn online. This kind of coaching is needed in both behaviorist and constructivist programs.

Learners who are either new to online learning or are new to constructivist strategies benefit from being coached in how to learn in these new environments. This is the gray area between technical support and help with learning. This is where students need to learn the skill for approaching an online course the way they have learned the skills for approaching traditional classroom courses, such as how to take notes, engage in classroom discussions, navigate a textbook, or create an outline. These are learning skills, not necessarily skills related to a specific course.

Metacognitive e-coaching is frequently found in higher education distance education degree programs. Online degree programs fund roles that are dedicated to supporting learners and coaching them to succeed.

Research done at Glenrothes College, Scotland, found that when using e-mail as part of online instruction learners needed clear guidelines such as the minimum number of e-mails to send during one week and acceptable online behavior and what constitutes an acceptable response for peer critique response (MacKinlay, 2000). Even programs that are considered "page-turners" benefit from coaching learners in how to get the most out of the program. In some cases it may be a simple welcome message, periodic check-ins, and feedback on performance. These coaching activities help learners build confidence and the skills needed to succeed.

When learners are exposed to constructivist instructional designs, such as problem-based, inquiry-based role play, and case-based learning, the instructor also needs to play the role of coach. Ron Oliver (2001) suggests "the role of the teacher . . . be defined as that of a coach and facilitator in place of the more didactic style often assumed. In contemporary settings, this form of learning support is called scaffolding in recognition of the way in which it helps to build knowledge and is then removed as the knowledge construction occurs" (p. 206). Learners unfamiliar with constructivist learning in the traditional world benefit from coaching that helps them assume an active role as learners and helps them make use of the resources available to them.

Upward e-Coaching

Upward e-coaching puts a new spin on coaching. In this strategy, younger workers who are technology savvy are part of a reverse coaching program. In this program e-coaches help more senior colleagues learn to navigate the Internet, coaching them on searching and using new applications. These junior staffers assist senior management in better understanding the potential of the new technologies and how these technologies are viewed and used by members of a generation that has grown up with the Web. The advantage of using the Internet in this kind of coaching is that tools such as instant messaging and application sharing allow coaches and students to share fast, short, and just-in-time questions and support.

John Joseph (2001), a Wharton Fellow in eBusiness, describes such a program at the General Electric Company. In the GE program, senior business leaders receive a coach drawn from a pool of younger talent within the company. Joseph reports, "GE chief executive Jack Welch ordered over 600 of his top managers, ranging in age from 30 to 60, to seek out young Internet-savvy professionals in the company and become their students." What might surprise some readers is that even Jack Welch has an e-mentor. (*Note:* GE chose to call the program e-mentoring, but given the definition used in this book, it is better described as a coaching role.)

Guidelines for Design for e-Coaching and e-Mentoring

e-Mentoring and e-coaching are in their infancy. There is a great deal to be learned about how to implement straight-up e-mentoring/e-coaching and blended programs. Some of the early adopters have gathered best practices and lessons learned and have created templates and other tools. Because programs vary widely in their use of technology, sophistication of participants, corporate culture, and goals, it is not practical to provide a recipe for success. This section provides general guidelines or "watch-points" for designing e-mentoring and e-coaching.

Assess the Cultural Match

One of the commonly cited challenges is the match of e-mentoring/e-coaching to the culture of the organization. e-Mentoring and e-coaching appear to be good solutions and easy to sell to management because the technology is ubiquitous and the infrastructure costs are low. The more difficult work is to assess whether mentoring and coaching can achieve the desired educational goals. Equally important is the cultural match to ensure that management values the program and is willing to support the costs that don't show up as line items in the training and development budget. Examples of support for mentoring are allowing meetings during regular work hours and recognizing and rewarding participation.

Management of the Program

The effort required to implement and nurture these programs should not be underestimated. There is a lot more work than simply announcing the program and circulating a sign-up sheet for mentors and protégés. Take the time to review best practices of traditional and e-programs to understand the steps needed to train participants, communicate goals and non-goals, maintain the ongoing monitoring and evaluation process, recruit mentors, and make mentor-protégé matches.

Consider Blending Mentoring Programs with Other Interventions

Mentoring programs should be seen as yet another strategy for employee development, but not the only strategy. Consider using these programs in combination with on-the-job training, formal management development programs, and executive MBA courses.

In Practice: Carol B. Muller: MentorNet

Carol B. Muller, Ph.D., is the founder, president, and chief executive officer of MentorNet, a nonprofit organization founded in 1997. MentorNet provides a one-on-one mentoring program pairing women in community college, undergraduate, graduate, and post docs as protégés with professionals as mentors for one-on-one, e-mail-based mentoring (e-mentoring) relationships. Dr. Muller is responsible for establishing and implementing the vision for the organization and its programs, developing needed resources, and managing those resources with the help of staff, volunteers, and partners. In addition to serving as MentorNet's president and CEO, she is a consulting associate professor of mechanical engineering at Stanford University. MentorNet has been awarded the Presidential Award for Excellence in Science, Mathematics, and Engineering Mentoring. The home page for MentorNet as of November 9, 2004, is shown in Figure 7.1.

Figure 7.1. Example of e-Mentoring

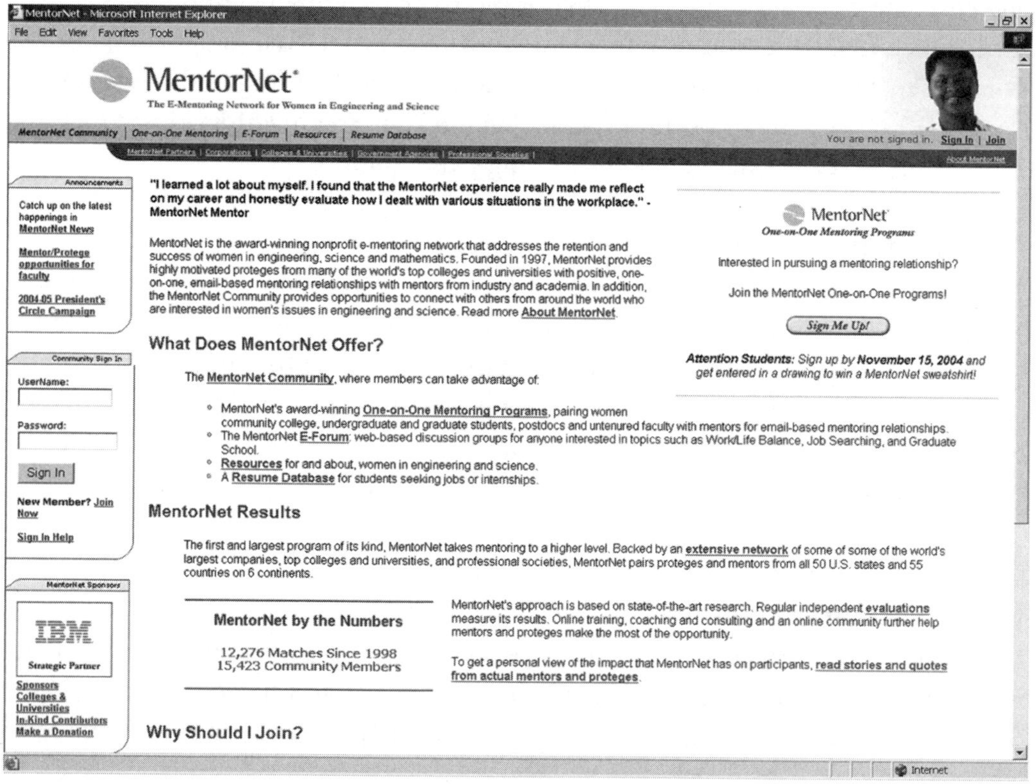

Source: MentorNet. www.mentornet.net. Retrieved from the Web on November 9, 2004.

Interviewing Dr. Muller was a privilege because she brings both the practical experience of leading an e-mentoring program that has made more than 20,000 matches and she is a recognized researcher, writer, and presenter on e-mentoring. The pragmatic issues of MentorNet operations and practices are well documented on the site (http://www.MentorNet.net) and more details can be found by reading the following:

- Alapati, M.R., Fox, S.J., Dockter, J.L., & Muller, C.B. (2003). MentorNet in depth: Structured mentoring practices (pdf). *Proceedings of the Women in Engineering Conference,* West Lafayette, Indiana. Chicago, IL: Women in Engineering Programs & Advocates Network.

- Boyle, P., & Muller, C.B. (n.d.). *Electronic mentoring programs: A model to guide best practice and research.* Australian e-Mentoring Reference Group. www.apesma.asn.au/mentorsonline/reference/pdfs/muller_and_boyle_single.pdf. [Retrieved July 22, 2004.]

- Single, P.B., & Muller, C.B. (2001). When email and mentoring unite: The implementation of a nationwide electronic mentoring program. In L. Stromei (Ed.), *Implementing successful coaching and mentoring programs* (pp. 107–122). Arlington, VA: American Society for Training & Development. [Also available online from www.mentornet.net/Documents/About/Media/papers.aspx]

Given the breadth of the topic, Dr. Muller took the lead and recommended we focus on the requirements for successful e-mentoring programs. Our discussion was shaped by a paper and presentation (Muller, 2004) she is working on that summarizes the factors for success and the related research.

Dr. Muller clearly knew where to start. Clutterbuck (2004), an expert in mentoring, estimates that at least 40 percent of mentoring programs fail, depending on the criterion used to judge success. Based on Dr. Muller's research, there are eight requirements for success. In the following section we look briefly at these requirements.

Research and Planning. Dr. Muller stressed the importance of "doing your homework." Included in this category is reading the literature and clarifying program objectives. She stresses that you need to know more than the "how to" logistical information. She suggests reading about the phases of mentoring relationships (Kram, 1983) and organizational issues (Clutterbuck, 2004).

She is also unambiguous about the need for clear goals, specific objectives, defined timeframes, and clarity regarding targeting participants. Clarity of purpose is essential to knowing whether you really need a mentoring program.

As an illustration of this point, Dr. Muller talked about an organization whose goal was to make the knowledge of experienced staff available to junior staff. Based on assessing the goal, it was clear that an "ask the expert program" was better suited to their needs than a mentoring program.

Resource Development. One of the mistakes organizations frequently make is underestimating the cost of resources for administering and staffing a mentoring program. These administrators, staff members, and program mentors require training for their roles. Dr. Muller also emphasizes the need to value the mentors' time.

Recruitment. If you have done your planning and researching well, you will have a blueprint for recruiting. Although you have a clear idea whom you are targeting for the roles of mentor and protégé, there are a few common recruitment problems to avoid. Limiting participation and failing to communicate expectations can result in a backlash against the organization and a backlash against mentors and protégés.

- *Targeting women and minorities.* If you are going to target women and minorities, avoid limiting the program to only women and minorities. If you limit the population, you will miss great opportunities for learning.

- *Failing to set expectations.* Communicate program expectations when recruiting mentors and protégés. These include more than program timeframes, frequency of contact, and objectives. One of the key expectations to set is that mentoring is a two-way learning experience. e-Mentoring is not based on the deficit model that assumes the learner is an empty vessel into which knowledge and skills must be poured.

Matching. Based on the literature, research findings, and personal experience; Dr. Muller cautions that not all matches will be successful. That being said, she suggests that matches work best when the mentor and protégé have more in common than superficial characteristics. When pressed to discuss these characteristics, she cautions that the characteristics will differ from situation to situation. (For more detail, see *Electronic Mentoring Programs: A Model to Guide Best Practice and Research* from the Australian e-Mentoring Reference Group available online at www.apesma.asn.au/mentorsonline/reference/pdfs/muller_and_boyle_single.pdf)

Training. Both mentors and protégés need training. MentorNet's online *Guide for Mentors* and *Guide for Students* provide suggestions for developing successful mentoring relationships.

Coaching/Program Facilitation. Training is not a one-time event. Developing mentors and protégés is an ongoing process. A skilled facilitator who can act as a problem solver is essential to success. A facilitator check-in should be conducted to determine whether there are problems due to a bad match, failed communication, or anything else. There are no guidelines for how often facilitators should check in. Check-ins depend on the duration, frequency, and goals of the program. Dr. Muller suggests that program creators consider designing their check-ins around the phases of mentoring relationships outlined by Kram (1983) until they are able to tune check-ins to their situation.

Closure. Dr. Muller stresses that mentoring relationship are not lifelong. She suggests a clear date of closure be established at the start. The closure date provides a tactful way for mentor and protégé to end the relationship. The closure date can also serve as the date at which the pair reevaluate their relationship and chooses to enter a new phase.

Evaluation. The evaluation phase brings the program full circle. Dr. Muller points out that if you have done a good job in the research and planning phase you have the benchmarks for established your program. She counsels that once you have completed the evaluation, you should write up the findings and share them with your program supporters and volunteers.

For those considering developing an e-mentoring program in an organization that has no history of traditional face-to-face mentoring or coaching programs, MentorNet is evidence that a successful program need not spring from a traditional program—as long as you do your homework.

Conclusion

e-Mentoring and e-coaching should be undertaken only after great consideration. At first glance these strategies may appear to be inexpensive ways of providing training and development. e-Mentoring and e-coaching are particularly attractive in environments in which the budget is tight and in organizations in which there is limited ability to address the developmental needs of middle management. In practice, e-mentoring and e-coaching require significant resources for planning, recruiting, making matches, and training and facilitating participants. There is also the cost of the mentors' and protégés' time.

When the organizational fit is good and the programs are well-managed, e-mentoring and e-coaching can provide outstanding development opportunities. Programs can leverage the best talent in the company regardless of geographical location, fit into schedules that would not other wise allow for training, and provide learning and career opportunities not possible in traditional management development programs.

Learn More About It

Clutterbuck, D. (2004). *Everyone needs a mentor: Fostering talent at work* (3rd ed.). London: Chartered Institute of Personnel and Development.

Clutterbuck looks at how mentoring can foster the development of talent and the benefits mentoring provides mentors, protégés, and organizations. Readers looking for models of mentoring and various approaches to managing the balance of formality and informal programs will find practical guidance. When assessing candidates for your program, the section on the behaviors of effective mentors and protégés will prove helpful.

Clutterbuck, D. (2002, December). Why mentoring programs and relationships fail. *Link&Learn Newsletter.* http://www.linkageinc.com/company/news_events/link_learn_enewsletter/archive/2002/12_02_mentoring_clutterbuck.aspx

This article succinctly outlines three pitfalls of mentoring programs and relationships: contextual, interpersonal, and procedural. He also provides guidance for how to avoid these pitfalls.

Goldsmith, M., Lyons, L. & Freas, A. (2000). *Coaching for leadership: How the world's greatest coaches help leaders learn.* San Francisco: Jossey-Bass.

This is a solid collection of chapters by experts in the field with real experience in coaching. You will not find this to be a how-to manual but rather an easy-to-read book full of war stories and case studies. The book focuses more on coaching executives rather than rank-and-file workers.

Kram, K.E. (1983). Phases of the mentor relationship. *Academy of Management Journal, 26,* pp. 608–625.

This article provides instructional designers with insights into the structure of mentoring that would be helpful when building a traditional mentoring program or an e-mentoring program. In this article Kram describes two mentoring roles (1) career function roles (sponsorship, exposure and visibility, coaching, protection, and challenging assignments) and (2) psychosocial functions (role modeling, acceptance and confirmation, counseling, and friendship). She also outlines the "phases" of a mentoring relationship: initiation, cultivation, separation, and redefinition.

Olson, M.L. (2001). *e-Coaching*.
www.learningcircuits.org/2001/sep2001/olson.html

If you want to read in detail about the differences between traditional coaching and e-coaching, this is the place to start. This article also provides terrific descriptions of the tools, such as assessment instruments, databases, and program management software.

Parsloe, E., & Wray, M. (2000). *Coaching & mentoring.* London: Kogan Page.

This book offers a balanced mix of theory and practical advice. If you agree with the authors that traditional training methods need to be changed or supplemented, then you will find the "Seven Golden Rules for Simplicity" a good roadmap. Readers will appreciate the tool-kit approach and proven best practice in this accessible how to book.

Single, P.B., & Muller, C.B. (2001). When email and mentoring unite: The implementation of a nationwide electronic mentoring program. In L. Stromei (Ed.), *Implementing successful coaching and mentoring programs* (pp. 107–122). Arlington, VA: American Society for Training & Development.

Readers seeking more than a bare-bones model of e-mentoring will find this chapter well worth reading. The authors have provided a simple model and then use the experience of MentorNet to provide examples. If you are seriously considering a mentoring program put a bookmark in page 120 and use the discussion questions. The authors put forward six questions that should be answered before writing your project plan.

Zeus, P., & Skiffington, S. (2001). *The complete guide to coaching at work.* New York: McGraw-Hill.

This is an easy-to-read book offering concrete steps for trainers and mangers interested in developing coaching programs. The blueprints are not focused on e-coaching, but the models and blueprints easily translate.

Websites of Interest

www.coachfederation.org. International Coach Federation

The International Coach Federation is the professional association of personal and business coaches that seeks to preserve the integrity of coaching around the globe.

www.coachingnetwork.org.uk. The Coaching and Mentoring Network

A community portal and resource center on the Internet for information and services relating to coaching and mentoring.

www.mentoring.org/. National Mentoring Partnership

MENTOR/National Mentoring Partnership is an advocate for the expansion of mentoring and a resource for mentors and mentoring initiatives nationwide.

REFLECTION AND APPLICATION

To reflect on the material presented in this chapter and apply it in a real e-learning situation, consider how you would respond to the following challenges. (Each of these challenges is intentionally left vague. If you are unsure about a piece of information, make an assumption about it and list the assumption.)

- The vice president of human resources in your company comes to you and says, "We need middle management training but can't really afford much. How about a mentoring program?" By the way, your middle managers are located in fifteen locations across three continents. Which mentoring strategy would you recommend? What challenges would you alert your vice president to?

- Create a job aid that will be distributed online to mentors that reminds them of the top responsibilities in their role.

- To support online training for a CAD/CAM application, you suggest that your organization provides an instrumental e-coach. But when you tell your manager about the idea, he hits the roof, saying, "We can't afford those coaches! Do you know how much they cost?" You immediately realize that your manager has confused the concepts of instrumental and professional coaching, as well as e-coaching and in-person coaching. How will you explain the differences to your manager?

Chapter 8

m-Learning

Every decade or so, learning and human performance technology get a new boost—a new medium through which it can inform, communicate, interact, empower, and enlighten. It seems that learning is getting poised to make yet another rush forward into the era of mobile and wireless learning!

Singh, 2003

In This Chapter

In this chapter we will

- Define m-learning and explains why it is considered a delivery strategy—not a learning strategy

- Differentiate among fixed line, m-learning, wireless learning, and disconnected use delivery strategies

- Explain what is fueling the growth of m-learning

- Describe the benefits and limitations of m-learning

- Describe three approaches to m-learning

- Consider the other educational tasks that mobile and wireless devices are being used to accomplish

- Provide a portfolio of examples of m-learning

Wireless learning is a *delivery* strategy; it is not a learning strategy. In the same way, *mobile learning or m-learning are also delivery strategies.* These delivery strategies support a range of instructional strategies and designs. Unlike other chapters in this section that offer techniques to help learners construct knowledge or techniques to speed the acquisition of knowledge, the m-learning strategies presented here focus on ways to use mobile devices.

Wireless learning, mobile learning, and m-learning are frequently asked for by customers who are in the process of selecting e-learning tools such as authoring software, learning management systems, and testing and assessment applications. The problem with looking for these capabilities before you understand what you need them to do is that you are shopping for a solution without a problem. This is the equivalent of shopping for ingredients without knowing what kind of meal you plan to prepare.

While the promise of this technology has a large "gee whiz" factor, it also has some very real limitations. Before picturing your learners equipped like James Bond, with the latest hand-held devices, it is important to ask the essential questions. What gap in skill and knowledge are you trying to fill? What are the options? What are the costs? How do the benefits and limitations of these options compare? Is your learning intervention part of a larger solution such as a documentation system, inventory management system, order entry system, or data collection solution? This chapter will give you skills needed to evaluate m-learning as a delivery strategy.

What Is m-Learning?

The question "What is m-learning?" is not rhetorical. The terminology used by people talking about wireless learning, mobile learning, and m-learning has a great deal of variability depending on the journal, website, consultant, or vendor. Because instructional design strategies are dependent on the capabilities of wireless and mobile devices, it is important to be clear about how the terms are used in this book. When developing solutions, make sure your technology suppliers share your definitions.

Wireless is a term used to describe telecommunications in which electromagnetic waves (rather than some form of wire) carry the signal over part or the entire communication path. Today common examples of wireless equipment (not all educationally useful) in the home and workplace are

- Cellular phones and pagers
- PDA-equipped wireless modems
- Laptops with wireless cards
- Global positioning systems (GPS)

- Cordless computer peripherals such as the cordless mouse or keyboard
- Remote garage-door openers
- Baby monitors

Mobile learning (m-learning) refers to learning that takes place on devices that are portable, have their own power supply, and can be easily used where there is no access to affixed lines, that is, a physical wire-based connection. Mobile learning devices can be connected to a wireless network or they can work in disconnected mode. In a disconnected mode, the device must have content downloaded in advance—so not all mobile devices are wireless. Likewise, not all wireless devices are mobile; many people consider a laptop PC with WiFi cards too cumbersome to be genuinely mobile. Examples of common mobile devices (not all educationally practical) are

- Mobile phones
- Pocket PCs
- Laptops
- Smart phones
- Tablet PCs
- Personal communication devices such as pagers

Table 8.1 contrasts the characteristics of traditional desktop e-learning to two kinds of mobile learning. *Fixed line* refers to an e-learning situation in which the learner is connected to a physical wire to achieve network connectivity. In contrast, the mobile systems free the learner from needing a physical wire and allow *situated learning*. The first kind of mobile learning, "disconnected use," relies on devices that have the content loaded on them in advance, making it possible to take devices such as pocket PCs, PDAs, or laptops anywhere. In contrast, wireless mobile learning uses a wireless high-fidelity network to connect learners to content without having to preload content.

There are pros and cons for each option. A multidimensional framework developed by Goh and Kinshuk (2004) suggests that the pros and cons for e-learning and m-learning fall into four dimensions: *content, device, connectivity,* and *collaboration.*

Content refers to more than what is being taught and the use of rich media such as streaming video, audio, or detailed graphics. Content considerations should include thinking about the context in which the learning materials will be used. A traditional desktop environment affords the learner time to explore related links, to engage in complex interactions, and to focus on learning programs that last fifteen to sixty minutes. In contrast, m-learning content is situated learning that takes place in context of doing a job. The learner focuses on content needed to complete a task and is not interested in exploring related links.

At the start of this chapter we emphasized that wireless is a delivery strategy, not a learning strategy. The importance of the device is evidence of this maxim. The functionality of the device in most cases will be the primary design consideration. Although it is technically possible, there is no such thing as "design once and reuse across multiple devices." Limitations such as screen size, resolution, input/output modes, navigation, and bandwidth require content be optimized for each device.

Anyone who has ever used the phrase "Can you hear me now?" knows about wireless connectivity. Traditional desktop programs delivered using a physical wire have both a reliable power supply and reliable connectivity. Wireless devices face challenges such as areas in which WiFi networks are not available, frequent lost connections, and poor bandwidth. Network issues are not a problem for disconnected users, but disconnected use means that content has to be downloaded in advance. In addition, a plan must be put in place to update that content on disconnected devices. Connectivity affects tracking. If knowing who is using the systems matters, mobile and fixed-line systems will deliver immediate results. On the other hand, disconnected use systems will require additional technology to upload information on how and what is being used.

Collaboration or the ability for the learner to send messages to fellow students, contact the facilitator, and query experts is a clear strength of fixed-line systems. Collaboration in the fixed-line system can include instant messaging, participation in a threaded discussion, and embedded e-mail. Disconnected users are without these collaborative and interactive tools. The degree of collaboration available to mobile wireless users will be dependent on the device.

If e-learning is in the early stages of development, m-learning is embryonic. The technologies are changing quickly, and the delivery strategies are evolving to take advantage of new features. One thing that is clear even at this embryonic stage is that m-learning will not be a stand-alone solution to fill gaps in skills and knowledge. As you read this chapter, consider m-learning as a tool for extending learning to where it is needed as a performance support strategy. Table 8.1 is a summary of this discussion.

Why Should You Use Wireless and Mobile Learning?

Wireless and mobile learning are enjoying a great deal of attention. The interest in this technology is being driven by the rapid growth of wireless and mobile devices. As Harvey Singh (2003), CEO of NavoWave, points out:

- More than 50 percent of jobs are mobile—away from a physical office.

- In the United States, an average worker spends only two days in formal training programs.

- To date, over 500 million Web-enabled mobile phones have been shipped to customers.

- Multipurpose hand-held devices, such as PDAs and cell phones, will outsell laptop and desktop computers combined by 2005.

- The enterprise market for mobile computing is estimated at $30 billion.

Benefits and Limitations of Mobile Learning

In this section, we'll review the benefits and limitations of m-learning for the two primary delivery strategies: the use of mobile devices to delivery performance support and the use of mobile devices to teach through communication. If you have ever used your cell phone to find a phone number, check the date and time, or calculate a tip, you have experienced m-learning as performance support. You also may have experienced mobile devices that teach through communication. If you have called using a cell while driving to a customer site to ask expert advice or if you have sent your team e-mails via your Blackberry during a client meeting asking for examples or definitions, you have experienced mobile devices that teach through communication. We will look at these strategies in more detail in the Portfolio of m-Learning Strategies section.

The Benefits

This section focuses on the benefits from two kinds of wireless mobile learning, m-learning as a form of performance support and m-learning as communication that creates knowledge. These are two very different strategies for using mobile devices. One assumes that benefits are derived from providing learners with a job aid in the context of their work. Of course, these job aids can be greatly enhanced depending on the device. The device can be wired so as to get the latest information, and it can use visuals, text, and audio to deliver performance support. In contrast, m-learning as communication takes a different approach. The benefits of this approach are based

Table 8.1. Comparison of Fixed-Line and Mobile Learning

E-Learning Delivery Options	Characteristics	Design Considerations
FIXED-LINE LEARNING (the traditional desktop experience using a PC)	**Content** • Rich media/exploration possible • Content access via streaming, browse, and download • Complex interactions possible **Device** • Full screen • Users are familiar with PC input/output and navigation **Connectivity** • Immediate tracking • Reliable connectivity and power • Bound to fixed lines **Collaboration** • Two-way collaboration (send/receive)	Take advantage of the ability to: • Provide weblinks to allow learners to explore additional material • Leverage rich media such as graphics and streaming visuals if appropriate • Encourage collaboration in class-based threaded discussions, e-mail messages to the facilitator, and team rooms for group work
M-LEARNING *Disconnected Use*	**Content** • Rich media possible • Embedded links and exploration is limited to what was downloaded • Content must be downloaded/ pre-loaded in advance • Complex interactions difficult due to use interface • Content can be consumed when and where it is needed (situated learning) **Device** • Limited screen size and resolution with mobile devices (not true for PCs or laptops that are operating in disconnected mode)	Take advantage of the ability to: • Deliver training at the point of need, situated learning, by providing just-in-time and just enough learning • Conduct a detailed needs analysis and learner analysis to ensure you understand the learner's environment and the essential content • Tailor content to optimize the device and connectivity capabilities

- Physical device limitations such as battery life, memory, and user interface input/output

Connectivity
- Not connected to network
- Delayed tracking
- Possible reliance on battery power

Collaboration
- No real-time collaboration

M-LEARNING	*Mobile Wireless*	

Content
- Task-focused content (no exploration)
- Content access via streaming audio or video
- Complex interactions difficult
- Situated learning/learning in context

Device
- Limited screen size and resolution
- Physical device limitations such as battery life, memory, and user interface input/output

Connectivity
- Dependent on network reliability and availability
- Frequent interruptions (incoming calls, network dead spots)
- Immediate tracking

Collaboration
- Two-way collaboration (send/receive) dependent on ease of input/output and device features

Take advantage of the ability to:
- Deliver short, well-targeted bites of training that are effective in environments in which learning must complete for attention
- Collaborate and interact in real time by simplifying interactions and navigation
- Deliver information using visuals, graphics, color, and sound to create effective communication

on constructivist theories of learning. The benefits of m-learning as communication stem from learners and experts constructing knowledge in an authentic context.

Wireless m-Learning as Performance Support

Wireless m-learning performance support systems (PSS) are similar to traditional PSS. m-Learning solutions integrate mobile devices with the work to help the user perform a task by providing information, guidance, and learning experiences when and where they are needed. Benefits of this use include the following:

- *Puts training and performance support where the actual work takes place.* Look for situations in which it would be helpful to have a performance support tool available as the job is being done. It might be the case of a repair person who has an iPAQ (hand-held computer) with documentation, job aids, and diagrams available to refer to as he or she does the repair.

- *Allows new skills or knowledge to be immediately applied.* Consider the use of these devices in a retail environment in which there are dozens of new products to learn to sell each month. Rather than taking sales associates away from the sales floor for new product training, think about putting product training on mobile devices. This would allow sales associates to learn about the products as the products become available for sale, instead of training associates weeks in advance. The device could also be used to look things up, such as product comparisons, warranty information, and other information vital to answering customer questions. Why ask sales associates to memorize information when they can reference it with accuracy?

- *Enables training when it is needed.* Wireless and mobile learning can empower "teachable moments," that is, times when those with a stake in a particular issue are attentive, willing, and receptive to learning. Using mobile devices, learners can access job aids, reference materials, or instruction when needed.

- *Allows use of rich media when appropriate.* Some of the wireless and mobile devices support rich media such as video, photographs, images, audio, and animation. If these media make instruction, reference material, or job aids more effective, they should be employed.

Wireless m-Learning as Communication That Creates Knowledge

The benefits of m-learning as communication may be controversial. The benefits discussed here are derived from collaboration with experts or collaboration among peers. The challenge for training professionals will be to acknowledge these benefits and realize that there is not a formal role for the trainer or instructional designer to play.

- *Provides access to experts.* Consider using wireless devices when there is a need to connect to and learn from experts. An example of this is service engineers working on a customer site. The service engineers are in the process of evaluating the customer's database and they need to learn more about the advanced options for securing data. Using a PDA with instant messaging and awareness (the ability to tell if someone is accessible via e-mail, instant messaging, or phone), learners can access expertise. The awareness option enables the learner to see which of the experts is available right now to dialog via e-mail, instant message, or phone. In this case the service engineers can call the expert and ask questions that will create knowledge and result in learning.

- *Builds a community of practice.* The term community of practice was coined by Etienne Wenger (Wenger & Snyder, 2000). It describes an informal network or group of people who exchange tips, best practices, and solutions to real problems. Using wireless devices, a community of practice can contribute to a forum or threaded discussion. Questions and answers posted to the discussion forum can be accessed from the field. Wireless devices can also be used to download tools like templates, sample letters, spreadsheets for estimating, sales scripts, and other documents that the team has developed over time. It can also be a tool for instant messaging, e-mail, or other communication and dialog. An example of this is an insurance adjuster who has a question about a claim she is working on. Using a cell phone with a camera, the adjuster sends images to a colleague from her team. Sharing the picture of the vehicle she is processing, the colleague can answer questions about how to process the claim.

- *Knows where your expertise is located by connecting and continuously sync training to back-end systems.* Wireless devices have the ability to push and pull data to and from learners. The ability to connect and sync means that you can have training records that are current and easy to report on. An example of this would be to use a wireless system to drive compliance and recertification training. In this case, a back-end system would track when learners need to take certification training and send the learner a reminder on the wireless device four to six weeks in advance of the certification expiration date. The leaner could then access the training and certification test online. The wireless device would send the certification test scores to a computer at headquarters and update the certification database. This means the records on certification are always up-to-date and a good source for reports to insurance companies and the government.

The Limitations

The limitation of m-learning are a combination of technical and education challenges. Some of these limitations may disappear as technology improves.

A Fragmented Learning Experience

A study done at Stanford University's Language lab (Qingyang, 2003) provides some insights into the fragmented experience of learning with mobile device. The lab staff chose foreign language study as the content area, hypothesizing that mobile devices could provide opportunities for review, listening, and speaking practice in a safe, authentic, personalized, and on-demand environment. The prototypes developed let users practice new words, take a quiz, access word and phrase translations, work with a live coach, and save vocabulary to a notebook—all in an integrated voice/data environment. The study warned that "Learning requires concentration and reflection. However, being on-the-go (riding a train, sitting in a cafe, walking down the street) is fraught with distractions. Students are in situations that place unpredictable but important demands on their attention. This leaves the mobile learner with a highly distracted, highly fragmented experience. The learning application must be designed with this in mind."

Lack of Well-Developed Metacognitive Skills

Metacognition refers to the ability of learners to be aware of and monitor their learning processes. Adult education literature counsels that the more learners understand about how they learn best, the better able they are to assess how well they are learning and to manage their own learning. The challenge in wireless and m-learning is that learners have little experience with this delivery mode and the related instructional strategies. Experts (Peters, 2000) have suggested that "some employees are unsure about evaluating their personal learning experiences. The lack of external feedback can cause learners to question their goals and achievements." Using m-learning delivery devices and strategies for self-directed learning compounds this challenge. When talking about metacognitive skills, a distinction needs to be made between the learners' ability to self-monitor and their ability to self-assess. Learners can easily monitor their progress against a plan that tracks task completion, time on task, and quiz scores. The more difficult metacognitive skill is self-assessment, the learner's ability to judge how well he or she has actually done learning and transferring new skill and knowledge.

Small Screens and Difficulty Accessing Information from the Web

Mobile and wireless devices have significant limitations relative to screen size and ability to access information designed for traditional PC-based Web viewing. If the mobile devices are accessing information from websites, Jacob Neilsen (2003b) advises

> Currently, the best we can hope for are websites that are basically scaled-down and redesigned to eliminate graphics and multi-column layouts. At worst, websites offer no mobile version, so you get crunched images and skinny columns that are almost impossible to read.
>
> Clearly, traditional websites are intended for a big-screen user experience. Putting them on a small screen is like the dog that sings: the miracle is that it does so at all. While a technical feat, usability is never going to be good. To cater to mobile devices, websites and services should offer much shorter articles, dramatically simplified navigation, and highly selective features, retaining only what's needed in a mobile setting.

High Costs

One of the biggest limitations and drawbacks for using a mobile wireless e-learning solution is cost. Recommending m-learning or wireless learning means investing in devices for each learner, paying for wireless service, budgeting for maintenance repair and upgrades, and support from an IT group to answer users' questions and resolve technical problems. It takes a compelling business case to implement this kind of technology for learning.

Challenges to the Security of the Device and Its Data

Security is a challenge in the office environment with desktop PCs, and that challenge is magnified with mobile devices. Because of their size and portability, they are easy to lose, subject to damage, and more likely to be stolen than desktop systems. There are also serious considerations regarding data security. In a *Computer World* article, Muir (2003) estimates that "probably fewer than 10 percent of mobile devices used by major organizations have serious protection for stored data. This vulnerability persists despite the annual Computer Security Institute/FBI studies that document substantial financial losses associated with theft and exposure of confidential data and despite federal regulations governing the security of private data collected by financial and health care organizations."

A Portfolio of m-Learning Strategies

m-Learning can be grouped into three delivery strategies: m-learning as e-learning, performance support, and communication. Each strategy is based on a different view of the role of the learners and different beliefs regarding how to design and deliver instruction. The first strategy is the least innovative, but probably the easiest to execute and most frequently used. The last two strategies are more innovative, but less frequently used. None of these delivery strategies is designed to be a stand-alone learning solution. As you think about these strategies, consider how they might be blended into larger programs to extend learning to the work site.

m-Learning as e-Learning

The first approach is to simply use wireless devices as an extension of desktop e-learning. Expressed as a math equation, m-learning = e-learning.

Given the proliferation of wireless devices and the prediction that the dominant form of Internet access will be via wireless devices, it follows that e-learning simply becomes m-learning. In this most simplistic view, e-learning and m-learning are the same; just the devices differ. An example of this would be a course that could be taken in an office by connecting to the physical local area network and that could also be taken on a PC equipped with a wireless card in a coffee shop. In either case it is the same course, taken on a the same PC notebook, and there is little need to re-think strategies because the device (the PC) remains constant; only the network connection changes.

A great example of m-learning = e-learning is the NETg courseware that runs on the IBM Lotus learning management systems. In this case, e-learning is available three ways, and two of the three options are mobile. The course can simply be taken at the employee's desk using fixed lines. Or the employee can bring a laptop to the cafeteria and take the course using a wireless network. Another alternative would be to download the course and take it in disconnected mode while on a plane. *Disconnected mode* is the ability to take a course without being connected to the network but maintain the scoring and tracking data until the PC is next connected to a network. In this case, the NETg courseware works in concert with the IBM Lotus LMS to track the learner's progress and uploads scores when he or she next connects to the network. The mobile options in this case rely on the same courseware and the same device as traditional e-learning.

A variation on this theme is the claim that e-learning developed for the desktop PC or laptop can simply be *ported* (moved from one platform to another) to PDAs and other mobile devices. Some vendors claim to have software that makes training universally available. Using their software, instructional designers are able to develop and deliver training content in multiple formats (Kossen, 2003). This strategy is often promoted as part of a learning-object vision that says "develop your content once and deliver it using multiple formats such as e-learning, CD-ROMs, and

PDAs." Clearly there are caveats to this claim. In this case, m-learning is not equal to e-learning. There are significant design considerations related to content reuse, device characteristics, connectivity limitations, and collaboration capabilities. This interpretation of m-learning = e-learning is beyond the scope of this chapter. Readers interested in this topic will find resources in the Learn More About It section at the end of this chapter.

Wireless and Mobile Learning as Performance Support

The second approach stresses that wireless m-learning is characteristically aimed at knowledge that is location-dependent and situation-dependent. In this case, traditional e-learning and m-learning are not the same. In this strategy, m-learning is focused on performance support, reference-based learning, or PSS solutions created specifically for remote access in the context of doing a task. Unlike the first case in which e-learning and m-learning are the same, this approach requires that e-learning and m-learning have distinct qualities. The design for performance support using mobile devices requires that content be optimized for the device and the connectivity capabilities.

Epocrates DocAlert® messaging is an example of m-Learning. Through this messaging, up to three short and timely news briefs are delivered to users each time they update their Epocrates® hand-held software. Messages include important medication safety alerts from the FDA, CDC, ISMP, and AHRQ, medical and practice management news, and valuable clinical news targeted by specialty.

Users can view additional information, save it to their PDAs, or request additional information via e-mail. Depending on the alert, this may include clinical abstracts, CME or conference event notification, comprehensive clinical guidelines, and links to useful websites and electronic reports.

Figure 8.1 shows a screen shot of an actual DocAlert message on a biological or chemical agent as it appeared on a hand-held device. The U.S. Department of Health and Human Services tested the Epocrates hand-held (or PDA) network as a method to alert frontline health care workers of bioterrorist attacks. This m-Learning solution puts information on some of the most life-threatening biological or chemical agents—such as smallpox, anthrax, and viral hemorrhagic fevers like Ebola—literally into the palm of a physician's hand. The overall ePocrates system delivers regularly updated clinical reference information to health care workers who use hand-helds and is particularly useful in emergency rooms, clinics, and doctors' offices.

Figure 8.1. Epocrates DocAlert® Messaging: Example of m-Learning

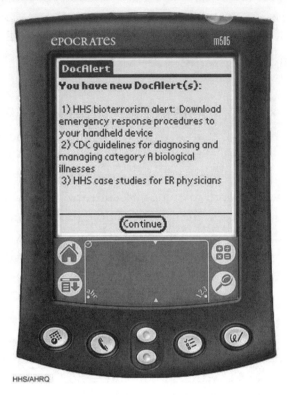

HHS/AHRQ

Source: www.space.com/businesstechnology/technology/pda_alert_030327.html

Communication as Learning in Context

The third approach stresses that m-learning is grounded in person-to-person communication. In m-learning, the learning arises through dialog (questions and answers) that takes place in context. Nyíri (2002), who has developed a philosophy of m-learning, argues that information and knowledge are not identical, but that there is a relationship between information and knowledge. He points out that questions arising in the course of mobile communication seek location-specific and situation-specific answers. These questions create a context, and thus the answers can give rise to knowledge. Knowledge and information are enriched in this case because mobile communication can combine voice, text, and live pictures.

Today this kind of learning is taking place with the IBM Lotus Instant Messaging Everyplace® solution. This solution allows mobile users to see who is available to collaborate via phone, instant messaging, and e-mail. The ability to see who is available is called presence awareness. Using presence awareness, employees are able to locate experts and see, in advance, whether a person is available to collaborate, share information, or chat. This technology enables learning in context and helps create knowledge.

Slightly Beyond the Scope of e-Learning

There are a number of educational uses of mobile and wireless devices that are not really "e-learning," but they are worthy of a short discussion. There is a significant amount of work being done to develop applications for the traditional classroom that use mobile devices because they are less expensive than laptops. Most of this work is limited to K–12 and higher education, where pilots are actively underway.

Traditional Classroom Assessment

Using PDAs and hand-held devices, a teacher beams a test or quiz to learners using a wireless network. The learners respond to the quiz and beam their responses back. The advantage of this process over passing out a paper-and-pencil test is that the data regarding elapsed test completion time, time to respond to a given item, detailed item analysis data, and other information is tracked in a database. Having data online enables teachers to do things like compare scores among classes, conduct item analysis, and look for trends. This is not an e-learning strategy but is talked about as something that would be possible if PDAs or hand-helds were available as a result of a larger e-learning initiative.

Administrative Tools

There are tools for making classroom administration easier for teachers. Examples of this are applications for tracking attendance, keeping seating charts, managing a grade book, storing lesson plans, providing references and notes for bus routes, birthdays, emergency contact information, and other important information. These tools can be used in connected or disconnected mode. The ability to synchronize information as it is uploaded and downloaded means that the information on a server/desktop PC and the information on the PDA are coordinated to ensure that the latest information is available to teachers and administrators. This is not a learning application, but it is often discussed in the popular trade magazines, so instructional designers should be aware of the possibilities.

Student and Tutor Notifications

A gray area in the use of mobile and wireless for e-learning is the use of hand-held devices for notification. This is the use of the notifications or messaging features that are part of learning content management systems (LMS). Many LMS systems send text messages, post items to online calendars, or send e-mail to wireless devices to notify students that they need to renew a certification, alert them to the offering a new class they might be interested in taking, or confirm they have been moved from a wait-list to an enrolled seat in a coveted course. There is even the possibility of having the system notify the learner when there are new postings to a threaded discussion. These uses are less about learning and more about tracking and managing learners.

The notification functions can also be used for instructors. In some cases a tutor or mentor can be notified that a student is seeking assistance. Using wireless notification devices such as a PDA or beeper, the tutor can receive a message without being seated in front of his or her PC.

Content "to Go"

Mobile devices also make it possible for learners to take materials with them. Materials designed for reading or listening to during short free periods like taking the train, having a coffee, or waiting to make a customer call can be turned into learning opportunities. This is slightly different than downloading an e-learning course that tracks date of download, scores of quizzes, the learner's progress, and other data. If you need to report on learner progress, comprehension, or mastery of materials content "to go" is not a good solution.

The content-to-go strategy encourages users to download reference materials, news, journal articles, speakers, interviews, maps, and more. While this is not learning in the traditional sense, it may be possible to ask learners to download a relevant newspaper story or journal article for discussion in class. For example, the American Medical Association (2003) offers its members PDA content for download on topics such as clinical practice, health care policy, and ethics.

Data-Gathering Tools for Project-Based Learning

In K–12 and higher education, hand-held devices are being used for project-based learning. In this context, the devices are used to allow students to go into the field and record observations, gather data, and make records (audio or visual). The data gathered in the field is then brought back into the classroom as the foundation of project-based learning An example of this is a grant-funded program at Manatee High School and Sea Breeze Elementary School (PalmOne, n.d.). Using pH meters attached to PalmPilots®, students gathered data in the field and then returned to the classroom to do advanced analysis. The pH meter enabled students to collect pH values, dissolved oxygen, and temperatures values for the water. The students could press buttons on their hand-helds to change the data into graphs or bar graphs. Then they were able to draw their own conclusions about the ecosystems they were studying.

Guidelines for Wireless and Mobile Learning

People who have implemented wireless mobile learning inevitably recommend that "newbies" master the basics first. What they are referring to is mastering the technical, organizational, and educational challenge of developing traditional desktop-based e-learning before moving to m-learning. This suggestion is based on the increased difficulty inherent in m-learning. Veterans will frequently tell you they leaned on their strong relationship with IT to overcome technical hurdles, developed confidence using authoring tools, and used lessons learned from selling e-learning programs and supporting the programs. Starting with basic e-learning, the veterans built alliances, a track record, or the skills needed to deal with m-learning.

The guidelines presented here are broken into high-level wireless m-learning recommendations for performance support and recommendations for communication as knowledge building. Instructional strategies for both must be crafted based on the context, the equipment, the learners, and the organization.

Performance Support

Designing performance support systems for mobile devices adds a level of complexity due to the size of the device and the technical challenges related to screen size, navigation, and interaction.

Focus on User-Centered Design

When designing content or materials for a wireless or mobile PSS device, focus on what the learner needs to do or know. Consider how you organize the material (that is, based on task, location, most to least common problems, time of year, product); the amount of detail required, and the value of rich media (video, sound, graphics).

Assess the Need for Connectivity

Does the content have to be retrieved from a network? If the content is subject to frequent changes and the changes are essential to performance, then wireless mobile connections are essential. If some of the content is stable and changes infrequently, consider a hybrid solution. Store the stable content locally and use a wireless connection to access perishable content and to send launch and tracking data.

Motivate and Prepare Learners to Use Performance Support

Adopting performance support requires more that distributing mobile devices. Allocate time to teach employees to technically use the devices and bolster their metacognitive skills. Conduct sessions that provide practice using the device to solve problems or work through scenarios that will build learner confidence.

Conduct a Formative Evaluation

Before rolling out any m-learning solution, be sure to test your program. Conduct walkthroughs with a small group of five people (Neilsen, 2000). Look at issues such as

- Does the performance support tool address a worthy problem?
- How easy is it for learners to use the program?
- Can they quickly complete typical tasks?
- What changes would users recommend to the navigation or user interface?

Communication-Based Knowledge Development

Encouraging m-learning through communications will require fewer instructional design skills and more skills in influencing line of business decisions.

Start with a Project That Matters

Choose a project that needs a learning strategy reliant on experts and tacit knowledge (that is, the organization's expertise and a knowledge that is not written down and not formally expressed but essential to the success of a project). If all the available skills and knowledge are explicit (written down and well-known) and there is no deep expertise to draw on, a communication-based mobile strategy adds no value.

Share Rewards

Implementing a communication-based form of m-learning requires an organizational culture that recognizes and rewards sharing. Allowances have to be made in people's work schedules to allow them to focus on responding to requests for assistance. There also have to be reward and recognition for those willing to share their expertise. Allocating time and overcoming organizational cultures in which knowledge is power can be significant obstacles.

Don't Expect Immediate Success

In most organizations this will be a new strategy and one that will take a while to take root. Learners must learn how to manage this kind of learning and come to see this tool much like documentation, on-the-job training, and other forms of learning.

Likewise, the experts must see how they can optimize their role in sharing knowledge and teaching as a result of dialog with learners.

Think Through How You Can Nurture the Process
of Encouraging m-Learning Through Communications

In this strategy there is little training professionals can do directly to deliver learning. The role training plays is behind the scenes doing things such as monitoring and cleaning up threaded discussions, keeping lists of experts' skills up-to-date, clarifying expertise of team members, and making managers aware of the benefits of the program.

In Practice: Chris von Koschembahr: IBM's Worldwide Mobile Learning Leader

In this section we look at a mobile learning solution designed for the retail environment. Chris von Koschembahr, an executive in IBM's Innovation and Transformation Group and the worldwide mobile learning leader, explains how to align the "corporate triad" and how to build the essential foundation for successful m-learning.

Chris was the project mentor for the development of a mobile learning solution for a large retailer. When we talked, he was very clear about the importance of understanding the economic and physical environment into which you are selling and deploying a mobile learning solution. He provided me with a brief overview of the economics of retail, that is, the selling of goods to consumers, usually in small quantities and not for resale. This environment is characterized by low margins (very competitive), and high store employee turnover that results in continuous and costly training. In addition, there is research suggesting some employee dissatisfaction is due to their lack of knowledge, and this may be part of the reason for high turnover. This is the backdrop to an electronics retailer who faced two added challenges. Selling in this environment required significant customer/sales associate interaction and a large selection of products that frequently changed.

Chris and his team focused on two challenges, integrating training into the sales process and making training continuous. As part of the sales process, the associates had Pocket PCs for checking inventory, reading corporate announcements, and referencing short descriptions of products. Adding training to these devices moved learning to the floor, integrated training with products, and made training just-in-time.

In retail, the expense of hiring trainers as well as the time associates spend away from the selling floor (either in a classroom or time spent sitting at a PC in the back room) are all costs. In an industry with low margin, any reduction in cost is valued, so mobile devices that put learners back on the selling floor was a desirable goal. In addition, mobile learning relieved managers of the challenge of scheduling trainers, arranging schedules for associates to be off the selling floor, and dealing with the scheduling challenges of juggling multiple shifts and part-time employees.

Once learning moved to the floor, it was redesigned to accommodate the sales environment. m-Learning lessons were designed in short five-to-seven-minute chunks that could be consumed during slow spells. Moving training to the floor also allowed associates to take advantage of having the actual merchandise in front of them during the lesson. In some cases, the lessons instructed the learner to complete hands-on exercises.

Just-in-time learning took on several meanings in this case. There was the obvious advantage of associates being able to learn as the need arose. In these cases, m-learning was used as a "Smart Assistant" that helped provide better service by acting as a job aid. A second take on just-in-time learning was the ability to provide a continuous "drip" of learning. Frequently changing products meant that new items were continually introduced. In the past, associates waiting for a scheduled class and classes were dependent on enough new products being introduced to justify an hour or half-day off the selling floor. m-Learning meant training about new products could be synchronized with the arrival of the new products.

Making training continuous required that learning be integrated into the sales process and career development. Figure 8.2 shows the menu from the pocket PC. In this solution, learning was integrated with corporate announcements, short descriptions of products, inventory checks, product comparisons, checklist of required/optional accessories, and learning modules. Learning was also personalized and managed based on profiles that prescribed training based on the learner's role. The devices allowed managers to track which associates were trained or cross-trained in different departments.

Lessons Learned

This highly ambitious project brought together expertise from throughout IBM, including retail and e-learning/m-learning expertise, pervasive computing, retail store solutions, sales and distribution, and IBM Global Services (IGS). Clearly, there were many lessons learned. I asked Chris to focus on lessons learned from the instructional design perspective. Chris stressed that the

Figure 8.2. m-Learning Integrated into the Sales Process

lessons learned can be generalized. He has seen three themes play out across multiple industries and various mobile devices. Chris advised instructional designers to do the following:

- *Build a corporate triad.* A training application alone is not enough to justify the cost of purchasing, deploying, and maintaining mobile devices. The best strategy is to become part of a corporate triad consisting of a line of business manager (for example, Sales, Customer Service, Distribution), the chief information officer (CIO), and chief learning officer or head of training. Look for line-of-business managers deploying wireless applications that improve profitability. Examples of these applications are sales force automation for placing sales and checking inventory, field force application for scheduling drivers and tracking packages, and service application for scheduling repairs, keeping service records, and tracking parts. Monitor how your CIO is going to address the demand for wireless access to popular applications such as e-mail, calendaring, and personal information managers (PIMs). Bring these people together and educate them about the value of m-learning. While training will not justify the cost of mobile devices, it may provide added value that tips the scale in favor of a mobile solution in some other realm. If you don't instigate the triad, at least take advantage of the call you will get to train employees to use these new devices. Once you're in the loop, bring in the CIO and see if the device can be used for more than the line-of-business application.

- *Be prepared to reengineer the back office.* Getting content from the training department to the mobile device is the last mile and probably the hardest part of the journey. Taking full advantage of m-learning is more than simply making content mobile. The most challenging and invisible part of the m-learning process is reengineering the back office. Back-office activities include developing content, profiling learners, and implementing programs. Mobile learning requires that content be chunked into appropriate units, learners be profiled so that the right content can be pushed to them, new authoring tools be deployed, and change management be undertaken to communicate expectations. Other back-office changes include a rigorous needs assessment process and a painstaking formative evaluation strategy that produces easy-to-interact-with and simple-to-navigate programs.

- *Assess the viability of m-learning.* m-Learning is not the solution for every problem. Look at the physical, economic, and technical environment. Is this a place where a mobile learning device makes sense? If you're training pharmaceutical reps, can it be used in a doctor's outer office while waiting to speak with the doctor? Does m-learning achieve return-on-investment by reducing time-to-market by shortening the time needed to train salespeople, or is there a positive cost-benefit ratio for providing continuous learning between major learning events? Is the environment conducive to mobile learning? Can learners move between learning and job tasks? Does the learning lend itself to short bursts of study?

Conclusion

Some people will argue that m-learning is not ready for "prime time." This chapter has explored and acknowledged the technical, educational, and financial challenges; but these should not be reasons for dismissing m-learning. Mobile devices are a growing part of the technical infrastructure of large and small enterprises. Industry watchers predict the convergence of wireless data and computing will give us true anywhere, anytime, and any device access to information (Mobileinfo.com, 1999). These devices are enabling enterprise applications for sales, distribution, and customer service, and they will provide the coattails on which training can ride. These devices are changing how work and learning are done. The leadership of training and development must monitor and align with the line-of-business functions considering mobile devices in order to take advantage of this new delivery mode. The strategies presenting in this chapter are a starting point for generating ideas for formal and informal mobile learning.

Learn More About It

Gayeski, D. (2002). *Learning unplugged.* New York: AMACOM.

This is a compact, easy-to-read technology primer written for training and development professions. Wireless and mobile technology is set in a context that instructional designers and training managers will understand.

Keegan, D. (2002). *The future of learning: From e-learning to m-learning.* http://learning.ericsson.net/leonardo/book.html. FernUniversitat, ZIFF, Postfach 940, D—58084 Hagen, Germany. ERIC Document Reproduction Service No. ED472435.

This online book provides an in-depth look at instructional design for four wireless devices (Screenphone HS210, Compaq iPaq, Smartphone R380, and WAP telephone R520) and the creation of a wireless virtual learning environment. It offers a solid historic context evolving from distance learning to e-learning to m-learning. Readers will also enjoy the realistic assessments of the limitations and decisions made for each environment.

Lambe, P. (2002). *The autism of knowledge management.* Green Chameleon website: www.greenchameleon.com/thoughtpieces/autism.pdf [Retrieved July 10, 2004.]

This article is required reading for those interested in learning about knowledge management, e-learning, and the assumptions related to treating knowledge as content, as object, and as an artifact to be manipulated. This has particular relevance to those who are considering a strategy of designing content once and porting to multiple platforms.

Rheingold, H. (2002). *Smart mobs: The next social revolution.* Boulder, CO: Perseus Publishing.

This is not a wireless or m-learning book, but it does paint a picture of how cell phones, pagers and PDAs are shaping modern culture. This is worth reading for training professionals because the drivers of wireless technology will probably not be training related. This is a good read to see where the on-ramps to wireless learning might appear.

Websites of Interest

www.academiccolab.org/projects/mobile.html. Academic (ADL Co-Lab) Mobile Learning (AML) Technology Center

The AML Technology Center will advance research, development, and implementation of mobile learning and communications technologies across academia.

www.handhelds.org/. Handhelds Organization

Encourages and facilitates the creation of open source software for use on handheld and wearable computers.

Solutionswww.mobilearn.org/. MOBIlearn

MOBIlearn is a worldwide European-led research and development project exploring context-sensitive approaches to informal, problem-based and workplace learning by using key advances in mobile technologies.

REFLECTION AND APPLICATION

To reflect on the material presented in this chapter and apply it in a real e-learning situation, consider how you would respond to the following challenges. (Each of these challenges is intentionally left vague. If you are unsure about a piece of information, make an assumption about it and list the assumption.)

- You are the account representative for a large instructional design agency. One of your new clients has requested a course and, in the discussions, regularly uses terms *wireless* and *mobile.* After about five minutes, you realize that the client is using these terms interchangeably. You know that they're not interchangeable, and your hair is starting to stand on the back of your neck. Now you can no longer take it and decide to explain that the terms wireless and mobile are not interchangeable. What do you say to make your point?

- Until now, you have not produced a learning program for a PDA because you could not justify the cost. (Your company has not supplied workers with PDAs, and the cost of the course would also have to include the cost of distributing PDAs.) But one of the members of the marketing programs staff has told you that the company will be automating the sales force with PDAs in the next year, knowing about your interest in developing a training application for PDAs. A new product will be launched a month after the PDAs are distributed to the sales force, and your friend in marketing thinks that the new product training would make a perfect opportunity for you to offer training on the PDA. But she says, "It's up to you to come up with the budget." And you know that the only way to get a budget is to develop a business case that formally justifies the investment in PDA-based training for the new product.

- Suppose you work in a university and are teaching a traditional classroom course. But the classroom itself has a wireless network, and students all have laptop computers. What strategies are available to you for incorporating wireless technology into your course? What capabilities are available that will interfere with your teaching? How would you address those issues?

Chapter 9

Live Virtual Classroom

It is less about the tool, and it's all about designing an effective, engaging and interactive learning experience.

Masie & Rinaldi, 2002

In This Chapter

In this chapter, we will

- Define the term live virtual classroom

- Discuss the economic versus the educational justifications for adopting live virtual classroom technology

- Describe the benefits and limitations of live virtual classrooms

- Provide a portfolio of communication- versus collaboration-based strategies and nine techniques

- Provide links to live virtual courses as well as examples of design issues for live virtual courses

Live virtual classroom (LVC) allows you to run a training program in real time in which the instructors and learners are online at the same time using the Internet. You might be more familiar with vendors of this kind of software, with names such as Centra, WebEx, IBM/Lotus Sametime, InterWise, Illuminate, and InterCall, than with the term live virtual classroom.

Live virtual classroom is an easy first step in e-learning because of the similarities between it and traditional classrooms. The skills needed by instructors, the use of slides, the support for lecture-based instruction, and classroom-like metaphors of hand-raising, question posing, and writing on a whiteboard are example of traits that make it easy to bridge from traditional classroom to LVC. Notice we did not say that these similarities result in creating good practices. As Elliot Masie points out, one of the top challenges for the virtual classroom is to create effective learning. He stresses that "it is less about the tool, and it's all about designing an effective, engaging and interactive learning experience" (Masie & Rinaldi, 2002).

In this chapter we look at two ways to approach a live virtual classroom: the *economic* and the *educational*. We also provide portfolio strategies for making the most of the delivery medium. Let's start by defining what we mean by a live virtual classroom.

What Is a Live Virtual Classroom?

The live virtual classroom (LVC) is an online learning experience in which the instructor and learners work together in real time. Working together, the instructor and students have live audio dialog while sharing slides, viewing a software application, surfing the Internet, working in virtual breakout rooms, conducting polls, and taking assessments. Live virtual classroom technology was one of the early e-learning delivery modes that caught everyone's attention for the *gee-whiz* factor. For a while, it looked like it might fade. However, what people quickly realized was that, of all the e-learning technology out there, live virtual classroom programs are the fastest and easiest to develop. In addition, LVC technology is an easy first step for instructors and learners and a simple sell to management. In some cases there is no need to sell management on LVC technology.

Organizations are installing live virtual classroom and e-meeting software on their internal networks or purchasing services from external providers who sell access to virtual classrooms by the hour and by the year. IDC, a leading technology consulting company, reports, "Worldwide, live e-learning is growing at an impressive rate, and IDC forecasts a compound annual growth rate (CAGR) of more than 50 percent between 2001 and 2006" (Anderson, Mahowald, & Brennan, 2002). This rapid growth means that in the next two to three years more organizations will have access to live virtual classrooms. These compelling facts ensure that LVC is here to stay. And an essential skill for educators will be a repertoire of strategies that make the most of this medium.

Why Use a Live Virtual Classroom?

The question can be answered from two angles: the economic perspective or the educational perspective—and the answers differ greatly.

The reasons for using live virtual classrooms are often rooted in the economics of this medium. The live virtual classroom has been championed by people who compare its economic advantages to traditional classroom programs and self-paced learning. The list below provides a summary of the economic reasons to adopt e-learning through LVC.

- LVC content is faster and less expensive to develop than self-paced instruction. The majority of live virtual classrooms programs are simply PowerPoint presentations with a lecture. In many cases subject-matter experts (SMEs) deliver the lecture, eliminating the need to capture the SME's knowledge in speakers' notes or the need to transform that knowledge into a self-paced program. Compared to the traditional metrics for hours of development work needed to produce an hour of self-paced video, instructor-led classroom materials, and self-paced e-learning, LVC is faster and less expensive.

- LVC programs provide group learning without the travel and expense of traditional classroom programs.

- LVC programs unlock and capture knowledge by creating an opportunity for SMEs to share skills and knowledge and to capture that knowledge. Many of the virtual classroom programs offer the option of recording a session and editing it for later viewing. This is a simplistic form of knowledge management and knowledge capture.

There is nothing wrong with these economic justifications, but it is important to understand that these are not educational reasons for choosing the virtual classroom as an instructional medium. As any instructional designer knows, the place to start is with a clear understanding of the skill or knowledge gap you are trying to fill and a profile of the learners and then choose a strategy best suited to fill the gap. Although this may seem obvious, it is not uncommon for organizations to select the medium and then define their learning needs.

About a year ago I received a call from an instructional designer who had attended a presentation I gave on designing lessons for the live virtual classroom. She was facing a challenge the lecture had not addressed and she needed some advice.

Her manager had purchased a live virtual classroom application for a project. The project was to train two thousand new employees acquired as the result of a merger. The employees were located in six East Coast states. The newly acquired employees had to learn how to use the phone system of their new parent company and learn the policies for processing calls. Despite the clear economic advantage of not having these employees travel, the instructional designer was struggling with creating a solution. The manager who had purchased the solution had made a business case that the software would eliminate the need to have employees travel, the training program could be rolled out quickly because it would not require the typical hundreds of hours of development, and it could be delivered by anyone in the parent company who knew the phone system and call handling process.

The dilemma for this instructional designer was that she was locked into a delivery medium without regard for what her needs assessment determined. In this case, short-term economics were used as the basis for decision making and not educational criterion.

In dealing with the dilemma of having the medium chosen before understanding the educational needs, this instructional designer did a great job. She was able to create a blended solution that used the LVC to deliver the key concepts and then followed-up with job aids, site-based local mentors, and a playback session of the LVC that could be viewed on demand.

The real strengths of a virtual classroom are its collaborative features and the ability to conduct group learning. The following sections will discuss the educational benefits and limitations.

The Benefits and Limitations of the Live Virtual Classroom

The Benefits

Many organizations are quick to grasp the economic benefits of the LVC, but they fail to understand the educational benefit. This section will look at the educational benefits and limitations. The next section, A Portfolio of Live Virtual Classroom Strategies, will explore how these benefits can be used in tactical designs.

When Learners Would Benefit from Sharing Life Experience

Adult education has a long tradition of valuing the life experience of learners. The live virtual classroom enables learners to share their experience in a virtual environment with tools that can take that sharing to a new level. The LVC allows learners to do things such as share their screens to demonstrate tricks and tips for searching a customer database or surf to helpful websites.

In a recent live virtual classroom session for customer service representatives (CSRs) on the topic of dealing with hostile customers, learning for life experience was amply demonstrated. In this session CSRs were asked to share how they would handle a number of types of hostile customer situations. The session was great because the textbook answers were far from satisfactory. The CSRs talked about how they had addressed hostile customer situations (and hearing them model the responses made this even better). The CSRs also shared experiences they had as *customers* of other firms' 1-800 service lines. The session was a great success because it expanded the canned and textbook answers and enriched them with learners' experience. The session was also a source of best practices that could be viewed by other CSRs.

To Extend the Access to Experts

A related benefit of the virtual classroom is the ability to make scarce resources accessible to a wider audience. How often have you attended a class delivered by an expert and told friends about the class? Later, as the program is more widely rolled out, it is delivered by people who are less skilled. When your friends attend the class they can't understand why you recommended it.

Highly technical programs offer some of the best examples of extending access to experts. A software company was launching a new version of a popular program. Through a series of glitches, the software took longer to develop than intended. In order to make the promised delivery date, the time allotted to designing and delivering training was cut in half and the SMEs who needed to help with training were not available. The live virtual classroom provided just the solution. With the help of the training department, the SMEs delivered a series of training sessions in which experts were able to demonstrate the new software and explain how it was similar to and different from the old program. The experts were also able to answer questions, allay customer concerns, and respond to questions. All of this led to great exchanges (and some last-minute adjustments to the product) between the expert instructor and the learners.

The LVC extended the availability of the experts by reducing the time they needed to spend traveling to multiple locations and it enabled optimal class sizes.

To Do Modeling and Application Sharing in Breakout Rooms

Educators have long known that learning is more likely to occur when the students can transfer learning from the abstract to the practical. In the virtual classroom there are tools that make it possible for students to run simulations or test models. That is rather simple talking about investment concepts such as dollar cost averaging, and Capital Asset Pricing Model students can learn about these concepts by conducting modeling exercises in the LVC.

A group adults studying personal finance were learning about the impact of credit card debt. As a means of demonstrating the impact of interest rates, late payment fees, and carrying debt, the group of fifteen learners was divided into five groups of three and placed in virtual breakout rooms. Each breakout room had a spreadsheet with a file that was a model of credit card debt. The exercise required each group to model the impact of different interest rates and debt load over two, five, and fifteen years. Working in small groups, the learners were able to see firsthand how these variables influenced personal finance and to talk about the issue of debt. Seeing the effect of interest payments over time made a point that could not have been made as effectively using a lecture.

To Deliver Short, Targeted Sessions

Take advantage of access to the live virtual classroom to deliver short lessons with an opportunity for practice between lessons. There is a wealth of well-known research regarding how much information learners can retain (Miller, 1956) and the importance of practice (Clark & Mayer, 2002).Use the live virtual classroom to teach short lessons (twenty to sixty minutes) and then allow learners time to apply the concepts, principles, and procedure before the next lesson. Short lessons are impractical in the traditional classroom setting due to the economics of travel.

A sales training manager for a Fortune 1000 company took this lesson to heart and went one step further. The manager not only made short lessons, but she targeted the lessons to small groups. Every year this company hired 150 to 200 new sales associates. The new hires required extensive training to learn the sales process and later to learn the product. Using the virtual classroom, the sales manager used a blended learning approach. She supported the three-week self-study curriculum with daily thirty-minute LVC sessions. During the three weeks in which the new sales people were studying a paper-based curriculum and shadowing an experienced sales rep. they were also invited to join a daily live virtual classroom program to review the paper-based curriculum from the previous day. When it came time to learn about the products, learners were placed into small groups of new hires who would be selling the same product. The product training was spread out over the first six months on the job, this provided short lessons over time and the opportunity to practice selling skills.

To Capture and Repurpose Recorded Sessions

If you are reading this and recall a corner of your office in which there is a pile of dusty videotapes of classes that no one has ever watched, I don't need to caution you. There is very little to recommend the recording of a typical live virtual session for playback at a later point. On the other hand, if you have the ability to add value by creating a program that has the purpose of being viewed later or if you have the ability to edit the key pieces of the program, then you may have an asset.

There is also the gray continuum in the use of the LVC that spans from training to reference to information. If you find the LVC is on that slippery slope, consider this pragmatic approach taken by one sales training manager who was asked to use the LVC as a communication vehicle versus a training vehicle. The training organization had a good track record for delivering new product introduction training; and skills training. This success was noticed by upper management. The VP of sales was so taken with the virtual classroom that he wanted to conduct monthly sales update "training" sessions using the LVC. This information-dump dubbed "training" was somewhat dubious. It included things such as communicating changes in dates for when reports were due, details on where to find things on the intranet, updates on new reference accounts, and the process for requesting loaner equipment. Given the challenge of delivering a live program to multiple time zones and the risk of damaging training's good reputation, the training manager chose to make the sales update programs recorded sessions. The sessions were recorded in such a way as to make it possible for reps to listen to the recorded programs in the background while they did other things. The programs were recorded in news magazine format with lots of short segments that could be randomly accessed, and programs ran only as long as it took to deliver the information (that is, he did not feel compelled to make the program thirty, sixty, or ninety minutes long).

The sales reps appreciated the recorded sales communication programs and referred to them as "sales radio." The programs ran in the background and the sales reps could tune the programs in and out. And the sales reps were aware of the difference between information programs (informal learning) and learning programs.

The Limitations

There is no limit the number of things that are not recommended in the live virtual classroom. The point of this section is to highlight some common practices and to explain why they should be avoided or used as little as possible.

Avoid Death by Overhead

According to a report by an industry expert (Masie & Rinaldi, 2002), the most popular feature of the live virtual classroom is to ability to show a slide presentation. Death by overhead refers to the experience in which learners are subjected to one-way information dumps delivered using overheads, PowerPoint® slides, and Freelance™

slides. These events are frequently referred to as "training." Some people metaphorically talk about them as online lectures. When possible, avoid this one-way deliver strategy; it squanders the opportunity for collaboration and dialog that is the strength of the virtual classroom. See the section Presenting Lectures in the Live Virtual Classroom in Chapter 11 to get pointers on how to deliver lectures that use slides in an effective manner.

Stay Away from Programs That Are Instructor-Centric

Technology-based training says a lot about the assumptions of the software developers who created the technology. The live virtual classroom is a wonderful case in point. The technology is based on a traditional view of the role of the teacher. Most LVC programs give instructors the ability to control who talks, what the learners can see, who can write on the white board and when, and to which breakout room a student is assigned. The instructor-centric set of tools makes it too easy for the program to become all about the teacher or, as the phrase, goes the "sage on stage" and not about the learners. Creating a learner-centric program requires two things: first, the design of the program must provide opportunities for the learners to interact, and second, the learners must be encouraged and rewarded for being engaged. Creating a student-centric program is easier said than done; learners have a long tradition of being passive.

Avoid Teaching Software Skills

Just because you can, doesn't mean you should. The ability to do application sharing means that you can teach software skills using the virtual classroom. Choosing to teach software skills such as Word, PowerPoint, or custom applications is tempting because it seems like such a natural use of the LVC. It is technically possible, but the virtual classroom adds a level of complexity that must be considered. If learners are not computer savvy and technically self-sufficient enough to manage the new application and the LVC application at the same time, you may overwhelm them. It is also boring to watch other students practice an application.

Limit Class Size for Optimal Interaction

Don't get confused by the recommended maximum number of learners who can attend a live virtual classroom versus the recommended number who should attend a live virtual classroom program. There is no magic number. The answer to how many people should be in a live virtual classroom is . . . it depends. The number of learners per session depends on how complex the content, how technically competent the learners, how skilled the facilitator, and how much interaction you have designed into the program. The answer is to pilot the program to find the right class size.

Differentiate an e-Meeting from an e-Learning Event

There is a great deal of overlap between the technology for e-meetings and e-learning. In most cases a live virtual classroom will have all the functionality of an e-meeting and then additional functions specific to learning. The industry is evolving so that these two applications are becoming almost identical. Software designed for learning has unique attributes, such as tools that let learners signal the instructor that he is going too fast or too slow or that the lesson is clear or confusing, and assessment features like quizzes and tests. If you are designing a program using a generic e-meeting application, you will probably be limited to hand raising, polling, and the typical e-meeting features. In either case, be sure the hallmarks of learning are there, including a goal or learning outcome, an opportunity to probe learners for understanding, and an assessment to determine whether your goal was achieved.

Anticipate That LVC Classes Will Take Longer to Deliver than Traditional Classroom Courses

There are longstanding statistics on the power of computer-based training to reduce the time it takes to train by 35 to 45 percent (Fletcher, 1990; Hall, 1995). These statistics do not apply to live virtual classrooms. The often-quoted statistic assumes that through pretesting, branching, and empowering learners to move at their own pace, the time spent learning can be shortened. In the live virtual classroom, pretesting and branching are of little help because the program requires all learners to go through the entire program at the same pace. The virtual classroom can theoretically take longer to deliver the same content than a traditional classroom. The LVC has the added burden of frequently stopping and checking on learners' understanding, which would be seen via nonverbal clues in the traditional classroom, and technical "speed bumps," such as waiting for screens to refresh and delays created by passing the microphone or waiting for the tally of a polling question.

A Portfolio of Live Virtual Classroom Strategies

Anyone planning to design live virtual classroom programs should attend as many "free" LVC programs as possible in order to see different styles of facilitation and to observe the features such as whiteboarding, application sharing, and polling being demonstrated to best advantage. Good places to find calendars for upcoming live virtual classroom programs are the websites of vendors such as Lotus, WebEx, Centra, Interwise, and IntraCall. If you can't find the time to attend in real time, you can often find a recorded session to watch in playback mode.

I recommend sampling programs at vendor sites because vendors have highly skilled facilitators capable of using the LVC tools to best advantage. The one drawback to free vendor-sponsored programs is the limited variety of instructional tactics demonstrated. Most of the free demonstration programs use the lecture format with some application sharing and polling. The following sections describe alternative strategies for using the live virtual classroom in other modes.

Tactics for the LVC can be divided into two groups: *communication-based tactics* and *collaborative-based tactics*. The two groups of tactics differ in their objectives and, more importantly, they differ in the degree of skill needed by both the facilitator and learners.

Communication-Based Strategies

Communication-based strategies are not considered "education" by many educators, but these tactics are well-suited to delivering awareness-level training. Communication-based tactics are good for making learners aware of facts, concepts, principles, and processes. For many organizations, communication-based tactics are an easy place to start. In some organizations, where traditional classroom objectives seldom get beyond "will be able to: identify, list, name, find, and cite," communication-based tactics will offer a solution with as much depth as their physical classroom programs..

It should not be surprising that most of the communication-based tactics draw on the metaphor of television or radio. These tactics focus on communicating information and therefore draw their inspiration from proven models. While lectures would fit well in this section, they will not be discussed because they are addressed in detail in Chapter 11, Exposition Techniques.

News Magazine

Like television news magazines such as "Entertainment Tonight" or "60 Minutes," the LVC news magazine format has a host or co-hosts and features a series of fast-moving segments. The goal is to deliver information and, if needed, to motivate the audience to seek additional information by going to a website or enrolling in a course. One of the key advantages of using the news magazine format in the virtual classroom is the ability to interact with the audience via live questions and answers and to poll the audience for instant feedback. This tactic requires good scripting skills and a sense of pacing.

Talk Show

Again, the inspiration is drawn from TV, but guests on these training-sponsored shows are unlikely to appear on "Oprah" or "The Tonight Show." The goals of this kind of program are to make a subject-matter expert accessible to learners and to communicate information. This might mean interviewing the salesperson of the year to learn best practices for prospecting or talking to the new CEO about a change in the strategic direction. In the live virtual classroom, the audience can be invited to send in questions in advance or interact with the guest by asking real-time questions. This format requires planning on the part of both the facilitator and the guest. The format may be talk show, but this is far more staged. Successfully communicating key points requires sharing the interview questions in advance. This can entail rehearsing or at least walking through the timing and transitions. It is also helpful to ask the guest for slides or graphics to support his or her responses. If the guest or SME knows what he or she wants to communicate, this is an easy program to produce.

Expert Panel

A variation on the talk show interview is a panel discussion. The goal of this tactic is to bring together a group of people to provide a broad perspective. This can be difficult to execute because the facilitator has less control. In the ideal situation, the panel would be well aware of the communication goal and, rather than simply agreeing with each other or restating the obvious, they would have differing and key insights to share. An example of this would be bringing in a panel made up of members of the customer service team to talk about the new call handling procedure. Each of the panelists would represent a different point in the process, be able to talk about his or her role, and add valuable comments relative to the other panelists. Strong facilitation skills are needed here to summarize the panel's comments and to manage and direct audience questions to the right panel member.

Doctor's Hours

This is a program that puts a recognized expert in front of the audience to answer questions and to solve problems. Technical audiences like this format because of its no-nonsense look and feel and the opportunity to see technical steps demonstrated.

The goal of this program is to make an expert available to answers questions that are too technical and too diverse to be addressed in a standard training program. This takes minimal skill to facilitate and it is easy to produce, but its success is dependent on the quality and volume of audience participation. It helps to ask the expert to provide two or three provocative questions and then to ask someone from the training staff to get the ball rolling by raising his or her hand and asking one or two of the expert's questions. In technical realms this is very effective because application sharing can allow the expert to bring up an application and demonstrate the solution, or the expert can pass the controls to the caller and ask him or her to demonstrate the problem and then share controls as they fix the problem. This differs from the talk show strategy because the audience dictates what is discussed during the scheduled program. Another key difference is the notion of "doctor's hours." The idea is that participants come to the doctor and the doctor will cure their problems, and they don't need appointments. Likewise, you don't have to stay after you have been *cured.*

Game Show

This can be dicey territory—audiences either love this tactic or hate it. The odds that the audience will like a game show are better if the audience is American, but this is not guaranteed. The goal of the program is to communicate factual information in a playful and fun manner. The tactics are simply to modify familiar game shows such as "Who Wants to Be a Millionaire?" "You Don't Know Jack" and "Lightning Fill in the Blank." The reason for imitating these popular shows is that imitation saves you a great deal of time explaining the rules. The system for responding must be modified to fit the available LVC technology, such as hand raising, polling, and using chat to send questions to the instructors. Special attention must be paid to strategies that involve hitting the response button first, due to the unfair advantage some learners will have based on the speed of their Internet connectivity.

The game show format is far more challenging than it first appears. Writing the questions requires as much effort as writing multiple-choice questions because the questions must be well-worded, each question must have only one right answer, and the level of difficulty must be consistent. Like gaming strategies in traditional training, the transfer of knowledge may be low if the learners cannot readily understand how to apply the information in the real world.

Communication-based tactics discussed in this section focus on delivering a message. Because of their nature, these tactics lack educational elements such as structured probes to determine whether the audience understands what is being presented, an opportunity for practice, and a final assessment to measure mastery. Communication-based tactics also tend to address the lower levels of Bloom's taxonomy (1956).

Collaboration-Based Strategies

Collaborative learning is defined as a style of teaching and learning where students work in teams toward a common goal. It has been argued that collaborative learning is more effective than most other approaches because the learner who learns best is the one who organizes, summarizes, elaborates, explains, and defends. The learner who does the intellectual work, especially the conceptual work, learns the most (Johnson & Johnson, 1993). The following strategies rely on some form of collaborative learning or group work. These strategies have corollaries in the traditional physical classroom and in most cases the LVC simply changes the medium. In the best of instructional designs, the live virtual classroom environment lends itself to things that cannot be done in a traditional classroom, such as surf the Web to find resources as needed, support application sharing to do modeling, build a presentation in real time as a team, or link to experts who might be too busy to attend a real class but who would be willing to be part of an LVC for twenty or thirty minutes.

Case Study

This tactic is tried-and-true (Einsiedel, 1995). It is a method for providing learners with an opportunity to apply concepts, principles, and practices to cases and then transfer that learning to real life (Galbraith, 1990). There are several ways to organize a case study, depending on the complexity of the topic, your resources, and the time available for delivery. The easiest way to do this is to provide a brief text-based case study as part of the live virtual classroom session. If the case study is more complex and requires learners to review numbers, tables, organizational charts, and financial statements, you may want to send the learners these items in advance. Focus the live virtual class time on discussions and case work. Draft a series of questions to guide the learners and highlight the key concepts and issues to be explored. If the LVC application allows breakout rooms, move virtually among the rooms to help clarify questions and keep the teams on track.

Action Learning

Action learning is a technique developed by Reg Revans (1980), a researcher at Cambridge University in the 1930s. In action learning, learners bring a real problem forward that must be solved by the learning group. The real problem must be an issue for which there is no known right answer. The problem must also be important enough to justify spending time solving it, have a deadline for resolution, and be significant enough that the solution will be implemented.

Action learning via the live virtual classroom allows learners from diverse backgrounds to come together easily. Because meetings do not place large demands for time and travel, managers can meet over an extended period of time to ask questions, design a solution, implement it, and reflect on the outcome. There is a need to acknowledge that action learning projects can take a great deal of time and that they should be part of a manager's regular duties. This learning strategy requires an organizational culture in which solving a genuine business problem via this method is valued.

Reciprocal Teaching

Reciprocal teaching is derived from health education (Palincsar & Brown, 1983) for low literacy patients. In the health care setting, learners (patients) are asked to "teach back," that is, in their own words repeat or teach back the instructions for things like taking medication and modifying their diets. As the patient delivers a teach-back, the medical professional monitors and corrects if needed.

In the live virtual classroom, learners can be given greater responsibility for their learning using reciprocal teaching. They can be asked to do more than simply repeat what they have learned. The facts, concepts, principles, and procedures they have learned can be extended and applied by asking the learners to prepare a lesson, develop exercises, and even assess their peers' understanding of what was presented. The reciprocal-teaching method allows students to become the teachers and to more thoroughly understand and internalize information. The interactive tools in the virtual classroom, such as the ability to ask questions, give a quiz, take learners to websites with additional resources and to use rich media like graphics and video to illustrate facts, concepts, principles, and procedures, makes this a powerful strategy.

Modeling and Role Play

Live virtual classrooms allow learners to hear and to see—if your organization has the bandwidth—how things are done. Using this method, it is possible to teach language skills, interviewing techniques, listening skills, and other competencies that require hearing and seeing skills demonstrated. Modeling and role-play-based lessons should be done with small groups, allowing for frequent and active participation, practice, and coaching.

Designing modeling/role-play lessons requires attention to two dimensions of the lesson. The first dimension is the model or role-play activity, and the second is what those learners who are not modeling or role playing are doing. For example, consider a role-play scenario for a manager who has to conduct an interview. After teaching the interviewing concepts and procedures, learners are provided an interview scenario, characters, and the characters' perspective on the situation. The learners then must act out the scenario as their characters and, in doing so, gain valuable experience in applying course concepts. The virtual observers should also have clear directions regarding what to listen for, and they should be expected to provide feedback and input on what they observed or heard. An LVC role play differs from a traditional role play in that the live physical aspects such as personal space and overall body language are not visible (most LVC systems are optimized for close-up shots of the learners' face) and the observers are virtual.

Where to Sample Live Virtual Classroom Technology

It is not possible to provide our readers with links to live virtual classroom programs that demonstrate the different strategies. Unlike the readily available e-learning examples of strategies for simulations, storytelling, and openings and closings, LVC examples require extra effort to sample.

We encourage readers to use the following information to visit vendors of live virtual classroom. Each of these vendors offers a wide variety ways to sample its technology. Visit these sites to look for free seminars, collaborative programs with professional organizations, and occasionally trial use of the application. Many of these vendors have archives of recorded programs. The recorded programs are better than not sampling LVC, but being part of a collaborative, interactive, real-time program is a very different experience.

This is a selected list of vendors, and by no means is it exhaustive or complete. These vendors have been chosen because they frequently host sample programs, provide free trial use of their applications, and are mentioned in analyst reports. Professional organizations such as the ones listed in Appendix B are also a good source for opportunities to participate in LVC programs.

Figures 9.1 through 9.5 below provide you with screen captures of the user interfaces and the URLs to locate vendors and to begin your exploration.

Figure 9.1. Centra Symposium

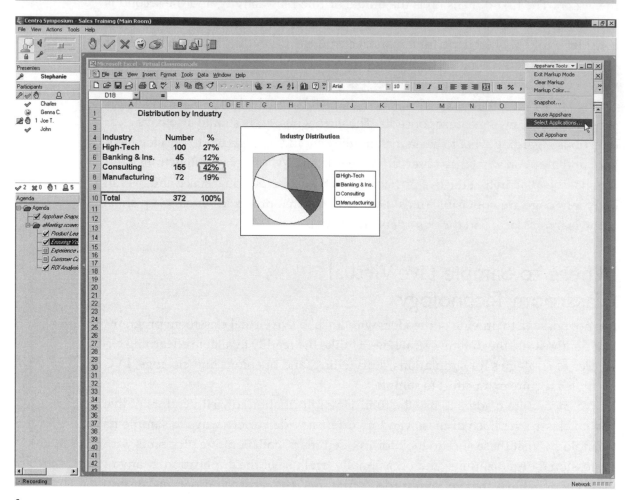

Source: www.centra.com

Figure 9.2. Elluminate Live!

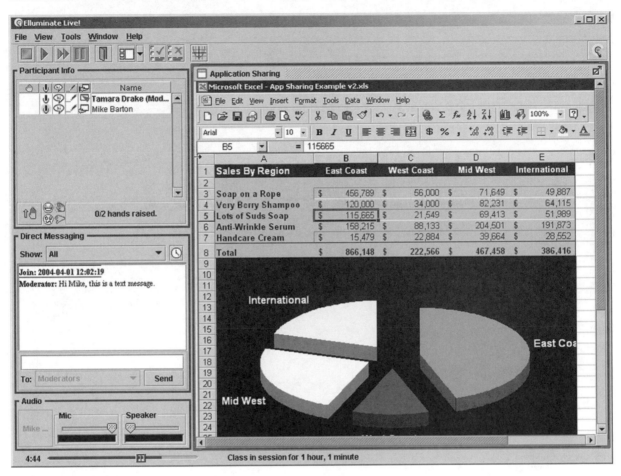

Source: www.Elluminate.com

Figure 9.3. IBM Lotus Live Virtual Classroom

Source: www.lotus.com

Figure 9.4. InterWise

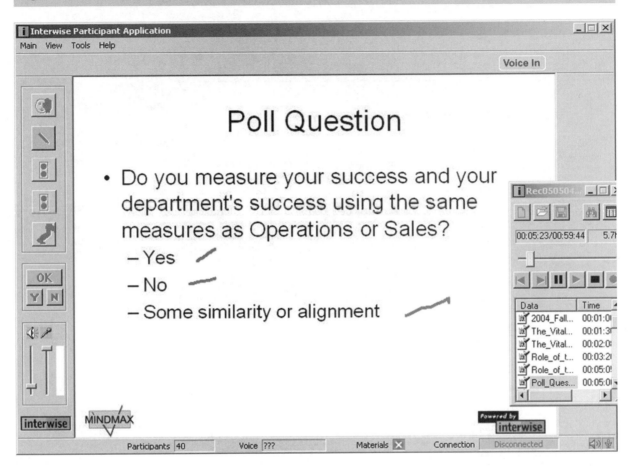

Source: www.interwise.com

Figure 9.5. WebEx

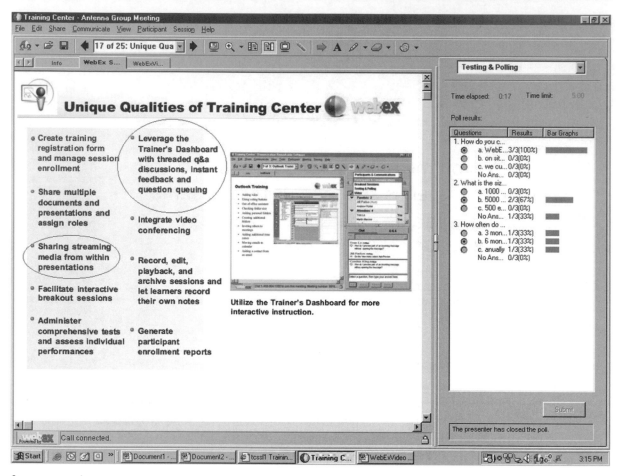

Source: www.webex.com

Guidelines for Designing for the Live Virtual Classroom

The tactics presented in this chapter vary greatly, but a number of guidelines apply to both the communication-based tactics and the collaboration-based tactics.

- Use a script, like the sample shown in Figure 9.6, to plan the program. The script will help you determine what graphics are needed, provide a sense of program flow, and provide a rough estimate of timing.

Figure 9.6. Sample Live Virtual Classroom Script

Elapsed Time	Time Remaining	Event	Audio	Visual	Comments
5 minutes prior to start	60 minutes	Program opening	Music	Title graphics and call in numbers for · conference call tel. number · help desk tel. number	Make sure the LVC is ready and running 5 minutes before official start time
3 minutes	57 minutes	Introduction	Host introduces Senior VP of Branch Bank Retail Sales	Photos of host and VP with captions	This program may be delivered three times. The third time the Junior VP will deliver the presentation. Create an alternative slide for this segment
4 minutes	53 minutes	Review the LVC user interface	Point out the four key buttons learners need to use and have them do the following: · answer yes/no · raise hand · send a message using chat	Make graphic with enlarged tool bar	Pre-script some yes/no questions to prompt the hand raise, and draft a meaningful question to provide practice using chat.
2 minutes	51 minutes	Program goals	Using an interview-style question and answer format, review the goals	Graphics with text outlining the two goals of today's program	
5 minutes	46 minutes	What is Freedom Checking	Ask the VP to explain what the new Freedom Checking Package includes	Text slide outlining features of Freedom Checking	
		How does Freedom Checking differ from Basic Checking and Gold checking	VP explains the chart and Hosts can ask clarifying questions	Text chart with a three-column comparison	

Figure 9.6. Sample Live Virtual Classroom Script, Cont'd

Elapsed Time	Time Remaining	Event	Audio	Visual	Comments
3 minutes	43 minutes	Invite questions	Host should remind the audience how to type and submit their questions	Start with a graphic with a question mark and be prepared to pull/move back to previous slides if needed	Get the ball rolling; either have the host ask the questions or have someone in the audience ask some pre-prepared questions
2 minutes	41 minutes	Probe for understanding	Host and moderator present three scenarios and ask the audience to determine if Freedom Checking is the right product using three scenarios		Fully script each of the scenarios
5 minutes	36 minutes	Scenario 1 College Student	Present scenario and ask audience to determine the right product and explain why Raise hand and call on people by name	Photo of college student looking perplexed Slide with key considerations for this customer	Be sure to debrief this scenario so the audience understands you would not recommend Freedom Checking
5 minutes	31 minutes	Scenario 2 Retired Couple	Present scenario and ask audience to determine the right product and explain why Raise hand and call on people by name	Photo of older couple sitting at typical branch service desk looking serious Slide with key considerations for these customers	Be sure to debrief this scenario so the audience understands you would recommend Freedom Checking

.
.
.

- Keep the program short. So how short should it be? There is no exact length for an LVC program. The answer depends on the topic, the audience, their level of technical skill, and how much content you must teach.

- Consider class size. So how many students should be in a class? The answer is "It depends." Look at all the factors related to your program, learners, and the culture of your organization. Remember to learn from experience; conduct post-program assessments to determine how thing went.

- First program or fiftieth program? Determine how familiar your learners are with the live virtual classroom. The first program should allow time to provide an orientation. Introduce the features such as polling, whiteboards, application sharing, assessments, hand raising, feedback, and yes/no responses slowly.

- Co-pilots or solo presenters? Becoming a skilled presenter takes time. In some cases, it makes sense to have co-facilitators. If the SME is not going to be a regular instructor, consider having an experienced facilitator manage the technology and have the SME do the teaching.

- Take time to check in with the audience. Use live virtual classroom tools such as pacing meters, hand-raising, and yes/no buttons to get feedback. You may need to script in these "speed bumps" for new facilitators. There is so much to contend with it is easy to forget to ask for feedback.

- Start and finish on time. Strive for the discipline needed to start and finish the program on time. This means having the instructor and program cued ten to fifteen minutes in advance and someone dedicated to act as time-keeper. It is easy to fall behind unless the script has markers to help the facilitators know how they are doing relative to the absolute time.

- Rehearse the program. Even if the content is familiar to the facilitator, running a rehearsal is important. Without a rehearsal, the facilitator can be surprised by the complexity of the interface and all the places on the screen that need to be monitored. It is also important to make notes during the rehearsal as to where the facilitator will stop and ask for feedback.

- Draft questions for the LVC. It comes as a surprise to many instructors to find that questions that work well in the traditional classroom such as "How many of you completed the prework?" and "Are there additional topics you hoped I would cover?" don't work in the LVC. Questions need to be carefully translated into questions that indicate how you want the students to respond, for example, "Please press yes if you completed the prework," and "Please use the questions dialog box to send me the additional topics you would like to discuss."

In Practice: Jennifer Hofmann: Leadership World Series

Jennifer Hofmann is the president of InSync Training, a company specializing in synchronous learning. She is not only a leading author and national speaker on the topic of designing and developing live virtual classroom programs, but she is a practitioner. As a program developer, Jennifer understands the challenges and is a pioneer in crafting work-arounds.

In this interview, we asked Jennifer to talk about a program she developed called *The Leadership World Series.* Figure 9.7 shows the opening screen that was used in the introductory exercise. The participants were asked to introduce themselves and "autograph" the baseball with their name. This exercise provided the participants with an interesting way to introduce themselves and practice using the whiteboard. This is an example of blended learning program that is based around the live virtual classroom experience. Like many instructional designers, Jennifer was asked to take an existing management program and redesign it. The goal was to revise the program to meet the needs of remote learners who logistically could not come together but who would benefit from the collaboration offered by the LVC. Jennifer is not able to name the customer, but we can tell you a little about her design challenge.

Jennifer was asked to work with a company that offered a large catalog of successful classroom-based training programs. She was part of a team tasked with revising the leadership program to make it an effective distance education program. The ultimate customer for the leadership program was a high-tech company whose staff could be characterized as working from home offices, geographically disbursed, and managing junior workers who were also working at home. The blended learning solution focused on the collaborative and interactive strengths of the live virtual classroom. In the solution you are about to read about, the LVC was essential to practice and feedback for the soft skills associated with leadership training.

Figure 9.7. The Leadership World Series

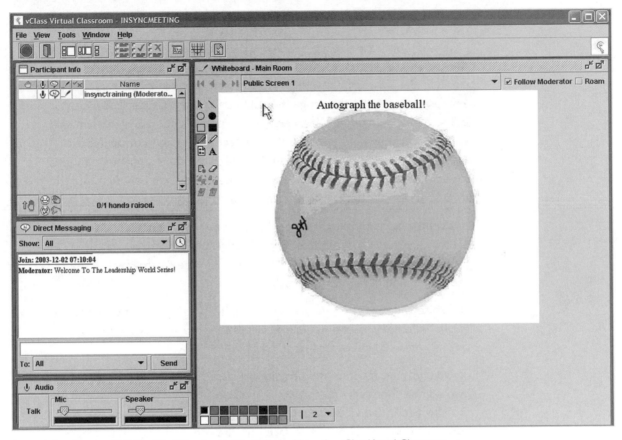

Source: InSync Training, LLC, The World Leadership World Series, Using the vClass Virtual Classroom

Here are the primary learning objectives for the curriculum. Note this was a curriculum, not a single course. The leadership curriculum addressed the fundamentals of:

- Coaching
- Giving feedback
- Providing reward and recognition
- Taking corrective action
- Delivering performance reviews
- Managing time
- Influencing management

We also asked about other learning issues underlying the project. Jennifer shared the fact that the team faced the daunting task of providing managerial training to three thousand new managers worldwide. The challenge was to provide consistent, relevant, and effective training in a cost-effective manner.

Knowing about the size and scope of the project, we asked Jennifer to start at the end and tell us about how the finished program was received by learners. She told us the program met with great success; all participants expressed overall enthusiasm for what the program could do for them. One telling indicator was a survey of her remote learners. In the survey, 75 percent of them said that, the program would enhance their "effectiveness and communication." Jennifer also noted that the program demonstrated the company's commitment to the managers. As evidence of this, she shared this comment for the end-of-course evaluations, which really captures the success of the program.

> "It's the whole ability to stop for that very brief moment and reevaluate where you are. I'm hoping that through this we'll have that brief second for us where you're able to focus not in the day-to-day, but the ability to kind of reinvent yourself."

Despite the rave reviews, we asked Jennifer to share with us what she might do differently next time. Jennifer shared a story about how they would choose a different kind of facilitator.

> "We chose an accomplished traditional classroom instructor, and we would not necessarily do that again. The skills and personality required to succeed in the virtual classroom are very different from the skills one needs in a physical face-to-face class. Before selecting the instructor, we would need to screen to ensure he or she has the appropriate attributes for the medium. There is also the issue of rehearsal in the LVC environment. It is not something that many traditional instructors do, but it is essential in the LVC."

She also confided that "the biggest lesson learned by the entire team was that re-creating learning online and determining the right blend isn't easy, or to be taken lightly." Jennifer stressed the importance of creating interactions that meet the same standards as traditional programs. She recommends investing the time to research the audience and the technology tools. Moreover, Jennifer offers some sage advice for LVC designers: "Most imperative, bring together the right team, either internal or external, and be willing to fail a few times in order to get the right blend."

Every strategy has different challenges, so we asked Jennifer for a short list of things that she would warn others to watch for if they produce this kind of blended LVC program:

- Budget for an assistant to co-facilitate the class. This person can help manage things like scribing on the whiteboard, responding to chat notes, launching surveys and breakout rooms, resolving technical questions and problems, and handling late arrivals and disruptive participants.

- Don't assume people know how to learn in a blended environment. Provide an orientation to the entire program.

- If you make a student guide to accompany the program and send it out via an Adobe PDF file, be sure to consider things like page size differences between the United States and the UK.

- Don't assume students will simply complete prework. Find creative ways to ensure that asynchronous modules and other preclass assignments are completed. For example, don't provide the password to the live session until a pretest has been completed.

- Keep asking yourself, "Is the LVC design using active learning?" Seek as many ways as possible to keep the learner engaged.

Despite the wealth of articles on the topic of LVC and the sample programs that exist, there is a shortage of sharing of the *numbers* regarding size, time, and resources. The numbers that Jennifer shares here are not presented as industry standards or as benchmarks. While these numbers are not generalizable, they do offer insights into the kind of statistics you might want to keep and a nice overview of how resources were applied.

The Numbers (and a Few Explanations)

Size of Audience: Fifteen to twenty per class

Time to Produce: This two-hour live virtual classroom module took fourteen days to produce and deliver. The time estimates in Table 9.1 include creating workbook templates, overall LVC design templates, and formatting layouts that were reused in subsequent programs, pilot time, and revisions, so the development time to deliver ratio may appear high.

Table 9.1. Time/Task Breakdown

Task Description	Number of Estimated InSync Person Days
Review existing classroom modules and complete tutorial	1.0
Create new LVC design	0.5
Design Meeting	1.0
Program Development (leader guide, profile, workbook, storyboard)	3.0
Program Development Group Review and Revisions	1.5
Media Development and Course Building	1.5
InSync Internal Pilot	1.5
InSync Internal Pilot Revisions	1.0
Pilot Set-Up, including Tech Checks and Learn How to Learn	1.0
Run pilot and make final revisions	1.0
Deliver program to customer	1.0
Total	14 Days Estimated

Primary Job Skills Used: Instructional designer, international SMEs, materials production and layout expert

Technologies Used: Live virtual classroom: Centra Software; self-paced e-learning: MacroMedia; Adobe PDF files

Conclusion

Live virtual classrooms have the potential to be either the best or the worst form of e-learning. The technology is becoming easy to use and readily available. The ubiquitous nature of this technology will enable well-meaning people to create Power-Point presentations that will be passed off as training. The challenge for instructional designers will be to create LVC experiences that demonstrate how the LVC can be engaging. It will also be up to instructional designers to tap into the collaborative power of the LVC and to demonstrate how instruction can be just in time, learner-centric, and a source of knowledge sharing.

Learn More About It

Barclay, K., Gordon, A., Hollahan, J., & Lai, Y. (2003). *The live e-l cookbook: Recipes for success.* Lincoln, NE: iUniverse.com.

This is a book that lives up to its title of being a "cookbook." Managers who are interest in an accessible "how to book" that is well organized, delivers the fundamentals quickly—this is the ticket. This book does not get bogged down in citations, or spend time explaining educational concepts; this is about following a recipe.

Driscoll, M., & Rocky, C. (2002, September). Teaching technical skills & knowledge in the live virtual classroom: 20 best practices for using application sharing. *ASTD Newsletter.* http://www1.astd.org/news_letter/September/Links/mindspan_elmg.html

This article focuses on the use of live virtual classroom technology for teaching software applications and technical information. Particular attention is paid to application sharing and interactions that keep learners engaged.

Hofmann, J. (2003). *The synchronous trainer's survival guide.* San Francisco: Pfeiffer.

This book goes the extra mile helping readers maximize the technical features found in virtual classrooms such as assessments, polling, feedback, breakout rooms, and other educational capabilities. In addition to helping the reader make the most of technology, this guide looks at the essential instructional design elements that differentiate an e-learning experience from an e-meeting experience.

Rothwell, W.J. (1999). *The action learning guidebook: A real-time strategy for problem solving, training design, and employee development.* San Francisco: Pfeiffer.

If you are going to push the envelope and use the live virtual classroom for action learning, this is an essential primmer. This book will provide the grounding that training professionals need to facilitate and evaluate action learning.

Websites of Interest

www.insynctraining.com. InSynch Training.

The archive of monthly Tips & Technquest is a wealth of information.

http://www.learningcircuits.org. Learning Circuits.

This site promotes and aids the use of e-learning by creating a body of knowledge about how to use technology efficiently and effectively for learning.

REFLECTION AND APPLICATION

To reflect on the material presented in this chapter and apply it in a real e-learning situation, consider how you would respond to the following challenges. (Each of these challenges is intentionally left vague. If you are unsure about a piece of information, make an assumption about it and list the assumption.)

- Your international dairy products company has workers scattered in 173 locations worldwide. After one of the executives was indicted for accounting fraud, the company agreed to a required business ethics curriculum for all management and senior staff. The course is now ready to teach, and every employee at these levels must complete the ethics curriculum by the end of the quarter. Because of the large number of employees to train and the limited window of training opportunity, management wants you to teach the course through a live virtual classroom and record the class session. Workers who are not able to attend the virtual class session will be required to retrieve the recording. What are the pros and cons of this approach?

- Nancy, your vice president of marketing and sales, is scheduled to teach a new product introduction class to the corporate sales force that she leads in a week by live virtual classroom. Nancy is an experienced presenter who often prepares her materials at the last minute, even if it's a training session. Consistent with Nancy's pattern, it's forty-eight hours before the webcast and Nancy has not yet rehearsed nor submitted slides. Because she said how excited she is about webcasting "for the first time," you know she has no experience with either the webcasting medium or the equipment and software. As producer of the webcast, what do you do?

- You are teaching deviant psychology for a local academic institution through live virtual classroom. To make sure that the course does not turn into a one-way conversation, you design the course around a series of problems. According to your plan, students read through and propose solutions to the problems as homework, then discuss their solutions and reach a resolution in the class sessions. By the second class session, however, you realize that students are not reading the problems and preparing solutions before class. Do you change your plans? Why or why not? If you change plans, what would you do while still creating an interactive learning environment? If you do not change strategy, what will you do to motivate students to do the homework?

Part IV

Portfolio of Detailed Design Strategies

Detailed design explores challenges in designing specific parts of e-learning programs. Some of these challenges focus on the presentation of content, such as introductions and closings. Other challenges center on engaging the learner, such as designing for interactivity. Specifically, the chapters in this section explore the following.

Chapter 10, Introductions and Closings, explores ways to open and close e-learning courses and units. It explores the several purposes of openings and suggests ways to address each. It also explores the several purposes of closings and offers suggestions on how to handle those sections, too.

Chapter 11, Exposition Techniques for Writing E-Learning Content, considers exposition, a term from the field of composition theory that refers to the way that authors "expose," or write, specific content. Relying on research from instructional design and the related fields of educational psychology and technical communication, this chapter specifically explores the educational and business value of the traditional lecture. Although our positive opinion of lectures probably seems out of step, the empirical evidence is clear: the lecture has a valuable role to play in learning. This chapter also presents ways to engagingly adapt the traditional lecture for both virtual classrooms and asynchronous e-learning to effectively present specific types of declarative content, including definitions, procedures, and explanations.

Chapter 12, Interaction, examines the holy grail of e-learning—how to engage learners. Although clients and designers alike advocate for interactivity in e-learning programs, few offer practical suggestions on how to engage learners and do so "on-topic." This chapter does so. It provides two schemes for approaching interactions. First is Moore's model of interaction, which draws distinctions among three types of interaction: learner-content interaction, learner-instructor interaction, and learner-learner interaction. The second scheme is Jonassen's, which suggests that learners use computers three ways: learning *though* computers, *from* computers, and *with* computers.

Chapter 13, Visual Communication Techniques, considers ways to enhance the impact of e-learning programs by presenting content visually, rather than verbally. The chapter first explains the educational and cognitive value of visuals, then presents strategies for presenting specific types of content visually, rather than with text. It closes with some technical considerations for presenting visuals.

Chapter 10

Openings
and Closings

You only get one chance to make a good first impression.

Anonymous

A good instructor "knows when to say hello and [how] to say goodbye."

Marilyn Marks, 1993

In This Chapter

In this chapter, we will

- State the purpose of openings and closings of both e-learning programs and sections of these programs.

- Describe the guidelines for designing openings and closings.

- Describe a portfolio of techniques for designing openings and closings

- Describe examples of effective introductions to e-learning programs

Educators have long recognized the strategic importance of introductions to learning programs. For example, in his nine events of instruction, Gagne (1985) devotes several to introducing a lesson. Similarly, Ausubel's (1960) research showed that starting a lesson with an *advance organizer,* which provides a preview of a lesson, improves learning.

An equally important point in a course is the end. How a lesson closes can set the stage for continued interest in, and learning about, the topic.

This chapter explores these two pivotal points in a lesson: openings and closings. In it, we start by exploring in depth the purposes of openings and closings. Then we explore the guidelines for designing openings and a portfolio of techniques for doing so. Next, we explore guidelines for designing closings and a portfolio of techniques for doing so. A bonus technique is also presented. We then present an example of a unique and inviting opening to an e-learning course.

What Are the Purposes of Openings and Closings?

Openings and closings play important roles in communicating content and developing motivation to learn, often in large disproportion to their size. Recognizing this, many designers invest extra effort in designing these parts of a course.

The Purposes of an Opening

Openings to learning programs (and openings to sections within these programs) serve these key purposes:

- To engage interest in the topic

- To communicate expectations about the content, often in the form of course objectives but not always (another option, for example, would be to open with organizing questions)

- To communicate expectations about the learning experience (for example, how long will the course take? And how will learners be assessed?)

- To ensure that learners can use the technology underlying a course

The specific content in an opening varies, depending on the type of course being taught. Usually, the required administrative content communicates expectations. Table 10.1 shows the administrative material presented in the openings of different types of learning programs.

In addition, openings need to make a motivational appeal to learners, which does the following:

- Grabs the attention of learners

- Establishes their comfort with the content

- Builds their belief that they can master the objectives

Table 10.1. Administrative Material Covered in the Openings of Different Types of Learning Programs	
Type of Course	**Specific Content to Be Communicated**
Academic	Present a syllabus (which is also formally distributed). The syllabus is a contract with students (in fact, in most institutions, a syllabus carries legal weight) and covers, at a minimum, the following topics: • Description of the course (usually taken from the course catalog) • Agenda (lesson-by-lesson or weekly plan with the topic, readings, and assignments due, if any) • Grading criteria, including the criteria for earning letter grades (like A, B, and C) and requirements for submitting assignments • Attendance policies and other administrative issues (if appropriate)

Corporate Training or Continuing Education	Present a variety of material known as *administrivia*. Administrivia include:
	
	• Course objectives
	
	• Intended audience
	
	• Prerequisites
	
	• Legal information, including:
	
	    List of trademarks, registered trademarks, and service marks used
	
	    Disclaimers (for example, about new products, corporations often state that the product might not be available in certain countries)
	
	    Copyright statement
	
	• Technical requirements, such as the system needed to run a course and plug-ins required

That type of motivation usually comes from giving learners a brief taste of the content in the opening moments of the e-learning program—kind of like content hors d'oeuvres or *tapas*.

In addition to introducing learning programs, instructional designers also need to design openings for each class session of a multi-session virtual course or each unit of an asynchronous e-learning program. Because each session of a live virtual course is taken individually, and because units (often called modules) of an asynchronous course might be taken out of order or a long time after taking the introductory one, designers must pay as much attention to the design of the openings of individual sessions and units as they do to entire learning programs.

Like openings to entire learning programs, openings to sessions or units must:

- Engage interest in the topic. But rather than introducing the general content of the entire learning program, the way that designers often engage interest in the content is by linking the content in the upcoming session or unit to the overall content of the learning program and, if possible, content already presented.

- Communicate expectations about the content—usually the objective(s) for the session or unit.

- Communicate expectations about the learning experience. In a session for a live virtual course, the most important expectations pertain to using the virtual classroom software. In a unit of an asynchronous course, the most important expectation is the anticipated length of the unit, so learners can figure out whether they have sufficient time to devote to the learning experience.

The Purposes of a Closing

Closings to learning programs (and sections within courses) serve these key purposes:

- To summarize the content presented, because this is the last opportunity for designers to communicate the content that they hope "sticks" with the learner after the lesson

- To assess the learner (formally or informally)

- To link learners to additional learning material, including the next program in the series (if the program is part of a curriculum) and other sources of content

- To provide reference material, including a glossary of terms used in the learning program, appendices with additional information, a bibliography of sources cited by the learning content, and a list of resources for further learning

The material presented is relatively similar among academic, training, and continuing education programs.

Designing Openings

Although they are often brief, their pivotal position as the first content that learners encounter gives openings a disproportionate role in an e-learning program in relation to their size. Because of this pivotal role, many instructional designers spend a similarly disproportionate amount of time preparing openings. The following sections describe the guidelines and a portfolio of techniques for doing so.

Guidelines for Designing Openings

Designers of e-learning programs face a number of challenges in designing the openings of learning programs and sections. Some are practical; others are motivational. The following guidelines help instructional designers address these challenges:

- For long-term courses, orient learners.
- For virtual classroom sessions, provide enough lead time for enrollment.
- Avoid an initial focus on "administrivia."
- Launch into the content as early as possible.

The following sections describe these guidelines in detail.

For Long-Term Courses, Orient Learners

In her study of a cohort of learners taking an academic course online, Conrad (2002) found that students had a high level of anxiety entering the course. To alleviate it, many wanted access to the course a week in advance so that they could see what was expected of them, become familiar with the technology, and find out who their classmates were.

The learners in Conrad's study are like many students in long-term academic courses. So, whenever possible, provide them with access to information in advance of the start of a course.

For Virtual Classroom Sessions, Provide Enough Lead Time for Enrollment

Similar orienting material is needed for virtual courses. As learners in classroom courses must often make arrangements for their absence from the office before a class or make travel arrangements to attend class, so learners in virtual classes must enroll in advance, receive passwords to gain access to the course, download software to run the course, and make sure that the software works on their systems and behind their firewalls (if any) before the course actually starts. Unfortunately, many administrators for online courses have learned that online learners—like classroom learners—wait until the last minute to enroll, not leaving sufficient time to prepare themselves to participate in the online session.

Avoid an Initial Focus on Administrivia

Although the course objectives, grading issues, payment issues (for public training courses), and similar administrative considerations play a key role in the ultimate success of a learning program, starting with these issues often serves as a demotivator. Learners are there to launch into the content and want to do so as soon as possible.

One key challenge for designers of e-learning programs is how much information they should provide on "how to take this course" at the very beginning of a course or unit. For example, in the early days of e-learning, many courses included twenty- to forty-minute units on how to take the course because the designers assumed that learners were not familiar with the keyboard, and courses used the systems in nonintuitive ways. This "overhead" frustrated many learners.

Of course it frustrated learners who were familiar with the course and wanted to work with the content as quickly as possible. But this overhead also posed a problem for those people going through a course for reasons other than learning. For example, one group of instructional designers submitted their course for a competition on e-learning. But because the course required all users go through a forty-minute introduction to the keyboard and the course, the judges could not get to the course content in a timely manner. Not surprisingly, the frustrated judges chose not to grant an award to the course.

Launch into the Content as Early as Possible

Readability research suggests that content designers must hook readers at the beginning of a learning program to increase the likelihood that readers will stick around to the end. This is especially true with e-learning because learners are often dropping out. For asynchronous e-training, some organizations have anecdotally reported dropout rates as high as 90 percent. Dropout rates are similarly high in e-courses offered by live virtual classroom and asynchronous discussion. Some universities have anecdotally reported dropout rates as high as 67 percent (though more institutions experience dropout rates closer to 33 percent).

One of the ways to avoid such high dropout rates is to grab the attention of learners from the beginning of a learning program. This suggestion is not unique to e-learning; Gagne (1985) lists grabbing the attention of learners as the first of his nine events of instruction, which he proposed long before e-learning earned its current popularity.

Journalists face the same problem. Readers of news stories generally read the first paragraph to decide whether they want to continue reading an article. Therefore, news stories are written in a format called "the inverted pyramid." That is, the most important information is at the top of the story, and information that follows is of decreasing importance. One journalism student reports that his professors said that 50 percent of readers stop reading by the end of the first paragraph; another 10 percent by the end of the second.

Because it must carry the most important information—and because it is the only paragraph that many people read—the first paragraph of a news story receives a disproportionate amount of attention in news writing. The paragraph is called the *lead*, because it leads the news story, and it must perform two functions:

- Report the main information about the story—who, what, where, when, why, and how

- Grab readers' attention so they continue reading

To ensure readers' attention, reporters limit the length of a lead paragraph. A common limit is thirty-five words.

Although content in an e-learning program does not necessarily follow the inverted pyramid, because it is often presented in order of complexity (elements of less complex content build on each other to be presented as more complex content), the need to grab the attention of learners at the beginning of an e-learning program, as well as the start of sessions of live virtual classes and units of asynchronous courses, is no less important than it is for a news story.

Many experienced designers suggest hooking learners first by giving them a small taste of the content, then presenting the administrivia of a course or lesson. At that point, learners should have developed an interest in the content and not only have the motivation to stick around, but the interest in validating their expectations of the content and learning the expectations about their participation in the learning program.

A Portfolio of Techniques for Designing Openings

Several techniques help instructional designers craft openings. The issues are listed in the order in which many instructional designers address them—and in which they present the material to learners. Specifically, these techniques address:

- Presenting initial administrivia
- Enticingly introducing learners to content
- Setting expectations about the content
- Setting expectations about the administration of the learning program

The next several sections explore each of these topics in detail.

Techniques for Presenting Initial Administrivia

As mentioned earlier, learners want to get into the content as quickly as possible, and the presentation of administrivia at the beginning of a course or unit delays that.

Only a few administrative matters must be addressed before presenting content. For example, instructions on how to contact an instructor or call for technical assistance are essential to a live virtual class and must be presented before a session begins. But information on grading policies is not, and it can wait until later in the session. In fact, the relevance of grades is higher after learners have been introduced to the content.

Similarly, although learners in asynchronous learning programs need to verify that they're in the intended unit, that information can be conveyed by the title alone, not a full description of the unit and its objectives. Such information can also wait until later in the unit, after the initial introduction of the content.

Techniques for Enticingly Introducing Learners to Content

As mentioned earlier, learners seem to respond best to a session if they can get into the content as soon as possible. This is true for both virtual classes and asynchronous learning programs. For most learners, getting into the content means interacting directly with it. Interaction is especially important to live virtual classes for breaking the ice and encouraging learners to interact throughout the session.

Some popular techniques for both introducing learners to content and encouraging interaction at the beginning of a program or unit include an opening assessment, an opening story, an opening case, and a vanity shot. The following sections describe these approaches.

An Opening Assessment. An opening assessment is much like a pretest in that it is criterion-referenced and gives learners a chance to assess how much they already know about a topic before taking a course. This type of assessment differs, however, in that the questions have a high fun factor, like the self-assessments in *Cosmopolitan* and, although scores are reported to the learner, they are not recorded for a record of learning.

An Opening Story. As stories often engage learners in the classroom, so stories often engage learners online. Several challenges exist with using stories to introduce content. First, learners must be able to see the direct relationship between the story and the topic of the course or unit. Off-topic stories not only confuse learners, but they also make the job of building interest in the content all the harder. (Basically, telling off-topic stories implicitly say, "Now the fun is over and the learning has to begin." On-topic stories make no implicit or explicit distinction between learning and fun.) Second, stories should represent a holistic view of the content in the learning program.

Two types of stories include personal accounts and simulations.

• *Personal accounts.* A personal account is an experience report. It describes a situation in which an individual applied the content taught in the learning program in his or her personal life. Two wide uses of personal accounts are to motivate learners with an interesting story and with one that describes successful application of the learning concepts in the real world.

Usually, the personal account comes from an instructor or one of the learners in the class. In the classroom, most personal accounts are a form of "war story." Fortunately, in most of these stories, the front lines are business environments, not actual battlefields in war. In virtual classrooms, instructors use war stories much as they do in classroom courses.

In asynchronous courses with videotaped lectures, war stories continue to appear. What's more common in asynchronous courses, however, are different types of personal accounts, such as accounts from individuals and organizations. This difference often results from the absence of the instructor's persona from asynchronous courses.

A third wide use of personal accounts is as a means of teaching, especially advanced technical material. For example, in a study of the education of hardware service representatives for a major manufacturer, researchers found that advanced learners learned more from sharing war stories around the water cooler than they did from formal classes. The reason that these advanced learners learned more around the water cooler is that they wanted to learn how to handle specific problems. Someone might ask, "How do you handle such-and-such?" Someone else would respond, "I had a problem like that. First we tried A, but it didn't work because of thus-and-so. So we tried this second approach and it worked." Through the story, participants not only learned how to fix the problem, they also learned the reasoning underlying the approach (Brown & Duguid, 2002).

• *Simulations.* Simulations are educational activities that place learners in a fictional situation that reproduces the key components of the real one it mimics. Within this situation, learners can act and experience the consequences and benefits of their actions as if they were in the real world, but without any of the harsh real consequences. As a result, each learner creates his or her own story. For example, The Virtual Leader, a management simulation course, lets learners develop principles of management by experiencing simulated business experiences. Based on their responses, each student experiences a unique "story" as he or she goes through this course. The challenge in designing such an experience is designing the debriefing and making sure that learners can identify their experiences, place labels on them, and identify broader concepts that they can apply. An example of this simulation is shown in Figure 10.1.

An Opening Case. A variation on the opening story is the opening case, in which learners are asked to respond to one or more cases related to the content of the course or unit. Case studies are detailed descriptions of situations in which an organization faces one or more crucial decisions. The cases describe the people, incidents, and context that led up to the decision—but do not include the solution in the materials originally given to learners. In a virtual class, instructors often present the case and let learners figure out how they would solve the problem based on the information available. Later, learners discuss their solutions and compare them with the actual solution that the organization in the case chose. A variation in asynchronous courses is that learners often complete the case, then see a description of the possible solution.

A case is essentially a story about an organization facing a particular challenge at a particular point in time. The story can be factual or fictional. A *formal* case study tells a factual story about a real organization and results from formal and extensive research that involves interviews with the key players in the case and an evaluation of reports and other documentation. A *fictional* case study is usually made up by the instructor and, although it exhibits many of the same characteristics of a formal case study, is not based on an actual organization or it does not emerge from formal and extensive research.

Case studies help learners synthesize concepts. By determining how they would solve cases, case studies provide learners with an opportunity to determine which concepts are relevant to a real-world situation and how they apply. Just as significantly, case studies also help learners determine which concepts do not apply to a

Figure 10.1. Example of a Simulation in an e-Learning Course

Copyright Simulearn, Inc. Used with permission.

given situation and help learners avoid the problem of the inappropriate application of principles.

Case studies are most widely used in management courses, both academic and corporate ones. For example, UNEXT, the online university, builds its business management courses around cases. Case studies are also used in other types of educational situations, including design courses (like instructional design, system design, and engineering design), training on customization, and troubleshooting, and medical education.

For example, the cases in Figure 10.2 opened a virtual course about the appropriate use of e-learning. Learners read through the cases, responded to a polling question about each case, then explained their answers.

Figure 10.2. Example of a Case-Based Activity to Start a Live Virtual Lesson on e-Learning

Opening Exercise

Instructions: Review each of the following situations and, based on the information given, determine whether the material should be presented online or not.

Situation 1: Thanks to huge demand for the all-natural breakfast cereals it produces, the Cedars Corporation is experiencing a huge growth in its manufacturing staff. Its one-day new employee orientation consists of modules on company's history and culture, products, management philosophy, and sanitation in food processing. In addition, each department offers training on its manufacturing process. Workers cannot begin their jobs until they have successfully completed the process training. Until the current growth spurt, the training department offered new employee training once a month. The training department now offers the course twice a month and feels that it needs to increase capacity to once a week to meet demand for the next four months, when the HR department predicts that the hiring spurt will slow down. One of the trainers suggested that, rather than add classes, the training department should convert new employee orientation to WBT.

☐ Appropriate online?

☐ Not appropriate online?

Situation 2: Cedars is not the only company experiencing a growth spurt. Morewood Technologies, a manufacturer of high-tech medical prosthetic equipment, is also experiencing a huge growth spurt in response to its innovative line of microprocessor-controlled artificial limbs. Like Cedars, Morewood is adding more staff than its classroom-based new employee orientation can handle. The HR department does not see a letup in hiring for at least the next eighteen to twenty-four months. New employee orientation consists almost exclusively of required technical training, such as modules on clean room procedures and right-to-know training. In fact, the manager of training laments that the course is so full of technical content that it permits little time for training on the corporate culture. But employees cannot begin work until they have successfully completed technical training, so the priorities are clear. Besides, the training department doesn't have the staff to handle a longer course. In addition to new employee orientation, the department conducts refresher training on many of the same topics as are covered in new employee orientation. One of the trainers suggests converting the new employee orientation to WBT.

☐ Appropriate online?

☐ Not appropriate?

Vanity Shots.   Some corporate designers typically begin courses and units with *vanity shots*—messages from corporate executives to learners, delivered as a video sequence (virtual classes and asynchronous courses) or a letter (asynchronous courses). In a few rare instances, these might be motivational to learners, such as corporate courses launching a major change initiative in a company.

In most cases, though, the message is nothing more than a vanity opportunity (hence, the name vanity shot). The executive's sponsorship of the content does not encourage motivation to learn and only serves the executive's own ego.

Techniques for Setting Expectations About the Content

Setting expectations is important to all types of courses. Instructors have commented that learners often do not read the course descriptions as thoroughly as they should and, as a result, start learning programs with unrealistic expectations about what will be covered. When a live instructor is available, such as in a classroom or live virtual classroom, clarifications and adjustments can be made on the spot. But in asynchronous learning programs, such adjustments are next to impossible.

To make sure that learners' expectations for the content match the actual plans for the course, early in the learning program instructors should review the plans for the content with learners. A number of techniques exist for doing so.

State Objectives.   The most direct way of setting expectations is listing the objectives early in the learning program. In one sense, objectives represent a contract, of sorts, between learners, sponsors, and the designers of the learning program. The instructional designer promises to cover the content named in the objectives and present the content in such a way that learners can master it. If learners invest time in the learning program and complete the activities, they should be able to master the content and achieve the stated objectives. Furthermore, sponsors receive the benefits that result from learners mastering the content.

Although objectives represent a contract of sorts, the terminology used in an effectively written objective should reflect the nature of the test question used to assess it. For example, if the test question is a matching question, the action in the objective should say "Match." Although precise from an instructional perspective, most learners are not interested in learning how to match something. They're usually interested in something more fundamental, like doing something. Therefore, designers might consider presenting the objectives in terms that would resonate more fully with learners. For example, rather than stating, "choose from a list the correct option for starting the computer," which is precise from an instructional design standpoint, write a more vernacular statement, like "start the computer." This approach is especially needed with asynchronous e-learning programs because they often rely on objective tests (tests with matching, multiple-choice, true-false, and fill-in-the-blank questions) to assess skills that are often more complex than can be tested through such tests.

Provide an Agenda. Instructional designers do not always need to present objectives to learners to set expectations about the content. These can be shared with learners in other ways. An agenda often serves a similar purpose. An agenda lists the topics and learning activities, which not only sets expectations about the content, but also about the order in which it will be taught. Table 10.2 shows the objectives and agenda for the same course.

Table 10.2. A List of Objectives and an Agenda for an e-Learning Program	
Objectives	**Agenda**

Main Objective: Supervise workers on a training or communication team.	1. Hiring
	    a. Recruiting candidates
	    b. Making offers

Supporting Objectives: To achieve the objective, you should be able to:	2. Performance planning, coaching, and evaluating
	    a. The performance cycle
	    b. Setting performance plans
	    c. Coaching employees
	    d. Writing appraisals
	    e. Delivering appraisals

• Recruit candidates for jobs
  • Explain how to write a job description
  • Describe the relationship between a job description and a job ad
  • Describe the different ways to recruit candidates
  • Describe at least three issues to consider in the interviewing process
  • Describe at least three issues to consider when selecting an employee
	3. Recognizing employees
	    a. Purpose of recognition
	    b. Ways to recognize employees

• State expectations of employees
  • Describe the performance cycle
  • Describe the points at which you can have impact in the performance cycle
  • Explain how to develop a performance plan for a training or communications professional
	4. Developing employees
	    a. Career development plans
	    b. Setting development plans
	    c. Career paths for training and communication professionals
	    d. Assessing success against plans

Table 10.2. A List of Objectives and an Agenda for an e-Learning Program, Cont'd	
Objectives	**Agenda**
<ul><li>Describe how to coach employees during the appraisal period</li><li>Explain how to write an employee evaluation</li><li>Explain how to deliver an employee evaluation</li></ul><ul><li>Provide recognition to employees<ul><li>Explain why different types of recognition are needed</li><li>Describe at least five ways to appropriately recognize employees</li></ul></li><li>Prepare a career development plan for an employee<ul><li>Describe the purpose of a career development plan</li><li>Describe the employee's role in setting and implementing a career development plan</li><li>Name the different types of opportunities that you can use to develop an employee</li><li>Describe career paths for training and communication professionals</li><li>Explain how to assess progress against a career development plan</li></ul></li></ul>	

Ask Learners to Complete an Information Form. For live virtual courses, ask learners to complete a student information form before the first session. Among the questions to ask are "What do you hope to learn in this course?" If the response to that question does not match the content of the course, the instructor can contact the learner to clarify expectations. In many cases, learners have not read through the course description and reached their own conclusions about the content to be covered.

Figure 10.3 shows an example of a student information form for an academic course. The form can be adapted for use with corporate training and continuing education courses.

Figure 10.3. Sample Student Information Form

Student Information Form

So that I can provide you with a learning experience that is of most value to you, I'd like to learn a little bit more about you before the first class session.

Instructions: Please copy these questions into an e-mail message, then send to instructor@courses.edu.

Who Are You?

1. Name: _____

2. Major and level (BA, MA, Ph.D.): _____

3. Previous Degrees (list degree and school): _____

4. Current employment: _____

About Your Interest in the Course

1. Why did you sign up for this course? _____

2. Describe your previous experience with the following

Using knowledge management systems	☐ Some ☐ None	If you have some experience, please describe it here:
Designing knowledge management systems	☐ Some ☐ None	If you have some experience, please describe it here:
Working with content management systems	☐ Some ☐ None	If you have some experience, please describe it here:
Working with learning management systems	☐ Some ☐ None	If you have some experience, please describe it here:

3. What is the one thing you hope to learn from this course?

_____

4. What excites you most about starting this course?

_____

5. What is your most significant concern entering this course?

_____

6. How do you think the knowledge learned in this course will benefit you in your career?

_____

Once again, copy these questions into an e-mail message; then send it to instructor@courses.edu.

Techniques for Setting Expectations About the Administration of the Learning Program

Although administrative details do not need to be presented first thing in a learning program, because the administration of a learning program often defines how success is assessed, instructional designers should make sure that this material is covered before the first lesson is presented (although it can happen after learners are introduced to the content).

As mentioned earlier, the type of content covered in the administration of the learning program varies, depending on whether the learning program is academic or a corporate training or continuing education program.

Administrative Material for Academic Courses. Administrative issues are covered in the syllabus. Academic institutions consider a syllabus to be a contract with the student so many institutions have guidelines regarding syllabi, including information that must be included and when and how they should be distributed.

For all types of courses, syllabi cover the following:

- Description of the course (usually taken from the course catalog)

- Agenda (lesson-by-lesson or weekly plan with the topic, readings and assignments due, if any)

- Grading criteria, including the criteria for earning letter grades (like A, B, and C) and requirements for submitting assignments

- Attendance and other class policies. (For example, many instructors include policies about learners with disabilities, requiring that they come forward in the first two weeks of a course to make the instructor aware of the issue so that learners cannot claim a disability later in the course if they have issues with grades.)

- How to receive assistance, such as how to contact the instructor with questions, and the availability of tutors and teaching assistants

In addition, syllabi for online courses should also state the technology requirements for the course:

- Hardware needed (including special audiovisual equipment, such as headphones and microphones)

- Software needed (such as the level of browser and plug-ins that learners should be using)

Because the syllabus is a contract, instructors have an obligation to review the syllabus with learners in the first class session. So when designing the first session of an academic virtual class, time should be set aside to cover the syllabus.

In terms of presenting the syllabus to students, many academic instructors like to begin the first session of an e-learning program with an interactive activity and close it by reviewing administrative issues.

See the website accompanying this book for examples of syllabi for academic courses.

Corporate Training and Continuing Education Courses. Although administrivia for training and continuing education programs are not considered to be a contract like the syllabi for academic courses, the issues raised often affect the quality of the learning experience so designers usually incorporate this type of material. These issues include

- Intended audience

- Prerequisites

- How to receive assistance, such as the availability of coaching and tutors

- Legal information, including trademarks, disclaimers, and a copyright statement (This information does not need to be verbally stated, but can be listed onscreen or in printed materials distributed to learners)

- Requirements for completing the learning program. These vary among programs and organizations. Some instructors merely track attendance, and learners receive credit for the learning program if they attend a given number of sessions (but the number must be stated up-front). Others require that learners complete an assessment at the end of the learning program, but have no attendance requirement. Others have both an attendance requirement and an assessment.

  Some online instructors find that learners in corporate and continuing education programs do not complete homework assignments, and suggest that assessment also include credit for completing homework.

  One system for tracking online learners has instructors offering points for attending class and completing assignments. Learners who receive a certain number of points (such as fifteen out of eighteen) receive credit for the entire program.

This information should be covered in the first class session of a live virtual class, or by the end of the first unit of an asynchronous course.

In addition, also make learners aware of the technology requirements for the learning program. The type of information needed is the same as that needed for an academic course (hardware and software needed) but must be provided before learners begin a course so that they know that they can take it. Some likely places to communicate this content include

- For learning programs distributed on DVD or CD, place the information on the outside cover of the box, so it is visible to learners before they purchase the program.

- For learning programs distributed online, include the requirements in the course description that learners read before enrolling.

Also include these requirements in the description of a learning program in a published catalog.

Designing Closings

Like openings, closings are brief but pivotal to e-learning programs. In this case they present the last material that learners encounter and are most likely to remember. Because of this pivotal role of closings, instructional designers should spend a similarly disproportionate amount of time preparing closings as they do openings. The following sections describe the guidelines and a portfolio of techniques for doing so.

Guidelines for Designing Closings

Designers of e-learning programs face a number of challenges in designing the closings of courses and units. Like the guidelines for designing openings, some are practical, others are motivational. The following guidelines help instructional designers address these challenges:

- Appropriately summarize the content.
- Appropriately assess the content.
- Build enthusiasm among participants for continued learning.

The following sections describe these guidelines in detail.

Appropriately Summarize the Content

One of the key purposes of the closing of a unit or course is summarizing the content. This summary is the last opportunity that designers have to reinforce key points with learners.

Several different approaches exist to summarizing content, from passive to active. A passively presented summary is one in which the instructor provides learners with a list of the key points in the lesson and states exactly how learners should remember them. An actively presented summary is one in which learners supply the key points they believe that they should remember.

Some common types of summaries include

- *A descriptive summary*, which states the topics covered in the learning program or unit as well as points that participants should remember about them. An example is, "This unit described hot and cold fields of opportunities. A hot field of opportunity is in which the industry is growing faster than the economy. A cold field of opportunity is one in which the industry is growing more slowly than the economy." Notice that, in addition to naming the topics, a descriptive summary also states what learners should remember about the topic.

- *A topic summary*, which names the topics covered in the course or unit, but gives no details about them. An example is, "This unit described hot and cold fields of opportunity." Notice that the topic summary does *not* define hot and cold, as the descriptive summary does.

- *A learner-supplied summary*, in which learners name the key points that they intend to take away from the unit. In some cases, learners may be prompted to state what they would remember with leading questions, in other cases, learners are asked to supply their own.

Figure 10.4 presents the types of summaries on a continuum.

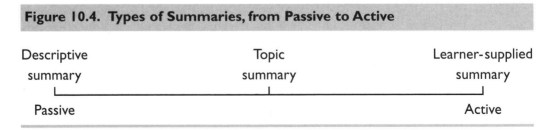

Figure 10.4. Types of Summaries, from Passive to Active

Descriptive summary	Topic summary	Learner-supplied summary
Passive		Active

The type of summary that you would use depends on the nature of the content and on the learning strategy chosen. For example, for units with highly technical content that learners must apply exactly as presented in the course, designers might choose a passive strategy to reinforce the key points that learners must remember. In contrast, for units teaching principles that have situational application, learners might benefit from supplying their own summaries as a means of helping to verify their own understanding.

Appropriately Assess the Content

One of the purposes of the closing sections of a course or unit is assessing learners' ability to master the objectives. Units of most e-learning programs include such an assessment. Merely including an assessment, however, does not ensure that it is an appropriate one.

Two issues arise in appropriately assessing content. One is the *approach to assessment.* Most instructional design is based on the principle of closing courses with criterion-referenced assessments. Criterion-referenced assessments are tests, quizzes, observations, and similar types of activities that emerge directly from the objectives for the course or unit. These objectives are the *criterion.*

Because the objectives state what learners should learn, a test assesses whether or not the learners can successfully achieve the objectives. Assessment questions should emerge directly from the objectives; in fact, objectives often suggest how the question should be stated. For example, if the objective says, "Describe at least four ways to structure content," the assessment question should ask learners to "Describe at least four ways to structure content."

Criterion-referenced testing emerges from the assumption that all learners should be able to master the material and that successful learning only occurs when learners master the objectives. Criterion-referenced testing is favored by corporate training departments.

Norm-referenced testing, favored by the academic system, assesses learners' abilities in a subject area along a continuum of strongest to weakest. In *norm-referenced tests,* the test questions should still emerge from the objectives but might include some questions that ask about situations that are dissimilar to the ones presented in the e-learning program. Although the questions still assess students' abilities to master the objectives, learners must also recognize that the concepts taught in class apply to dissimilar situations. Testing learners about their ability to handle dissimilar situations assesses their ability to transfer concepts broadly and separates those who have merely memorized the content from those who have fully integrated it.

The second challenge of preparing assessments at the ends of units is the *type of assessment used.* In some instances, formal, scored tests are appropriate. These are useful in instances in which learners receive a grade for the course or are formally passed and failed. For similar reasons, scored tests are also useful in training that leads to certification.

But in many instances, instructional designers do not want to include a test at the end of a course or unit. In some instances, that's because the course is not graded. In other instances, formal testing creates legal problems. In some countries, employers must be able to demonstrate that tests used to make personnel decisions (such as promotions and new job assignments) are unbiased or face the possibility of a legal challenge. To avoid such legal challenges, many companies simply choose not to use formal tests in training programs.

But even when not formally testing, many instructional designers would like to provide learners with a way of assessing for themselves whether or not they can master the objectives. Rather than provide formal tests, designers create a variety of other types of assessments. These include:

- Quizzes and self-tests, which are like tests. Quiz questions emerge directly from objectives, just as test questions do. The difference is that, although scored, quiz scores either play a minor role in a final grade (as they do in most academic courses) or scores are only reported to learners; they are not recorded or reported to instructors (as is typical of corporate training and continuing education courses).

- Self-assessments, which are "fun" quizzes (like those in *Cosmopolitan* magazine). Although based on the objectives, the questions and possible responses have a high level of humor. Also, rather than merely provide a score, the system provides learners with an interpretation of the score. In other words, if learners score 80 percent or higher, that means they're knowledgeable of the subject, but if they score 50 percent or lower, they still have some skill development to do. See "How Close Are You to the Performance Zone?" and other samples on the website accompanying this book to see what a self-assessment looks like.

Build Enthusiasm Among Participants for Continued Learning

The last key purpose of the closing is encouraging learners to continue studying the topic, if they choose. Learners might continue studying a topic for several reasons:

- They don't feel they have mastered the topic and want to continue practicing it. This is called *remediation*. In some instances, the learner initiates remediation but, more commonly, the instructor (or system) recommends it.

- They would like to better understand how the content of the unit or course applies to their unique situation. For example, the basic skills of presentation graphics programs like PowerPoint® apply in a wide variety of situations. People who prepare business presentations and training programs might like to learn about specific features of PowerPoint that can enhance their work, but the features that they would use differ.

- They would like to learn about the topic more in-depth. In some instances, learners are fascinated by a topic and one experience with it motivates interest in more experiences. This is called *enrichment.* For enrichment, learners might not only be interested in additional formal courses, but in other sources of information about the topic such as other websites, seminal works of literature, and associations that support it.

A Portfolio of Techniques for Designing Closings

Several techniques help instructional designers craft closings. The issues are listed in the order in which many instructional designers address them—and in which they present the material to learners. Specifically, these techniques address each of the three guidelines for closing a course or unit:

- Summarizing the content presented

- Assessing the learner (formally or informally)

- Linking learners to additional learning material

The following sections describe these techniques in detail.

Techniques for Summarizing the Content Presented

The techniques for writing summaries depend on the type of summary you are writing.

To write a *descriptive summary,* first return to the objectives of the course or unit. Then identify the content that learners should remember about each main (terminal) and supporting (enabling) objective. For example, if the objective is "Name the three uses of the ABC Copier," the descriptive summary would name the three uses of the ABC Copier. For example, "The ABC Copier has three uses: copying, scanning images from outside sources, and faxing documents." Notice how the sentence incorporates as many words from the objectives as possible. The consistency of using the same words to express the same points further enhances learning.

To write a *topic summary,* go back to the objectives to create a list of topics covered in the course or unit. Then list the topics. For example, if the objectives of the unit were (1) Describe the purpose of the ABC Copier, (2) Name the three uses of the ABC Copier, and (3) Identify the key customers for the ABC Copier, the summary would say, "This unit covered the purpose of the ABC Copier, the three uses of it, and the key customers for this product." Notice how the topic summary does *not* provide the level of detail that a descriptive summary does.

To prepare a *learner-supplied summary,* prompt learners to state what they learned in the lesson. This is often posed as a question to the learner, such as "State the most important things you learned in this course" or "What are the take-away lessons from this unit?" In a live virtual class, learners can type this information into the discussion area and share their responses with the entire class. In an asynchronous course, learners can be prompted to complete this information, though it will not be processed by the computer. Figure 10.5 shows a sample slide from a live virtual class that requests such input.

Figure 10.5. An Example of a Slide from a Live Virtual Class Asking Learners to Provide the Summary

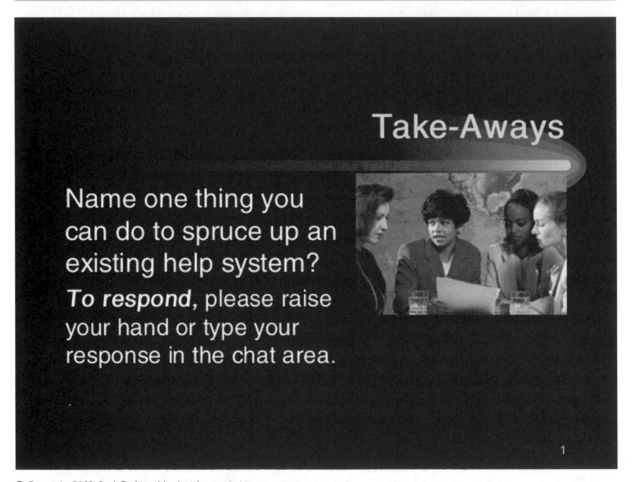

Techniques for Assessing the Learner (Formally or Informally)

When assessing the learner, choose an assessment that is consistent with the goals of the learning program. Guidelines for writing test questions and providing feedback are covered on the website accompanying this book. Also see the website for examples of end-of-unit and end-of-course assessments.

Techniques for Linking Learners to Additional Learning Material

The techniques for linking learners to additional material vary, depending on the purpose of creating the link.

Linking for Remediation. The primary issues in encouraging interest in further study vary, depending on the purpose motivating the learner. When encouraging learners to consider remediation, a number of issues arise:

- If the suggestion emerges from poor performance on a learning assessment, the motivation must help learners work past feelings of disappointment and failure.

- Pinpointing the specific content to review. One of the advantages of using criterion-referenced assessment is that it lets designers identify when learners have mastered material and when they need remediation. Learners who perform well on questions about a particular objective have probably mastered it; learners who do not perform well on questions about a particular objective probably need remediation. Learners who perform well on some questions about a particular objective but not on others might also benefit from remediation on those questions that they did not answer correctly.

- The presentation of the remedial material must *not* repeat the earlier one. In many self-study programs, remediation consists of sending learners through the material a second time, such as sending them through a section of an asynchronous web-based training program. This is probably a useless approach. If learners did not understand the material the first time through, they are not likely to understand it on a second read-through. Instead, prepare an alternate presentation of the content. It might be simpler, include more and different examples, and include more checks for understanding to make sure that learners can master the objectives before they move forward.

Linking to Apply Content in Specific Situations. Link learners to tailored units for their specific purposes. (In some cases, the material already exists. In other instances, you'll need to create it.) For example, "If you are using PowerPoint to create marketing presentations, see 'PowerPoint for Marketing Presentations.' If you are using PowerPoint to create training programs, see 'PowerPoint for Training Presentations.'" Notice in the sample statements that the linking begins with words that would attract learners' attention: "If you are using. . . ." Use that format, rather than merely listing the titles. In this instance, the titles of the additional material are clear. Because learners might not always see the link, your explicitly stating it helps them.

Linking for Enrichment. When recommending enrichment material, instructional designers can motivate interest in a number of ways. First, they should provide links to material that logically extends the learning experience, including:

- Glossary of terms used in the program
- Bibliography of sources cited in the program

Second, instructional designers can link to other websites, articles, and books of interest. When compiling this list, note that learners are more likely to check references and website on a small list than on a long one because the long one is likely to overwhelm them. Similarly, learners are more likely to check a website or reference if the designer explains why the reference is worth checking. More than "Check this reference," learners need to see "Check this reference *because* . . ."

Bonus Technique: Using Templates to Ensure Consistency in Openings and Closings

Although the introduction to the content is unique in each unit of a course and in each course in a curriculum, many of the other elements of openings and closings are remarkably similar. To ensure that the information is presented consistently— and to increase the efficiency of designing and developing openings and closings— many instructional designers prepare templates. Templates codify design plans for similar content into a series of fill-in-the-blank forms (where feasible) so developers do not have to re-enter information that needs to be consistent.

Designers usually create templates in their primary authoring program (such as Word or Dreamweaver). The content that is consistent is entered exactly as it would appear. Blanks and instructions for filling them in are placed where developers should add information. Text is formatted and illustrations inserted exactly as they should appear. Specifically, a template includes the following:

- Text that is the same in every part of the learning program.

- Formatting for headings, body text, examples, figures, and other text elements; this formatting includes typography, margins, and placement of consistently placed items, such as the text of a title or a line that might appear in the same place on every screen.

- Navigation bars (if they are separately coded in each frame). Note that some or all of the navigational material may be provided by the authoring tool or by the learning content management system (LCMS) used to create the e-learning material.

In Practice: The Opening to Jones International University's "Managing the Design, Development, Delivery, and Evaluation of e-Learning"*

General Description of the Project

Title: Managing the Design, Development, Delivery, and Evaluation of e-Learning

Publisher: Jones International University
www.jonesinternational.edu
info@jonesinternational.edu

Producers: William and Kit Horton
William Horton Consulting
www.horton.com
william@horton.com

Description: Managing the Design, Development, Delivery, and Evaluation of e-Learning (EDU 721) is an online academic course designed by William and Kit Horton. The course is unique in that it is given as a role-playing simulation of a "real-life" situation.

At the beginning of class, the learner is told that he or she is the new chief learning officer (CLO) of a fictional company that is "owned" by the instructor. The student (employee) learns that he or she has been hired to replace an incompetent CLO who submitted a poor eLearning proposal to the company.

*This In Practice was prepared by Patrick Devey.

In the opening to the course, the learner is merely presented with the problem and left to his or her own devices to figure out how to proceed with the project. The learner is supposed to realize that he or she needs to communicate with the instructor. This element of surprise and figuring out what to do makes this course unique for an academic course, in which learners are usually led through the material.

The opening also sets the tone for communication in the course. Rather than presenting material as assignment sheets and readings, all material is presented as a series of interoffice memos and reports between the employer and the employees. The challenge of the opening section is getting learners to realize that they are in charge of their learning experience and that the experience is designed for them to initiate interaction with the instructor.

In the course, learners explore each component of the proposal before rewriting it until the entire report is prepared. Learners address human resource management, interviewing skills, and budgets as they work through the various aspects of the proposal, which is submitted as their final assignment for the course. Learners communicate with one another through the occasional online meetings and the discussion board. They are also able to contact their "boss" (the instructor) through e-mail. In the end, learners should have mastered the skills needed to manage the process of designing, developing, delivering, and evaluating e-learning programs.

Intended Audience: Master's of education students enrolled in the eLearning generalist degree program at Jones International University (an online university).

Size of Audience: Twelve students per term, four terms per year.

About the Learning Goals

Primary and Secondary Goals of the Project: Traditional learning.

Primary Learning Objectives:

- Describe the benefits and limitations of e-learning.

- Identify the members of an organization who need to implement e-learning.

- Compare and contrast e-learning options based on educational, technical, and organizational considerations.

- Estimate cost and time for development of e-learning.

- Assess the organizational issues related to internationalization, infra-structure, and change.
- Write a needs assessment plan.
- Write a design document or request for proposal (RFP) for an e-learning project.

Learning Issues Underlying the Project

The instructor observed that, for whatever reason, students tended to do their work on Saturday nights. That meant that the subject-matter experts would not be immediately available to answer questions. Because one of the purposes of the opening is to help learners establish an e-mail relationship with the instructor, the response could be delayed by a couple of days because of practical matters.

The Numbers

Approximate Number of Development Hours Per Finished Hour of Instruction: Estimated to be five development hours per hour of finished instruction

Schedule (from Beginning to End of the Project): Eight weeks for the content (Horton) plus eight weeks to produce (Jones development team), which equaled four months

Skills Used on the Project: Instructional design, writing, programming, graphic design, editing

Other Business Issues Affecting the Project: An initial needs assessment conducted by Jones International University found that a significant group of their learners use dial-up Internet connections. The Horton group had to consider this low bandwidth when designing the course and, as a result, chose to exclude high-end multimedia (such as video and audio).

Technology Infrastructure

Delivery Medium: Internet

Media Used in the e-Learning Program: Text, graphics, animation, audio

Delivery Platform: Web browser-based

Authoring Environment: Jones Knowledge, the Jones International University's virtual classroom system

Supporting Software: Macromedia Flash®, JavaScript®

Results of the Course

- *How Did You Market the Course?* The course was marketed through the University's traditional marketing process.

- *What Were the Results of the Course?* Between one-half and three-quarters of the students involved in the course enjoyed their experience, according to Kit Horton. She adds that learners relish their role in the fictional company. Most also admitted that they invested more time in the course than they had originally thought and found the experience challenging.

- *What Would You Do the Same on a Future e-Learning Project?* Bill and Kit Horton comment that the role-playing simulations worked extremely well and put learners in a real-life situation. They could immediately recognize the value of the content and apply it in their work and other courses. However, learners could just as easily veer off-track in the simulation, so instructors need to monitor discussions and, if needed, intervene to keep discussions on-topic. Bill and Kit Horton also found it was important to clearly and adequately define the terminal objectives in the course.

- *What Would You Do Differently?* The Hortons would prepare answer keys and other tools to assess learners beforehand to save time. Doing so would also standardize feedback to learners and smooth the transition among instructors (The Hortons taught the course once. Since then, others have taught this course using the material that the Hortons designed and developed.)

Conclusion

Openings and closings provide the first and last opportunities to present content to learners. As a result, they require special care in designing and developing. To reach this conclusion, this chapter explored the following points:

- The purposes of openings and closings of courses and units (sections within courses) are

  - Openings engage interest in the topic, communicate expectations about the content, communicate expectations about the learning experience, and ensure that learners can use the technology underlying a course.

- Closings summarize the content presented, assess learners formally or informally, link learners to additional learning material, and provide reference material.

- When designing openings:

  - Consider these guidelines: (1) for virtual classroom sessions, provide enough lead time for enrollment; (2) avoid an initial focus on administrivia; wait on that until after introducing the content; (3) launch into the content as early as possible.

  - Consider these techniques: (1) limit the amount of administrivia presented at the very beginning to the minimum that is required to get started with a learning program; (2) enticingly introduce learners to content through techniques such as assessments, opening stories, opening cases, and similar interactive techniques; (3) set expectations about the content by stating either the objectives or agenda for the course or unit; also distribute a student information form in advance of an academic or live virtual course to make sure that learners' expectations are in line with the actual content of the course; (4) set expectations about the administration of the learning program by sharing the requirements for completing the learning program and how to receive assistance.

- When designing closings:

  - Consider these guidelines: (1) appropriately summarize the content, choosing either a passive summary, like a topic or descriptive summary, or an active summary in which learners summarize content on their own; (2) appropriately assess the content, using formal assessments such as tests and observations for graded courses and informal assessments such as quizzes and self-assessments; assessments should be criterion-referenced, that is, derived from the course objectives; (3) build enthusiasm among participants for continued learning by providing useful enrichment, showing learners how to adapt generalized content taught in a learning program to the specific needs of the learner, and linking learners to enrichment.

  - Consider these techniques: (1) summarize the content presented appropriately, choosing a strategy that is consistent with the goals of the course and following related writing guidelines; (2) assess the learner (formally or informally); (3) link learners to additional learning material without overwhelming them.

- Also, in the process of designing openings and closings, designers might prepare templates for content that is similar across units or courses.

As this chapter explored how to compose the ends of a learning program, the next chapter explores how to compose the middle. Specifically, it explores exposition— or writing—techniques for composing e-learning content.

Learn More About It

Ausubel, D. (1963). *The psychology of meaningful verbal learning.* New York: Grune & Stratton.

Ausubel's book introduced the concept of advance organizers. Since then, others have followed up on Ausubel's work.

Conrad, D. (2002). Engagement, excitement, anxiety and fear: Learners experiences of starting an online course. *American Journal of Distance Education, 16*(4), 205–226.

Conrad's study follows learners who took an online course and describes a variety of feelings that they experienced before the course began. In response, Conrad offers a number of specific suggestions for effectively launching an academic course online.

Website of Interest

www.netnet.org/instructors/design/goalsobjectives/advance.htm. Creating and using advance organizers for distance learning. Tyler, TX: Northeast Texas Network Consortium Coordinating Office.

Provides step-by-step instructions for creating advance organizers and samples.

REFLECTION AND APPLICATION

To reflect on the material presented in this chapter and apply it in a real e-learning situation, consider how you would respond to the following challenges. (Each of these challenges is intentionally left vague. If you are unsure about a piece of infor- mation, make an assumption about it and list the assumption.)

- You are teaching an online course about information design. The term "in- formation design" has a number of meanings. To some, it means organizing and structuring content and presenting it in a way that is most usable to the intended reader. To others, it simply refers to the visual design of pages and screens. Your course approaches information design from the first perspective (organizing and structuring content). You are concerned that some learners will think that the course is primarily focused on the visual design of pages and screens, and those students will be disappointed by the course. What can you do to address these unrealistic expectations?

- You are preparing an asynchronous web-based course about new sales force automation software that your company will be using. Sales force automation software is used by organizations to help marketing representatives, current and past customers, and prospective customers. The system tracks past contact with, and orders by, customers and lets marketing representatives record personal information about customers (such as their birthdays) and keep in regular contact with them. This is the second contact management software that your company has installed. The first application was not successful; only 40 percent of the marketing representatives ever used it. The new software is much better than the old, and should be of value to marketing representatives because it will truly simplify the daunting task of keeping in touch with clients and prospects, without all kinds of annoying "computer stuff," as was the complaint with the first application. To ensure that the new software is successfully launched in the organization, the new director of sales thought that the course should open with a letter from him and include his photo at the top of the letter. What do you think? Do you think that this will be a useful way to start the course? Why or why not? If not, how would you begin this course?

- You are designing a course for a large bank that introduces new college graduates to personal finance for working adults. The course addresses such issues as paying off student loans, furnishing a first home, buying a first business wardrobe, saving for a first house, saving for retirement, and doing all of this without going into debt. Because of the voluntary nature of the course, it is intentionally brief. You hope to whet learners' appetite in the course, so that they'll continue learning afterward. What can you do to increase the likelihood that learners will continue the learning process?

Chapter 11

Exposition Techniques for Writing e-Learning Content

Facilitating learning through oral exposition and illustration does not need to violate the principles of adult learning.

Shirley J. Farrah, 1990

In This Chapter

In this chapter, we will

- Define the term *exposition techniques*

- Describe the role of exposition in transferring technical content to learners

- Describe the role of the lecture as an exposition technique

- Describe the economic, financial, and educational benefits of lectures as an exposition device

- Describe three challenges in exposing (writing) content

- Explain how to compose the following types of declarative content: definitions, procedures, examples, and analogies

- Describe an example that effectively presents content

◆ ◆ ◆

Carrie has been asked to develop an e-learning program about a new personnel policy for her state government. The new policy affects every state employee. The deputy secretary of human resources for the state plans to announce it in four weeks. The program that Carrie is developing tells managers how to apply the policy and explains how to handle the ten most common challenges in implementing it.

As Carrie considers the instructional strategy for this course, one of her co-workers suggests that she consider simulation training—placing learners in a work situation in which they must administer the policy—and use that situation to discover the basic issues about the policy. Although she likes the idea of rooting the instruction in real work situations, Carrie quickly realizes that she cannot develop a high-quality simulation; she has only four weeks to design, develop, and launch the entire learning program. Creating the simulation alone requires more than four weeks of effort. Carrie is also concerned that, if learners were to "discover" the policy, they might not discover the correct components of the policy. Because the governor expects that each manager in state government will implement each policy consistently, Carrie believes that managers must be exposed to the policy as written, as well as the same explanations of how to implement the policy.

As a result, Carrie decides to use the electronic equivalent of a lecture as her instructional strategy. The program opens with a brief video from the governor that explains the policy and why the state is implementing it. The program continues with material about the specific components of the policy that learners will read on-screen. The program closes with a series of scenarios. Each screen explores a different scenario. On each, Carrie asks managers how they might respond to the scenario. Learners type their response and, on the following screen, Carrie compares common responses with the actual policy.

In other words, Carrie opted for an electronic equivalent of the traditional lecture for presenting the learning material in her lesson. The process of presenting learning content is called *exposition*. The term comes from the field of composition and refers to the act of exposing ideas. Although the lecture—and its online equivalent, the page-turner—have horrible reputations among instructional designers, perhaps those reputations are worse than they should be. Lectures are among the most efficient and least expensive forms of instruction to develop, making them attractive to instructional designers on tight schedules or budgets, or both. Lectures also ensure a more consistent presentation of content than is feasible with other methods of exposition, ensuring that each learner is exposed to the content in a consistent way.

This chapter explores the lecture and other means of exposing learning content. Specifically, we describe what lectures and other types of exposition techniques are and the benefits of using these techniques. Next we describe some general exposition principles and then describe a number of specific exposition techniques, including techniques for presenting examples, analogies, procedures, definitions, and explanations. The chapter closes with an example of a course using effective exposition techniques.

What Are Exposition Techniques?

Exposition techniques complement instructional strategies. An *instructional strategy* is the plan for presenting the content to learners in a way that they can achieve the stated objectives. The instructional strategy addresses the way that designers plan to present the content itself as well as the way that they plan to reinforce it and provide practice and assessment opportunities to learners.

In contrast, *exposition techniques* solely focus on the way that instructional designers present the content itself to learners. It does not address other aspects of instruction, such as reinforcement, practice, and assessment.

Consider this issue in practical terms. An instructional designer might be presenting a unit on how to perform a particular surgical technique. The lesson might use an instructional strategy of mastery learning, in which learners continue practicing a skill until they master it (hence the name). A mastery lesson has many parts corresponding directly to Gagne's Nine Events of Instruction (1985). These events include an opening intended to gain learners' attention, followed by a description of the skill to be taught and the concepts underlying it. Next, learners see a demonstration of the skill, then have opportunities to practice the skill with increasing independence until they master it. Exposition techniques solely address one part of that mastery lesson: the part in which the skill to be taught and its underlying concepts are described. Instructional strategies generally address design at a higher level of focus; they do not address such specific issues.

In a case like this, several options for presenting the content exist. The designer can merely explain it in a series of paragraphs or as a step-by-step procedure. When presenting the related concepts, the designer may need to define some of them. For others, the designer may need to provide analogies to more common concepts to help learners more quickly grasp the ideas.

What Are the Challenges of Using Exposition Techniques?

Although popular educational thinking encourages designers to let learners discover many learning points for themselves, at some point learners need—and often seek—clear explanations of content from an instructor. For example, the concept of self-directed learning—crucial to informal learning online—assumes that learners will search out content of interest. But at some point, these learners must find lucid explanations of the content they seek to learn. If a learner wants to learn about the different investment choices available in a pension plan, for instance, at some point the learner needs to see clear explanations of what the choices are and the criteria for choosing among them.

A core task in exposition is the transfer of information. Sometimes, this is called *lecture,* because when this transfer happens, the instructor does most of the presenting and learners primarily absorb the content. According to Farrah (1990), the lecture involves facilitating learning through oral exposition and illustration.

In the circles of both academics and practicing professionals, the lecture has a poor reputation. In oral presentations (including ones in virtual classrooms), the lecture is often characterized as "spray and pray": "spray" as much content as possible at the learners and "pray" that some of it sticks. In asynchronous courses, in which learners often read endless screens of PowerPoint® presentations with little or no opportunity to interact, the lecture has the reputation of "Death by PowerPoint."

But perhaps the lecture has a far worse reputation than it deserves. The next several paragraphs present some of the benefits of the lecture, and the next section presents a portfolio of creative approaches to the online lecture.

Rather than thinking about all of the deficiencies with lectures as means of presenting learning content, consider, for a moment, all of the positive aspects of lectures. To start, think about some of the best instructors you have had. If yours are like ours, one of the qualities that make most of these instructors great is that they are excellent lecturers. When they lecture, these instructors speak in a way that holds your attention. They present the content entertainingly, clearly, and effectively. The lectures are interruptible—in fact, these instructors encourage learners to ask questions. When learners do so, these great instructors answer those questions completely.

In other words, lectures can be exciting learning experiences, if handled properly. Consider the additional benefits of lectures stated in Table 11.1.

Table 11.1. The Benefits of Lectures

Benefit	Explanation
Most accurate means of communicating content	According to some educational studies, the lecture is the most effective way of ensuring that content is communicated clearly (Arthur, Bennett, Edens, & Bell, 2003)
Most efficient way of communicating content	Although *discovery learning* techniques (ones in which learners find—or discover—key concepts on their own) often provide high learner involvement, learners often take a long time to reach the intended conclusions. Learners must go through the activity and a lengthy debriefing before the learning points are raised. In a lecture, learners get the information immediately, resulting in shorter lessons. In training courses and other time-constrained learning situations, time-to-learning-the-concept is one that designers must consider.
Most consistent way of presenting content	As one education professor noted, "The problem with learning by experience is that some learners don't." In other words, despite a strong design, some learners may not get the point, or the points that learners conclude may differ from one another and from the one that the instructional designer intended. For learners to get the point in the way that the instructional designer intended, the designer must explain it directly to the learners.
Allows for presentations by experts	One of the misconceptions about the transfer of information is that the transfer must always come from the instructor. In classroom courses, many instructors invite guest speakers who are experts in their fields to present content. Their experience and credibility add value to the learning experience. The same can happen online. For example, medical training courses offered by Medsn.com often include videotaped lectures or asynchronous "consults" by leading medical experts. These courses also incorporate primary source materials, such as journal articles and reports.
Learners know how to process lectures	Because learners are exposed to the lecture early and often—starting with primary school—they are "wired" to process lectures. Learners know how to record information from lectures by taking notes and clarify confusing issues by comparing notes with other learners or asking the instructor. In other words, processing content from a lecture is a metacognitive skill that learners already have.

Sometimes the challenge with lectures is not its effectiveness as a teaching form, but learners' familiarity with lectures. Because learners are exposed to so many lectures, learners can get bored with them, just as diners would |

Table 11.1. The Benefits of Lectures, Cont'd	
Benefit	**Explanation**
	become bored with meatloaf if they ate it every night for dinner. Similarly, because of the quantity of lectures they are exposed to, learners are exposed to numerous high-quality lectures, raising their impatience with poor ones.
Some lecture formats are popular	Among the most popular forms of learning over the past thirty years has been the audiotape—a one-way, recorded lecture (*Training* magazine annual industry surveys between 1985 and 1998). A similarly popular format is the book-on-tape (now book-on-CD), in which a narrator reads a book (sometimes the narrator is the author). Learners like these formats because they are portable (learners can take them anywhere) and let them use time like commuting time that would otherwise be wasted as more productive learning time.
Most efficient to design and develop	One of the reasons that instructional designers rely so heavily on the lecture is that it is the most efficient type of presentation to design and develop. For example, in asynchronous e-learning, conversion of a PowerPoint presentation to an electronic format can take between 50 and 150 hours of development effort for every one hour of finished instruction, while development of a fully interactive, highly graphic hour of instruction requires as much as 450 hours of development (Chapman, 2002).
Some of the easiest to use authoring tools support the development of lectures	Some of the newest and most popular authoring tools for creating asynchronous e-learning programs at the time this book was written are ones that convert PowerPoint presentations to e-learning programs. Basically, these tools transfer PowerPoint lectures online by adding a soundtrack of a recorded lecture and a few interactive elements and are intended to significantly reduce the average of 223 hours of development effort required on average for one finished hour of asynchronous e-learning (Chapman, 2002). The lecture is also popular in the live virtual classroom. Part of the issue is practical; because of technical constraints, most designers rely on PowerPoint slides to present content and, because some people have difficulty receiving presentations using voice over Internet protocol (that is, sound on the Internet), many instructors must rely on designs that only allow participants to communicate with them through text messages and polling questions.

A Portfolio of Exposition Techniques

In other words, lectures have many benefits for instructional designers. Because learning involves the transfer of knowledge, eventually all instructional designers turn to lectures, at least in part, to present content to learners. The challenge, therefore, is not avoiding the lecture; the challenge is in using the lecture effectively.

Addressing that challenge involves:

- *Effectively using the medium.* Although designers of e-learning programs lose some of the immediacy of the classroom when teaching online, they can compensate by taking advantage of opportunities online that designers would not have in the classroom, like the opportunity to show animations, simulate software (if appropriate), and, in live virtual classrooms, use polling questions and whiteboarding techniques.

- *Effectively communicating the content.* Communicating technical content, called technical communication, involves following conventions—or standard forms—in communication. By following these conventions, designers provide learners with the material in a well-understood format and can take advantage of research on how people work best within some of these forms.

The following sections explore these challenges and help you build a portfolio for lecturing online. The first sections explore ways to effectively use the online medium. The sections that follow explore how to present some of the most common forms of technical content: definitions, procedures, examples, and analogies.

Some Preliminary Issues to Consider

Before exploring these issues, however, consider, first, these general issues with lecturing online.

First, consider the length of the online lecture. In short doses, online lecture can effectively and efficiently transfer information. But a lecture that goes on too long fatigues learners. Overloaded with content, learners reach their saturation point and they tune it out. This situation is called *information overload* (Wurman, 1989). Lectures that go on too long give the online lecture a bad name.

To avoid overloading learners, designers of e-learning programs should limit the length of these lectures. Although no firm lengths exist as they do for video (the ideal instructional video is twelve to eighteen minutes long (Floyd, 1987)), some rules of thumb have emerged.

- According to a discussion of readers of *Online Learning E-News,* the preferred length of a live virtual class is thirty to ninety minutes. Within classes of that length, instructors should vary techniques frequently, and limit a "lecture" to twelve to eighteen minutes (the length of an instructional video).

- The ideal length of an asynchronous lesson is brief. Although the definition of brief varies among instructional designers, the consensus ranges from five to thirty minutes. This time includes time for exercises.

A second issue to consider applies specifically to asynchronous courses. According to some studies of reading patterns online, learners do not read lectures word-for-word. Instead, they skim. People typically read the headings at the top of the screen and the first line, then skim downward. People typically skim the first line of each paragraph and item on a bulleted or numbered list.

People read in depth when they encounter material of interest. In practical terms, that means that designers cannot trust learners to read online prose carefully. To address this problem, designers of online materials usually do the following:

- Limit the number of words on the screen. The fewer the number of words, the less burdensome reading appears to be and the more likely that learners will finish the text online.

- Design screens so that all material appears when the screen appears—and no material appears "below the fold" (that is, requires learners to scroll). In some instances, learners do not scroll. In cases when they do, the quality of reading decreases as the length of the screen increases.

Third, learner motivation matters. When learners feel an incentive to learn, and feel that they can do so online, they are more likely to finish the lecture material. According to some studies, certain subject matter works more effectively online, such as end-user training and training for technical certifications (such as training for Microsoft and Cisco certifications) (Barron, 2002). In other instances, access to unique sources, such as material by authorities in a field, raises motivation levels.

Strategies to Consider to Make the Most of the Online Medium

One of the challenges of designing online lectures is that, online, the lecture has morphed into different types of presentations, depending on the type of e-learning. The following sections explore some ways to use the unique features of the computer in online lectures—first in the live virtual classroom, then in an asynchronous e-course.

Presenting Lectures in the Live Virtual Classroom

In the live virtual classroom, the lecture resembles the traditional classroom lecture in many ways. This has happened partly because the live virtual class relies on a live instructor, who usually presents PowerPoint slides, as has become the norm in the traditional classroom.

But as mentioned earlier, instructors lose the immediacy of the traditional classroom online and, to effectively lecture online, must compensate. Consider these strategies for addressing the loss of immediacy:

- Because instructors cannot see learners' faces to determine how learners are responding to a lecture (not even with two-way video capability), instructors can use the polling features available with most live virtual classroom software to take interim assessments. At the end of a lesson, for example, an instructor might ask learners to rate their understanding. When doing so, consider using extreme measures on the scales of understanding—partly as a technique to gain attention and partly as a technique to help learners accurately assess their understanding. For example, you might use a scale like this:

    1 = Clueless

    2

    3 = I could probably follow a discussion

    4

    5 = I should be leading this discussion

- In addition to polling learners on their understanding of a topic, also poll them on the following issues:

    - Speed of the lecture (is it too fast, too slow, or just right)

    - Depth of the content (enough, too little, too much)

- If possible, integrate animations that are relevant to the content into the lecture. Less expensive to produce and less likely to cause system crashes than videos, these animations can be used to describe processes and demonstrate procedures. You can create simple animations in PowerPoint.

Chapter 9 explores in-depth the issues of planning for the live virtual classroom. Chapter 13 explores ways to incorporate visuals into a course.

Presenting Lectures in Asynchronous Courses

In asynchronous courses, lectures seem more like books or PowerPoint slide shows than lectures in the classroom. But effectively using the online medium helps enliven these presentations of content so that they do not appear to be monotonous.

Consider these strategies for communicating lecture material in asynchronous courses:

- When appropriate, direct learners to original source material (journal articles, magazine articles, and reports about the topic of the course). Although such material is often more "dense" than material written for presentation online, it has the authority of the original author and provides an authentic learning experience. Because the learning occurs from the original reference, it is called *reference-based learning*. In practical terms, many of these original sources are available in the portable data format (PDF), which learners usually print and read offline. Encouraging reading offline is an effective learning strategy because reading speeds are faster offline than on (Rubens and Krull, 1985). This technique is often used in academic courses, such as courses on instructional design that are taught online.

- In some instances, consider having both a written and an oral presentation (that is, have a narrator record a reading of the written material) of the learning content. When presenting materials to learners whose first language is something other than the language of instruction, having both written and oral presentations of content helps learners "get" the content, because it is *double-coded* (that is, it is sent through two sensory channels into the brain). This technique of recording the narration has been used in training for bank tellers and other customer service jobs that attract second-language speakers. When the majority of learners speak the same language as the one in which materials are written, such double-coding may not be necessary because learners can read through the material far more quickly than the narrator can do so aloud. As a result, learners are often far ahead of the narration in their reading. (If you must record the narration, give learners at the least the opportunity to turn it off.)

- Record a subject-matter expert who has excellent presentation skills. Access to such expertise motivates learners. Training on medical topics uses this technique; instructional designers often record lectures by leaders in the field whom learners might not otherwise have the opportunity to learn from.

One issue to consider when recording experts: try to avoid the *talking head,* in which the video sequence almost exclusively shows the expert talking (hence, the name). Such a technique is considered to be monotonous and is known to bore learners.

Table 11.2 summarizes lecture techniques for asynchronous courses.

Table 11.2. Lecture Techniques for Asynchronous Courses	
Situation	**Lecture Technique to Use**
To efficiently present concepts to learners	Text on screen that learners are expected to read
When learners have limited reading skills in the language of the course	Display the text on screen and also have a narrator read it, so learners can follow along
When learners need to see the original source of ideas (such as a key medical study or an announcement of a new policy)	Send learners to the original
To provide learners with in-course access to experts	Lecture (either video or voice-over audio), plus related visuals (such as PowerPoint slides)

Strategies to Consider When Presenting Content

Although using the medium effectively plays a crucial role in maintaining the interest of learners in lectures, effectively presenting content plays an even more crucial role. One of the reasons that learners have such difficulty following entire lectures is that they often have difficulty following the material that is presented.

One of the primary purposes of learning is the transfer of cognitive information. To do so, Farrah (1990) observes that an effective lecture should do one or more of the following:

- Present information in an organized way and in a relatively short time frame

- Identify, explain, and clarify difficult concepts, problems, and ideas

- Analyze a controversial issue

- Demonstrate relationships between previously learned and new information and among apparently dissimilar ideas
- Think aloud for learners (modeling thoughts)
- Challenge beliefs of learners

Designers make these things happen by presenting clear definitions, thorough procedures, and effective examples and analogies.

Presenting Clear Definitions

A definition provides a formal statement of the meaning of a term. The term may be a single word, such as the term, *learning,* or it may have several words, such as *constructivist learning theory.*

Because learners may not know terms used in the learning material or may work with different definitions of terms than the designer uses, defining terms clearly is one of the most fundamental issues that instructional designers face. If instructional designers do not define terms, learners work with an incomplete or incorrect base of knowledge and incorrectly learn the additional material. This is an especially serious problem in asynchronous courses, in which learners have limited access (at best) to instructional assistance and are not likely to have their incorrect understanding clarified.

Many subject-matter experts and some instructional designers advise against defining define basic terms. These people claim that providing basic definitions "insults" learners.

We feel differently—and we feel strongly about this. In many cases, learners do not know what a term means but would not admit it. For example, in research that Saul has conducted with training directors (Carliner, Groshens, Chapman, & Gery, 2004), only a third claimed to have a comfortable working knowledge of key terms used in our field, such as human performance technology, knowledge management, and learning content management systems. By defining terms, you not only provide a common base of knowledge to less experienced learners, but also address the issues of learners who may be working with incorrect or incomplete definitions.

When determining which terms to define, consider that the learning content must cover all objectives that begin with the phrase, "Define the term. . . ." But designers should also define those terms for which they anticipate that learners might have incorrect or incomplete definitions. These include terms that are less commonly used. Learners might have heard the term before but might not recall the definition. Also define terms that have several meanings within the context of the technical content so learners are aware of which definition you are referring to.

When writing definitions, consider the extent to which you plan to define a term. According to Pfeiffer (1999), three types of definitions exist:

- *In-text definition.* A parenthetical phrase that immediately follows the unfamiliar technical term and that sufficiently explains the term so that readers can comprehend the sentence. (A parenthetical phrase is a phrase inside of a sentence that is preceded and followed by commas, parentheses, or m-dashes (—).) Use when presenting terms that may be easily confused, or with terms introduced earlier that learners might have forgotten (for example, a term was mentioned briefly in Unit 1, and you use it again in Unit 6, but have not used it in the units in-between).

  Example: The *journal,* a record of all changes made to the database, . . .

- *Basic definition.* A one- or two-sentence definition. It may appear in the body of the text as well as in a list of terms called a glossary or dictionary. The glossary or dictionary entry might include all of the relevant definitions. In such instances, each definition is separately numbered. Use a basic definition within the body of the text when presenting significant terms, especially those covered by an objective. Use a basic definition in the glossary for all of those terms. Also prepare a basic definition when preparing glossary entries for each term defined with an in-text definition.

  Example of a Basic Definition in the Body of the Text: A *journal* is a record kept by the computer of all changes made to the database between the time the database is opened and the time it is closed.

  Example of a Basic Definition in a Glossary: Journal: (noun) a record kept by the computer of all changes made to the database between the time the database is opened and the time it is closed.

- *Expanded definition.* A one- to three-paragraph description of the term. It begins with a definition in the style of a glossary or dictionary entry and continues with additional explanatory information. The information may be visual (pictures) or verbal (words), and adds clarity to the brief definition. For example, an expanded definition of a car might include a line drawing of a car and the identification of its key components, such as a steering column and engine. Use an expanded definition when defining a term as part of fulfilling a broader instructional objective.

Example:

Journal: (noun) a record kept by the computer of all changes made to the database between the time the database is opened and the time it is closed.

If the system unexpectedly stops before you close the database file, the journal serves as a backup. The filename for a journal file is XXXXXXXX.jrn, where XXXXXXXX is the name of the database file that you were working on. The system automatically erases the journal when you close the database file. See also *backup.*

You might incorporate all three types of definitions into a learning program. You might include an in-text definition so learners can continue reading without looking up a term in the glossary entry, use the basic definition in the glossary itself, and use the expanded definition when you describe the concept in-depth.

Consider these suggestions for writing definitions:

- Do not include the term being defined, or a variation of the term, in its definition. For example, rather than saying a "a software application is software" you might say "a software application is a type of computer program. . . ."

- Provide an in-text definition for each term the first time learners encounter it. You do not need to repeat the definition in subsequent passages if you can assume that learners have completed the earlier passages. However, if you are designing an online course with several units, you might define a term the first time it is used in each unit, because you cannot assume that learners will have seen the previous units.

- For basic definition, follow this structured format:

  - Term, usually emphasized with bold type

  - Part of speech, telling users whether the term is a noun, verb, adjective, or adverb. This is especially useful information for terms that are familiar to users but are used in unfamiliar ways. Place the part of speech immediately after the term.

  - Definition: One or two sentences that explain the term. The definition need not be a full sentence; it can be a phrase.

  - References to similar terms (called "see also" references) and contrasting terms (called "contrast with" references). Highlight the expressions "see also" and "contrast with" in italic type. Make sure the additional terms are also in the glossary.

- For an expanded definition, include all of the components of a basic definition, as well as:

  - Expanded description (details that extend beyond the first two sentences)

  - Visuals that show what something looks like, especially a physical object

  - Examples that clarify abstract terms and terms that are similar to other terms

- Test the draft of a definition with a typical learner to make sure that it is clear.

Presenting Thorough Procedures

A procedure is a set of instructions for performing a task. The task can be *physical,* such as installing a modem, or *cognitive,* such as calculating the profit margin on a product. Procedures are among the best-known formats for presenting information. Procedures tell learners how:

- To do something, such as changing the oil filter in a car

- Various parts of a task relate to one another, such as how a bill passes through a legislature

- Something was done so learners can then verify what happened (For example, a researcher can review the procedures another researcher used to determine whether the analysis is valid.)

- Something will be done so learners can then make necessary plans (For example, a procedure might state the plan for an e-learning project. Reviewers can then determine when they must distribute review copies [or receive them for review] and plan their time accordingly.)

Do the following to write procedures:

1. First, state the goal of the procedure as succinctly as possible. For example:

   This procedure explains how to start your car.

   This procedure tells you how we conducted the study.

Often, a good heading will suffice, such as:

   Starting Your Car

   How We Conducted the Study

2. If readers need knowledge, supplies, or assistance to perform the procedure, next state that information in a Read Me First section, which precedes the procedure. Present supplies needed as a check-off list. The checkbox signals readers that they need to do something. For example:

> **Before starting the procedure, get these supplies:**
>
> ☐ Tape
>
> ☐ Scissors
>
> ☐ Construction paper

3. Explain only "must-know" terminology and concepts in a procedure. Learners use procedures to do something; this is not the time to present concepts and terminology underlying the procedure. That material belongs in another lesson.

For example, learners must know what a command is before they can use it. But they do not need to know how a computer processes the command. A procedure for learners, then, might define the term *command* but not explain the steps the system follows to process a command.

4. Mention "Who should perform the procedure." For example:

> **Who should perform the procedure?**
>
> ☐ Technical writers
>
> ☐ Technical editors
>
> ☐ Technical illustrators

5. Provide an estimate of the time needed to complete the procedure. Provide an estimate that is a little bit longer than the typical learner needs to complete the procedure. If learners complete the procedure in less time, they will feel a sense of success. (But if they complete the procedure in more time, they may feel a sense of failure.) Timed usability tests (pilots of the procedure) provide the best means of estimating the length of a procedure. By providing an estimate of the time needed, learners can plan to make sure that they have sufficient time when they perform the procedure in their work.

6. Then present the steps of the procedure. Consider these guidelines as you write a procedure:
    - Write procedures as numbered lists. That is, begin each step with a number. The number tells readers the sequence for performing the steps. For example:

1. Open the car door.

2. Sit behind the wheel.

3. Insert the ignition key.

4. Turn the key to start the engine.

- Because users can handle only a limited amount of information at any given time, limit the length to ten steps. If your procedure has more steps, break them into a "mini-procedure" within the larger procedure. Present mini-procedures in one of these ways:

  - As a separate procedure, with its own title. For example, suppose you are writing the procedure for solving problems with a computer, called a "problem determination guide." Few computer problems can be solved in ten steps. So you might present an initial procedure that helps readers identify the nature of the problem (such as a hardware or software problem), then have separate procedures for solving the different types of problems.

  - As a "procedure within a procedure." That is, you might write the mini-procedure as a series of steps within the larger procedure. When writing it, you indent the mini-procedure within the step of the main procedure. To distinguish the steps of the mini-procedure from those of the main procedure, begin each step of the mini-procedure with a letter. For example:

    1. Open the car door.

    2. Sit behind the steering wheel.

    3. Start the engine.

       a. Insert the key into the engine.

       b. Turn the key away from you.

       c. Wait for the engine to start. You will hear a noise.

    4. Begin to drive.

- Consider the following when writing the steps in a procedure:

  - Limit each step in a procedure to one task. If the step has several tasks, break the step into several steps or write a mini-procedure. Real-world experience indicates that users stop reading as soon as they encounter the first action to be performed in a step.

- Present conditional information as a clause at the beginning of a step; do not place it after the action. Learners usually stop reading as soon as they encounter the action and perform it. Placing the conditional information before the action is one way to make sure that learners see it. For example, if learners need to use both hands to hold a piece in place on an assembly line, say it at the beginning of the step, like this:

  Holding the piece with both hands, place the assembly in the drying machine.

  Do not write the clause like this:

  Place the assembly in the drying machine and hold it with both hands.

- Write each item on the list as a self-contained task. A task is an action that can be performed physically or cognitively. For tasks that learners are expected to perform, write in the imperative mood. That is, begin with an action verb and tell readers what to do. Research shows that learners read these types of directions faster than ones that do not begin with actions (Mirel, 1991). Examples of writing in the imperative mood include:

  Turn the power on.

  Subtract expenses from revenues.

- For procedures that learners are not expected to perform, include the agent (person who is expected to perform the task) for each action so learners know who or what is responsible for that task. For example:

  The Training Department will distribute the training plan by January 22.

  The Programming, Product Test, and Marketing departments must submit their review comments on the plan by January 29.

  Rather than:

  The training plan will be distributed by January 22.

  Review comments must be submitted by January 29.

  In this second version, readers do not know who is responsible for performing the steps. It's possible that they themselves are!

- When several people perform a procedure together, you need to state who performs each step and how responsibility passes among people performing the procedure. John Brockmann (1990) calls this a *playscript*. Following is an example of a playscript.

1. The technical writer writes the document.

2. The technical writer electronically transmits the document to the editor.

3. The technical editor:

   a. Prints the document.

   b. Identifies the passages that need to be illustrated.

   c. Completes an Art Request Form for each illustration needed.

   d. Submits the Art Request Forms to the technical illustrator.

- End a procedure by

  - Telling learners that they have finished the procedure. Consider writing, "You should now see the Program Manager of Windows with the New Program Icon on it. This is the end of Procedure," or "Your VCR should now be installed and ready for use."

  - Stating anticipated problems and how to address them. For example, you might say, "If the Program Manager appears but you cannot find the New Program Icon, then you should . . ." Note that you should describe anticipated problems (results that are incorrect, but likely to occur anyway from a minor mistake at the learners' end to a major foul-up) at the place where they would likely occur, so learners receive immediate feedback and can easily correct problems themselves.

  - Referring users to related procedures and other information of interest.

Here's an example of a procedure that readers are expected to perform:

To choose a task from the action bar without using a mouse:

1. Press F10.

2. Move the cursor to the task you would like to perform.

3. Press Enter.

Notice that each step begins with a number and is written as a command to the reader.

Here's a procedure that readers are not expected to perform:

1. Using the analysis of covariance test, Miller analyzed the data.

2. Miller presented the results to Richards and Defoore for verification.

3. Richards and Defoore certified the results.

Notice that each step begins with a number and that the agent for each step is identified (the agent is the person who performed the step).

Notice, too, that the conditional clause in step 1, "Using the analysis of covariance test," appears at the beginning of the step.

Also consider this example of what you should *not* do.

To choose a task from the action bar without using a mouse: the F10 should be pressed, then the cursor should be moved to the task to be performed. Once the cursor is there, the Enter key should be pressed.

Notice in this example that the procedure is presented as a paragraph and that the paragraph is written in passive voice. This tells learners what should be done, not what they should do.

Presenting Effective Examples

An *example* represents a concept being taught. It provides learners with a concrete representation of that concept.

Because they help learners make abstract concepts concrete, examples play a central role in all types of learning programs, especially online ones. The following sections describe the key uses of examples as a means of exposing learning material. Specifically, they cover how to use examples to help learners distinguish examples from non-examples, show learners a continuum of examples, help learners prepare for the near and far transfer of concepts in examples, demonstrate the proper techniques of performing tasks, and additional teaching issues to consider.

Help Learners Distinguish Examples from Non-Examples. As examples help learners recognize an instance of a concept when they see it, *non-examples* help learners distinguish the concept under study from instances of similar—although different—concepts. Non-examples possess many characteristics of the concept being taught, but either possess a significant additional characteristic or lack one or more key characteristics of the concept. For example, coffee table and kitchen table are examples of the concept table, because each has four legs and a smooth top. A desk is a non-example of a table. Although it has four legs and a smooth top, it also has drawers for storing materials and is therefore not a table.

Instructors can carefully sequence the presentation of examples in a lesson to make sure that learners distinguish examples from non-examples. Becker (1986) suggests the following specific sequence for presenting a series of examples so that learners can distinguish between examples and non-examples:

1. Present a non-example that is very different from the concept, one that learners can easily distinguish.

2. Present another non-example that is very close to the concept, but differs in one key detail.

3. Present an example that is similar to the second non-example presented, so learners can easily see the one key characteristic that differs among the two.

4. Present another example that differs substantially from the previous one so learners begin to see the breadth of instances covered by the concept.

5. Present a third example that differs from the other two examples presented to further demonstrate the breadth of instances covered by the concept.

This sequence is followed by a mix of six additional examples and non-examples. Based on what they learned in the first five examples, the instructor asks learners to identify whether each of the six is an example or non-example. This type of instruction works well online, because it is visual and offers an opportunity for interaction with learners.

Show Learners a Continuum of Examples. In addition to helping learners distinguish examples from non-examples, one of the purposes of presenting examples is helping learners see the range of instances or situations covered by a concept. To show this range, designers turn to *continuum-based examples.*

Continuum-based examples earn their name because they show examples across a range, such as worst to best, first to last, and one of the most common, simple to difficult.

For example, consider the examples of addition that ranges from simple to difficult, shown in Figure 11.1.

Figure 11.1. A Continuum of Examples

		44.2
2	98	3987.56
+ 3	+125	+ 894.50
Simple: Involves two single digits.	**Intermediate:** Involves two numbers with at least two digits each, plus "carrying" (8 + 5, 9 + 2).	**Complex:** Involves three numbers, each with additions and several places. Also involves "carrying."

Notice that in the presentation of examples and non-examples given earlier, the three examples of an instance are each expected to vary widely from one another. Many instructional designers use a continuum to choose examples.

Help Learners Prepare for the Near and Far Transfer of Concepts in Examples. A third purpose of examples is to help learners transfer the concepts to the real world. *Near transfer* refers to situations in which learners transfer the concepts to situations that are similar to the ones initially presented in the classroom. *Far transfer* refers to situations in which learners transfer the concepts to situations that differ substantially from ones initially presented in the classroom. Far transfer is considered to be more complex than near transfer, because learners must recognize the example in a situation that appears very different from those presented in the instructional materials.

One of the challenges of presenting examples of near and far transfer is making sure that learners can successfully recognize and understand cases of near transfer before presenting examples of far transfer, especially if you want to build to complexity one step at a time. One way to do so is to present examples of near transfer to learners first, and ask them whether or not each is an example. Ask learners to explain their answers to check for understanding. If learners answer correctly, move to the more complex example.

Ultimately, instructional designers hope to prepare learners for far transfer of concepts so that learners can make the widest—and most appropriate—use of the material learned. E-learning lends itself well to presenting examples of near and far transfer, because these examples provide opportunities for interaction in both live virtual classes and asynchronous learning programs.

Demonstrate the Proper Techniques of Performing Tasks. A fourth purpose of examples is to help learners develop proper technique for performing a task. Learners do so by observing an expert performing that task. Proper technique is especially important with psychomotor skills, like welding or inserting a needle, and highly structured cognitive skills, such as processing a standard insurance claims form or answering a call to a customer service center. Performing the task with improper technique could cause serious, and perhaps costly, problems.

Demonstrations provide an opportunity for learners to observe proper technique. Demonstrations are usually more involved than typical examples because, in addition to showing correct technique, the demonstration often includes a commentary on performing the task. For psychomotor skills, the commentary describes exactly how the task should be performed. For cognitive skills, the commentary describes the thinking process that learners should follow to successfully achieve the task. Both live virtual classes and asynchronous e-learning programs lend themselves well to presenting demonstrations. The audiovisual capabilities of the computer let instructional designers present the demonstrations through video, animation, or a sequence of computer screens (for demonstrations of software). Narration accompanies all of these types of demonstrations.

Additional Teaching Issues to Consider with Examples. Following are some additional issues to consider when using examples.

In addition to helping learners distinguish examples from non-examples, showing learners a continuum of examples, helping learners prepare for the near and far transfer of concepts in examples, and demonstrating the proper techniques of performing tasks, examples are a key element of several learning strategies. For example, designers structuring lessons according to Gagne's (1985) Nine Events of Instruction notice that presentation and demonstration are two important parts of presenting material to learners.

Similarly, examples play a key role in the debriefing of discovery learning exercises, such as simulations and case studies. The "lecture" in the debriefings places concrete labels on the concepts that learners encounter in the activity, and the examples help learners transfer learning from the discovery learning exercise to other environments.

Presenting Analogies

Closely related to the concept of examples is that of *analogies.* Like an example, an analogy helps make an abstract or unfamiliar concept concrete. Specifically, an analogy is a comparison that relates an unfamiliar concept to a familiar one and explains what the similarity is. An analogy can provide "a shortcut means of communication if it is used with care" (Brusaw, Alred, & Oliu, 1976, p. 37).

Learners often understand new information best when it is linked to something that they already know. Learners "attach" the new material to information already stored in memory. They easily store and retrieve the new information and, as a result, are more likely to retain and use the information.

Analogies are most effective when the comparisons are the relevant to learners. For example, to compare a new computer concept to an existing one might be useful to an audience of software engineers, but useless to a group of painters. The better you understand your learners, the more relevant your analogies.

According to Stepich and Newby (1990), you can use the formula shown in Figure 11.2 to create analogies.

Figure 11.2. A Formula for Creating Analogies			
SOMETHING NEW	IS LIKE	SOMETHING OLD	QUALIFIER
Subject	*Connector*	*Analog*	*Ground*
A live virtual class (LVC)	is like	a classroom course	in that both the instructor and learner are online at the same time

Note the *ground* in the formula. The ground explains how the two concepts are similar. The use of a ground distinguishes analogies in instructional materials from those in fiction, which merely state the comparison. As Newby and Stepich also suggest, you should use a visual to reinforce analogies when appropriate.

Table 11.3 shows examples of several analogies.

Table 11.3. Examples of Analogies	
Example of an Analogy	**Elements of That Example**
A computer file is like a file folder in that both hold information	subject = computer file analog = file folder ground = both hold information
A person's short-term memory is like a computer's random access memory in that it is an intermediate stop in the flow of information to long-term storage and has a limited capacity	subject = person's short-term memory analog = computer's random access memory ground = an intermediate stop . . .
A professional organization is like a trade guild in that it is an organization for people with similar job skills.	subject = professional organization analog = trade guild ground = organization for people with similar job skills
Webcasting is like television in that you see a picture and hear sound as it is being sent from the studio. But you receive the webcast on a PC rather than a TV and turn to a website rather than choosing a channel.	subject = webcasting analog = television ground = see a picture and hear sound

In Practice: Plimoth Plantation's "You Are the Historian"*

General Description of the Project

Title: You Are the Historian

(Learning program available at www.plimoth.org/olc./)

Publisher and Producer: Plimoth Plantation
Plymouth, Massachusetts
http://www.plimoth.org

Description:

Plimoth Plantation is a living history museum in Plymouth, Massachusetts, that presents the story of the interaction of the first English colonists (the Pilgrims) with the Wampanoag natives in 1620s New England.

When creating a website to supplement the museum, Plimoth Plantation included an online learning center that was intended to expose students and teachers in elementary and middle schools to the concepts underlying the historical story told by the museum.

Telling this story involves exposing substantial quantities of information. Instructional designers accomplish this by having learners experience life during that era—learners take an active role as an historian piecing through the evidence of life in 1621 and presented to them by a host of interactive activities and multimedia "testimonials." In each activity, the designers "expose" additional facts that website visitors piece together to uncover the story of the colonists and Wampanoags in the 1620s and the meaning of that interaction today.

See Figures 11.3 through 11.6 for sample screens from this program.

Intended Audience:

- *Primary:* Students (specific objectives are geared for grade 3 through 5 students in Massachusetts)

- *Secondary:* Teachers and parents of the students.

Size of Audience: Tens of thousands

About the Learning Goals

Primary and Secondary Goals of the Project: Support of traditional learning. Students use the resource center to increase their knowledge about the events

*This In Practice was prepared by Patrick Devey.

Figure 11.3. Introduction to the Guide-Interpreters, Shown in Twenty-First Century Clothing

Source: Plimoth Plantation Online Learning Center (www.plimoth.org/olc./)

surrounding the harvest, as well as to enhance their problem-solving and analytical skills. Specifically, the program had these learning goals:

- *Primary learning goal:* To make use of new evidence to educate students and teachers about the origins and the evolution of the Thanksgiving holiday.

- *Secondary learning goal:* To demonstrate the enduring effects of the relationship developed between the first settlers and the Wampanoag people in the seventeenth century on people living in the twenty-first century.

Figure 11.4. Example of a Screen Where Learners Can Investigate the English Immigrants

Source: Plimoth Plantation Online Learning Center (www.plimoth.org/olc./)

Primary Learning Objectives: Designed to meet standards for third-grade through fifth-grade social studies courses in the Commonwealth of Massachusetts and the United States.

- Students will understand how historians use multiple primary sources and educated guesswork to research the past and create history.

- Students will understand how the Wampanoag and the English colonists of 1621 represented distinct cultures with their own points of view.

Figure 11.5. Example of a Screen Where Learners Can Investigate the Wampanoag People

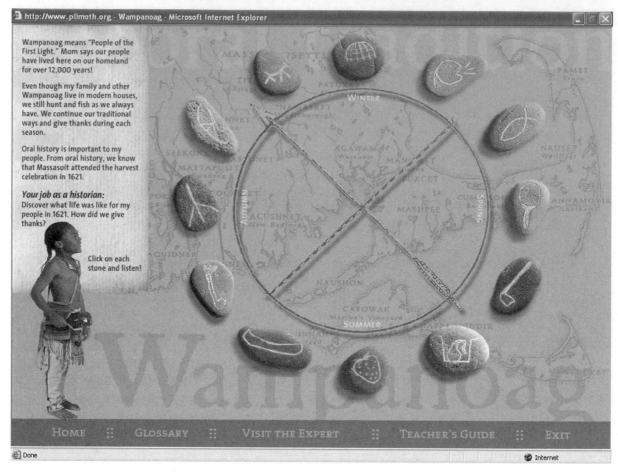

Source: Plimoth Plantation Online Learning Center (www.plimoth.org/olc./)

- Students will understand how the seventeenth-century English colonists and the Wampanoag may have interacted during the harvest celebration of 1621.

- Students will understand how to respectfully celebrate the Thanksgiving holiday.

Learning Issues Underlying the Project

- Finding a way to bring the rich, authentic, personal experience online that one gets when visiting the facilities, but at the same time, not substituting for it either.

Figure 11.6. Example of a Personalized Page in Which Learners Demonstrate Their Learning by Creating an Online Exhibit of Their Own

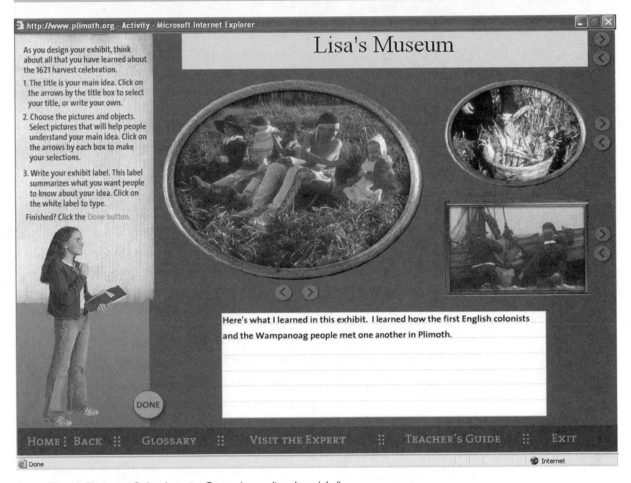

Source: Plimoth Plantation Online Learning Center (www.plimoth.org/olc./)

- Making the website fun and engaging, all the while remaining educational for the students who visit it.

- Making the website appealing to both the target users (the students), as well as to the target customers (the teachers).

The Numbers

Schedule (from Beginning to End of the Project): Eighteen months

Approximate Number of People Who Worked on the Project: Thirty, although most worked on a part-time basis.

Skills Used on the Project:

Instructional design

writing

programming

graphic design

usability engineering

editing

audio engineering

video production

video direction

photography

acting

Other Issues Affecting the Project: Although limitations in bandwidth were considered a possible obstacle for learners (especially those who would participate using dial-up connections from home), the team decided to go with a rich (high bandwidth) multimedia experience anyway because:

- By the time the project would be completed, the minimum computer configurations at the students' homes could have improved.

- Many of the students would be completing these activities at school, where the high-speed computer labs are available.

Technology Infrastructure

Delivery Medium: Internet.

Media Used Within the Learning Program: Text

graphics

animation

audio

video

photographs

Delivery Platform: Web browser

Primary Authoring Environment: Macromedia Flash®

Supporting Software: Image editing, sound editing, and video editing software.

Results

How Did You Achieve the Learning Objectives?

- Guided by a curriculum design tool called Teaching for Understanding (TfU). This technique makes use of the introductory, guided inquiry, and culminating performance stages to help learners ultimately achieve the understanding of the goals established by the instructional design team.

- Inspired by goal-based and scenario-based learning, the designers decided to mold the online learning center into a problem-solving experience in which the visitor is put into the shoes of a historian trying to solve the mystery of "What really happened in 1621."

- To connect with the primary audience, the program uses two children as the main characters of the site. These main characters serve as guide-interpreters throughout the visit to the site. The two guide-interpreters first appear in modern-day clothes (as guides) and then "transform" into 1621-era attire to become interpreters.

- Motivated by the success of movies like *Spy Kids* and the Harry Potter series, the designers decided to include hidden information, surprises, and rewards throughout the website to keep learners engaged and, according to site designer Lisa Neal, "promote a sense of mystery."

- Recognizing the knowledge and skills of the staff at Plimoth Plantation, the designers incorporated this expertise in segments called "visit the expert." These segments include audio clips (with transcript for students who may not be able to hear) in which these experts offer interesting tidbits and other information about the topic off the screen. Some of the narration is in authentic accents.

- Concerned about captivating and interacting with the learners and maintaining their attention (and making the experience as realistic as possible), the designers made extensive use of multimedia such as graphics, audio, and animation.

- To assess learning, the designers opted for a culminating activity in which learners demonstrated their understanding of the material by creating their own online museum exhibit. They decided against assessing learners with multiple-choice and similar objective questions because that type of assessment is inconsistent with their goal and scenario-based approach to learning.

How Did You Market the Course?

- Direct link to the Online Learning Centre on Plimoth Plantation's website

- Word of mouth

- Publicity at the museum

What Were the Results of the Course?

- In terms of reception, the response has been overwhelmingly positive.

- The designers received very positive feedback from the teachers, parents, librarians, and especially the learners.

- The site has received several awards, including the Massachusetts Interactive Media Council (MIMC/MITX) 2003 award for best education site, and it has also been voted Site of the Day (Macromedia) and Site of the Week (Blue Web'N).

What Would You Do the Same on a Future e-Learning Project?

- Complete a competitive analysis, perform formative and heuristic evaluations, as well as extensive usability testing.

- Conduct a formative evaluation. In our case, we tested the website with one hundred children and teachers. As a result of their responses, we made significant changes to the website. Although the initial reaction was positive, both students and teachers wanted to see more audio, which was appreciated by students who are not strong readers. Students and teachers also wanted more activities and an enhanced role for the guide-interpreter children, whom the students identified with.

- In addition to the increased audio and an increased presence of the "guides," the revision to the designs included more interactive activities and less text. The heuristic evaluation, and subsequent usability testing, resulted in an added attempt to personalize the experience for the learner by using personal stories. They also included pictures of the guides in more active poses, which the students could better relate to.

What Would You Do Differently?

- Hire a smaller team of individuals to work on the project, and hire them on a full-time basis.

- Establish an online community to give children a chance to share their experiences (and projects) with others.

- Establish online communities for teachers to share best practices and experiences regarding the way they incorporated this material into their classrooms.

Conclusion

One of the key components of any e-learning course is clear explanations of the learning content. This often happens during an information exchange, which may serve as the centerpiece of the lesson or as a debriefing of a learning activity. Regardless of how the exchange occurs, the more effective the presentation—or exposition—of the content, the more likely that learners will "get" the material in the manner intended by the instructional designer. To reach this conclusion, this chapter explored the following points:

- Exposition refers to the means of presenting content to learners.

- Because a key purpose of learning programs is to transfer technical content to learners and because learners do not always accurately or completely learn this content from experiential learning activities, the presentation of content plays an essential part of the learning process.

- The lecture is the traditional means of transferring content in learning programs. The lecture takes a variety of forms in e-learning programs:

  - In live virtual classes, the lecture often takes the form of an instructor narrating a presentation of PowerPoint slides. A lecture in a live virtual class might also take the form of a videotape of an expert.

  - In asynchronous learning programs, the lecture often takes the form of a sequence of slides that learners are intended to read in their entirety. But lectures might also take the form of recorded sequences of narration, either by an anonymous narrator or a subject-matter expert, who might be narrating a script that also appears online. In addition, an online lecture might also take the form of a reading from an original source, such as an article from a scientific or management journal.

- Although much maligned in popular writing about education, the lecture continues to offer many benefits as an exposition technique. These include the following:
  - Most accurate means of communicating content
  - Most efficient way of communicating content
  - Most consistent way of presenting content
  - Allows for presentations by experts
  - Learners know how to process lectures
  - Some lecture formats are popular
  - Most efficient to design and develop
  - Some of the easiest to use authoring tools support the development of lectures
- A portfolio of exposition techniques includes these considerations:
  - Limiting the amount of information to a manageable quantity (so limit the length of a live virtual session and the number of screens in an asynchronous lesson)
  - Using imaginative presentations, such as animations and stories, to maintain the interest of learners
  - In asynchronous learning programs, taking advantage of an Internet connection to direct learners to original sources and address the reduced reading speed and accuracy of online readers
- One of the most significant challenges of exposition is choosing the appropriate format for exposing content. Some of the most common formats for learning materials include:
  - Definitions, which provide formal and agreed-on meanings to terms. Definitions can take three forms: in-sentence, basic, and expanded.
  - Procedures, which describe a sequence of tasks or actions. A procedure has three main parts: a beginning that describes the purpose of the procedure, its length, and important advance warnings; the procedure itself, which presents material as numbered steps; and a closing, which describes the intended results and how to respond to common errors, variations in the procedure, and links learners to related procedures.

- Examples, which help learners see concrete applications of abstract concepts, apply the concepts broadly and distinguish from similar concepts.

- Analogies, which help learners attach new concepts to existing knowledge by making a comparison between the new concept and the known one.

Learn More About It

Foshay, W.R., Silber, K.H., & Stelnicki, M. (2003). *Writing training materials that work: How to train anyone to do anything.* San Francisco: Pfeiffer.

Explains how to write specific types of training material.

Price, J., & Price, L. (2002). *Hot text: Web writing that works.* Indianapolis, IN: New Riders.

Explains how to write material for the Web. Presents both general principles and guidelines for writing specific types of content.

Strunk, W., White, E.B., & Osgood, C. (1999). *The elements of style* (4th ed.). New York: Macmillan.

Known in communication circles as the little book with big ideas on how to communicate ideas effectively. It primarily does so by identifying problems with usage (that is, problems with using terms effectively).

Williams, J. (2002). *Style: Ten lessons in clarity and grace* (7th ed.). Reading, MA: Longman.

An interactive book that first presents principles of writing clearly and gracefully, then gives readers an opportunity to revise dense, poorly written prose.

REFLECTION AND APPLICATION

To reflect on the material presented in this chapter and apply it in a real e-learning situation, consider how you would respond to the following challenges. (Each of these challenges is intentionally left vague. If you are unsure about a piece of information, make an assumption about it and list the assumption.)

- You are designing a course for a pharmaceutical company about a new drug; the course is intended for doctors who might prescribe this drug. The drug is based on advanced gene research and, according to public news reports, represents a "quantum leap forward in care" for this particular disease. In developing the drug, the company worked with Dr. Yvonne Chang, the leading expert in this subspecialty of gene research. As part of her research contract, she is expected to lecture about the research underlying the product. Your boss has given you three challenges when designing this course: (1) It must be ready within twenty-five working days; (2) doctors must view the course as credible; and (3) you have been given five days of services from the corporate video team. How would you present the material about the new drug?

- You are working in the sales training department for the same company that is producing the new drug. On the day that the new drug is announced, your company is planning a major sales presentation that includes presentations by the CEO, chief medical officer, regulatory compliance officer, and live testimonials from five participants who participated in the trials. Your course is supposed to cover what the product is, regulatory issues related to the product, use in clinical situations, and how patients have responded to the drug. The course must be ready for download two weeks after the announcement. The program cannot exceed forty minutes, but you receive a bonus if the course does not exceed thirty. How will you leverage existing content in a lecture format to meet these objectives?

- You have been asked to develop the overview course for a new manufacturing process. Before people can learn about their particular roles in the process, they must demonstrate an understanding of the general manufacturing process, because—in addition to their primary task—each worker will be cross-trained to perform at least three other tasks in the manufacturing process. The course on the general manufacturing process will be taught through an asynchronous e-learning program. How would you present the information about the manufacturing process? For example, what approach would you take to present the process? What can you do to enhance the specific presentation of that content?

Chapter 12

Interaction

Telling is not teaching: listening is not learning.

Anonymous

In This Chapter

In this chapter we will

- Define the three kinds of interaction in Moore's model
- Explain the value of interactivity in learning
- Evaluate the benefits and limitations of using interactions
- Discuss the difference and similarities among: learning through computers, learning from computers; and learning with computers
- Provide several examples of interactions

A common experience of veteran e-learning program producers is having a client or sponsor stress the need for interactivity. What is so challenging about this is that *interactivity means different things to different people.*

Interactivity takes on distinctive meanings in different contexts. Interactivity is found in computer games, e-commerce sites, user-interface designs, online media, and education. Clients have experienced interactivity that set their expectations and definitions. Consider the following experiences: interacting with MapQuest to get driving directions, interacting with the *Wall Street Journal* Interactive Edition to tailor the presentation of news, and interacting with La-Z-Boy's online design studio to design a room. And those clients who grew up with GameBoy and PlayStation may be more familiar with the interactions of games such as *Grand Theft Auto*® and *Medal of Honor*®.

Table 12.1 lists a number of websites with different types of interactivity.

Table 12.1. Examples of Web-Based Resources with Strong Interactivity

Context	Example
e-Commerce	La Z Boy www.lazboy.com/ The Design Center link offers an interactive application for placing furniture in a room and arranging it.
Reference	MapQuest www.mapquest.com Offers driving directions with maps that allow the user to zoom in and zoom out for detail.
Media	*Wall Street Journal* Online http://online.wsj.com/public/us *The Wall Street Journal* Online allows readers personalization of news. Readers have access to content 24/7 that is tailored their individual needs.
Entertainment	MTV www.mtv.com Use the site search engine to find interactive games, entertainment, skits, and program schedule.
Games	EverQuest http://everquest.station.sony.com/ Try this 3D role-playing game. Prepare to enter an enormous virtual environment—an entire world with its own diverse species, economic systems, alliances, and politics.
Database	The Internet Movie http://imdb.com/ This is an interactive movie database that lets users search for local show times, read reviews, search for old movies, find names of movie characters and the stars who played them, and search for movies by type.
Banking	Bank of America www.bankofamerica.com/ The nature of online banking is interactive. BoA offers interactive personal banking that includes checking balances, paying bills, applying for a loan, working with mortgage calculators, and tracking investments. Explore their tools and calculators.

These experiences create challenges for instructional designers because they muddy the definition and establish expectations regarding interactions that may not have direct transference to interactive online learning.

So when you encounter a request for interactivity, stop and ask what the client means. Be specific; ask your client or sponsor for some examples of interactivity so that you have a solid gasp of how he or she is using the term and what he or she is expecting in an e-learning program. What you may soon discover is that interactivity, like beauty, is in the eye of the beholder. Some people will tell you interactivity is having students do things such as click, mouse-over, or select a radio button; others will tell you that it involves students working together or feedback from the instructor-to the student. Based on one of the many definitions of interactivity and interaction, each of these examples is technically correct.

What Is Interaction?

According to Gilbert and Moore (1998), an accepted definition of interactivity in the literature on computer-mediated instruction is a reciprocal exchange between the technology and the learner, a process they refer to as "feedback." This reciprocal exchange can be categorized into three kinds of interactions:

- *Learner-content interaction* refers to the interaction between the learner and the content being studied. The action in this type of interaction results from the learners having conversations with themselves regarding the content. The material being studied triggers an internal dialog. Thus, learner-content interaction occurs when the learner reflects on the content and questions the material in order to analyze, synthesize, and evaluate it.

- *Learner-instructor interaction* refers to interaction in which the learner and the instructor have exchanges in which the instructor seeks to stimulate interest, clarify questions, guide, motivate, and dialog with the learner. This kind of interaction can take place in a class or in a one-on-one setting. The key difference between this and the learner-content interaction is that the instructor can give feedback on the application of new knowledge and assess the learner's understanding of the material.

- *Learner-learner interaction* refers to the interaction among students. Given the range of technology options available, learners can experience this type of interaction in real time or asynchronously—as part of a threaded discussion or in an exchange of e-mail; with an instructor present or not present; and one-on-one or one-to-many.

This model of interaction has its critics. It has been argued that there is a difference between "interaction" and "interactivity" (Wagner, 1994). Wagner points out *"interaction* is an interplay and exchange in which individuals and groups influence each other" (1994, p. 20). She argues that because interaction requires a reciprocal exchange it is only possible to have this kind of relationship between people, that is, learner(s)-learner(s), and learner(s)-instructor. In contrast, Wagner observes that "interactivity" seems to have emerged from "descriptions of technological capability for establishing connections from point-to-point . . . in real time" (p. 20). Thus, interaction focuses on people's behaviors, while interactivity focuses on characteristics of the technology systems.

Collins and Berge (1996) suggest there are two kinds of interaction in learning, the student individually interacting with content and the student engaged in social interaction about the content with others. In their view, "Interacting with content means actively processing and combining this content with prior knowledge."

Terry Anderson (2003), a professor and Canada Research Chair in Distance Education at Athabasca University, has developed a theory called the Equivalency of Interaction. His theory sidelines this debate by suggesting that:

> Deep and meaningful formal learning is supported as long as one of the three forms of interaction (student–teacher; student-student; student-content) is at a high level. The other two may be offered at minimal levels, or even eliminated, without degrading the educational experience. High levels of more than one of these three modes will likely provide a more satisfying educational experience, though these experiences may not be as cost or time effective as less interactive learning sequences.
>
> This theorem implies that an instructional designer can substitute one type of interaction for one of the others (at the same level) with little loss in educational effectiveness—thus the label of an equivalency theory [Anderson, 2003].

Why Use Interaction?

Interaction is a vital part of the learning process (Tu, 2000), and the level of interaction has an impact on the quality of the learning experience (Navarro & Shoemaker, 2000; Vrasidas & McIsaac, 1999).

Instructional designers should make learners active participants, not passive spectators in the process. Active learning has been described as "providing opportunities for students to meaningfully talk and listen, write, read, and reflect on content, ideas, issues, and concerns" (Meyers & Jones, 1993, p. 6). This is not a small mandate. Interaction shifts the instructional focus from the facilitator and materials to the learner, who must actively engage with peers, materials, and the instructor.

A review of the literature reveals other reasons for using interactions. It has been shown that higher levels of interaction are associated with improved achievement (Gokhale, 1995; Kekkonen-Moneta & Moneta, 2002) and positive learning attitudes (Althaus, 1997; Fulford & Zhang, 1993).

Before we leave readers with the impression that interaction is a silver bullet for online learning, we must discuss the flip side of interaction. Interaction requires that students bring metacognitive skill to the task of learning. Many adult learners are accomplished in the role of passive learning, but the role of active learning is foreign and uncomfortable territory. There is also the issue of motivation. Simply designing interactions does not ensure learners will engage in discussions, read, write, or reflect on the content.

The Benefits and Limitations of Interactions

Understanding the benefits and limitations of educational interactions is essential for educators who are advising clients and developing programs. When client have so many definitions and ideas of interactivity, being able to assess the value of using interaction is an essential skill. As Roderick Sims (1997) points out, understanding "interactivity is the one element which can distinguish what we produce as educational technologists [and instructional designers] from what other developers' of-so called interactive products produce" (p. 159).

The Benefits of Interactions

The value of using interactions depends on your instructional goals, audience, and budget. As discussed earlier, interactions are essential to the learning process and can lead to increased learner satisfaction when used well. This section reviews the benefits of adding interaction to your program.

Motivation

Interactions have a great deal of impact on learner motivation and learner success. In e-learning, as in any distance education, attrition can be high, so strategies need to be used that encourage completion. Research has shown that learner-instructor interaction is perceived as being most highly valued by students (Fredericksen, Pickett, Shea, Pelz, & Swan, 2000).

Gaining Attention

A well-known component of many instructional design models is the need to gain and keep the learners' attention.

Practice and Increased Retention

Interactions provide the learner with an opportunity to practice new skills in a safe and structured environment. The value of interaction is that it prompts learners to retrieve information from memory, and it's this retrieval practice that prompts the learning improvements (Bjork, 1988).

Promoting Reflection

Many of the learner-to-learner and learner-to-instructor interactions promote reflections. Opportunities for learners to express their own points of view, explain the issues in their own words, and formulate opposing or different arguments have always been related to deep-level learning and the development of critical thinking (Mason, 1994).

The Limitations of Interactions

Interactions are not a silver bullet for e-learning. The following section summarizes the limitations.

Not as Fast as Direct Instruction

Engaging in meaningful interaction with other learners and the instructor takes time. If the goal of moving instruction to the Internet is to reduce the time it takes to complete training, interactivity may not deliver. Waiting for reciprocal exchanges with peers and the instructor may mean the dialog takes days or weeks to evolve. Of course, interacting with materials is still a viable option.

Time-Intensive

Those who teach in higher education have demonstrated that online courses with high levels of interaction take more time to teach than traditional classes do. Interacting with students is a critical part of the learning process and has been shown to increase student satisfaction. The challenge of delivering learner-instructor interaction is that instructors must write content-laden, responsive messages tailored to the learner (Graves, 2001; Newman & Scurry, 2001). This kind of written interaction takes longer than verbal interaction provided in the traditional classroom. Students and instructors also find learner-learner interaction time-consuming. These peer-to-peer experiences require effort from learners and instructors to monitor threaded discussions, post responses, and referee group work.

Does Not Scale

Due to time demands, learner-learner and learner-instructor interactions do not scale well. That is, what works well for a small group does not work as well when the group is large. The instructor is over-stretched to respond to a large number of students, and the process for keeping the dialog running becomes more challenging. Students are also at a disadvantage because large classes require students to spend more time reading and responding to threaded discussions.

Unrealistic Expectations Regarding Level of Interaction

It is not unusual for instructional designers to mandate the number of postings a week or to assign group projects in an effort to up the level of interaction. In some cases, the design of the course reflects an unrealistic expectation regarding the time learners have to engage. Instructional designers should consider whether the level of interaction is reasonable when comparable to a traditional classroom program. If a topic would not have supported a spirited in-class discussion, it seems unreasonable to expect the topic to be highly interactive on the Web. There is also no substitute for a good audience analysis. How much interaction is reasonable if the learners are taking e-learning because of demanding work schedules or personal lives? What are reasonable expectations regarding participation in threaded discussions? Do group projects that depend on other learners create undue burdens?

Costly to Develop

The disadvantages we have looked at so far have focused on learner-learner and learner-instructor. These are relatively inexpensive to develop because they rely on existing infrastructure such as e-mail and threaded discussion. The third kind of interaction, learner-content, can be costly to develop. We encourage you to try as many of the learner-content interactions as possible. Even the ones that do not appear to have high production values are deceiving in the amount of effort required to design, test, and write.

A Portfolio of Strategies for Interacting with Learners

This portfolio of strategies is organized differently than previous sections. When we set out to write this book we wanted to create a book for instructional designers that would be the equivalent to the books near the cash registers at Home Depot or Lowe's. We wanted to create an idea book like the books with the glossy examples of kitchens and bathrooms. Like those books, we have devoted chapters to specific areas such as simulations, m-learning, live virtual classrooms, e-coaching and e-mentoring. This chapter is more like the home decorating book for selecting color and using lighting. Like the topics of color and light, interactions are not limited to single rooms or areas of instruction. And like color and lighting that are used in all rooms, interactions are widely used in online instruction. Because of the pervasive nature of interactions, we want to talk about interactions both in the context of specific strategies such as simulations and look at interactions as individual elements such as team spaces and visualization software.

To organize this section, we are relying on concepts of interactivity derived from Yacci (2000) and Jonassen and Reeves (1996). This framework suggests there are three ways learners interact with computers. Learners can

1. Learn through computers

2. Learn from computers

3. Learn with computers

The section opens with a review of how students learn *through* computers, that is, how students use computers to get information, and from that information they learn. The second strategy, learning *from* computers takes a brief look how learners use the computer as a tutor or guide. We won't spend much time on the computer as a tutor or guide because the topic is well addressed elsewhere in the book. Finally we will look at how student learn *with* computers. Jonassen, Carr, and Hsiu-Ping (1998) refer to strategies for learning with computers as mindtools. Mindtools such as calculators, team spaces, and modeling offer many possibilities for constructivist learning. Table 12.2 provides an overview of how these categories differ and the strategies associated with each.

Strategies for Learning *Through* Computers

The first groups of strategies are related to learning that takes place when computers are used as communication devices or as a means of providing information. These interactions are learner-directed. Let's be very clear here . . . one can learn without a teacher, and that is what learning though computers is all about. The learning is interacting with raw information and content. In this case, the content has not been organized, chunked, or sequenced by an educator. (In learner-content interactions, the assumption is that the content has been chosen, ordered, designed, or has in some way benefited from the attention of an educator.)

Table 12.2. Comparison of Interaction Categories			
	Learning *Through* Computers	**Learning *from* Computers**	**Learning *with* Computers (Mindtools)**
Role of computer	Provides information and communication	Acts a guide, tutor, and teacher	Mindtools helping learners interpret and organize their personal knowledge
Primary philosophy	Humanistic; self-directed learning projects	Behaviorism	Constructivist
Instructional designer's role	None	Create materials	Coordinator, facilitator, resource advisor, coach
Unit of learning	Individual	Individual	Individual or group
Time for learning	At the learner's discretion	Any time, anywhere; learner sets pace	The learner is part of a group; the pace is regulated and dependent on peers and instructor
Assessment of success	Defined by learner	Defined by program developers	Defined by learner
Interactions	Learner-materials	Learner-materials	Learner-materials; learner-learner; learner-instructor
Interactions/ Strategies/Tactics	Reading e-books Visiting news sites Using databases Taking virtual tours Interacting with experts	Self-paced instruction Simulations • Attitudinal simulations • Case study • Game-based simulations • Physical simulations • Process (step) simulations • Role play • Software simulation • Symbolic (invisible) simulations • Virtual reality • Recorded LVC program	Mindtools include: • Agents (intelligent agents) • Blogs • Calculators • Concept mapping • Digital cameras • Databases • Expertise locators • Instant messaging • Modeling tools • Organizers • Presentation tools • Productivity applications • Surveys • Team spaces • Threaded discussions • Visualization

Learning through computers spans the entire range of Bloom's taxonomy (1956) from simple knowledge to sophisticated evaluation. Table 12.3 shows a range of sample resources such as the *CIA World Fact Book* that answers simple questions such as "What is the life expectancy of adults in Chile?" or the sites like breastcancer.org that provide the information needed to analyze, synthesize, and evaluate treatment options.

Learning through computers is about using content and information without a facilitator. Resources include articles, databases, virtual tours, e-books, and reference sites. The prevalence of this mode of learning is highlighted by a Pew Foundation (2001) study on Internet usage. The report found that both adults and teens use the Internet to teach themselves new things or to satisfy their curiosity about a subject. What may be surprising is how much self-directed learning is taking place. The study found that 80 percent of all Internet users have done an Internet search to find the answer to a specific question. A more telling statistic is that 16 percent of adult Internet users go online in a typical day to get an answer to a question.

Although we have included "learning through computers" in this chapter, it is not a strategy for which educators design programs. By the very nature of this strategy, it is self-directed learning and managed by the learner. This kind of strategy is best aligned with the definition of self-directed learning (Candy, 1991) that stresses learning projects organized, executed, and evaluated by learners without the assistance of a facilitator.

Strategies for Learning *from* Computers

The second group of strategies is related to using the computer as the primary guide, tutor, teacher, or facilitator. Within this category there may be dialog with the instructor and other students, but the majority of the lesson's structure and feedback are delivered via the computer. Strategies that fit in this category are focused on learner-content interactions. In these programs, learners generally work alone, work at their own pace, and work toward mastery of predefined skills and knowledge. The goal of these programs is to enable students to learn 24/7 and speed the process of learning by allowing students to opt out of material they have mastered.

The most common philosophy of design with this strategy group is behaviorism. These programs are best for teaching lower-level skills such as knowledge (such as define, order, name, recall, state, and list), comprehension (such as classify, describe, report, select, and discuss), and application (such as demonstrate, solve, use, write, and apply).

Strategies in this category rely on instructional designers and developers to spend significant time defining what is to be learned and then sequencing, chunking, and

Table 12.3. Sites Demonstrating Learning *Through* the Computer

Site	Description
Center for Disease Control www.cdc.gov/cancer/	The Center for Disease Control (CDC) is recognized as the lead federal agency for protecting the health and safety of people—at home and abroad. It provides credible information to enhance health decisions and to promote health. Within the CDC site is the Cancer Prevention and Control site; it is an example of a site visited by people who want to learn about cancer treatment, survival rates, and drug trials.
Smithsonian www.si.edu/	The Smithsonian is an information-rich site providing self-directed learners a multimedia resource needed to learn about things ranging from African-American culture to zoology.
CNN.com www.cnn.com/	News sites with archives are important resources for self-directed learners. The CNN site allows learners to search for relevant new articles and older articles from its database. This site makes it possible to follow topics like terrorism or the outsourcing of jobs back for two or three years.
CIA World Fact Book www.cia.gov/cia/ publications/factbook/	The *CIA World Fact Book* is an outstanding example of a well-organized e-book featuring navigation that is intuitive. Learners can quickly find answers to their questions about any country in the world.
U.S. Capital Virtual Tour of the Library of Congress http://lcweb.loc.gov/jefftour/	This highly interactive site allows learners to read about the building and to navigate using cutaways, text, and images.
Databases The EServer http://www.eserver.org	This is a community of writers, artists, editors, and scholars who gather to publish and discuss their works
Breastcancer.org www.breastcancer.org/	BreastCancer.org is a nonprofit organization dedicated to providing reliable, complete, and up-to-date information about breast cancer. Their mission is to make sense of the complex medical and personal information about breast cancer, so that readers can make the best decisions for their lives.
Home Depot www.homedepot.com/	Home Depot provides customers with a Know-How center that provides garden advice, plant finders, calculators, and access to gardening experts.

organizing information. In these strategies, the computer acts as teacher and a guide. The computer provides structure and reinforcement in lessons through pretests, post-test, exercises, personalized feedback, and other tactics. The popularity of these kinds of programs is demonstrated by the large number of companies that have purchased content libraries such as those offered by SkillSoft or Thomson NETg.

The interactions that take place when learning from computers can be divided into several broad categories:

- Self-paced instruction
- Simulations
- Recorded lectures

These categories are not mutually exclusive. When designing programs, instructional designers often mix these strategies. For clarity's sake, they will be presented as distinct groups below.

Self-Paced Instruction

Self-paced instructional programs range from simple text-based programs to sophisticated multimedia programs featuring complex branching. The text-based programs are analogous to online workbooks. These programs rely on the printed word to deliver the content and feature questions that help the learner assess his or her mastery of the content. More sophisticated programs use rich media and branching strategies based on pretest scores, learner's preferences, and responses to exercises to present a personalized learning experience. These programs can offer opportunities to contact an instructor for assistance via e-mail, instant messaging, threaded discussion, or telephone, but the primary role of the instructor is played by the e-learning program. Table 12.4 provides URLs for programs that illustrate the tactics typically used. Sampling these programs will give readers personal experience with the interactions that follow.

The following interactions are options for those developing self-paced instruction.

Pretest/Post-Test. Testing is an interaction that learners have come to expect in the physical as well as the virtual classroom. Testing can be a powerful tool in self-paced instruction. If pretests are part of the program, they can be used to determine what sections a learner has already mastered and opt them out of those sections. A good pretest saves learners time and prevents potential boredom and frustration created by studying material that has already been mastered.

Table 12.4. Examples Demonstrating Self-Paced Instruction
SkillsSoft www.skillsoft.com/ Take a sample course from their e-learning library.
NETg Thomson www.netg.com/ Take a demo from the NETg library of free courses and tools.
Internal Revenue Service (IRS) www.irs.gov/app/vita/content/intro/lesson01/0001_00_005.html Volunteer Income Tax Assistance (VITA) and Tax Counseling for the Elderly (TCE) program
Howard Hughes Medical www.practicingsafescience.org/ Knowing how to practice safe science
The Bureau of Alcohol, Tobacco, Firearms and Explosives (ATF) www.atf.gov/firearms/ffrrg/index.htm
The Learning Theatre www.learningtheatre.co.za

Practice Exercises. The best interactions in self-paced programs are ones that enable learners to practice what is being taught. Research has shown that practice moves skills and knowledge from short-term to long-term memory. Designing practice interactions may seem easy and straightforward, but this is one of the most challenging interaction types to build. The strategy should be to develop practice items that actually allow learners to practice the behavior specified in the lessons objectives. In many cases the objective is at a higher level than the practice item.

Let's look at an example. If the objective reads "the learner will be able to create and edit a watermark in a Microsoft Word document," what should the practice include? The interaction should feature practice items in which the learner embeds a watermark and edits a watermark. In the case of software training, the cost of creating practice interactions can be prohibitive. When cost becomes too much, developers use interactions that are at a lower level of Bloom's taxonomy. So instead of practicing at the *application* level, developers create exercises at the *know* level. In this case, rather than creating or editing, the learner identifies, locates, and describes how to create and edit a watermark.

Practice exercises are delivered using a variety of techniques. Production value (slickness) and the expense of developing these vary widely. The practice exercises are constrained by what the authoring software is capable of and your budget. That is, the more complex the answer, the more challenging, costly, and time-consuming it is to develop exercises. Some practice formats include the following:

- *Drag and drop.* Use this when you want learners to practice building, assembling physical items, or arranging conceptual information. For example, you ask a learner to assemble a PC by dragging the monitor, keyboard, mouse, and cable to the right places or you may ask learners to sequence the steps in responding to a code red emergency.

- *Fill in the box.* Use these exercises to develop the learner's ability to recall and apply information. For example, the learners may be asked to name foods that are high in fiber.

- *Multiple-choice questions.* When well-written, multiple-choice questions can provide learners with practice of higher-level skills than simple recall. For example, a question to test the learner's ability to apply percentages might read, "Customers who are SYMS Preference Customers get 5 percent off all items. Margaret is a preferred customer and the $100 shoes she is purchasing are reduced 15 percent for the President's Day sale. What is the price of the item after all discounts?" All of the answers must be plausible and test the learner's ability to actually apply the percentages and not support a guess, so answers might include (a) $15.00; (b) $75.75 (c) $80.00; (d) $80.75; (e) $85.00.

- *Application simulation.* Use application simulations to allow learners to practice using software in a safe environment. For example, provide an application simulation of a customer billing system. Allow the learner to practice finding a customer's payment history and updating a record.

Hyperlinks. An inexpensive tactic to enable the learner to interact with the content is to provide hyperlinks. Using a hyperlink, an image or piece of text can link to another web page. This type of interaction must be undertaken with care and consideration for the experience level of the learners and the complexity of the content. For example, if learners are new to a content area, save the links for the end of the page or unit. Those who are new to a content area would expect the lesson to be self-contained and would probably not benefit from links for enrichment sprinkled through the program. The developer would also want to make sure that the links don't take the new learner to another website or lose the learner in a jumble of pop-up windows and related sites.

Tactics for advanced learners may be different. Advanced learners may need links embedded in the text to allow them autonomy to pursue some topics in greater detail or to verify the source of a recommendation in the text.

Interactive Animations and Media. If budget permits, the uses of animation segments or video clips to show a process are powerful interactive strategies. A highly instructive method for teaching procedures is allowing the learner to play, replay, or slow down the playback of a process captured on video or illustrated in an animation.

Covert Questions. Not all interactions are overt and require clicking, dragging, or interacting with an application. Some of the interaction can be delivered by drawing on internal interactions, such as posing a covert question. Covert questions are questions that learners answer or consider in their minds rather than respond to in an overt way such as selecting a multiple-choice distracter, filling in a box, or dragging items across the screen.

Pop-Ups. When onscreen real estate is at a premium, pop-up boxes on the screen allow learners to drill down to see additional information. As learners mouse over hot spots on the screen, additional information is revealed. The learners interacts with the content in the sequence they want.

Probes Within the Unit. Questions can be used with the lesson to assess the learner's understanding of content. Unlike test questions that are simply graded, probes can be used to provide remediation. For example, if students are studying multiplication, a probe may ask what is $3 \times 2 =$. The choices may be (a) 5, (b) 1, or (c) 6. Based on the answer chosen, the remediation is more sophisticated than simply telling the learner he or she is right or wrong. Questions or probes can be used to do more than send the learner back to review the last few screens of content. In this case, the remediation would differ for each answer: (a) 5 would assume the learner needs help distinguishing between addition and multiplication. Remediation for answer (b) 1 would clarify the learner's confusion between subtraction and multiplication.

Evaluation-Free Responses. There may be times when it is not possible to evaluate a learner's response but there is value in having the learner think about a question and formulate a written response. For example, you may ask a medical student to draft five questions to ask during a patient's annual physical. While there may be no single set of correct questions, the learner can interact with the system by writing the questions down and then have the system return a list of the five questions recommended by the American Family Practice Association. Citing the AFP answers, while not evaluating the learner's responses, does give the learner a benchmark against which to judge his or her work.

Optional Communication-Based Interactions. Many self-paced learning programs have options for sending e-mail to an instructor or joining a threaded discussion. When learning *from computers*, these are secondary interactions. In some cases you may not want to encourage this interaction because it can be expensive to staff or impossible to scale when a program is being taken by thousands of people. In self-paced instruction, the role of the instructor is not to facilitate the learning but rather to help the learner with problems or questions the computer cannot answer.

Simulation

Simulations are another strategy of learning *from* computers. In this category, as in self-paced programs, the computer acts as a teacher and strategies focus on accomplishing defined goals. What sets simulations apart from self-paced learning is the context; simulations are generally less analogous to textbooks and classrooms. Simulations place the learning in roles such as manager, doctor, and sales representatives.

Simulations are representations or simplified representations of the real world that help the learner explore ideas, processes, concepts, and principles in controlled environment. When people think about simulators. what often comes to mind are flight simulators or other sophisticated and expensive applications. In practice, simulation-based strategies range from simple text-based programs to sophisticated media-rich programs costing millions of dollars. Readers interested in more learning about simulations are encouraged to read Chapter 6 and sample additional programs.

The challenge in developing simulations is to design feedback or debriefings that are meaningful. The learner's solution must be evaluated by the system, which means that designers must either anticipate a very large range of solutions or find a way to provide feedback that is less specific but still valuable. In addition, there is the challenge of transferring the learning from the simulation (game, role play, case study . . .) to the real world. Table 12.5 provides a sampling of programs that use simulations to learn from computers. Readers are encouraged to sample as many of these as possible and take note of the feedback and debriefing interactions as well as the ease of transfer from the learning environment to real-world application.

Table 12.5. Examples Demonstrating the Use of Simulations to Learn *from* Computers	
Simulation Type	**Sample and Description**
Case Study	Case Studies in the Evaluation and Management of Dyspepsia www.aafp.org/x21055.xml This simulated patient encounter uses multimedia to emphasize key aspects of the case and to provide supplemental learning. Rationale and references are supplied for additional self-directed learning. Participants assess their progress through the case using instantaneous feedback comparing their results with expert analysis.
Game-Based Simulations	Mobile Phone Safety www.orange.co.uk/safety/game.html Orang™, the European Union mobile phone company, is providing an online game to teach customers about the dangers of mobile phone crime. Street Smart is an interactive game that scores the learners for recognizing and avoiding potential dangers.
Physical Simulations	Animated Tooth.com http://animatedtooth.com/ This site provides simulations of dental processes.
Process (Step) Simulations	Virtual Earth Quake www.laep.org/target/technology/secondary/earthquakes/
Role Play	WebQuests http://webquest.sdsu.edu/ Look at the examples of programs that ask learners to assume the role of personal trainer, reporter, or expedition leaders. e-Negotiations www.enegotiation.org/2004/index.html University and college students taking courses in conflict resolution, labor relations, industrial relations, law, or general business are the target audience for this program. The International eNegotiation Tournament provides students from across the world a means of showcasing their negotiation skills by role playing business negotiations.
Software Simulation	Robodemo from Macromedia www.macromedia.com/software/robodemo/ Visit the Robodemo in Action and click on the Customer Demos link. This site offers software simulation examples and case studies.

Table 12.5. Examples Demonstrating the Use of Simulations to Learn *from* Computers, Cont'd

Simulation Type	Sample and Description
Symbolic (Invisible) Simulations	Goldratt's Theory of Constraints: Online Simulation www.ganesha.org/leading/toc.html This simulation lets learners play with variables to see how the theory of constraints can bring about big changes by leveraging a few things that "constrain" or limit you. Roller Coaster Physics www.learner.org/exhibits/parkphysics/ This site for grade school students demonstrates the laws of physics in the context of building a roller-coaster ride.
Virtual Reality/ Sims	http://thesims.ea.com/us/index.html?content=about/bustinout/index.html www.historychannel.com/ellisisland/index2.html

Recorded Lectures

Recorded programs are becoming a common form of self-paced instruction. A popular strategy is to reuse live virtual classroom (LVC) programs. LVC programs are recorded and then made available for viewing as recorded lectures. As one might imagine these programs generally have the appeal of watching a video of a live traditional classroom program.

These lectures may have had interactions when they were first delivered in real time, such as live question and answer (Q&A), real-time polling, application sharing, and dialogue among learners, breakout rooms, and text chat. Recorded or playback versions of these program do not offer much interaction. But they can be effective self-paced instruction if designed well. In some cases, the playback version can offer a pretest and post-test, tools for navigating the lecture via a table of contents, and links to additional resources and threaded discussions. Table 12.6 lists some sites for recorded lectures. Sample the programs and compare the production values, the content presentation strategies, and the technical requirements relative to bandwidth and players.

There are many variations on these basic strategies of learning *from* computers. This is an important strategy because companies value the ability to allow learners access to training on-demand and the freedom of being able to offer training without scheduling an instructor, forming a class, and booking a room. The strategies

Table 12.6. Using Lectures to Learn *from* Computers

GE Medical Systems: Imaging/Physician/Nursing
www.gehealthcare.com/education/
GE Healthcare offers a variety of continuing education courses on the Web for healthcare professionals.

Job Interview Skills
http://education.lsuc.on.ca/ess/apo/apoPlacementHelp.jsp
This site uses a combination of text, audio and video.

Shaping Health Care Policy
www.uic.edu/depts/accc/itl/realmedia/rm-SMIL-samples.html
This program uses video and audio to deliver what they call a case study, but it is really a good example of learning from a lecture. The program uses a news program format to accommodate a large number of speakers.

Title V: Needs Assessment Workshop (A live program recorded for playback later)
www.uic.edu/sph/cade/mch_needs_workshop/
Notice the production values and consider the relevance of the content to the intended audience.

Hernia
www.herniasolutions.com/audio/audio.html
Try this lecture-based program that features an interview format and offers the program in both English and Spanish. Listen to Robert Enteen, Ph.D., health care expert and talk-show host, interview Arthur Gilbert, MD, an expert in hernia repair.

Chief Learning Officer Magazine e-Seminars
www.clomedia.com/eseminar/
Records of live seminars on training topics are archived on this site.

CE3000
www.ce3000.com/
This site provides continuing education units for medical professionals using lecture-based, self-paced instruction.

MIT Open Courseware: Media, Education, and the Marketplace
http://ocw.mit.edu/OcwWeb/Comparative-Media-Studies/
CMS-930Media—Education—and-the-MarketplaceFall2001/VideoLectures/index.htm
A collection of video lectures from a number of business and education experts.

highlighted here can be tracked and measured. These programs have traditional classroom analogs that make it easier to persuade management to support them than learning *with* computers strategies. Generally, learning *from* computers is behaviorist by design with predetermined goals and a singular perspective of reality.

Strategies for Learning *with* Computers

The last groups of strategies are best described as constructivist in orientation. Learning *with* computers refers to learners using their computers as tools for learning rather than relying on their computers to act as reference books or as teachers. Interactions in learning *with* computers rely on the computer's computation power to do things such as calculate, remember, retrieve information, sort, organize, and graphically present. Jonassen (1996) has coined the term "mindtools" to describe this kind of learning strategy. He defines mindtools as "computer applications that, when used by learners to represent what they know, necessarily engage them in critical thinking about the content they are studying" (Jonassen, Carr, & Hsiu-Ping, 1998, p. 24).

The research and application of learning with computers has focused on using computers as mindtools in traditional K–12 and higher education classrooms. The importance of this is that learners are more and more working in physical spaces equipped with computers, Internet access, and other technology and so are able to build or construct knowledge working with others. The group learning aspect of learning with computers cannot be discounted. Steketee (2002) researched students' perceptions of cognitive tools in this kind of environment to understand why, despite the impressive qualities of cognitive tools, the tools have largely failed to deliver a transformation in learning. Her findings suggest that successful use of mindtools requires more than a single learner using the computer to enhance his or her thinking. The real value of learning *with* computers is realized when a group of learners uses the tools in a collaborative effort to achieve a common goal. This has implications for the design of instruction and strategies that employ mindtools.

Instructional designers who want to use mindtools a part of an e-learning program have several options. The tools can be used in live virtual classrooms, in asynchronous group learning, and as part of a blended learning program.

Strategies for learning with computers are most effective for group learning, as opposed to self-paced instruction. Using the computational power of the computer to offload work means groups can focus on higher-order learning such as analyzing, synthesizing, and evaluating information in order to construct knowledge. These programs will also require a significant change in roles for learners and facilitators. Learners must take responsibility for their learning and be willing to work with others. Facilitators, meanwhile, must shift to the role of posing authentic problems, encouraging learners to value diverse points of view, and encouraging learners to compare their personally constructed meanings with those of a larger community of experts.

Before looking at strategies for learning *with* computers, it should be noted that constructivist strategies are not frequently found in corporate or professional development. A review of the literature by Thompson suggests that "adult learners tend to want to learn skills quickly without entering into the kinds of reflection and elaboration brought about in a constructivist learning environment" (2001, p. 109). He also notes that corporate training primarily utilizes an objectivist model for learning.

The following section provides a sampling of the mindtools available for designing programs that encourage group learning and the construction of knowledge.

Agents or intelligent agents are programs that gather information or perform some other service without the user's immediate presence and on some regular schedule. These programs are also called *bot,* short for robot, because, like a robot, they can be given directions (parameters) and sent off to search the Web for information. To see example of bots, visit the Bot Spot at www.botspot.com/ to see search bots, chatter bots, and tracking bots.

Blogs or *Web logs* are journals kept on the Web. A blog is a web page made up of usually short, frequently updated postings arranged chronologically. The content and purposes of blogs varies greatly—from links and commentary about other websites to news about a company/person/idea. Blogs can have a single author or they can be shared by a group. Because they are easy to access and use, they offer a tool for promoting critical reflection and insight.

Calculators are online programs that perform computational operations via data input. The processing is done on a remote computer and does not require the learner to have any software. The result is displayed onscreen. Examples of calculators range from the frivolous to the fantastic. There are discipline-specific calculators for astronomy, engineering, medicine, and finance. These calculators can be used to model problem solving and, in some cases, the calculators graph the data to make visualization possible.

Concept maps offer a way to represent information visually as means of making complex information understandable "at-a-glance." As a tool, concept mapping applications allow learners to construct, communicate, share, navigate, and critique knowledge in a representative model.

Digital cameras offer yet another means of engaging learners with visuals. Learners can document events, gather information for later analysis, clarify their communication, and add dimension to their presentations with digital images.

Databases offer students powerful tools for storing, organizing, managing, and sorting information. Creating the database requires reflection and a tangible conceptualization of information. Once the database is designed, learners can manipulate large amounts of data and see relationships and trends not possible without a computer.

Expertise locator applications link learners to experts in a domain. These sites allow learners to access knowledge from an expert that may not be available elsewhere. Learners can use the Internet to expand their resources for learning.

Instant messaging applications make learners aware that colleagues and experts are online and allow them to communicate with others in real time through private chat areas. These programs enable learners to get quick answers and tap into resources that might not otherwise be available.

Modeling tools are applications that enable one to enter variables and observe the outcomes. Examples of this are spreadsheets where one can explore the impact of supply and demand by observing what a change in demand will do to price, project management software where one can see the impact of changing items on the critical path, and financial applications that show the impact of changing the interest rate.

Organizers are templates and applications that allow learners to plan in a structured fashion. The organizers can include fishbone diagrams, Venn diagrams, storyboards, flowcharts, and family tree software. These online tools can help students visually organize data and share it with other learners.

Presentation tools encompass a number of web-based applications that enable learners to organize and communicate their knowledge. Give serious consideration to alternative presentation software such as digital video, audio-based tools that produce radio-style documentaries, and other technologies that force learners to organize information and critically reflect on communicating the information.

Productivity applications such as word processing, spreadsheet, databases, and other tools can be used to support learners in constructing knowledge. The files created by these applications can be shared via e-mail, stored in a shared directory, or posted to a website.

Surveys online allow learners to gather data using Internet-based data-gathering applications such as interviews and focus groups. The value of these kinds of tools is limited by the nature of what is to be studied. Facilitators must assist learners by providing a clear understanding of research design and analysis for this medium (Hewson, Yule, Vogel, & Laurent, 2003).

Team spaces are applications that create a virtual workroom in which learners can assemble collective materials, check documents in and out, keep a calendar, post notes, create a library, and manage who has access to the room. Team spaces are ideal for collaborative learning and resource sharing.

Threaded discussions, forums, and discussion boards enable learners to post a topic and engage peers in a running dialog about the topic. Notes are posted and dated so that participants can see the dialog evolve. In some cases, old threads can be data-mined for best practices and lessons learned. These forums can also be places for communities of practice where new members can ask questions of those more experienced.

Visualization tools graphically display data to facilitate better understanding of its meaning. Graphical capabilities range from simple scatter plots to complex multi-dimensional representations. Examples of the visualization tools can also be found in Chapter 6.

Table 12.7 lists examples of mindtool software for each of the categories previously discussed. These programs share one characteristic; it is that the learners' data is what make the tool of value. For example, database software, organizer software, and modeling programs are of no real value until the learner uses them to solve problems by displaying data, allowing a comparison of alternatives, and illustrating patterns. If you have not tried some variant of each type of mindtool, visit the sites and experience demos and take virtual tours. In some cases you can get a free trial copy or you can use a hosted version of the service for thirty days.

This list of tools and applications is just a small sample of what is available to extend the mental capabilities of the learner by employing the computer and Internet. These tools can be used as part of online courses, as components of blended solution, or as tools in a traditional classroom.

This section has classified three ways computers can be used in interactions: learner-material, learner-learner, and learner-instructor. The challenge is to sort through the interactions to understand the available options. There is no magic formal for interactions; there are simply a number of strategies available to instructional designers.

Table 12.7. Tools for Learning *with* Computers	
Tools	**Examples**
Agents (Intelligent Agents)	BotSpot www.botspot.com/
	1st SPOT: Agents, Robots and Spiders http://1st-spot.net/topic_agents.html
Blogs	WebLogs.com www.weblogs.com/
	LearningCircuits Blog: hosted by Jay Cross www.internettime.com/lcmt/
Calculators	Clinical Calculator www.intmed.mcw.edu/clincalc/bayes.html
	Body Mass Index http://nhlbisupport.com/bmi/bmicalc.htm
Concept Mapping	Cmap Tools http://cmap.ihmc.us/
	Inspiration www.inspiration.com/home.cfm
Digital Cameras	HP www.hp.com
	Kodak www.kodak.com
	1001 Uses for Digital Cameras http://pegasus.cc.ucf.edu/~ucfcasio/qvuses.htm
Databases	Microsoft Access www.microsoft.com
	FileMaker Pro www.filemaker.com/
Expertise Locators	Ask an Expert www.askanexpert.com/
	IBM Community Tools http://community.ngi.ibm.com/
Instant Messaging	America Online Instant Messaging www.aim.com/

Table 12.7. Tools for Learning *with* Computers, Cont'd

Tools	Examples
	IBM Lotus Instant Messaging and Web Conferencing www.lotus.com
Modeling Tools	3D Garden Composer www.gardencomposer.com/
	Retirement Estimator www.asec.org/ballpark/ballpark.htm
Organizers	Adobe PhotoShop Album wwww.adobe.com
	Paper Tiger www.thepapertiger.com/
Presentation Tools	Microsoft PowerPoint www.microsoft.com
	Macromedia RoboDemo www.macromedia.com/software/robodemo/
Productivity Applications	Microsoft Office www.microsoft.com
	WordPerfect Office www.corel.com/
Survey	Zoomerang http://info.zoomerang.com/
	SurveyMonkey.com www.surveymonkey.com/
Team Spaces	Lotus Team Workplace (QuickPlace) www.lotus.com/
	Documentum eRoom www.documentum.com/eroom/
Threaded Discussions	Discusware www.discusware.com/index.php
	12Planet www.12planet.com/en/software/forum/
Visualization	Visual Thesaurus www.visualthesaurus.com/

Conclusion

Interactivity is not a silver bullet, but we do know that it is essential for learning and we know it leads to greater learner satisfaction. It is the holy grail of e-learning; clients are hard pressed to explain what it is (but they insist on it); educators can't agree on a definition of it; and learners only notice it when it is missing.

The chapter has provided a starting point for your critical reflection on a definition for interaction. Two models for classifying interactions have been presented: Moore's model and a framework for using computers to learn through, from, and with. An abundant number of URLs and examples were provided to help you build a portfolio of interaction examples and ideas on which to draw. Using a problem-centered approach to designing, the right mix will be influenced by your philosophy of education, the learning theories you subscribe to, and the organization climate in which you work.

Learn More About It

Hirumi, A. (2002). The design and sequencing of e-learning interactions: A grounded approach. *International Journal of e-Learning. 1*(1), 19–27.

This is a must-read for practitioners who want answers to the questions such as "How does e-learning differ from other modes of instruction?" "What are meaningful e-learning interactions?" and "How do you design and sequence meaningful e-learning interactions?" This article chronicles knowledge gained from seeking answers to these fundamental questions and posits a five-step process for designing and sequencing e-learning interactions based on a combination of research, theory, and experience.

Jonassen, D.H., Carr, C., & Yueh, H.P. (1998). Computers as mindtools for engaging learners in critical thinking. *TechTrends, 43*(2), 24–32.

Readers interested in learning more about mindtools will find this article easy to read and rich in examples.

Schwier, R.A. (1995). Issues in emerging interactive technologies. In G. Anglin (Ed.), *Instructional technology: Past present and future* (2nd ed.). Englewood, CO: Libraries Unlimited, Chapter 10, pp. 119–130.

Outstanding chapter that looks at interactive media design from a constructivist and a behavioralist perspective. Although the book is dated, many of the research citations call out the seminal work in the field. In a brief chapter, Schwier provides guidance for design of interaction, which is succinct and well-grounded.

Sims, R. (1997). Interactivity: a forgotten art? *Computers in Human Behavior, 13*(2), 157–180.

This article provides a taxonomy of interactivity and examples that include object interactivity (object activation via mouse clicks), linear interactivity (forward/backward movements through a predetermined linear sequence), hierarchical interactivity, support interactivity (general or context-sensitive help), update interactivity (dynamic responses, feedback), construct interactivity (manipulation of components), reflective interactivity, simulation interactivity, hyper-linked interactivity (traveling through a knowledge base), nonimmersive contextual interactivity (microworlds), and immersive virtual interactivity (complete virtual worlds).

Wagner, E.D. (1994). In support of a functional definition of interaction. *The American Journal of Distance Education, 8*(2), 6–26.

This is a classic article for those interested in learning more about interactions. The article will help you reflect on and come to your own conclusion regarding what should constitute an educational interaction.

Websites of Interest

www.elearningguild.com/. The eLearning Guild.

The Resource Directory offer links to articles and case studies related to interactivity.

www.ncolr.org/. *Journal of Interactive Online Learning.*

Provides a forum for the dissemination of research on interactive online education.

www.tlt.ab.ca/tltresources/mindtools_new.html. Teaching and Learning with Technology.

This is a meta resource page for information related to mindtools.

REFLECTION AND APPLICATION

Visit three of the sites listed in Table 12.1. Then view an e-learning course of your choice. (If you do not have access to an e-learning course, try a demonstration course at www.netg.com or www.skillsoft.com.) Then consider the following:

- What are the similarities among interactions in e-commerce and e-learning interactions?
- In what ways do these types of interactions differ?
- How might they set expectations for learners? For sponsors? For you?

- What best practices that you saw in e-commerce sites can you apply to e-learning sites?

- What worst practices did you see that you would not want to repeat?

To reflect on the material presented in this chapter, and apply it in a real e-learning situation, consider how you would respond to the following challenges. (Each of these challenges is intentionally left vague. If you are unsure about a piece of information, make an assumption about it and list the assumption.)

- You're asked to teach a new software application for filing expense reports within your company. Your course is intended for end users, who are likely to be starting this course the first time they complete an expense report with the new application. What types of interactions would you include?

- You are designing a bare-bones e-learning program. It's bare bones because that's about the size of your budget. Your sponsor has little experience with e-learning, but has heard that it should be interactive to be effective. She has demanded that you develop a "highly interactive learning experience," an expression that you also heard during an e-learning seminar sponsored by your local chapter of the International Society for Performance Improvement (ISPI). What questions would you ask the sponsor and what issues would you consider before recommending a solution?

- You are an instructor for an introductory course on calculus, which will be taught through a live virtual classroom. You expect to have one hundred students in the class for the semester. Your colleagues have told you that you're "crazy" to be teaching this course. "You'll never have any interaction with your students." You're intent on demonstrating that they're wrong. How do you do that?

Chapter 13

Visual Communication Techniques

Where did the idea come from that words communicate better than pictures? Since they were first invented to communicate complex thoughts, words and pictures have been locked in a struggle for dominance with words being the clear-cut leader. . . . However, the invention of television and the computer— and the recent spread of desktop publishing and the World Wide Web— dramatically changed the role of visual messages in communication.

Paul Martin Lester, 2000, p. ix

In This Chapter

In this chapter, we will

- Define visual communication

- Explain why you should use visuals

- Describe a portfolio of visual communication techniques for e-learning

- Describe the guiding principles underlying visual communication for e-learning

- Describe examples of effective visual communication in e-learning programs

◆ ◆ ◆

"It looks like crap," Michael commented to himself about the appearance of his first e-learning lesson.

Although he had extensively researched the content and developed what he thought was engaging text, unfortunately that's what the lesson looked like . . . text. Endless text. Lengthy paragraphs followed by even lengthier paragraphs, requiring that learners scroll, and scroll, and scroll some more.

In other words, the lesson looked like a book dumped online.

Michael thought he should produce something that was more visually interesting. After all, most of the literature on e-learning recommends the use of visuals and lauds visually attractive courses. But designing a course that primarily communicates through visuals is challenging because most instructional designers are trained to use words as the primary means of communication. Those with backgrounds in the classroom rely on the spoken word. Those with backgrounds in publishing rely on the written word.

Because most instructional designers primarily rely on words, when they do use visuals, they use them as a supplemental means of communicating content or as adornment—something to visually attract learners. These designers usually look for clip art that visually enhances the screen. Rarely does it communicate content; text does that.

This chapter is intended to help you use visuals in your e-learning programs. First, we explain what visuals are, why they are effective in teaching online, and how they can both communicate technical content and motivate learners. Next, we suggest specific situations that should trigger you to communicate visually. Then we offer some practical issues to consider when using visuals. Last, we show an example of effective visual communication in e-learning.

What Are Visuals?

Some general confusion surrounds the concept of visuals. First, many people confuse PowerPoint® slides (or slides produced in similar graphics programs) with visuals. That these slides are often called "visuals" only adds to the confusion. In most organizations, PowerPoint slides almost exclusively consist of text. These are not visuals. Visuals are pictures, illustrations, photographs, videos, charts, and symbols that communicate messages through images rather than words.

Second, many people confuse visuals with graphic design. According to the American Institute of Graphic Arts (2002):

> Graphic design is a creative process that combines art and technology to communicate ideas. The designer works with a variety of communication tools in order to convey a message from a client to a particular audience. The main tools are image and typography.

Although presenting content visually is an important skill of graphic designers, it is not the only skill they bring. Good graphic design also encompasses the effective use of typography, efficient and effective design of the screen, navigation among screens in the learning program, and the *corporate identity* (also called *brand*)—the visual characteristics that uniquely link the e-learning program with a particular organization. Certain specialists focus exclusively on specific types of visual communication. *Illustrators* draw still pictures of people, places, and things to make these concepts easier to understand (WordNet® 1.6). *Animators* prepare moving images (such as presentations created in Macromedia Flash®) from drawn pictures of people, places, and things. *Photographers* take still photographs of people, places, and things. *Videographers* take moving photographs of people, places, and things.

Visual communication is a term that refers to using visuals and graphic design.

Why Should You Use Visuals?

Visuals are essential to learning, because 83 percent of what is learned is learned through sight. Only 11 percent of what is learned is learned through hearing (Stolovitch, 2004).

Because the technology underlying computer displays is the same as that used for television, the computer is technically a visual medium and, like other visual media such as television and film, it communicates most effectively through visual images.

In addition to taking advantage of learning patterns and the computer screen, focusing on visual communication in e-learning programs offers a number of other learning benefits, including these:

- Visuals best communicate inherently visual content
- Visuals communicate some ideas more efficiently than text
- Learners remember visuals
- Visuals appeal to the affective domain
- Visuals accommodate learners with a need for visual content

The next several sections explore these benefits.

Visuals Best Communicate Inherently Visual Content

In many instances, the content covered by the learning program is visual. For example, objects such as computers, testing equipment, and airplanes are visual. Learners best understand them by seeing them.

Some other topics are easier to understand through visual presentation. For example, research suggests that learners easily overlook numbers buried within paragraphs, but easily comprehend them when presented as charts and graphs. For example, consider the two presentations of a budget shown in Figure 13.1.

Figure 13.1. Comparison of Verbal and Visual Presentations of Numbers

Version One (Text): The annual budget will be allocated in the following way.

Twenty-four percent will be spent on facilities and overhead.

Forty-two percent will be spent on salary and benefits.

Twenty-three percent will be spent on programming.

Ten percent will be spent on marketing and promotion.

One percent will be spent on evaluation.

Version Two (Visual):

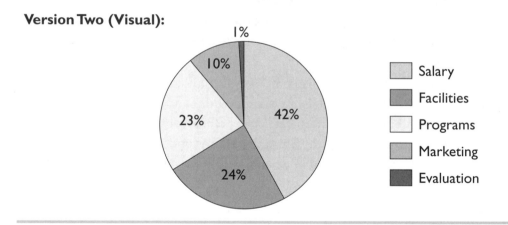

Similarly, family trees and organization charts more efficiently communicate relationships among people than do lengthy paragraphs that attempt to describe the relationship. For example, consider the two presentations of the reporting structure of an organization shown in Figure 13.2.

As visuals more efficiently present relationships between people, visual devices also more efficiently present processes. For example, consider the two presentations of a procedure shown in Figure 13.3.

Note that the simple use of step numbers and paragraphs makes the procedure easier to follow. The procedure could also be depicted as a flow chart, like that shown in Figure 13.4.

Figure 13.2. Comparison of Verbal and Visual Presentations of Relationships in an Organization

Version One (Text): Mary, Lisa, Michael, Ryan, and Jeff are instructional designers. They report to project manager Jim. Carey, Chloe, Sundray, Michelle, and Tess are technical writers who report to project manager Phyllis. Jim and Phyllis report to Jane, the manager of training and documentation development. Jane reports to Charlene, the director of training, who reports to Andre, the vice president for human resources. Andre reports to Charlie, the senior vice president for operations. Charlie reports to Carleton, the CEO of the corporation.

Version Two (Visual):

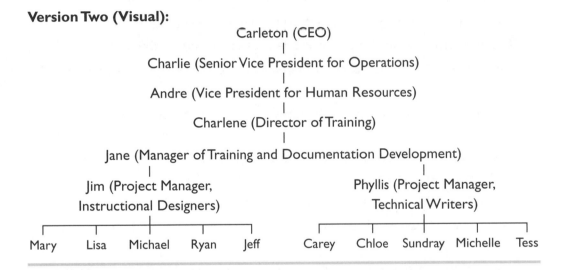

Figure 13.3. Comparison of Verbal and Visual Presentations of a Procedure

Version One (Text):

The process for recommending and approving policies is as follows. An operating unit proposes a policy to its lowest-level executive. The executive reviews the policy and returns comments to the unit. The unit then sends the policy to all other units that will be affected by the policy for review. Units have ten days to respond and present their comments at a formal review meeting. After the review meeting, the people proposing the process prepare a response to the comments and a revision to the policy (if needed). The policy is then sent to the senior management council

Figure 13.3. Comparison of Verbal and Visual Presentations of a Procedure, Cont'd

for review. Senior management sends comments to the unit, which responds within ten business days. The unit returns the revised policy to the senior management council for final review and approval. After receiving it, the unit is responsible for preparing a management communiqué about the policy and sending it to all affected employees, suppliers, and customers.

Version Two (Visual):

The process for recommending and approving policies is as follows:

1. An operating unit proposes a policy to its lowest-level executive.

2. The executive reviews the policy and returns comments to the unit.

3. The unit then sends the policy to all other units that will be affected by the policy for review.

4. Units have ten days to respond and present their comments at a formal review meeting.

5. After the review meeting, the people proposing the process prepare a response to the comments and a revision to the policy (if needed).

6. The policy is then sent to the senior management council for review.

7. Senior management sends comments to the unit, which responds within ten business days.

8. The unit returns the revised policy to the senior management council for final review and approval.

9. After receiving it, the unit is responsible for preparing a management communiqué about the policy and sending it to all affected employees, suppliers, and customers.

Figure 13.4. Presenting Procedural Information as a Flow Chart

1. An operating unit proposes a policy to its lowest-level executive.

2. The executive reviews the policy and returns comments to the unit.

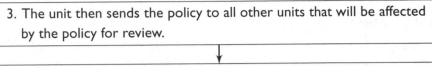

Figure 13.4. Presenting Procedural Information as a Flow Chart, Cont'd

3. The unit then sends the policy to all other units that will be affected by the policy for review.

4. Units have ten days to respond and present their comments at a formal review meeting.

5. After the review meeting, the people proposing the process prepare a response to the comments and a revision to the policy (if needed).

6. The policy is then sent to the senior management council for review.

7. Senior management sends comments to the unit, which responds within ten business days.

8. The unit returns the revised policy to the senior management council for final review and approval.

9. After receiving it, the unit is responsible for preparing a management communique about the policy and sending it to all affected employees, suppliers, and customers.

Visuals Communicate Some Ideas More Efficiently than Text

In many instances, a well-labeled visual communicates content more efficiently than text. In some instances, efficiency is defined in terms of space. A visual might take up less physical space on the screen than text. In a medium in which space on the screen (called *real estate*) is at a premium, this efficiency is valued.

In some instances, however, the visual explanation takes up more physical space than the verbal explanation, but it is still more efficient because learners are more likely to comprehend the content on the first read-through. Learners might need to reread the same paragraph(s) several times to comprehend the verbal explanation.

This type of efficiency is called *cognitive efficiency* (Cobb, 1997) because it reduces the time learners need to acquire new technical content.

Learners Remember Visuals

A growing body of research suggests that learners remember content as visuals rather than as words. For example, in one study, people were shown pictures of seagulls. People who lived near the seashore (and, therefore, frequently saw seagulls) recognized the image more quickly than those who lived inland (Columb, 1991). What this research suggests is that learners do retain visual images and, the more memorable or the more frequently they interact with those images, the more likely they are to recall the content.

Visuals Appeal to the Affective Domain

With their use of color, line, and images, visuals reach the affective domain in ways that text alone cannot. Specifically, visuals can do the following:

- *Gain and hold attention.* Through the use of eye-catching images and sharp colors, visuals can attract the attention of learners. In some cases, like photographs, the image encourages learners to look and linger. In other cases, an image appears more inviting than text.

  For example, to make a dry subject like renal analysis seem more appealing to learners, the producers of The Seven Deadly Perils used a comic-book-like approach in the course. Figure 13.5 shows a sample screen from the course. See the In Practice section toward the end of this chapter for a detailed description of this visually attractive course.

- *Build trust.* Visuals enhance the credibility of a learning program in a number of ways. First, visuals provide evidence of concepts presented in the text. For example, the text might have explained a complex procedure. A flowchart that accompanies that text helps readers see the relationships between the steps in that procedure, as shown in Figure 13.4. Similarly, the text might have recounted an event. Or consider the illustrated procedure in Figure 13.6, in which a picture explains how to change the look of a software application.

  Second, visual images can enhance the credibility of an e-learning program. For example, beginning an e-course with a letter from an executive on company sta-

Figure 13.5. A Course That Uses Cartoon-Like Images to Gain and Hold Attention

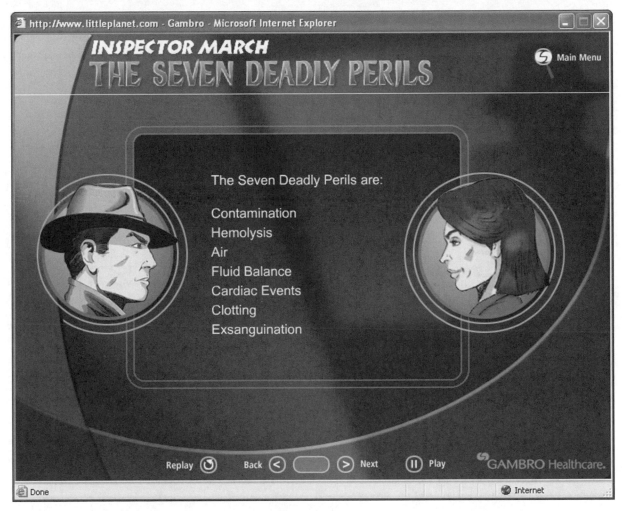

Source: Little Planet. www.littleplanet.com/clients_gambro.html. Used with permission.

tionery or an image of the executive as he or she narrates an introduction demonstrates upper management support for a lesson. This upper management support is especially important to the success of learning programs associated with complex change management initiatives. (This supporting statement contrasts with the vanity shot mentioned in Chapter Ten, in which upper managers open e-learning programs merely to see pictures of themselves but for no other apparent purpose.)

Figure 13.6. Example of an Illustrated Procedure for Changing the Look of an Application

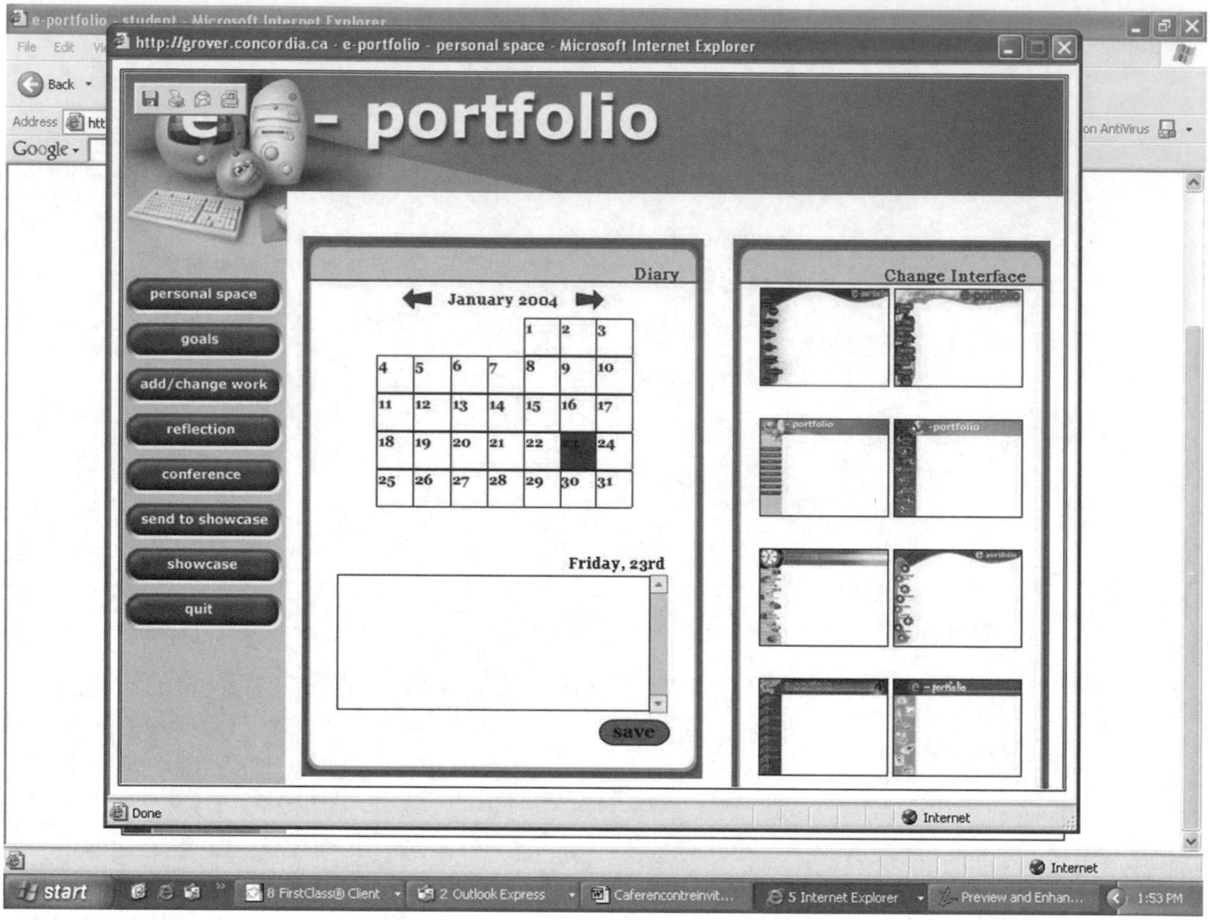

Source: Centre for the Study of Learning and Performance website on e-portfolio software, http://grover.concordia.ca/eportfolio/promo/imgs/StudentImgs/JPEGs/Interface_3.jpg. Used with permission.

Visuals Accommodate Learners with a Need for Visual Content

In some instances, learners cannot understand words because they lack the language skills needed to read them. Many people assume that those who lack language skills are illiterate. That is, they cannot make sense of the letters and use them to form words and meaning. In some cases, this is true.

In many other cases, however, learners are literate in their primary language, but not in the language of instruction. For example, suppose that learners speak and read French as their primary language, but the instruction is in English. Learners might have difficulty following the text.

In such instances, instructors rely on wordless communication. For example, most PC manufacturers prepare the instructions for setting up the computer as wordless instructions. Learners merely need to follow the drawings to set up their computers.

A Portfolio of Visual Communication Techniques

Visuals can be categorized in two ways: by the types of content they address and by their form. The following sections explore both types of visuals.

The Different Types of Visuals for Content

You can choose among groups of visuals for:

- Representing quantitative information
- Representing concrete concepts
- Representing abstract concepts
- Directing learners' attention

The next several sections describe these types of graphics.

Visuals for Representing Quantitative Information

Although not the first to use visuals to present numbers, Yale professor Edward Tufte (2001) made people aware of the power of presenting quantitative information visually. He showed the power of graphs and charts in communicating information. Visuals can specifically show relationships of parts to a whole, changes over time, and comparisons. Table 13.1 shows the most common types of graphs and charts.

Table 13.1. Types of Visuals for Communicating Quantitative Information

Purpose	Visual
To show relationships of parts to the whole	Pie charts

Pie chart legend: Salary, Facilities, Programs, Marketing, Evaluation

Table 13.1. Types of Visuals for Communicating Quantitative Information, Cont'd

Purpose	Visual
To show trends over time	Histograms

Purpose	Visual
To compare two items	Bar charts

Purpose	Visual
To compare several items	Table

	Year 1	Year 2
Salary	42	39
Facilities	24	25
Programs	23	25
Marketing	10	10
Evaluation	1	1

Visuals for Representing Concrete Concepts

The second category of content for which you can use visuals involves representing concrete concepts such as things (products), processes, and relationships among people. Presenting this information visually, you provide learners with a sense of the whole and how each of the parts fits in. Table 13.2 shows the most common categories of concrete concepts and the types of visuals used to represent them.

Table 13.2. Types of Visuals for Communicating Concrete Concepts	
Concept	**Example**
People	Both real (such as subject-matter experts cited in courses and top executives) and imagined (such as characters in role plays)
Finished products	Pictures that represent the object, such as a drawing of a fax machine. 
Product plans	Schematic drawings. These drawings often use a symbolic language to represent different components of the proposed product. In engineering, the drawings are called schematics, because they show the schemes for the inner workings of the product. In architecture, the drawings are called blueprints, because they are usually printed on a special blue paper.
Procedures	Flowcharts. Flowcharts are a type of illustration that show the flow of a process or procedure. They can merely have boxes representing the various steps in a procedure, use illustrated boxes, or use the symbols designated for programming. Each type of step in the procedure has its own symbol. (See Figure 3.4 earlier in this chapter for an example of a simple flowchart.)
Relationships	Family trees and organization charts. (See Figure 13.2 earlier in this chapter for an example of an organizational chart.)

Visuals for Representing Abstract Concepts

Sometimes instructional designers need to explain abstract ideas, like symbols. *Symbols* are visuals that represent abstract concepts. In many instances, the symbols do not look like the concept they represent and learners must be told what the symbols mean. In some instances, however, the symbols are so widely used that learners know their meaning immediately upon looking at them. Such symbols are called *icons*. (Software interfaces often use symbols to represent actions. Software designers call these icons, but in the graphic sense of the word, they are not because users must often be told what the symbols mean.)

Table 13.3 shows the most common categories of abstract concepts and the types of visuals used to represent them.

Table 13.3. Types of Visuals for Communicating Abstract Concepts	
Concept	**Example**
Travel	Symbols such as road signs provide people with travel instructions and warnings. In many instances, the shape of the sign communicates information, such as a stop sign. 
Organizations	Symbols are often associated with organizations. For example, the "swoosh" is linked to Nike.
Control of equipment	Symbols direct readers to perform certain actions with equipment. For example, the controls for video and audio equipment are nearly universal, like these:

◄◄	►►	■	►
Backward	Forward	Stop	Play

Visuals for Directing Learners' Attention

Some visuals primarily direct the attention of learners. In some cases, the visual images help learners move about the course. In other cases, the visual images direct learners' attention to a certain part of the screen. Table 13.4 lists the common issues in directing learners' attention and suggests visuals that can do so.

Table 13.4. Types of Visuals for Directing Learners' Attention	
Form of Direction	**Examples**
Navigation or wayfinding	Symbols that help people move forward and backward in a computer program, shopping mall, or airport. For example, symbols like these: ← → instruct learners to move forward and backward in an e-learning program.
Directing learners to a particular part of the screen	Symbols like directional lines, arrows, shading, and boxes draw learners' attention to a specific part of the screen. For example, the oval in the following example directs learners' attention to the space between two lines of text. Note, too, the directional line that draws attention to the explanatory text beside the oval.

Line of text number 1

⬭ —— Leading, the space between

Line of text number 2

The Different Forms of Visuals

Visuals come in two general forms: photographs and illustrations.

Photograph

According to the University of Arizona library, a photograph is an image "made with a camera by exposing film to light" (1999). The image mimics the scene the person hoped to capture and is recorded either on paper (traditional photography) or in a digital storage device (digital photograph).

Research suggests that photographs are ideal for presales or motivational purposes, because they are the more eye-catching of the two types of visuals. Studies suggest that learners spend more time looking at photographs than at other types of visuals.

Illustration

An *illustration* is "a visual representation (a picture or diagram) that is used to make some subject . . . easier to understand" (http://dictionary.reference.com). An illustration that merely shows the outline of the content drawn is called a *line drawing,* because it only has lines, and little or no shading. Instructional designers usually reproduce line drawings in black and white, but do not have to do so. They can use shading to enhance the appearance of line drawings.

Research suggests that illustrations in general, and line drawings in particular, are better for teaching content than photographs. Photographs contain extraneous details; line drawings only present the salient ones. As a result, learners are not distracted by irrelevant information and are more likely to retain the content (Eugenio, 1994; Kostelnick & Roberts, 1998). So if you're planning to use visuals to show service representatives how to repair a washing machine, you would choose line drawings to show the repair procedures because they will be most effective in this situation.

Static and Moving Images

Visuals can also be static or moving. Moving images of photographs usually take the form of a film or video. Moving images of illustrations take the form of animation. In reality, these moving images are actually sequences of static images that change ever so slightly from one moment to the next and, by playing them quickly (a typical video shows twenty-nine images per second), viewers get the sense of movement.

Guidelines for Using Visuals

For visuals to have the most impact in your learning program, keep the following guidelines in mind. The guidelines come in two categories: guidelines regarding the learning experience and guidelines regarding technology and production.

Guidelines Regarding the Learning Experience

The first set of guidelines focuses on making sure that visuals effectively communicate with learners, and that they only convey the messages that you intend. Specifically, these guidelines include:

- Pay attention to aesthetics

- Balance visual appeal with usability

- Make visuals comprehensible

- Note the cultural meanings your visuals might convey

- Avoid using visuals solely for adornment

The next several sections explore each of these guidelines. We conclude this discussion with some guidelines for designing screens.

Pay Attention to Aesthetics

Aesthetics refers to the guiding principles underlying the design of graphics, especially regarding their appearance. Although aesthetic sensibilities vary among people, most graphic designers agree that graphics should have an attractive, pleasant appearance to learners. Furthermore, following some general aesthetic principles helps ensure that the largest number of learners perceive your visuals as attractive.

For example, one principle of aesthetics is simplicity. Simplicity suggests that visuals contain only necessary elements; designers should remove extraneous details and unnecessary adornment.

Another principle is balance. That is, on the whole, the different parts of the visual do not compete for learners' attention. The focal point (the part of the visual that learners should attend to first) should be clear, and other parts of the image should not distract attention from it.

One specific technique for making visuals aesthetically pleasing to learners is to make them interactive. You can do so in a variety of ways.

If you are showing a procedure or an organization chart, you can reveal the procedure or the organization one part at a time. After learners finish reading about that part, the next part appears on the screen. Consider the example in Figure 13.7. It shows a procedure that is revealed one step at a time. Also note that the newest step is shaded to call attention to it.

This type of image is called a *build sequence.* In a build sequence, let learners press Enter before the next part appears on the screen. Some learners read more slowly than the information appears on the screen, and the faster pace can be discouraging to them.

When using animation, however, avoid annoying special effects. For example, although flashing definitely catches the eye on the first or second flash, continued

Figure 13.7. Example of a Build Sequence

Part One (steps 1 thru 3):

1. An operating unit proposes a policy to its lowest-level executive.

2. The executive reviews the policy and returns comments to the unit.

3. The unit then sends the policy to all other units that will be affected by the policy for review.

Part Two (additional step 4):

1. An operating unit proposes a policy to its lowest-level excutive.

2. The executive reviews the policy and returns comments to the unit.

3. The unit then sends the policy to all other units that will be affected by the policy for review.

4. Units have ten days to respond and present their comments at a formal review meeting.

flashing quickly becomes annoying. Similarly, flying images that appear on the screen definitely create an effect, but the effect grows tiresome after the first use. Ideally, items should just appear on the screen.

If you are showing a product or place that has many parts, show the entire product or place, then let learners click on a particular part to learn more about it. The additional information appears in a pop-up window. For an example, see the website accompanying this book.

Balance Visual Appeal with Usability

One of the greatest tensions in the wired world is that between graphic designers and usability experts. Graphic designers advocate that the visual appearance of web pages takes priority. In contrast, usability experts advocate that the speed of loading pages and the ease of locating content and moving about websites take priority. This tension is a classic one: that between form (graphic designers) and function (usability experts). A similar tension existed in the French art community in the mid-nineteenth century, between the Formalists and the Naturalists.

In reality, good e-learning programs balance the two. In the sense that a learning program is visually appealing, it has good form. In the sense that the program is intuitive to use (that is, requires no instructions) and learners can easily find information of interest and move about, it has a useful function.

Make Visuals Comprehensible

Although a picture is presumed to be worth a thousand words, the reality is that many require a few words of explanation before readers can make full sense of them. Consider the following guidelines to ensure that learners can appropriately interpret the visuals in your e-learning program.

Remove Extraneous Details from Images. *Extraneous* details are ones that do not directly support the learning objectives. For example, in an older photograph, outdated fashions and hairstyles immediately catch learners' eyes. Although these details might be relevant in a program about history or culture, they are often irrelevant to programs about technology and other subjects (unless these programs explore the history of the subject). Learners attend to pictures that now seem humorous in their aging, rather than the subject at hand. In a medium where getting and holding onto learners' attention is already difficult, irrelevant details only make the situation more challenging.

The method of removing details varies, depending on the type of image that you have:

- For photographs, you would crop out the irrelevant details. *Cropping* means cutting out parts of photograph or picture. Most photo refinishing software (like PhotoShop® and Microsoft Photo Editor®) let you crop a photo.

- For line drawings, instruct the illustrator to include only the most relevant parts. Unnecessary shading and detail would not be included. (This is the general practice in technical illustration.)

Properly Label Visuals. Well-placed words help learners properly interpret visuals. These words, called *captions* and *legends*, tell readers the purpose of particular visuals and help them interpret them. The specific placement and formatting of these words follow publishing *conventions* that have been around for years. *Convention* refers to publishing practices that are widely followed and well-understood by learners, without additional coaching or instruction (Kostelnick & Roberts, 1998).

Specific conventions for visuals include:

- *Providing captions for all visuals.* A caption is a title, sentence, or short paragraph that explains the purpose of a visual. It usually appears below the visual. The caption usually starts with the figure number (for example, Figure 1.1) and is either formatted in bold type or the type face used for headings. For examples, look at the figures in this chapter.

- *For figures showing graphs, provide the following additional documentation:*

    Label the two axes. Indicate what type of information is tracked along a given axis (such as money or years) and the units of measurement (for example, each point represents $U.S. 1 million or 1 year).

    Provide a legend, especially in bar charts. Use different colors or shading to differentiate among items. For example, if you are plotting the sales of regular and decaf coffee, the bar for regular might be coffee colored and the bar for decaf might be mint green.

- *For figures showing maps or plans for equipment, indicate the scale.* That is, indicate the relationship each inch or millimeter to actual units, such as 1 inch = 1 mile or 1 millimeter = 1 kilometer.

- *In diagrams, label key parts so users can associate names with different parts of a product or process.* In flow charts, the labels are typically placed directly within the boxes. In diagrams, the labels take one of two forms:

    Identifiers, such as A or B, which appear on the drawing. A key below the drawing or on the next screen tells readers how to decipher these identifiers. Use these only when needed; most learners find the task of matching identifiers with labels to be laborious.

    Callouts, which are lines that are drawn from a point on the illustration to the explanation elsewhere on the page. Learners prefer these because they require no effort to decipher.

Place Visuals Immediately After or Beside the Reference to Them in the Text or Narration. When you refer to a visual in text or narration, learners expect to see it on the same screen. But designers of e-learning programs often place visuals elsewhere to conserve real estate on the screen, either on the next screen or in a pop-up window.

These practices annoy learners, so avoid them. Instead, place the visual immediately on the same screen as the text reference. You might place the visual to the side, or immediately beneath the text.

Note the Cultural Meanings Your Visuals Might Convey

Because cultural messages are often encoded in visuals, you may inadvertently communicate an unintended message if you are not aware of the other meanings of the visual images. Two common issues (but by no means all of them) are:

- *Hand gestures.* Hand gestures vary widely among cultures. Hand gestures that have a positive meaning in one culture might have a negative meaning in another. Carefully use them.

  Note that, when showing hands in the middle of performing a physical task, the hand is in movement and learners typically interpret it as such. They do not interpret it as a hand gesture.

- *Colors.* Meanings of colors vary widely among cultures. For example, in Western cultures, white is a color of purity and used for marriage. In contrast, red is a sign of passion and black is a color for mourning. As a result, a typical Western bride prefers a white wedding gown and is not likely to get married in red. In Western cultures, people wear black at funerals. In Eastern cultures, white is a color of mourning and red is the color of love. Brides prefer wedding gowns colored red, and white is widely worn at funerals.

Avoid Using Visuals Solely for Adornment

Although aware of the value of visuals in e-learning programs, some course designers and developers have difficulty choosing appropriate images, so they use visuals solely for adornment—that is, to spice up the screen.

Although these images may enhance the appearance of the screen, they have no educational value and, as a result, ultimately distract learners from the learning program instead of enhancing their learning experience.

Therefore, make sure that every visual image used directly relates to the learning experience.

Screen Design Guidelines

Although this chapter primarily focuses on using visual images, many instructional designers have questions about the effective design of screens. Table 13.5 summarizes some of the conventions for screen design.

Table 13.5. Summary of Screen Design Guidelines for Web-Based Materials

Convention	Guidelines

Design screens for easy navigation	Make sure that each screen has the following:
	• Title in the title bar at the top of the screen, usually indicates the name of the course or unit.
	• Heading (different than the title), which usually indicates the title of the topic.
	• Screen number. If possible, indicate the number of the screen in sequence (such as 1 of 20).
	• Icons for the following: forward, backward, exit, and help. When placing the icons:
	  • Place them toward the bottom of the screen, so users see this when they finish reading the material on the screen and are most likely to be interested in moving to another screen.
	  • Place the forward icon on the bottom right corner. Learners would physically touch that spot in a book to turn the page, so they think to look there for navigational devices.
	• White space (for a basic page, 25 percent. For a page that will be translated, 50 percent).

Use emphasis type appropriately	• **Bold**
	  • Headings (such as section headings, headings on charts and tables).
	  • Captions.
	  • Avoid using bold for emphasis within paragraphs. Instead of calling attention to the words, it calls attention away from headings.
	• *Italic*
	  • Titles of published works (books, videos, CDs, software). Example: *The Grapes of Wrath.*
	  • Words that are appropriated from other languages and have not become standard English (words such as *détente*), or that are being defined in text.
	  • Avoid using italic type to merely emphasize words. Although different, italic type is harder to read on screen than regular type and, as a result, instead of calling attention to text, the use of italic type makes the words harder to read.

Convention	Guidelines
Table 13.5. Summary of Screen Design Guidelines for Web-Based Materials, Cont'd	
	• Underscore only to indicate hyperlinks. Avoid any other use.
	• Color: to indicate hyperlinks. Be careful about other uses because users often confuse colored text with hyperlinks, even if they do not have underscores.
	• ALL CAPS: Never use. Looks like you're screaming at someone.
Use heading type appropriately	• Headings can be in a different typeface than body type, but all headings should use the same typeface.
	• Heading 1 is 4 points larger than body type.
	• Heading 2 is 2 points larger than body type.
	• Headings 3 and 4 are the same size as body type.
	• Use only 1 type font for heading type (More makes your document look like a ransom note).
Use body type appropriately	• Use sans serif type, considered the easiest to read online (serif fonts are considered easier to read in print). Serif fonts are ones that have hooks on the letters (the hook is called a serif, hence the name). Example of serif fonts are Times New Roman and Century Schoolbook. Examples of sans serif fonts are Arial and Helvetica.
	• Use either 11- or 12-point type for body type.
	• Use black type on a white background for the sharpest contrast.
	• Align all body type on the left margin.
	• Do not justify the right margin.
	• Use only one type font for body type (More fonts make your web pages look like a ransom notes).
	• Note that the ideal line length is approximately fifty characters.
Align headings and text along the left margin	Because readers scan text, they are likely to miss any text aligned elsewhere.
Present information in lists	• Bullets or numbers:
	• For ordered lists (in which list items must be considered in a particular order), use numbers

Convention	Guidelines
Table 13.5. Summary of Screen Design Guidelines for Web-Based Materials, Cont'd	
	• For unordered lists (in which list items may be considered in any order), use bullets.
	• Margins:
	• Bullet or number against the left margin.
	• Text indented .25 inches from the left margin.
	• Nested lists (lists within lists):
	• Align dingbat (number or bullet) with the beginning of text from the basic list.
	• If using an ordered list within an ordered list, items on the nested list should begin with letters.
	• If using an unordered list within an unordered list, items on the nested list should begin with m-dashes.
Design tables	• Use grid lines and borders, or alternate colors of rows and shading on columns, to help readers scan across rows and down columns without losing their places.
	• Use headings at the top of columns to help readers decipher what's below.
	• Use lists within cells, to further help readers in scanning.

Source: Little Planet. www.littleplanet.com/clients_gambro.html. Used with permission.

Guidelines Regarding Technology and Production

Although they may communicate ideas more efficiently than text in a cognitive sense, in a technical sense graphics are much larger than their text. A typical text file might only have 2 to 150 kilobytes of data, while a file with graphics covering the same material could easily have one to two megabytes of data. In practical terms, that means that graphics files have much more data to transmit and, as a result, can load more slowly, especially on dial-up connections.

This reality prompted one instructional designer who believes strongly in using graphics to declare, "I wouldn't consider accepting an assignment if the client refuses to require that its learners have high-speed Internet access."

Unfortunately, such requirements are rarely feasible. Many e-learning programs are designed so that learners can take them at home or in hotels. At the time this book is being written, the majority of homes do not have high-speed access, and many hotels charge a connection fee that is much higher than the cost of a telephone call. Still others must design materials for global use, and in some countries Internet access by telephone is difficult and high-speed access is either nonexistent or has extremely limited availability.

Designers who have such cut-and-dry requirements for their assignments not only limit themselves, but also limit the learners they want to serve. In a practical world, e-learning programs must balance the need for graphics with the practical realities of dial-up connections to the Internet, or no connection at all.

Similarly, corporate, government, and academic environments typically present other technical limitations that designers should consider when preparing e-learning programs.

The following guidelines are intended to help balance the use of graphics with the realities of learners' technologies. So when planning to use visuals, consider the following guidelines for technology and production:

- Watch the size of visuals
- In the space in which a visual is supposed to appear, provide descriptive information to alert learners while the image loads
- Avoid nonstandard plug-ins for viewing visuals
- Make sure you have permission to use images before publishing them

The next several sections describe these guidelines in detail.

Watch the Size of Visuals

Although, in terms of time, visuals communicate more efficiently than text, in terms of computer resources, visuals take up more space than the text they replace. Visuals take up space in two ways:

- *Physical space on the screen.* For example, a flowchart might take up an entire screen while the text procedure it replaced only needed an eight-line paragraph.
- *Storage space, because visual almost always uses more bytes than storing text.* A typical text-only file takes between 2 and 15 kilobytes of storage. A formatted text file takes between 20 and 150 kilobytes of storage. A graphics file, in contrast, can take up to 1 or 2 megabytes of space.

This larger size has significant implications for the technical performance of the learning program and for storing it. In terms of technical performance, the more bytes in the file, the more time needed to transmit it over the Internet. Therefore, e-learning programs with many graphics generally run slower. Performance over a telephone line is prohibitively slow, but performance over a high-speed network might also be slow. Unfortunately, learners have little patience waiting for graphics to load.

To avoid long loading times, keep graphics files as small as possible. You can do so by:

- *Limiting the amount of detail in graphics.* In addition to the learning benefits already described, limiting the amount of detail minimizes the amount of information that must be transferred. For example, files with line drawings are typically smaller than those with photographs.

- *Using the JPG format for photographs.* The size of JPG files is smaller than photographs stored in other formats.

In the Space in Which a Visual Is Supposed to Appear, Provide Descriptive Information to Alert Learners While the Image Loads

These messages, such as a text description that appears in a little yellow balloon when learners move their mouse over the area of the graphic, set learners' expectations about the graphic and, even without saying so, invite learners to wait for the visual to appear.

This description also benefits learners who are visually impaired. Adaptive technology can read the description of the visual to them, so that they can understand what they have difficulty seeing. Providing alternative presentations for persons with disabilities is a requirement by several government agencies, corporations, and school systems. This is called *universal design* because it provides all people with access to web pages, regardless of physical ability. Universal design results from an enhancement to the Americans with Disabilities Act (ADA), which is intended to ensure that people with disabilities can use web-based materials. Although ADA originated in the United States, it is an internationally recognized guideline for producing universal materials.

Avoid Nonstandard Plug-Ins for Viewing Visuals

Plug-ins refer to specialized software that handles certain types of information in an e-learning program. The most common types of plug-ins are used for presenting media, such as plug-ins for playing animation, music, narration, and video.

Standard plug-ins are ones that you can readily assume to be installed on learners' computers. In corporate environments, a centralized information systems (IS) department often installs software on each computer and generally has a list of plug-ins that are installed on each computer. These departments often prevent users from installing other plug-ins. Similarly, certain plug-ins are included standard on home and private computers, too, but there are fewer of them.

Using nonstandard plug-ins creates several problems. In some instances, learners will still not be able to use them. For example, to ensure that large video files do not slow down overall system performance, some computer networks forbid users from viewing them. In such instances, learners cannot see video sequences, regardless of the viewer.

In other instances, learners must download the plug-in program from another website. Many learners prefer not to download software. Some are not familiar with the downloading process; others are concerned about acquiring software viruses.

Even if learners do download the software, the download process takes time. In some instances, learners must restart their computers before the downloaded software becomes operational, adding to the time and complexity of taking the course.

This limits the use of plug-ins to ones known to be installed on learners' computers. If you are developing material for use on your organization's computers, check with the IS department to learn which plug-ins are widely available. The most typical plug-ins include:

- For viewing print files, Acrobat® Reader (Macintosh® computers have their own viewer for files in the portable data format [PDF])

- For viewing animation and special graphics: Flash® viewer and Shockwave®

- For viewing movie clips: QuickTime®, Real®, and Windows Media players®

Make Sure You Have Permission to Use Images Before Publishing Them

Preparing visuals can be expensive, especially if you need to have drawings custom made (an original line drawing might cost approximately $US 1,000) or custom photography (a professional photographer and assistants can cost upwards of $US 5,000/day, before rights to use the photographs). No wonder that many designers consider clip art (which can cost as little as $US 10/disk) and stock photography (which can cost as little as $US 350 for a disk of several hundred photos) or reuse drawings and photographs that were already prepared for their organizations.

Although copyright laws allow you to use a limited number of words of text without requesting the permission of the author, they also require that you receive permission to use all images that have been prepared elsewhere, whether you use them in full or in part.

Therefore, if you are using clip art stock specifically, consider these issues:

- If you are developing materials about a product or service from your company, chances are that someone has already produced the graphics in the engineering, graphics, marketing, or communications departments. Check with them.

- If you are developing other types of materials, you can find stock images in clip art libraries and on CDs with stock photos.

- Even if you paid for it, do not assume that you have blanket permission to use graphics and photos from clip art libraries, photo CDs, and other departments in your organization. Many clip art libraries have copyright restrictions and require that you pay a royalty before using them. Similarly, most custom graphics and photography firms provide material for one-time use; organizations must pay royalties for additional uses. For information on the policy with the clip art, check the documentation that comes with it or contact its publisher. For restrictions on using work prepared for another department in your organization, contact the graphics firm or photographer who created the image.

In Practice: The Seven Deadly Perils*

General Description of the Project

Title: The Seven Deadly Perils

Publisher: Gambro Healthcare, Department of Safety and Compliance

Producer: Little Planet Learning
www.littleplanet.com
info@littleplanet.com

Brief Description: Gambro Healthcare is one of the three largest renal care providers in the United States, providing more than six million dialysis treatments annually to roughly 40,000 chronic kidney disease (CKD) patients. Gambro employs nearly 13,000 people in the United States to provide hemodialysis, peritoneal dialysis, and acute care to patients with renal disease. This online learning project was developed to increase the employees' awareness about the importance of their tasks due to the fact that mistakes on their part can be fatal for

*This In Practice was prepared by Patrick Devey.

their patients. In particular, the online course aimed at informing them about the "7 Deadly Perils" regarding their jobs (such as contamination).

Intended Audience: Employees at Gambro other than those in the Safety and Compliance Department (who were already familiar with the material)

Size of Audience: The 13,000 employees of Gambro working in its 550 clinics across the United States

About the Learning Goals

Goals of the Project: Traditional Learning: employees use the learning program to increase their awareness of the importance in the well-being of their company's patients.

- *Primary goal:* Increase employees' awareness of the importance of safety in their jobs, especially when carelessness can cause serious harm to patients

- *Secondary goal:* Put a "human face" on the employees in the Safety and Compliance Department

Primary Learning Objectives:

- Describe primary risk factors associated with renal analysis

- Help employees avoid behavior that would lead to potentially adverse consequences.

Learning Issues Underlying the Project

Employees have been disenchanted with the previous attempts to "educate" them. They sometimes found the material boring, a waste of their time, and even insulting to their intelligence. In other words, they were fed-up with the classic "corporate video" approach.

Learners have access to computers at the workplace, and were encouraged to view the learning session during work hours.

The Numbers

Budget Range: High. Expenses included a Hollywood-based script writer and an illustrator who works with Marvel Comics and DC Comics. These expenses are seen as an investment by Gambro. If the learning session saves a life, the rewards are both intrinsic and financial (reduction of liability, which can be substantial in medical cases).

Schedule (from Beginning to End of Project): Ninety days

Approximate Number of People Who Worked on the Project: Ten

Skills Used in Project:

scriptwriting

programming

graphic design

illustration

editing

directing

audio engineering/composing

acting (voice-over work)

Other Business Issues Affecting the Project: Because Gambro employees viewed the Safety and Compliance Department as the company's "cops," employees expected the "same old" training from them, devoid of emotion and tedious in technical detail.

To challenge this image, the designers decided to play on this perception of the department and add a human element to it. The main character of the online course (or scenario) is Inspector March, a private eye modeled after the classic gumshoe (such as in "Dragnet" and "Dick Tracy"), complete with fedora hat and trench coat. This character served as a "virtual caricature" of the Safety and Compliance Department employees.

The dialogue is riddled with humorous innuendoes and jokes, all delivered with a straight face by the protagonist in the story used in this training program. As project manager and director of development Carter Andrews at Little Planet Learning, which produced the course, commented, "The viewer cannot help but feel an emotional attachment to Inspector March. We took the cop image and put a human face on it, hoping that the employees would appreciate the fact that he is just doing his job, yet with dry humor and wit. In other words, we use soulful communication techniques to get the point across to the learner, and at the same time, they relate to and feel for our hero."

This character was merged with a script tailored to the learners and, in addition to humor, used emotion, an engaging plot and, most significantly, content that learners could relate to and care about. Learners followed the trials and tribulations of the detective and, in doing so, would see the relevance of the material with their own work at Gambro.

Andrews also commented that learners needed to notice as early as possible that this online course was much different from others they have seen.

In other words, gaining their attention and maintaining it was very important for the design team. That's why visual appeal was so important. Animation begins on the first screen, as does sound. The designers hoped that this initial "wow" would propel the learner into the learning experience. But designers were also cautious about bombarding learners with a multimedia show that distracted learners from the serious technical content. "If you're going to take a swing at this project, you don't want to miss," Andrews concluded.

Technology Infrastructure

Delivery Medium: Internet (or intranet)

Media Used Within the Learning Program:

text

graphics (Vector Art)

audio (music, sound effects, narration)

animations

Delivery Platform: Macromedia Flash® (standalone, or as a plug-in in a Web browser)

Authoring Environment

- Primary software: Macromedia Flash®

- Supporting software: Programs supporting vector graphics (Adobe PhotoShop®, Adobe Illustrator®); audio editing software for the voice and music components; minor JavaScript® programming

Results of the Course

Marketing of the Course: Although the Safety and Compliance Department at Gambro encouraged employees to view the online course, ultimately, word of mouth from employees who were delighted with the learning materials was ultimately the most powerful marketing tool.

Response to the Course: Employees were generally pleased with the course and thought it to be a good excuse to take a break from work. The consensus was that the course was entertaining and fun, and at the same time, informative.

What Would You Do the Same on a Future E-Learning Project? The use of multimedia effects to accompany the fantastic visuals takes advantage of the creative strengths of the employees of Little Planet, Andrews commented. Through the directing, producing, writing, and preparing special effects, the talents of the staff went a long way to captivate their target audience and maintain their attention throughout the learning session. In other words, Andrews compliments his colleagues on knowing how to make effective use of "bells and whistles," not only to entertain but to get the message across to learners.

What Would You Do Differently? Time constraints were an issue with this project and the development team ended up using a character (Inspector March) that had been previously created for another project. Although Gambro had approved the use of this premade character, added time could have allowed the creation of a unique persona that better represented the Gambro company. But as things turned out, this image—used to save development time—was an appropriate one to the task at hand.

Figures 13.8 and 13.9 show sample screens from the program.

Figure 13.8. Sample Screen from Inspector March: The Seven Deadly Perils

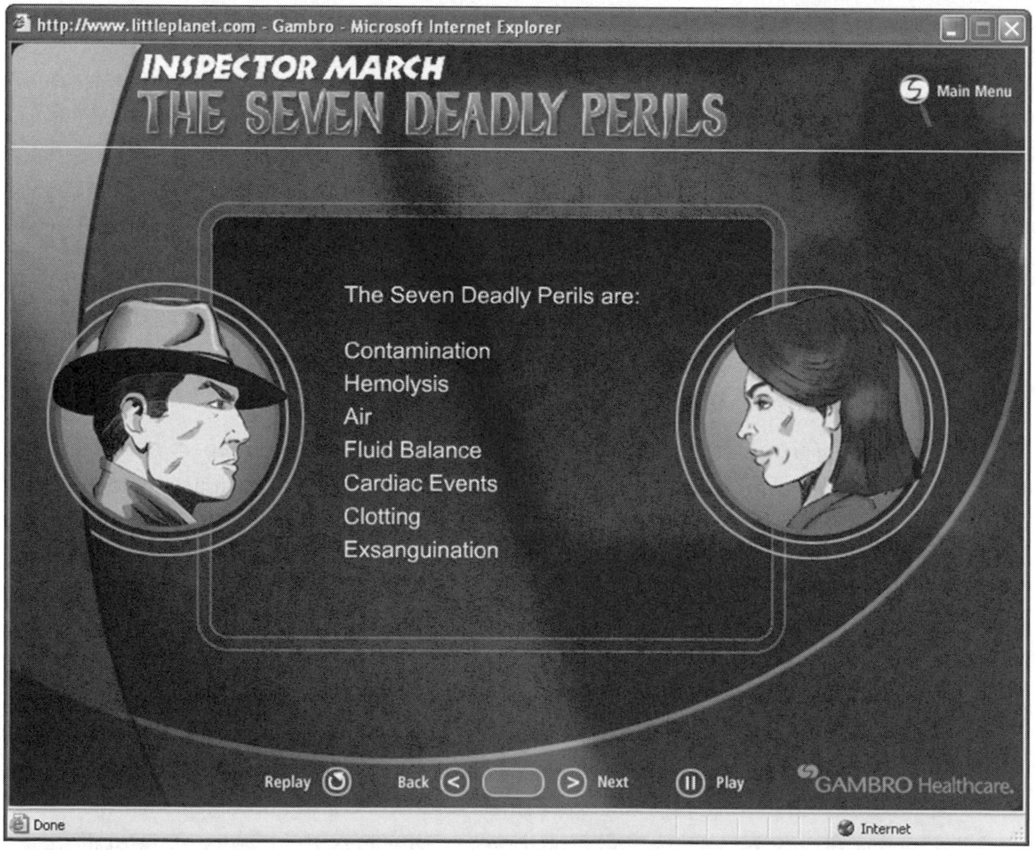

Source: Little Planet. www.littleplanet.com/clients_gambro.html. Used with permission.

Figure 13.9. Another Screen from Inspector March: The Seven Deadly Perils

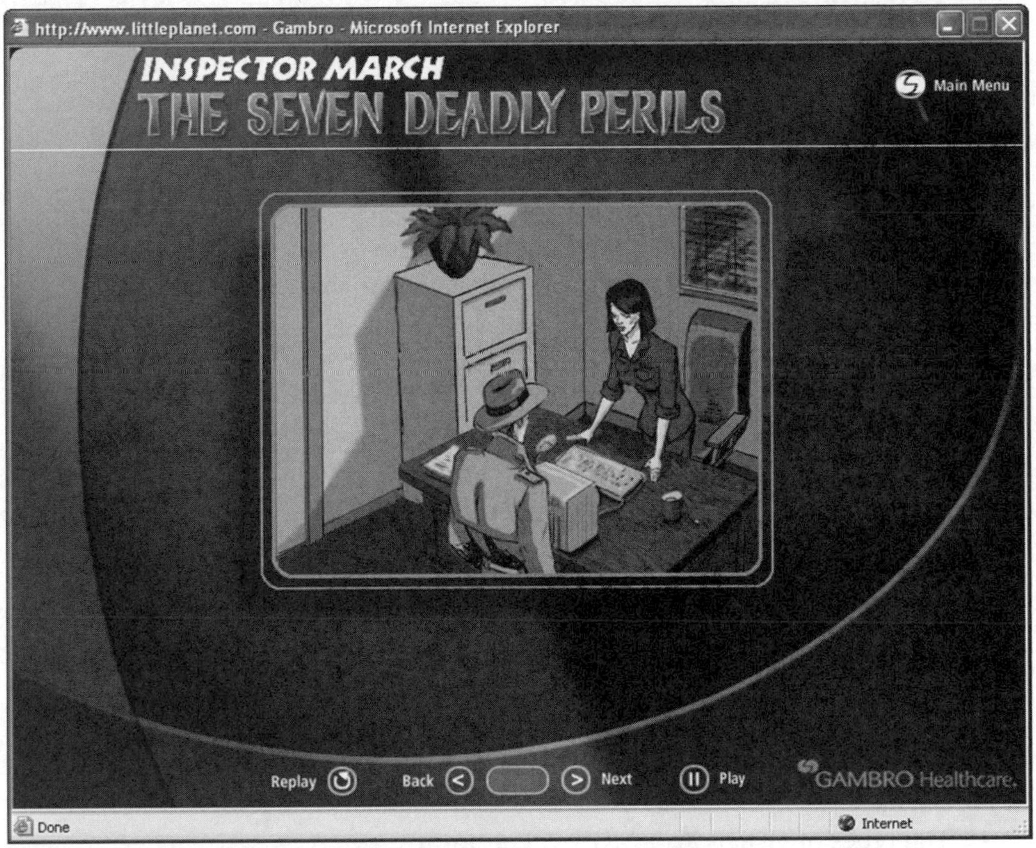

Source: Little Planet. www.littleplanet.com/clients_gambro.html, Used with permission.

Conclusion

Visuals enhance the online learning experience in a number of ways, from putting a human face on an otherwise anonymous learning experience to more efficiently and effectively communicating technical content than is possible with words alone. To reach this conclusion, this chapter explored the following points:

- Visuals are pictures, illustrations, photographs, videos, charts, and symbols that communicate messages through images rather than words.

- Use visuals because:

  - The computer is an inherently visual medium; its technology is the same as that used in television.

- Visuals best communicate inherently visual content, such as a product, a process, and the comparison of financial results.

- Visuals communicate some ideas more efficiently than text, such as what actually happened at an event.

- Learners remember visuals, especially images that they interact with frequently.

- Visuals appeal to the affective domain by gaining and holding attention and by building trust.

- Visuals accommodate learners with a need for visual content, such as second- and third-language learners.

- The types of visuals vary by their content.

  - Some present quantitative information, such as pie charts (showing relationships of parts to the whole), bar charts (comparing two items), and histograms (showing performance over time).

  - Some present concrete concepts, such as people, finished products, product plans, procedures, and relationships.

  - Some represent abstract concepts, such as travel, organizations (corporate identity), and control of equipment.

  - Some direct learners' attention, such as navigational images and images that direct learners' eyes to a particular part of the screen.

- The types of visuals also vary by their form:

  - Photographs

  - Illustrations

  - Static (photographs and illustrations) or moving (videos and animations)

- Consider these guidelines to make sure that visuals effectively enhance the learning experience:

  - Pay attention to aesthetics by using simplicity and balance to ensure that visuals are attractive to learners and make them interactive whenever possible.

  - Balance visual appeal with usability by making sure the material is aesthetically pleasing, yet easy to follow and understand.

- Make visuals comprehensible by removing extraneous details from images, properly labeling visuals, and placing visuals immediately after or beside the reference to them in the text.

- Note the cultural meanings your visuals might convey, such as hand gestures and the meanings of color.

- Avoid using visuals solely for adornment.

- Consider these technical and production guidelines for using visuals:

  - Keep the size of graphics files as small as possible to ensure efficient use.

  - Provide descriptive information about visuals to guide learners while an image is loading and to make images accessible to people with disabilities.

  - Avoid nonstandard plug-in software.

  - Make sure that you have permission to use images produced for your e-learning programs, especially ones prepared by sources outside of your organization, such as clip art and illustrations and photographs prepared by outside contractors.

Learn More About It

Clark, R., & Lyons, C. (2004). Graphics for learning: Proven guidelines for planning, designing, and evaluating visuals in training materials. San Francisco, CA: Pfeiffer.

The first book on graphics specifically for e-learning.

Horn, R. (1999). *Visual language: Global communication for the 21st century.* Bainbridge Island, WA: MacRovu.

From the same man who gave us the information mapping approach to organizing and preparing content comes a book about the effective use of visuals. Horn explores how visuals communicate and offers good insights and practical tips on how to apply them in everyday communication.

Kostelnick, C., & Roberts, D. (1998). *Designing visual language: Strategies for professional communicators.* New York: Allyn & Bacon.

Although primarily geared toward communicating visually in print, this is the only book primarily focused on communication within corporations and on technical content.

Tufte, E. (2001). *The visual display of quantitative information* (2nd ed.). Cheshire, CT: Graphis Press.

Shows good and bad examples of graphic design, and popularized the importance of using visuals to convey quantitative information.

Williams, R. (1994). *The non-designer's design book.* San Francisco: Peachpit Press.

A quick read that introduces you to some of the key principles of design and shows how to apply them in practical situations, such as e-learning programs.

Websites of Interest

www.aiga.org/loop/ *Loop: The Online Journal of Experience Design.*

An online journal by and for graphic designers that explores a combination of practical and theoretical issues in designing online communication. Even for us nondesigners, stretches thinking about the topic and offers good insights into current practice. Updated quarterly.

www.usability.gov.

A website prepared by the U.S. National Institutes for Health that provides guidelines both for effective web-based design and design that accommodates the needs of persons with disabilities and complies with the Americans with Disabilities Act.

REFLECTION AND APPLICATION

To reflect on the material presented in this chapter and apply it in a real e-learning situation, consider how you would respond to the following challenges. (Each of these challenges is intentionally left vague. If you are unsure about a piece of information, make an assumption about it and list the assumption.)

- You are designing a course that describes the process for incorporating a business. The course explains, in detail, the steps involved in doing so, such as choosing a unique name, getting an employer identification number, writing articles of incorporation, and choosing a type of corporation. Your colleague looks at your first draft and says, "That's cool stuff, but couldn't you make it more visual?" So could you make this procedure more visual? If so, how could you do it?

- You are designing an e-learning course that tells your company's staff how to set up a new machine that the company is marketing. The subject-matter expert has asked whether you intend to use visuals to present the set-up instructions. So do you intend to use visuals? What would they show? What type of visual would you use—a photograph or a line drawing? Why?

- Terry is developing an online course on corporate identity for a university. In the course, Terry plans to show the logos of several organizations. Terry plans to find these logos by going to the websites of these organizations, copying the logos, and pasting them into the course materials. Do you have any concerns about Terry's getting logos in this way? If so, what concerns do you have? How could they be addressed?

Part V

Closing

The book concludes with Chapter 14, Seeking Ideas Outside the Norm, in which we suggest how to continue building your portfolio of e-learning techniques. We first identify some specific ways of finding ideas to add to your portfolio, then suggest a way to keep abreast of the admittedly voluminous and confusing changes in technology.

Chapter 14

Seeking Ideas Outside the Norm

Sometimes, the best ideas come from noncompetitors.

Stead, 1999

In This Chapter

In this chapter, we will

- Identify fields outside of instructional design to which instructional designers can look for guiding theories

- Identify sources other than other e-learning programs that instructional designers can consult for ideas for their own programs

- Explain how designers of e-learning programs can prepare for new developments in e-learning

◆ ◆ ◆

In this book, we have used the problem-solving approach to design to frame the challenge of designing e-learning programs. We have explored several specific approaches and opportunities in design, such as the use of storytelling techniques to enhance understanding of learners and the learning problem, how to provide coaching services online through e-mentoring, and frameworks for integrating interactivity into e-learning programs. For each, we explained what the approach or opportunity is, how it benefits the learning process, issues to consider when applying this approach or taking advantage of this opportunity, a portfolio of techniques associated with it, and examples of it "in practice" from other e-learning programs.

Until now, we limited our search for approaches, opportunities, guidelines, and examples primarily to other learning programs. Sometimes, however, the best design ideas come from outside the field or noncompetitors. That is, the best ideas might not come from other e-learning programs or the field of instructional design, but from other disciplines and other types of content.

In fact, many of the examples in this book come from people whose formal training comes partially or fully from outside the field of instructional design. For example, the designers of the World Bank's MoneyMatters have backgrounds in corporate copywriting. The designer of the Plimoth Plantation program has a Ph.D. in computer science—and three young children of her own. One of the designers of the Jones University course on instructional design is a registered electrical engineer and has a master's degree in technical communication.

The influences on instructional design are many, and most come from outside of the field. This chapter explores those influences, and we suggest how to explore these influences further. We first identify outside influences on the field of instructional design. Then we suggest activities that might help designers conceive of additional ideas for e-learning. Last, we explore ways to keep abreast of changes to e-learning, especially changes outside of the field of instructional design and e-learning that would have a strong impact on the work.

Looking Outside for Theory

In the academic world, instructional design is considered an applied field. That means it is based on theory developed from other fields and applies those theories to practical problems, such as the design of curricula and courses. Some of the core theories on which we base instructional design come from other disciplines in education—or other fields entirely.

For example, the systematic approach used in the instructional systems design process comes from the field of cybernetics, a discipline closely aligned with computer science and management theory. Similarly, some of the basic theories about how the brain processes information come from the field of cognitive psychology. Because cognitive psychology explores how humans learn, some scientists study it within the context of education, through a discipline called educational psychology.

In other words, when looking for theories to guide the development of e-learning programs, course designers need not limit themselves to the field of instructional design (also called educational technology and instructional technology—with technology referring to the hardware and software and, most important, the thinkware [theory] underlying the design of instruction). Many other fields inform our work. In the sub-specialty of instructional message design, Pettersson and Fager (2002) found nearly fifty fields alone.

Table 14.1 lists some of the most relevant disciplines for finding ideas, but you need not limit your choices to them.

Table 14.1. Different Disciplines Whose Ideas Inform the Design of e-Learning Programs	
Discipline	**How It Informs Instructional Design for e-Learning**
Adult and Vocational Education (from the Field of Education)	Explores how adults learn and how to teach vocational topics. Some of the greatest contributions of this discipline include the principles of *andragogy* (the principles of adult learning, as contrasted with *pedagogy*, the principles for teaching children) and self-directed learning. Applying concepts of adult and vocational education are helpful in designing meaningful job-training and continuing-education programs. To learn more about adult education, visit the site of the American Association for Adult and Continuing Education (www.aaace.org).
Anthropology and Sociology	Explores the study of cultures. Anthropology focuses primarily on the study of cultures in their own environments (including corporate and occupational cultures), while sociology explores the interaction of cultures. Among the great contributions of anthropology are observational research techniques, which prove useful in conducting needs assessments. Applying concepts of anthropology and sociology provides designers with a framework for considering the overt and implied cultural issues in their e-learning programs. To learn more about anthropology and sociology, visit the American Anthropological Association's list of resources (www.aaanet.org/resinet.htm).
Artificial Intelligence (from the Field of Computer Science)	Explores ways to design computers so that they appear to have human intelligence. Among the contributions of artificial intelligence are search engines, especially those that accept terms in "natural language" (language that ordinary humans speak), personalization (systems that can identify the needs of specific learners and adapt to them), and intelligent tutoring systems. Applying the principles of artificial intelligence, designers can prepare e-learning programs that better

Table 14.1. Different Disciplines Whose Ideas Inform the Design of e-Learning Programs, Cont'd	
Discipline	**How It Informs Instructional Design for e-Learning**
	meet the unique needs of individual learners. To learn more about artificial intelligence in education, check the International Journal of Artificial Intelligence in Education (www.cogs.susx.ac.uk/ijaied/), an online journal.
Cognitive Psychology (from the Field of Psychology)	Explores how humans acquire, process, and recall information. Applying cognitive psychology in learning programs is a bit like using LactAid®.* LactAid pre-digests lactose so people who have a lactose intolerance can handle dairy products. Similarly, applying cognitive psychology involves presenting content to learners in a way that some of the tasks of human information processing have been started, so learners are more likely to acquire, comprehend, and retain the content. To learn more about cognitive psychology, especially as it relates to education, visit either the American Educational Research Association (www.aera.net) or the American Psychological Association (www.apa.org).
Computer Graphics and Data Visualization (from the Field of Computer Science)	Explores the technologies needed to create and present graphics online, as well as the principles needed to represent data visually. Among the key contributions of this discipline are three-dimensional graphics and scaleable graphics (graphics that can be easily re-sized). Applying the principles of computer graphics and data visualization, designers can create e-learning programs that effectively present visuals. To learn more about computer graphics, visit the Special Interest Group on Graphics of the Association for Computing Machinery (www.acm.org/siggraph).
Early Childhood and Elementary Education (from the Field of Education)	Explores the principles for teaching children in primary and preschool. Specifically explores issues such as childhood development (and age-appropriate activities), reading development, and special education. Applying these principles, designers of e-learning materials intended for young children in pre- and primary schools can adapt and employ strategies that have proved successful with learners in this age range. To learn more about early childhood and elementary education, visit the website of your local school system.

Table 14.1. Different Disciplines Whose Ideas Inform the Design of e-Learning Programs, Cont'd	
Discipline	**How It Informs Instructional Design for e-Learning**
Educational Evaluation and Pyschometrics (from the Field of Education)	Explores the principles and practices of assessing learning and learning programs. Specifically, this discipline explores the various ways to evaluate educational programs and individual learning achievement and develops and validates methodologies and instruments for doing so. Applying the principles of educational evaluation and psychometrics, designers can prepare effective evaluations of learners and e-learning programs. To learn more about educational psychometrics and evaluation, check the journal, *Educational Evaluation and Policy Analysis,* published by the American Educational Research Association (www.aera.net/pubs/eepa/)
Human-Computer Interaction (HCI) (Usability) (from the Field of Computer Science)	Explores how humans interact with computers and generates principles for designing interactions that are most likely to be performed correctly on the first try. Most of the focus of this sub-discipline of ergonomics is on the design of computer interfaces. Applying concepts from HCI, designers can prepare screen designs and interactions that clearly communicate with learners. To learn more about computer-human interaction, visit the Special Interest Group on Computer-Human Interaction of the Association for Computing Machinery (www.acm.org/sigchi).
Human Performance Improvement (Technology) (HPI) (from the Discipline of Instructional Design)	Explores a systematic approach to improving the effectiveness and efficiency of workers in organizations. Although primarily focused on businesses, the principles can be applied elsewhere. Originally called *human performance technology,* but more recently called human performance improvement, because the technology is an intellectual one (rather than hardware or software) and few people outside of the field understand that. Two of the greatest contributions of HPI are the acknowledgement that training cannot always improve human performance in the workplace if learners do not have the resources or motivation to effectively perform and electronic performance support systems. Applying the concepts of HPI, designers only prepare programs likely to result in learning and suggest other approaches (called interventions) for those situations in which learning will not

Discipline	How It Informs Instructional Design for e-Learning
Table 14.1. Different Disciplines Whose Ideas Inform the Design of e-Learning Programs, Cont'd	
	achieve the desired performance. To learn more about human performance improvement, visit either the International Society for Performance Improvement (www.ispi.org) or the American Society for Training and Development (www.astd.org).
Human Resource Development and Management (HRD/HRM) (from the Field of Management)	Explores the principles and practices of developing, rewarding, and managing individuals and groups in organizations. Specifically, human resource *development* explores training, career development, and similar approaches to building the capacity of individuals and human resource *management* explores issues such as recruitment, compensation, and benefits to recruit and retain employees. Applying the principles of HRD and HRM, designers of corporate training can prepare programs that link to larger systems in organizations. For more information about human resource development, visit the American Society for Training and Development (www.astd.org). For more information about human resource management, visit the Society for Human Resource Management (www.shrm.org).
Industrial Design (from the Field of Graphic Design)	Explores the design of everyday objects for both practical use and aesthetic pleasure. Most products are designed by industrial designers, and some of the most famous industrial designers work on a wide range of products, ranging from furniture to computers. One interest of industrial designers is the design of information. Applying the concepts of industrial design, designers can prepare courses and related packaging that are both practical to use and aesthetic. For more information about industrial design, visit the Industrial Designers Society of America (www.idsa.org).
Industrial Engineering (from the Field of Engineering)	Explores the efficient design of processes in business organizations. Although once associated with the efficiency of manufacturing, industrial engineers have expanded their focus to a wide array of business processes. One of the great contributions of this discipline was its influence on the field of instructional design to create the subdiscipline of human performance improvement (also described here).

Table 14.1. Different Disciplines Whose Ideas Inform the Design of e-Learning Programs, Cont'd	
Discipline	**How It Informs Instructional Design for e-Learning**
	Applying the principles of industrial engineering, designers can integrate learning programs with larger efforts to improve efficiency in organizations, especially businesses and government agencies. For more information about industrial engineering, visit the Institute for Industrial Engineers (www.iienet.org).
Information Design (Interdisciplinary Field, Emerging from Graphic Design, Human-Computer Interaction, and Technical Communication)	Explores the principles of effectively communicating content, especially online. This interdisciplinary field explores the structure of content (called information architecture), the aesthetics and practicality of screen and interface design, and the strategies for effectively presenting and writing content. For more information on information design, visit InfoDesign (www.bogieland.com/infodesign/).
Management	Explores the principles of managing organizations. Two of the greatest contributions of this field are the principles and practices for performance planning and evaluation in the workplace and change management, which pertains to the issues of managing the introduction of change in organizations to address not only the intended benefits, but also the likely consequences. Applying the principles of management theory, designers in business organizations can prepare learning programs that link effectively with jobs and, when they introduce change to those jobs, address that change in a responsible way. For more information on management, check with the business school at a nearby university.
Middle-Secondary Education (from the Field of Education)	Explores the principles for teaching in specific content areas to middle and secondary level students. Specifically explores educational strategies in particular subject areas, such as science and math. Applying these principles, designers of e-learning materials intended for middle and secondary students can adapt and employ strategies that have proved successful with learners in this age range. For more information about middle-secondary education and the field of education, visit the website of your local school system.

Table 14.1. Different Disciplines Whose Ideas Inform the Design of e-Learning Programs, Cont'd	
Discipline	**How It Informs Instructional Design for e-Learning**
Technical Communication (from the Field of Rhetoric)	Explores the principles of transferring scientific and technical knowledge from those who know (such as scientists and engineers) to those who need to know (such as end users). One of the greatest contributions of technical communication is the principle of task-oriented writing, writing that is focused on communicating how to perform a task that readers need to do, rather than describing functions and features of a product or concept and letting readers figure out for themselves how to perform the task. Another contribution of technical communication is the principles of writing content for presentation online. Applying the principles of technical communication, designers can prepare online materials that communicate concisely and clearly. For more information about technical communication, visit the eServer on Technical Communication (http://eserver.org).

*LactAid is a trademark of McNeil Nutritionals, a Division of McNeil-PPCc.0

Looking Outside for Ideas

In addition to looking outside of the field of instructional design for theories and research to guide work, designers can also look outside the field of instructional design for ideas on how to effectively prepare e-learning programs. Following are some ideas to get you started.

Visit a Museum

Although many see them as warehouses of artifacts, museums consider themselves institutions of free-choice learning—that is, informal learning in which learners choose what they would like to learn and what they choose to ignore. Because museum exhibits need to appeal to broad audiences with varying levels of interest in the subject of an exhibition (and equally varying levels of interest in being in the museum itself), exhibition designers face a challenging prospect. Recognizing that interest levels are generally low and that visitors spend less than thirty seconds at any label (descriptive text) in the exhibit, exhibit designers use a variety of techniques to grab visitors' attention and entice them to learn more (Carliner, 2001). Designers should find these ideas useful for preparing asynchronous courses.

Shop—in a Mall, Not an e-Store

Designers of retail spaces also face a broad public, but their customers are either highly focused (looking for a particular product) or highly unfocused (just browsing, planning to make a purchase later). In addition, individual retailers face competition from others selling similar merchandise in nearby stores. To appeal to prospective customers, brick-and-mortar retailers and malls use a variety of techniques to entice shoppers in and keep them shopping for hours (Carliner, 2002b). Designers should find these ideas useful for preparing asynchronous courses.

Watch a Talk Show on Television

Unlike panels in academic and professional conferences, in which four speakers divide up their hour by each speaking for twelve minutes, and leave five minutes at the end for general questions, talk shows on television design similar types of panels to move much more quickly and with a high level of interaction with the studio and viewing audiences to gain and hold viewers' attention. For example, daytime talk shows like "Live with Regis and Kelly" and "The View" keep interviews brief (no more than eight minutes). Between interviews, hosts often have other types of activities, such as fashion shows and interactive sequences with audiences. Although fast-paced, this format does not allow for in-depth exploration of topics. Late-night talk shows, such as "NightLine," allow for more in-depth exploration of topics, but still keep the pace going. "NightLine" typically begins with a background report, so that viewers all have a basic familiarity with the topic of discussion. That is usually followed with a discussion of some sort, either between the host and the reporter, or between the host and one or more experts. The discussion is conducted as an interview rather than a formal presentation. Designers should find these ideas useful in designing live virtual classes.

Play a Game—Computer Game, That Is

Although we expressed concern at the beginning of this book that games are not necessarily the only way to reach younger learners, we were responding to others who suggest that games are the only way to teach. But as one of many ways to present content online, games offer a number of ideas. Many people believe that games are the most effective interactive programs on the market. Designers should find these ideas useful in designing asynchronous and live virtual courses.

Learn a Topic on Your Own Online

That's right. Decide to learn about something online. Conduct an online search for websites on the topic and see which ones actually yield information of interest. Reflect on what made the useful sites "good hits," and the other sites "weak hits." On the useful sites, consider how they present content. Consider what makes the presentation effective and what encourages learners to stick around. Designers should find these ideas useful in designing informal learning experiences.

Preparing for New Developments in e-Learning

One of the ongoing questions in the field of e-learning is "What's next?"

To be honest, who knows? Although e-learning has grown steadily over the past several years, it has not grown as fast as early predictions indicated it would. Similarly, despite substantial efforts to develop technical standards so that organizations can easily find and exchange e-learning content, the standards do not yet work seamlessly as of the writing of this book.

In contrast, other technical developments come out of nowhere to take over the field. For example, Macromedia Flash® became a popular authoring tool almost from the day it was introduced. A prediction written months in advance probably would have missed that one.

So rather than make a prediction about technology, we want to suggest ways that you can make your own predictions and assessments. Specifically, we suggest that you do the following:

Critically Consider Technology Predictions

Throughout the year, industry analysts and others publish predictions about the growth of technologies. At the least, these predictions help designers—who are pressed for time just keeping up with their regular workload—stay abreast of changes in technology.

In addition to following predictions about e-learning technology, we recommend that you also look at predictions in the broader areas of information systems in general, and content and document technologies in particular. The trends affecting information systems in general often affect e-learning. For example, as e-learning spending was challenged in the years 2002–2004, so information systems spending has been challenged. Similarly, related technologies such as content and document technologies are among the biggest affecting e-learning.

So when reading these predictions, don't merely take them for granted. Read them with a critical eye. To help you develop your critical eye, we suggest that you consider these issues while reading predictions:

- Do you believe the prediction? Why or why not? In many instances, the analysts predict uses of technology that substantially differ from your own experience. In some instances, that change is likely to happen because the technology offers a better and cheaper way of performing work. In other instances, the change doesn't seem to make sense. The technology does not offer a substantially improved way of performing work or does not offer a cost savings. Trust your instincts.

- How did the analyst arrive at this conclusion? Is it just a "gut instinct," or does it result from scientific study?

- What support does the analyst offer for the prediction? If the prediction is based on a gut instinct, does the analyst have sufficiently broad experience on which to base predictions? If the gut-instinct prediction is based on someone else's data, when was the data collected? Have things changed since then? For example, when analysts base 2004 predictions of growth in e-learning based on studies conducted in 2001, the data is tainted. If the analyst conducted a study on his or her own, what types of organizations were included? Was it a broad cross section or just larger organizations? If it is just larger organizations, does your organization approach training and development like these larger organizations? Was it a study of *best* practice or *real* practice? Saul's research of real practice suggests that it differs so substantially from best practices that best practices can only be used for inspiration, not necessarily a prediction of how ordinary organizations will operate in the future.

Follow Economic and Business Trends

Regardless of the type of e-learning developed, spending on education and training in general, and on e-learning in particular, is shaped by larger economic forces. For example, when the economy is growing, tax revenues increase and more funds are available for public primary and secondary education, as well as public university education. Similarly, in an economic downturn, budgets for corporate training departments are cut (although, contrary to popular belief, studies suggest that the amount of budget cuts received by training departments are the same as those by other departments, we are not necessarily the first to be cut and we don't receive larger cuts than others).

To follow business trends, follow the economic trends from central governments and central banks. In contrast to the predictions of technology forecasters, predictions of general economic growth in an economy seem to emerge from prediction formulas developed and refined through the years. Specific figures to follow include:

- General economic growth rates (often predicted by a central bank, like the U.S. Federal Reserve) and validated through the economic forecasts of private bankers

- Employment trends, especially unemployment rates (like those reported monthly by the U.S. Department of Labor)

Also explore growth rates in particular industries in which you work. These are generally reported by the business press. For example, some business magazines, like *Business Week,* provide general outlooks by industry at the beginning of each year, then follow up with updated forecasts later in the year.

When exploring business trends, consider them broadly. Look beyond your own country, because the global economy means that events in places like Hong Kong can have an impact on places like Toronto, Ontario.

Also look beyond the industry in which you work, because industries are as linked as national and regional economies. For example, a downturn in air travel affects not only other branches of tourism, but also aircraft manufacture. An upturn in housing sales also affects mortgage banking, home furnishings, and appliance manufacturing.

Follow Developments in the Field of Education

Most significantly, whatever branch of education you work in—early childhood, primary, secondary, higher, adult, or corporate—follow industry trends in education. That's business developments, such as increases and decreases in spending and changes in policy, as opposed to intellectual developments, such as a new philosophy or theory or the latest research. Certainly new intellectual developments can have a profound impact on the work, but business developments often have a more profound effect on the educational environment. Government policies usually affect funding and workloads and, in the long term, set the agenda for corporate training and vocational education. For example, much of the focus on standards in education is the result of U.S. government policy.

Because educational developments in primary and secondary education are local, and often covered by the press, check for coverage locally.

For broader trends affecting higher education, check the *Chronicle of Higher Education*, a weekly newspaper that reports trends in U.S. higher education.

For trends affecting corporate training, check the annual industry report from *Training* magazine (www.trainingmag.com), as well as the annual industry report from the American Society for Training and Development (www.astd.org).

Conclusion

A problem-solving designer brings a broad range of knowledge and experiences to a given instructional design challenge and, as a result, can call on a broad portfolio of ideas and techniques to address that challenge. To reach this conclusion, this chapter explored the following points:

- When looking for theories to guide the development of e-learning programs, look to the following fields in addition to the field of instructional design: adult and vocational education, anthropology and sociology, artificial intelligence, cognitive psychology, computer graphics and data visualization, early childhood and elementary education, educational evaluation and psychometrics, human-computer interaction, human performance improvement (technology), human resource development, human resource management, industrial design, industrial engineering, information design, management, middle-secondary education, and technical communication.

- The following activities might suggest new ideas for e-learning programs:
  - Visit a museum
  - Shop at a mall (not an e-store)
  - Watch a talk show on television
  - Play a computer game
  - Learn a topic on your own online

- Prepare for new developments in e-learning by:
  - Critically considering technology predictions
  - Following economic and business trends
  - Following developments in the field of education

REFLECTION AND APPLICATION

To reflect on the material presented in this chapter and apply it in a real e-learning situation, consider how you would respond to the following challenges. (Each of these challenges is intentionally left vague. If you are unsure about a piece of information, make an assumption about it and list the assumption.)

- From the list of disciplines affecting instructional design and e-learning, pick any three. Visit the primary source listed and, if time permits, visit at least two additional sources about that discipline. Name at least three ways that each discipline can influence your designs for e-learning.

- After designing six e-learning programs, you have concluded that they all look the same. Name three things you can do to prevent the seventh from looking like a clone of the other six.

- You have read a prediction that use of reusable learning objects will increase five-fold in the next three years. How do you decide whether or not that prediction is valid? If it is valid, how would that affect the way that you design e-learning programs?

Appendix A

Rubric for Assessing Interactive Qualities of Distance Learning Courses

Directions: The rubric shown below has five (5) separate elements that contribute to a course's level of interaction and interactivity. For each of these five elements, circle a description below it that applies best to your course. After reviewing all elements and circling the appropriate level, add up the points to determine the course's level of interactive qualities (low, moderate, or high).

Low interactive qualities	1 to 9 points
Moderate interactive qualities	10 to 17 points
High interactive qualities	18 to 25 points

Scale (see points below)	Element #1: Social/Rapport-Building Designs for Interaction	Element #2: Instructional Designs for Interaction	Element #3: Interactivity of Technology Resources	Element #4: Evidence of Learner Engagement	Element #5: Evidence of Instructor Engagement
Low interactive qualities (1 point each)	The instructor does not encourage students to get to know one another on a personal basis. No activities require social interaction, or interaction is limited to brief introductions at the beginning of the course.	Instructional activities do not require two-way interaction between instructor and students; they call for one-way delivery of information (instructor lectures, text delivery) and student products based on the information.	Fax, Web pages, or other technology resource allows one-way delivery of information (text and/or graphics).	By end of course, most students (50–75 percent) are *replying to* messages from the instructor, but only when required; messages are sometimes unresponsive to topics and tend to be either brief or wordy and rambling.	Instructor responds only randomly to student queries; responses usually take more than forty-eight hours; feedback is brief and provides little analysis of student work or suggestions for improvement.
Minimum interactive qualities (2 points each)	In addition to brief introductions, the instructor requires one other exchange of personal information among students, for example, written bio of personal background and experiences.	Instructional activities require students to communicate with the instructor on an individual basis only (for example, asking/responding to instructor questions).	E-mail, listserv, conference/ bulletin board, or other technology resource allows two-way, asynchronous exchanges of information (text and graphics).	By end of course, most students (50–75 percent) are *replying to* messages from the instructor and other students, both when required and on a voluntary basis; replies are usually responsive to topics but often are either brief or wordy and rambling.	Instructor responds to most student queries; responses usually are within forty-eight hours; feedback sometimes offers some analysis of student work and suggestions for improvement.
Moderate interactive qualities (3 points each)	In addition to providing for exchanges of personal information among students, the instructor provides at least one other in-class activity designed to increase communication and social rapport among students.	In addition to requiring students to communicate with the instructor, instructional activities require students to communicate with one another (for example, discussions in pairs or small groups).	In addition to technologies used for two-way asynchronous exchanges of information, chat rooms or other technology allows synchronous exchanges of primarily written information.	By end of course, all or nearly all students (90–100 percent) are *replying to* messages from the instructor and other students, both when required and voluntarily; replies are always responsive to topics but sometimes are either brief or wordy and rambling.	Instructor responds to all student queries; responses usually are within forty-eight hours; feedback usually offers some analysis of student work and suggestions for improvement.

Scale (see points below)	Element #1: Social/Rapport-Building Designs for Interaction	Element #2: Instructional Designs for Interaction	Element #3: Interactivity of Technology Resources	Element #4: Evidence of Learner Engagement	Element #5: Evidence of Instructor Engagement
Above average interactive qualities (4 points each)	In addition to providing for exchanges of personal information among students and encouraging communication and social interaction, the instructor also interacts with students on a social/personal basis.	In addition to requiring students to communicate with the instructor, instructional activities require students to develop products by working together cooperatively (for example, in pairs or small groups) and sharing feedback.	In addition to technologies used for two-way synchronous and asynchronous exchanges of written information, additional technologies (for example, teleconferencing) allow one-way visual and two-way voice communications between instructor and students.	By end of course, most students (50–75 percent) are *both replying to and initiating* messages when required and voluntarily; messages are detailed and responsive to topics and usually reflect an effort to communicate well.	Instructor responds to all student queries; responses usually are prompt, that is, within twenty-four hours; feedback always offers detailed analysis of student work and suggestions for improvement.
High level of interactive qualities (5 points each)	In addition to providing for exchanges of information and encouraging student-student and instructor-student interaction, the instructor provides ongoing course structures designed to promote social rapport among students and instructor.	In addition to requiring students to communicate with the instructor, instructional activities require students to develop products by working together cooperatively (for example, in pairs or small groups) and share results and feedback with other groups in the class.	In addition to technologies to allow two-way exchanges of text information, visual technologies such as two-way video or videoconferencing technologies allow synchronous voice and visual communications between instructor and students and among students.	By end of course, all or nearly all students (90–100 percent) are both *replying to and initiating messages,* both when required and voluntarily; messages are detailed, responsive to topics, and are well-developed communications.	Instructor responds to all student queries; responses are always prompt, that is, within twenty-four hours; feedback always offers detailed analysis of student work and suggestions for improvement, along with additional hints and information to supplement learning.
Total each:	_____ **pts.**	_____ **pts.**	_____ **pts.**	_____ **pts.**	_____ **pts.**
Total overall:	_____ **pts.**				

Appendix B

Websites
for Training
Professionals

Site/URL	Description
Advanced Distributed Learning Organization (ADLNET) (www.adlnet.org)	This is the site for the Advanced Distributed Learning (ADL) Initiative, sponsored by the Office of the Secretary of Defense (OSD), a collaborative effort between government, industry, and academia to establish a new distributed learning environment that permits the interoperability of learning tools and course content on a global scale. This is an excellent site to find information on SCORM standards and accurate information on which vendors are certified and compliant.
Alert Box (www.useit.com/alertbox/)	A bi-weekly column self-published by well-known Web usability expert, Jacob Nielsen. The advice on usable Web design emerges from Nielsen's company's usability studies.
Association for Computing Machinery (ACM) Special Interest Group on Human Computer Interaction (SIGCHI) (www.acm.org/sigchi/)	An association that promotes usable design in computers, software, and websites. This website links to some of the association's publications, which report recent research and theory on usability and related topics.

Note: These links can also be found on the book's companion website www.advancedwbt.com.

AutoUnfocus (www.reusability .org/blogs/david/)

David Wiley at Utah State University runs this blog. He describes it as a nonperiodic oscillation between learning objects, informal online communities, self-organization, peer learning, instructional technology, open source culture, and intellectual property law. A great place to engage in dialog.

Blues News (www.bluesnews.com/)

This is a gaming site providing great insights into what the cutting edge of gaming, simulations, and multimedia are and a forum to read about what is to come.

Boxes and Arrows (www.boxesandarrows.com)

A web-zine for information architects (people concerned with the structure and navigation of websites) and information designers (people concerned with the appearance and understandability of content).

Center for Online Learning and Pedagogy (www.nyucolp.org/)

The Center for Online Learning and Pedagogy site is designed to further the field of education by providing access to the most current knowledge and best practices in online education, by providing tools and resources for educators and by encouraging discussion among active practitioners.

Chief Information Officer Magazine (www.cio.com)

This is the companion website for *CIO Magazine* a publication serving information technology executives. It is a great place to learn more about technical topics such as ERP, CRM, and knowledge management. It provides a strategic perspective and offers articles, interviews, and webcasts that will ensure you are technically current.

Chief Learning Officer Magazine (www.clomedia.com)

A print and online magazine intended for executives in corporate learning, training, and performance improvement. The magazine regularly features articles about learning technology.

Chronicle of Higher Education, **Distance Education Column** (http://chronicle.com/)

The major trade paper of higher education. Features a weekly column on issues in learning technology and distance education in colleges and universities.

David Davies' Weblog (http://david.davies.name/ weblog/categories/edtech/)

Fans of blogging recommend this site. David Davies offers m-blog posting and traditional postings, and the subjects range from e-learning to general technology.

EdTechNot.co (www.edtechnot.com/)

This site is designed to encourage debate on the merits and pitfalls of using educational technology in real schools. The site has links to research sites, blogs, news, and articles.

Educause (www.educause.edu/)

One of the leading associations promoting the use of computing in education. Through its widely recognized awards program, the organization annually recognizes excellence in the use of educational computing. The site links to various Educause publications, among others.

e-learning Europa (www.elearningeuropa.info/)

Supported by the European Union, this site offers e-learning resources to academic institutions. The resources, practices, forms, and events are EU-centric.

e-Learning Forum (www.elearningforum.com/)

A noncommercial, global community of people who make decisions at the intersection of learning, technology, business, and design.

e-Learning Guru (www.e-learningguru.com/)

This site offers practical information in a plain-language format. Readers will find "how to" articles, white papers, tools, and links to other sites.

e-Learning Post (www.elearningpost.com)

A Singapore-based website with news about the e-learning industry. Although much of the news emerges from North America, the Asia-specific news provides a unique view of e-learning applications.

eLearningGuild (www.elearningguild.com/)

A U.S.-based organization for e-learning designers and developers. The site includes a subscription-only web-zine about e-learning issues.

EPSS Central
(www.pcd-innovations.com/)

A portal on all aspects of electronic performance support systems. Includes links to articles about EPSS design and implementation, case studies of EPSSs, and articles on related topics.

ERIC (www.eric.ed.gov/)

The Educational Research Information Clearinghouse, a U.S.-government-funded clearinghouse of all scholarly publications on educational topics (such as early childhood education, educational foundations, and educational technology). Provides a database of all publications. Occasionally has published summaries of research in particular areas.

First Monday
(www.firstmonday.dk/)

This is a free, monthly, Internet-only journal providing thought-provoking articles about the Internet and its future.

Gamasutra
(www.gamasutra.com/)

If you are thinking about games and simulations, this is a good place to get a view of the cutting edge and the insights into game developers thinking.

IBM User Centered Design
(www-3.ibm.com/ibm/easy/
eou_ext.nsf/Publish/570)

This site addresses all aspects of soft engineering related to user-centered design. There is a great deal of information that has relevance for instructional designers.

Instructional Technology
Forum hosted by University
of Georgia (http://it.coe.uga
.edu/itforum/index.html)

ITFORUM is an electronic listserv where people from around the world discuss theories, research, new paradigms, and practices in the field of instructional technology.

InternetTime
(www.internettime.com/e.htm)

Check out the InternetTime Jump Page, an outstanding site for finding a links to a wide variety of e-learning related sites. The site also offers a blog.

InfoDesign: Understanding
by Design (Formerly
Information Design Community)
(www.informationdesign.org/)

A portal on all aspects of information design, a discipline concerned with the appearance and understandability of content. Links to articles and organizations of interest and provides a comprehensive listing of upcoming events.

International Review of Research in Open and Distance Learning (www.irrodl.org/)	This is a referred e-journal to advance research, theory, and best practices in open and distance learning worldwide.
Learnativity (www.learnativity.org/)	A portal on learning, with a focus on e-learning. Provides brief primers on key topics in learning and links to related articles that explores the topics in-depth.
Learning Circuits (www.learningcircuits.org/)	A web-zine published by ASTD about e-learning. Articles provide practical tips for handling specific design issues, advice for purchasing learning technology, and industry outlooks.
LearningCentre (www.e-learningcentre.co.uk/)	This site contains links to thousands of selected and reviewed e-learning articles, white papers, and research reports; examples of e-learning solutions; vendors of e-learning content, technology, and services; as well as e-learning conferences, seminars, workshops, and other e-learning events.
MERLOT (www.merlot.org/Home.po)	A database of learning objects. These learning objects are primarily materials that can be integrated into classroom lessons and are geared toward primary and secondary teachers.
MIT Future of Learning Group (http://learning.media.mit.edu/)	This site offers links and papers that explore how new technologies can enable new ways of thinking, learning, and designing. The group creates new "tools to think with" and explores how these tools can help bring about change in real-world settings, such as schools, museums, and under-served communities
No Significant Difference Study (www.nosignificantdifference .org/nosignificantdifference/)	This site provides selected entries from the book, *The No Significant Difference Phenomenon,* as reported in 355 research reports, summaries, and papers—a comprehensive research bibliography on technology for distance education.

Online Journal of Distance Learning Administration (www.westga.edu/~distance/ jmain11.html)

An online journal about the issues of managing distance learning. Articles primarily explore issues associated with administering distance education in colleges and universities.

Penn State American Center for the Study of Distance Education (www.ed.psu.edu/acsde/)

A compilation of useful resources for teaching academically and online.

Pew Research Center (http:// people-press.org/reports/)

The Center's purpose is to serve as a forum for ideas on the media and public policy through public opinion research. The site frequently publishes surveys related to learning, e-learning, and the Internet.

Pitch **Journal** (www.pitchjournal.org)

Pitch is a peer-reviewed online journal in instructional and learning technology. Articles in *Pitch* focus on pedagogical, technological, sociological, legal, and moral issues related to opening access to educational opportunity.

Reusable Learning Objects (www.reusability.org/)

The first, and most visited, website on reusable learning objects. Includes access to the seminal book on the topic, as well as related resources.

Significant Difference (www .aln.org/publications/jaln/ v4n1/pdf/v4n1_joygarcia.pdf)

This link takes you to a paper that is a response to the Thomas Russell "No Significant Difference Study."

Singapore's e-Learning House (www.elearninghouse.com)

e-Learning House is a Singapore-based site that provides forums, news, and resources that are relevant to Asia.

Sloan-C Foundation: Web Center for ALN Research (www.alnresearch.org/index.jsp)

This private foundation supports research on online learning, including a seminal study on the five pillars of quality online learning. This site offers tutorials, research papers, forums, and links to researchers and students in Asynchronous Learning Networks. ALNs are online classes that include extensive class discussion materials.

Society for Human Resource Management (SHRM) (www.shrm.org/)

Website of a professional association that addresses another side of human capital development in organizations—benefits, salaries, and similar issues. The website provides access to SHRM's magazine, *HR,* which frequently covers topics about corporate learning, especially e-learning.

Stephen Downes site (www.downes.ca)

An impeccably kept log about all aspects of e-learning. Downes provides links to countless articles on e-learning, as well as commentary about them.

Syllabus **(www.syllabus.com/)**

This is the companion site to *Syllabus* magazine. The site and magazine focus on delivering news, case studies, and best practices drawn from higher ed.

Teleeducation (http://teleeducation.nb.ca/english/)

Available in both French and English, this site offers useful resources and references to assist faculty and developers, K-12 teachers, and workplace trainers in the development and delivery of e-learning courses.

Training Journal **(www.trainingjournal.co.uk/)**

This UK-based site provides training professionals and others interested in training with timely articles on key issues of the day.

Training **Magazine (www.trainingmag.com/)**

The leading and longest running privately published magazine about the field. The website provides links to some of the current articles; subscribers to the print magazine have online access to all current content and the archives.

Training Outsourcing (www.trainingoutsourcing.com)

This site is dedicated to all things related to the outsourcing of training. It is vendor-driven but also offers some good resources.

University of Twente Collaborative Project (http://users.edte.utwente.nl/collis/homepage03/newres.htm#Shell)

Follow the links from Dr. Betty Collis's home page to Shell. The Shell site provides papers on the Shell University of Twente Collaborative Project.

Usability.gov
(www.usability.gov)

Usability.gov, from the U.S. Department of Health and Human Services, provides a comprehensive listing of guidelines for designing usable websites, with a special focus on designing websites that are accessible to persons with disabilities (especially visual and hearing impairments, as well as older users).

U.S. Dept of Education
(www.ed.gov/index.jhtml)

This is a one-stop shopping site for all things related to the U.S. Department of Education. This is a great place to find statistics on distance education, literacy rates, the state of school infrastructure, and grants.

U.S. Distance Learning
Association (www.usdla.org/)

This site offers resources for distance education (broader than just e-learning), including statistics, reports, and a glossary of terms.

VNU Business Media
(www.vnulearning.com/)

VNU Business Media's site provides events, publications, and resources focused on job-related, employer-sponsored training and education.

Wisconsin-Extension DE
Clearing House
(www.uwex.edu/disted/)

The Distance Education Clearinghouse is a comprehensive website bringing together distance education information from Wisconsin, national, and international sources.

Appendix C

Professional Organizations

Developing e-learning brings together the skill and knowledge of many different kinds of professionals. Because of the cross-disciplinary nature of the field, many organizations provide resources to developers. The major ones are listed below:

American Association for Higher Education (AAHE)
1 Dupont Circle, Suite 360
Washington, DC 20036
Tel: (202) 293–6440
Fax: (202) 293–0073
URL: www.aahe.org
AAHE's conferences and publications highlight a broad range of issues. They have developed many in-depth, long-term commitments to specific programmatic areas, such as quality, service-learning, teaching/peer review, and technology. AAHE's Technology Projects seek to mainstream the effective use of technology for instructional purposes.

American Society for Training and Development (ASTD)
1640 King Street
Box 1443
Alexandria, VA 22313–2043
Tel: (703) 683–8100
Fax: (703) 683–8103
URL: www.astd.org
ASTD's mission is to provide leadership to individuals, organizations, and society to achieve work-related competence, performance, and fulfillment.

Association for Educational Communications and Technology (AECT)
1800 North Stonelake Drive, Suite 2
Bloomington, IN 47407
URL: www.aect.org
The mission of AECT is to provide leadership in educational communications and technology by linking professionals with a common interest in the use of educational technology and its application to the learning process.

**Association for Information and Image Management
International (AIIM International)**
1100 Wayne Avenue, Suite 1100
Silver Spring, MD 20910
Tel: (301) 587 8202
Fax: (301) 587 2711
URL: www.aiim.org
AIIM International is the leading industry association and trade show for IT professionals in document-intensive businesses. Its mission is to help institutional users understand document technologies and how they can be applied to improve critical business and exploding enterprise and web-based processes. AIIM's focus is information and process management, including web-enabled document management, workflow, and industry-specific solutions.

Australian Society for Educational Technology (ASET)
P.O. Box 2024
Hawthorn VIC 3122
Melbourne, Australia
URL: www.aset.org.au
The Australian Society for Educational Technology is a national organization for people with professional interests in educational technology. Our members come from all walks of life. We hold regular meetings with a diverse range of guest presenters where members can mingle and relax over a coffee, nibbles, or a glass of wine.

British Educational Communications and Technology Agency (BECTA)
Millburn Hill Road
Science Park
Coventry, England
CV4 7JJ
Tel: 024 7641 6994
Fax: 024 7641 1418
URL: www.becta.org.uk/corporate/index.cfm
BECTA's purpose is to apply the power of information and communications technology (ICT) to support learning. We provide strategic leadership on ICT and learning, helping to develop a world-class education system. BECTA guides and coordinates the necessary changes in policy and practice and brokers effective partnerships to establish and exploit reliable and sustainable educational technology.

Computer Education Management Association (CEdMA)
Nancy Lewis
Association Manager
P.O. Box 749
Scotch Plains, NJ 07076
URL: www.cedma.org
CEdMA's goal is to provide formal and informal forums for education managers to discuss critical training and business issues encountered in high-tech companies. CEdMA also provides opportunities for members to participate in initiatives to shape excellence in education and training.

Distance Education Australia and New Zealand (DEANZ)
Nola Campbell
DEANZ President
School of Education
University of Waikato
Private Bag 3105
Hamilton, New Zealand
URL: www.deanz.org.nz
DEANZ is the New Zealand association for professionals working in flexible, open, and networked education. DEANZ is committed to fostering growth, development, research, and good practice in these areas.

Education Online
Street Loyes House, Suite 1000
20 St. Loyes Street
Bedford MK40 12L
United Kingdom
URL: www.edon.org.uk
The mission of Education Online is to promote multimedia access to education and training in European society and establish by consensus a standard for online learning.

Educause
4772 Walnut Street, Suite 206
Boulder, CO 80301–2538
Tel: (303) 449–4430
Fax: (303) 440–0461
URL: www.educause.edu
The consolidation of the training organizations CAUSE and Educom, Educause's mission is to help shape and enable transformational change in higher education through the introduction, use, and management of information resources and technology in teaching, learning, scholarship, research, and institutional management.

The eLearning Initiative of the European Commission
European Commission
Directorate General for Education and Culture
Multimedia Unit
200, rue de la Loi
B-1049 Brussels, Belgium
URL: europa.eu.int/comm/education/index_en.html
The **e**Learning Initiative of the European Commission seeks to mobilize the educational and cultural communities, as well as economic and social players in Europe, in order to speed up changes in the education and training systems for Europe's move to a knowledge-based society.

The Human Resource Planning Society
317 Madison Avenue, Suite 1509
New York, NY 10017
Tel: (212) 490–6387
Fax: (212) 682–6851
URL: www.hrps.org/home/index.shtml
The Human Resource Planning Society's mission is to improve organizational performance by creating a global network of individuals who function as business partners in the application of strategic human resource management practices.

Institute of Educational Technology
Walton Hall
Milton Keynes MK7 6AA
United Kingdom
URL: www-iet.open.ac.uk
The institute is the largest center for educational technology in the world and has top rankings for its contributions to teaching and for its research. In addition to its work on courses across the Open University, the institute is engaged in many collaborative projects in all parts of the world, as part of its mission and objectives.

Instructional Technology Council (ITC)
One Dupont Circle, NW, Suite 360
Washington, DC 20036-1143
Tel: (202) 293-3110
Fax: (202) 293-0073
URL: www.itcnetwork.org/joinitc.htm
The Instructional Technology Council provides leadership, information, and resources to expand and enhance distance learning through the effective use of technology.

International Society for Performance Improvement (ISPI)
1400 Spring Street, Suite 260
Silver Springs, MD 20910
Tel: (202) 408–7969
Fax: (202) 408–7972
URL: www.ispi.org
ISPI is the leading association dedicated to increasing productivity in the workplace through the application of performance and instructional technologies.

Knowledge Management Consortium International (KMCI)

P.O. Box #41

Vernon, CT 06066

URL: www.kmci.org

Knowledge Management Consortium International is an organization and individuals coming together to develop a shared vision, common understanding, and aligned action about knowledge and knowledge management.

New England Learning Association (NELA)

P.O. Box 1323

Melrose, MA 02176

Tel: 617-558-5566

Fax: 617-558-5599

URL: www.nelearning.org

The New England Learning Association (NELA) brings together professionals in industry and education for the purpose of advancing the successful adoption of technology for learning. NELA leverages New England's position as a leader in education and technology innovation to enhance the human potential of individuals and organizations.

Philadelphia Area New Media Association (PANMA)

PANMA: a division of the Eastern Technology Council

Attn: Ida Marie Higgins

435 Devon Park Drive

Building #600, Suite 613

Wayne, PA 19087

Tel: (610) 975-9430, ext. 3157

URL: info@panma.org

PANMA's primary objectives are to increase the visibility of the local new media industry, to facilitate career growth of new media professionals, and to enhance the ability of local new media companies to hire locally trained and educated professionals. To achieve its objectives, PANMA offers ongoing professional development and social programs.

Prometeus
Prometeus Support Service
ARTTIC
58a rue du Dessous des Berges
75013 Paris
France
Fax: 33 1 53 94 54 70
URL: www.prometeus.org
The goal of Prometeus is to support effective use, take-up, research, and development in the field of technology-enabled learning. Prometeus plans to create a European forum and a global knowledge resource dedicated to identifying, sharing, and disseminating knowledge and best practices relating to all significant activities in this field and to identifying any gaps in knowledge, experience, capability, and tools across Europe.

Society for Applied Learning Technology (SALT)
50 Culpepper Street
Warrenton, VA 20186
Tel: (540) 347–0055
URL: www.salt.org
The society is oriented to professionals whose work requires knowledge and communication in the field of instructional technology. SALT provides a means to enhance the knowledge and job performance of an individual by participating in society-sponsored meetings and through receiving society-sponsored publications. It enables one to achieve knowledge in the field of applied learning technology by association with other professionals in conferences sponsored by the society.

Society for Human Resource Management (SHRM)
1800 Duke Street
Alexandria, VA 22314
Tel: (703) 548–3440
Fax: (703) 535–6490
URL: www.shrm.org
The mission of SHRM is to lead, encourage, and financially support research and educational activities that further the growth and development of the HR profession.

Society for Technical Communication (STC)

901 North Stuart Street, Suite 904

Arlington, VA 2203–1822

URL: http://www.stc.org

The mission of STC is to advance the arts and sciences of technical communication by addressing emerging issues in technical communications.

United States Distance Learning Association (USDLA)

140 Gould Street, Suite 200B

Needham, MA 02494–2397

URL: www.usdla.org

The association's purpose is to promote the development and application of distance learning for education and training. The constituencies served include K through 12 education, higher education, continuing education, corporate training, and military and government training.

References

ABC News. (2004). *War games: The military uses its combat simulators for Afghanistan training.* http://abcnews.go.com/sections/scitech/DailyNews/pt_STRICOM_01115.html. [Retrieved February 15, 2004.]

Adkins, S. (2003). Workflow-based e-learning: Next-generation enterprise learning technology. *Learning Circuits, 4*(8). www.learningcircuits.org/2003/aug2003/adkins.htm. [Retrieved January 4, 2004.]

Aldrich, C. (2003). *Simulations and the future of learning: An innovative (and perhaps revolutionary) approach to e-learning.* San Francisco: Pfeiffer.

Alessi, S., & Trollip, S. (2000). *Computer-based instruction: Methods and development.* New York: Allyn & Bacon.

Allen, L. (2000). *Scholarly publication as an indicator of change. Proceedings of the 47th Society for Technical Communication Annual Conference.* Washington, DC: Society for Technical Communication. www.stc.org. [Retrieved September 15, 2003.]

Althaus, S.L. (1997). Computer-mediated communication in the university classroom: An experiment with online discussions. *Communication Education, 46,* 158–174.

American Institute of Graphic Arts. (2002). *What is graphic design?* www.aiga.org/content.cfm?contentalias=whatisgraphicdesign. [Retrieved June 9, 2002.]

American Medical Association. (2003). PDA content available for download. www.ama-assn.org/ama/pub/category/9630.html.

Anderson, C., Mahowald, R., & Brennan, M. (2002, August). *Bulletin: The future of live e-learning vendor challenges and recommendations.* IDC Document #27769.

Anderson, T. (2003). Getting the right mix right again: An updated and theoretical rationale for interaction. *International Review of Research in Open and Distance Learning, 4*(2). www.irrodl.org/content/v4.2/anderson.html. [Retrieved December 16, 2003.]

Arthur, W., Bennett, W., Edens, P.S., & Bell, S.T. (2003). Effectiveness of training in organizations: A meta-analysis of design and evaluation features. *Journal of Applied Psychology, 88*(2), 234–245.

Atkinson, R.C., & Shiffrin, R.M. (1968). Human memory: A proposed system and its control processes. In O. Spence & O. Spence, *Advances in the psychology of learning and motivation.* New York: Academic Press.

Australian Association of Professional Engineers, Scientists, and Managers. (n.d.). *Development of e-mentoring programs.* www.apesma.asn.au/mentorsonline/reference/pdfs/mol1.PDF. [Retrieved November 11, 2004.]

Ausubel, D.P. (1960). The use of advance organizers in the learning and retention of meaningful verbal material. *Journal of Educational Psychology, 51,* 267–272.

Barbian, J. (2002). Screen play. *Online Learning, 4*(5). www.onlinelearningmag.com/onlinelearning/magazine/article_display.jsp?vnu_content_id=1480770. [Retrieved June 11, 2004.]

Barron, T. (2002). Learning object approach is making inroads. *Learning Circuits.* www.learningcircuits.org/2002/may2002/barron.html. [Retrieved November 12, 2003.]

Becker, W. C. (1986.) *Applied psychology for teachers: A behavioral cognitive approach.* Chicago: Science Research Associates.

Billhardt, B. (2004). The promise of online simulations. *Chief Learning Officer, 3*(2), 38–41.

Bjork, R.A. (1988). Retrieval practice and the maintenance of knowledge. In M.M. Gruneberg, P.E. Morris, & and R.N. Sykes (Eds.), *Practical aspects of memory: Current research and issues* (Volume 1). New York: John Wiley & Sons.

Bloom, B.S. (1956). *Taxonomy of educational objectives: Cognitive and affective domains.* New York: McKay.

Bloom, B.S., Englehatt, M.D., Furst, E.J., Hill, W.H., & Krathwohl, D.R. (1956). *Taxonomy of educational objectives. Handbook I: Cognitive domain.* New York: Wiley.

Boren, T. & Ramey, J. (2000). Thinking aloud: Reconciling theory and practice. *IEEE Transactions on Professional Communication, 43*(3), 261–278.

Bowie, J.S. (1996). Information engineering: Using information to drive design. *Intercom, 43*(5), 6–10, 43.

Bradford, A. (2003, Spring/Summer). e-Learning simulations: Bringing case studies alive. *Rotman management: The alumni magazine of the Rotman School of Management,* pp. 41–42.

Brockmann, R.J. (1990). Writing better computer user documentation from paper to hypertext, version 2.0. New York: Wiley.

Brodsky, M. (2003). Four blended learning blunders and how to avoid them. *Learning Circuits, 4*(11). www.learningcircuits.org/2003/nov2003/elearn.htm. [Retrieved July 19, 2004.]

Brown, J.S., and Duguid, P. (2002). *The social life of information.* Cambridge, MA: Harvard Business School Press.

Bruner, J. (2002). *About constructivism.* http://tip.psychology.org/bruner.html. [Visited May 17, 2002.]

Brusaw, C.T., Alred, G. J. & Oliu, W. E. (1976). *Handbook of technical writing.* New York: St. Martin's Press.

Candy, P.C. (1991). *Self-direction for lifelong learning.* San Francisco: Jossey-Bass.

Capuzzi-Simon, C. (2003, Tuesday June 10). A coach for "team you." *Washington Post Online.* www.washingtonpost.com/ac2/wp-dyn?pagename=article&node=&contentId=A36862–2003Jun9&notFound=true. [Retrieved July 28, 2003.]

Carliner, S. (1995). *Every object tells a story: A grounded model of design for object-based learning in museums.* Doctoral dissertation. Atlanta, GA: Georgia State University.

Carliner, S. (2001). Modeling information for three-dimensional space: Lessons learned from museum exhibit design. *Technical Communication, 48*(1), 66–81.

Carliner, S. (2002a). *Designing e-learning.* Alexandria, VA: ASTD Press.

Carliner, S. (2002b). Inconspicuous consumption: Lessons for web design from mall and retail design. *Boxes and Arrows.* www.boxesandarrows.com/archives/inconspicuous_consumption_lessons_for_web_design_from_mall_and_retail_design.php. [Retrieved January 15, 2003.]

Carliner, S. (2003). *Online or off the map? When e-learning will work and when it won't.* Presented at Online Learning 2003. VNU Business Media. Los Angeles, California, September 22, 2003.

Carliner, S. (2004). *An overview of online learning* (2nd ed.). Amherst, MA: HRD Press.

Carliner, S., Groshens, J., Chapman, B., & Gery, G. (2004, June 7). Strategic trends: An analysis of 5 years of the Training Director's Forum survey. *Training Director's Forum.* Phoenix, AZ: VNU Business Media.

Chapman, B. (2002). Keynote presentation at the *Online Learning Asia Conference,* Singapore, May 15, 2002.

Christensen, T.K., & Osguthorpe, R.T. (2004). How do instructional-design practitioners make instructional-strategy decisions. *Performance Improvement Quarterly, 17*(3), 45-65.

Clark, J.M., & Paivio, A. (1991). Dual coding theory and education. *Educational Psychology Review, 3*(3), 149–170.

Clark, R.C. (2003). *Building expertise* (2nd ed.) Silver Spring, MD: International Society for Performance Improvement.

Clark, R.C., & Mayer, R.E. (2002). *e-Learning and the science of instruction: Proven guidelines for consumers and designers of multimedia learning.* San Francisco: Pfeiffer.

Cloninger, C. (1999). *Usability experts are from Mars; Graphic designers are from Venus.* From the website, A list apart. www.alistapart.com/stories/marsvenus/index.html. [Retrieved June 9, 2002.]

Clutterbuck, D. (2002). Why mentoring programmes and relationships fail. *Link&Learn, 2*(12). www.LinkageInc.com [Retrieved July 9, 2004.]

Clutterbuck, D. (2004). *Everyone needs a mentor: Fostering talent at work.* London: CIPD Press.

Cobb, T. (1997). Cognitive efficiency: Toward a revised theory of media. *Educational Technology, Research and Development, 45*(4), 21–35.

Cognition and Technology Group at Vanderbilt (CTGV). (1990). Anchored instruction and its relationship to situated cognition. *Educational Researcher, 19*(6), 2–10.

Collins, M., & Berge, Z. (1996). *Facilitating interaction in computer mediated online courses.* www.emoderators.com/moderators/flcc.htmlm. [Retrieved July 22, 2004.]

Columb, G. (1991). Visual communication. Paper presented at a meeting of the Society for Technical Communication, Atlanta, GA, February 9.

Conrad, D. (2002). Engagement, excitement, anxiety, and fear: Learners experiences of starting an online course. *American Journal of Distance Education, 16*(4), 205–226.

Cooper, A. (1999). *The inmates are running the asylum.* Indianapolis, IN: Sam's.

Corrosion Doctors. (2003). *Material adapted from Bloom's taxonomy for corrosion training.* www.corrosion-doctors.org/Training/Bloom.htm. [Retrieved January 11, 2004.]

Dabbagh, N.H., Jonassen, D.H., Yueh, H.P., & Samouilova, M. (2000). Assessing a problem-based learning approach to an introductory instructional design course: A case study. *Performance Improvement Quarterly, 13*(3), 60–83.

Dick, W., Carey, L., & Carey, J. (2000). *The systematic design of instruction* (5th ed.). Reading, MA: Addison-Wesley.

Driscoll, M. (2002). *Web-based training: Using technology to design adult learning experiences* (2nd ed.). San Francisco: Jossey-Bass.

Duin, A. (1993). Test drive: Evaluating the usability of documents. In C. Barnum & S. Carliner (Eds.), *Techniques for technical communicators.* Upper Saddle River, NJ: Prentice-Hall.

e-Learning Guild. (2003). *The blended learning best practices survey.* Available online at www.elearningguild.com. [Retrieved July 14, 2003.]

Einsiedel, A.A., Jr. (1995). Case studies: Indispensable tools for trainers. Training & Development, 49(8), 50–54.

Elias, J., & Merriam, S. (1980). *Philosophical foundations of adult education.* Malabar, FL: Robert E. Krieger.

Eugenio, V. (1994). The effect of experience level and visual image type on the time required to master a task within an interactive multimedia job task simulation. Doctoral dissertation. Atlanta, GA: Georgia State University.

Farrah, S.J. (1990). Lecture. In M.W. Galbraith (Ed.), *Adult learning methods: A guide for effective instruction.* Melbourne, FL: Robert E. Krieger.

Field, S. (1984). *Screenplay: The foundations of screenwriting.* New York: Dell.

Fletcher, J.D. (1990). *Effectiveness and cost of interactive videodisc instruction in defense training and education.* Washington, DC: Institute for Defense Analyses.

Floyd, S. (1987). Visualization: The key to effective scriptwriting. *Technical Communication, 34*(1), 8–10.

Fredericksen, E., Pickett, A., Shea, P., Pelz, W., & Swan, K. (2000). Student satisfaction and perceived learning with online courses: Principles and examples from SUNY learning network. *Journal of Asynchronous Learning Networks, 4*(2). www.aln.org/publications/jaln/index.asp. [Retrieved January 13, 2004.]

Fulford, C.P., & Zhang, S. (1993). Perceptions of interaction: The critical predictor in distance education. *American Journal of Distance Education, 7*(3), 8–21.

Gagne, R. (1985). *The conditions of learning* (4th ed.). New York: Holt, Rinehart & Winston.

Galbraith, M.W. (1990). *Adult learning methods.* Malabar, FL: Krieger.

Gatto, D. (1993). The use of interactive computer simulations in training. *Australian Journal of Educational Technology. 9*(2), 144–156.

Gilbert, L., & Moore, D.R. (1998). Building interactivity into web courses: Tools for social and instructional interaction. *Educational Technology, 38*(3), 29-35.

Goh, T., & Kinshuk. (2004). Getting ready for mobile learning. In L. Cantoni & C. McLoughlin (Eds.), *Proceedings of ED-MEDIA 2004—World Conference on Educational Multimedia, Hypermedia & Telecommunications.* June 21–26, 2004, Lugano, Switzerland.

Gokhale, A.A. (1995). Collaborative learning enhances critical thinking. *Journal of Technology Education, 7*(1), 22–30.

Gold, M. (2003). Enterprise e-learning. *Learning Circuits, 4*(4). www.learning circuits.org/2003/apr2003/gold.htm. [Retrieved June 27, 2004.]

Graham, A.W. (1991). Persistence without external rewards: A study of adult learners in art museum and planetarium education programs. Doctoral dissertation, Northern Illinois University.

Graves, K. (2001). A framework of course development processes. In D.R. Hall & A. Hewings (Eds.), *Innovation in English language teaching* (Vol. 3, pp. 178–196). London: Routledge.

Guerra, I.J. (2003). Key competencies required of performance improvement professionals. *Performance Improvement Quarterly, 16*(1), 55–72.

Gustafson, K.L., & Branch, R.M. (2002). *Survey of instructional design models* (4th ed.). Syracuse, NY: ERIC Clearinghouse on Information.

Hall, B. (1995). Return-on-investment and multimedia training: A research study. *Multimedia Training Newsletter.* July-August, p. 2.

Harvard Business Online http://harvardbusinessonline.hbsp.harvard.edu/ [Retrieved Feb 15, 2004.]

Hewson, C., Yule, P., Vogel, C., & Laurent, D. (2003). *Internet research methods: A practical guide for the social and behavioral sciences.* Thousand Oaks, CA: Sage.

Horton, W. (2000). *Web-based training: How to teach anyone, anything, anywhere, any time.* New York: John Wiley & Sons.

International Society for Performance Improvement (ISPI). (2004). Principles of human performance technology. www.ispi.org/ hpt_institute/#What. [Retrieved November 11, 2004.]

Ioannidou, A., & Repenning, A. (1999). End-user programmable simulations. *Dr. Dobbs Journal, 24*(8), 40.

Johnson, D.W., & Johnson R.T. (1993, Winter). Cooperative learning: Where we have been, where we are going. *Cooperative Learning and College Teaching, 3*(2).

Jonassen, D. (1994, April). Thinking technology. *Educational Technology, 34*(4), 34–37.

Jonassen, D.H. (1996). *Computers in the classroom: Mind tools for critical thinking.* Columbus, OH: Merrill/Prentice-Hall.

Jonassen, D., Carr, C., & Hsiu-Ping, Y. (1998). Computers as mind tools for engaging learners in critical thinking. *TechTrends, 43*(2), 24–32.

Jonassen, D.H., & Reeves, T.C. (1996). Learning with technology: Using computers as cognitive tools. In D.H. Jonassen (Ed.), H*andbook of research for educational communications and technology.* New York: Macmillan.

Joseph, J. (2001). Upward mentoring. *Wharton Leadership Digest.* http://leadership .wharton.upenn.edu/digest/01–01.shtml#Upward%20Mentoring:%20%20The%20 Wharton%20Fellows%20in%20eBusiness%20. [Retrieved June 11, 2004.]

Joyce, B., & Weil, M. (1986). *Models of teaching* (3rd ed.). Englewood Cliffs, NJ: Prentice-Hall.

Karrer, A., Laser, A., & Sund-Marit, L. (2002). Instruction and feedback models for software training. *Learning Circuits, 3*(3). www.learningcircuits.org/2002/mar2002/karrer.html.

Kekkonen-Moneta, S., & Moneta, G.B. (2002). e-Learning in Hong Kong: Comparing learning outcomes in online multimedia lecture versions of an introductory computing course. *British Journal of Educational Technology, 33*(4), 423–433.

Keller, J.M. (1987). Strategies for stimulating the motivation to learn. *Performance and Instruction, 26*(9), 1–8.

Kirkpatrick, D.L. (1998). *Evaluating training programs: The four levels* (2nd ed.). San Francisco: Berrett-Koehler.

Knowles, M.S. (1980). *The modern practice of adult education: Andragogy vs. pedagogy.* Wilton, CT: Association Press.

Knowles, M. (1990). *The adult learner: A neglected species.* Houston, TX: Gulf.

Kossen, J.S. (2003). Mobile e-learning: When e-learning becomes m-learning. *Palm Power Magazine* (Enterprise Edition). www.palmpowerenterprise.com/issuesprint/issue200106/elearning.html. [Retrieved July 10, 2004.]

Kostelnick, C., & Roberts, D. (1998). *Designing visual language: Strategies for professional communicators.* New York: Allyn & Bacon.

Kram, K.E. (1983). Phases of the mentor relationship. *Academy of Management Journal, 26,* 608–625.

Lester, P.M. (2000). *Visual communication: Images with messages* (2nd ed.). Belmont, CA: Wadsworth.

Lewin, K. (1951). In D. Cartwright (Ed.), *Field theory in social science: Selected theoretical papers.* New York: Harper & Row.

Lipschutz, R.P. (2004). The ABCs of e-learning. *Portal Magazine.* [Retrieved July 30, 2004, from www.portalsmag.com/articles/default.asp?ArticleID=5629]

Longmire, W. (2004). A primer on learning objects. *Learning Circuits, 1*(3). www.learningcircuits.org/2000/mar2000/Longmire.htm. [Retrieved June 27, 2004.]

Lowry, C.M. (2002). *Supporting and facilitating self-directed learning.* NTLF.COM. www.ntlf.com/html/lib/bib/89dig.htm [Retrieved December 21, 2003.]

MacKinlay. (2000). Planning to use e-mail to support the learning process? www.globaled.com/articles/MacKinlayKarelena2000.pdf [retrieved January 17, 2005].

Mager, R. (1975). *Preparing instructional objectives* (2nd ed.). Belmont, CA: Lake Publishing Company.

Marks, M. (1993). Remarks to the Buckhead Business Association leadership development class. Atlanta, Georgia. May 1993.

Marsh, J. (2001). *How to design effective blended learning.* Santa Clara, CA: Brandon Hall.com. www.brandonhall.com/public/execsums/execsum_blended.pdf. 5. [Retrieved July 13, 2003.]

Masie, E., & Rinaldi, H. (2002, February). *Virtual classroom technology scan.* The Masie Center Presents eLearning Consortium, Saratoga, New York.

Mason, R. (1994). *Using communications media for open and flexible learning.* London: Kogan.

Mergel, B. (1998). *Instructional Design and Learning Theory.* http://www.usask.ca/education/coursework/802papers/mergel/brenda.htm [retrieved December 31, 2003].

Merrill, M.D. (1994). *Instructional design theory.* Englewood Cliffs, NJ: Educational Technology Publications.

Meyers, C., & Jones, T.B. (1993). *Promoting active learning: Strategies for the college classroom.* San Francisco: Jossey-Bass.

Miller, G.A. (1956). The magical number seven, plus or minus two: Some limits on our capacity for processing information. *Psychological Review, 63,* 81–97.

Mirel, B. (1991). Designing manuals for active learning styles. *Technical Communication, 38*(1), 75–88.

Mobileinfo.com. (1999). *Mobile computing's 10 most important trends.* www.mobile info.com/Market/market_trends.htm. [Retrieved July 23, 2004.]

Mobley, K., & DeLoach, S. (2003). Embedded help: An overview of this special section. *Technical Communication. 50*(1), 11–12.

Moldenhauser, J. A. (2002/2003). Storytelling and the personalization of information. *Information Design Journal & Document Design. 11*(2/3), 230–242.

Morris, B. (2000). So you're a player. Do you need a coach? *Fortune, 141*(4), 144–154.

Muir, J. (2003). *Decoding mobile device security.* ComputerWorld Online. www .computerworld.com/securitytopics/security/story/0,10801,82890,00.html [Retrieved May 15, 2004.]

Muller, C. (2004). MentorNet: Large-scale e-mentoring to advance women in engineering and science. Panel presentation at the Academy of Management, New Orleans, August 9, 2004.

National Education Association. (2000). *A survey of traditional and distance learning higher education members.* www.nea.org/he/abouthe/dlstudy.pdf [Retrieved April 11, 2002.]

Navarro, P., & Shoemaker, J. (2000). Policy issues in the teaching of economics in cyberspace: Research design, course design, and research results. *Contemporary Economic Policy, 18*(3), 359–366.

Neilsen, J. (2000). *Designing web usability.* Indianapolis: New Riders Publishing.

Neilsen, J. (2003a). Mobile devices: One generation from useful. *Alertbox.* www.useit.com/alertbox/20030818.html [Retrieved August 18, 2003.]

Neilsen, J. (2003b). Usability 101. *Alertbox.* www.useit.com/alertbox/20030825.html [Retrieved May 15, 2004.]

Newman, F., & Scurry, J. (2001). Online technology pushes pedagogy to the fore-front [Electronic version]. *The Chronicle Review, 47*(44).

http://chronicle.com/weekly/v47/i44/44b00701.htm. [Retrieved July 4, 2002.]

Nyíri, K. (2002). *Towards a philosophy of m-learning.* IEEE International Workshop on Wireless and Mobile Technologies in Education (WMTE 2002), August 29–30, 2002, Teleborg Campus, Växjö University, Växjö, Sweden. http://21st.century.phil-inst .hu/eng/m-learning/nyiri_m-learn_philos.htm. [Retrieved: July 10, 2004.]

Oliver, R. (2001). Developing e-learning environments that support knowledge construction in higher education. In S. Stoney & J. Burn (Eds.). *Working for excellence in the e-conomy.* Churchlands, Australia: We-B Centre.

Palincsar, A., & Brown, A. (1983). *Reciprocal teaching of comprehension-monitoring activities.* Bethesda, MD: National Institute of Health and Human Development.

PalmOne: Manatee High School & Sea Breeze Elementary School. (n.d.). www .palmone.com/us/education/studies/study58.html. [Retrieved July 21, 2004.]

Peters, M. (2000). Does constructivist epistemology have a place in nurse education? *Journal of Nursing Education, 39*(4), 166–170.

Pettersson, R., & Fager, G. (2002). *Information design at Malardelen University.* Presented at Infodesign Ed 2002. Reading, United Kingdom, September 16–17, 2002.

Pew Foundation. (2001). *The internet and education: Findings of the power internet & American life project.* www.per.internet.org. [Retrieved September 1, 2001.]

Pfeiffer, W.S. (1999). *Technical writing: A practical approach* (4th ed.). Upper Saddle River, NJ: Prentice-Hall.

Prensky, M. (2002). *Digital game-based learning.* New York: McGraw-Hill.

Price, J., & Price, L. (2002). *Hot text: Web writing that works.* Indianapolis, IN: New Riders Press.

Princeton University. (1997). *Wordnet 1.6.* As viewed on Dictionary.com, January 11, 2004. http://dictionary.reference.com/search?q=competency

Qingyang, G. (2003). M-learning: A new development towards more flexible and learner-centered learning. *Teaching English with Technology: A Journal for Teachers of English 3*(2). Source: www.iatefl.org.pl/call/j_nt13.htm [Retrieved May 8, 2004.]

Reigeluth, C., & Stein, F. (1983). The elaboration theory of instruction. In C. Reigeluth (Ed.), *Instructional design theories and models.* Hillsdale, NJ: Erlbaum Associates.

Revans, R.W. (1980). *Action learning: New techniques for management.* London: Blond and Briggs.

Robinson, R. (2000). Interview with Rick Robinson. *Loop: The journal of interaction design education, 1*(1). http://loop.aiga.org. [Retrieved July 4, 2002.]

Rossett, A., & Czech, C. (1996). They really wanna but . . . : The aftermath of professional preparation in performance technology. *Performance Improvement Quarterly, 8*(4), 114–132.

Rossett, A., & Gautier-Downes, J. (1991). *A handbook of job aids.* San Francisco: Pfeiffer.

Rossett, A., Douglis, F., & Frazee, R.V. (2003). Strategies for building blended learning. *Learning Circuits, 4*(7).

Rowland, G. (1993). Designing and instructional design. *Educational Technology Research and Development, 41*(1), 79–91.

Rubens, P., & Krull, R. (1985). Application of research on document design to online displays. *Technical Communication, 32*(4), 29–34.

Rumelhart, D.E. (1980). Schemata: The building blocks of cognition. In R.J. Spiro, B. Bruce, & W.F. Brewer (Eds.), *Theoretical issues in reading and comprehension.* Hillsdale, NJ: Erlbaum.

Rummler, G.A., & Brache, A.P. (1995). *Improving performance: How to manage the white space on the organization chart.* San Francisco: Jossey-Bass.

Russell, T. (Ongoing publication). *No significant difference website.* www.nosignificantdifference.org.

Schmucker, K. (1990). *A taxonomy of simulation software: A work in progress.* www.apple.com/education/LTReview/spring99/simulation/. [Retrieved February 8, 2004.]

Sims, R. (1997). Interactivity: A forgotten art? *Computers in Human Behavior, 13*(2), 157–180.

Singh, H. (2003). Leveraging mobile and wireless internet. *Learning Circuits, 4*(9). www.learningcircuits.org/2003/sep2003/singh.htm

Single, P.B., & Muller, C.B. (n.d). *Electronic mentoring programs: A model to guide best practice and research.* www.apesma.asn.au/mentorsonline/reference/pdfs/muller_and_boyle_single.pdf. [Retrieved November 12, 2004.]

Skinner, B.F. (1961, July 15). The theory behind teaching machines. *Journal of the American Society of Training Directors,* pp. 27–29.

Smith, P.L., & Ragan, T.J. (2000). *Instructional design* (2nd ed.). Upper Saddle River, NJ: Prentice-Hall.

Society for Storytelling. (2004). *What is storytelling?* www.sfs.org.uk/. [Visited July 23, 2004.]

Spiro, R.J., Feltovich, P.J., Jacobson, M.J., & Coulson, R.L. (1992). Cognitive flexibility, constructivism and hypertext: Random access instruction for advanced knowledge acquisition in ill-structured domains. In T. Duffy & D. Jonassen (Eds.), *Constructivism and the technology of instruction.* Hillsdale, NJ: Erlbaum.

Spool, J.M. (1997). Why on-site searching stinks. http://www.uie.com/articles/search_stinks. [Retrieved November 21, 2004.]

Spool, J.M. (2001). Users don't learn to search better. http://www.uie.com/articles/learn_to_search. [Retrieved November 21, 2004.]

Starcevich, M.M. (1998). *Coach, mentor: Is there a difference?* www.coachingandmentoring.com/Articles/mentoring.html [Retrieved May 30, 2004.]

Starr, P. (1994). Seductions of SimPolicy as a simulation game. *The American Prospect, 5*(17).

Stead, J. (1999). Keynote presentation. Training Director's Forum, VNU Business Media, Phoenix, Arizona, June 8, 1999.

Steketee, C. (2002). Students' perceptions of cognitive tools and distributed learning environments. In A. Goody, J. Herrington, & M. Northcote (Eds.), *Quality conversations. Proceedings of the 2002 Annual International Conference of the Higher Education Research and Development Society of Australia (HERDSA).* July 7–10, 2002. Perth, Western Australia: HERSDA Publications, pp. 626–633.

Stepich, D.A., & Newby, T.J. (1989/1990). Designing instruction: Practical strategies. *Performance and Instruction, 28*(7) through *29*(4).

Stolovitch, H. (2004, June 14). *Telling ain't training.* American Society for Training and Development seminar, Alexandria, Virginia.

Stolovitch, H., & Keeps, E. (2004). *Training ain't performance.* Alexandria, VA: ASTD Press.

Stone, D. & Villachica, S. (2004). RAPRO: Employ a rapid ISD approach like the pros! Paper presented at the International Society for Performance Improvement Performance-Based Instructional Design Conference, Chicago, IL, September 30, 2004.

Sugrue, B. (2003a). Validated practice: The research base for human performance technology. ISPI European Conference. Paris, France, September 26, 2003.

Sugrue, B. (2003b). *Use better practice activities, not simulation.* http://66.89.55.104/synergy/emailmgmt/moreinfo/moreinfo.cfm?member_id=309002&sponsor_id=376&content_id=3173&b1=192&b2=194&b3=194. [Retrieved April 4, 2004.]

Sugrue, B. (2004). *ASTD state of the industry report.* Alexandria, VA: American Society for Training and Development.

Thalheimer, W. (2004). Review of research on the seductive-augmentation effect. http://www.work-learning.com/seductive_augmentations.htm. [Retrieved November 10, 2004.]

Thompson, K. (2001). Constructivist curriculum design for professional development: A review of the literature. *Australian Journal of Adult Learning, 41*(1), 94–109.

Thomson Learning. (2002). *Thomson job impact study: Next generation of corporate learning.* Available at www.netg.com. [Retrieved July 14, 2003.]

Tough, A. (1971). *The adult's learning projects: A fresh approach to theory and practice in adult learning.* Toronto: OISE.

Tristram, C. (1996). Wanna be a player? Get a coach! *Fast Company, 5,* p. 145.

Tu, C. (2000). *Strategies to increase interaction in online social learning environments.* Society for Information Technology and Teacher Education International Conference. 2000(1), 1662–1667. [Available: http://dl.aace.org/741.]

Tufte, E. (2001). *The visual display of quantitative information* (2nd ed.). Cheshire, CT: Graphis Press.

University of Arizona Library. (1999). *Glossary.* www.library.arizona.edu/branches/ccp/education/guides/reframe/glossary.html. [Retrieved November 21, 2004.]

University of Minnesota. (2003). *Connecting to success: Mentoring through technology to promote student achievement.* National Center on Secondary Education and Transition Institute on Community Integration (UCEDD). http://ici.umn.edu/ementoring/CTS_Training_Manual.pdf [Retrieved January 4, 2004.]

Van Buren, M.E., & Erskine, W. (2002). *ASTD state of the industry report.* Alexandria, VA: American Society for Training and Development.

Van Buren, M.E., & Sloman, M. (2003). *e-Learning's learning curve: Will they come, will they learn?* American Society for Training and Development International Conference and Exposition. San Diego, California, May 18, 2003.

Vrasidas, C., & McIsaac, M.S. (1999). Factors influencing interaction in an online course. *American Journal of Distance Education, 13*(3), 22–36.

Wagner, E.D. (1994). In support of a functional definition of interaction. *The American Journal of Distance Education, 8*(2), 6–26.

Wallace, G. (2004). *ISPI presidential task force to redefine human performance technology.* 42nd Annual International Society for Performance and Improvement Conference, Tampa, Florida, April 23, 2004.

Watson, J.B. (1913). Psychology as the behaviorist views it. *Psychological Review, 20,* 158–177.

Website development for mentoring programs: Reasons and strategies for being online. (2004). www.nwrel.org/mentoring/elearning.html. [Retrieved January 4, 2004.]

Wedman, J., & Tessmer, M. (1993). Instructional designer's decisions and priorities: A survey of design practice. *Performance Improvement Quarterly, 6*(2), 43–57.

Wenger, E., & Snyder, W. (2000, January/February). Communities of practice: The organizational frontier. *Harvard Business Review,* Reprint R00110.

Westbrook, J.I., & Braithwaite, J.(2000). The health care game: An evaluation of a heuristic, web-based simulation. *Journal of Interactive Learning Research, 12*(1), 89–104.

Wickham, D.P. (Ed.). (2001). Designing effective wizards: A multidisciplinary approach. Upper Saddle River, NJ: Prentice-Hall.

Wilson, C. (2001, March). *Presentation to advanced technical writing class.* Waltham, MA: Bentley College.

Wurman, R. (1989). *Information anxiety.* New York: Doubleday.

Yacci, M. (2000). Interactivity demystified: A structural definition for distance education and intelligent CBT. *Educational Technology, 40*(4), 5–16.

Zemke, R., & Lee, C. (1987). How long does it take? *Training, 24*(6), 75–80.

Zemke, R., & Rossett, A. (2002). A hard look at ISD. *Training, 39*(2), 26–35.

Zinn, L.M. (1983). *Philosophy of adult education inventory.* Boulder, CO: Livelong Learning Options.

Name Index

Subject Index

About the Authors

Margaret Driscoll is a consultant with the human capital management practice of IBM Global Services. In this role she works with organizations interested in strategic planning, e-learning, instructional technology, blended learning, competency modeling, and return on investment. Margaret has worked with pharmaceutical firms, financial services, high-tech, and retail organizations to design, develop, and deliver programs leveraging technology to teach adults. She has also applied her expertise in adult education and instructional technology to inform the development of software for e-learning. Her work has influenced product specifications, competitive analysis, and product direction for learning management systems, authoring tools, and live virtual classroom products.

Margaret is often a featured speaker at national and international training events, such as Online Learning, TRAINING, and the ASTD International Conference and Exposition. She is the author of the best-selling *Web-Based Training: Using Technology to Design Adult Learning Experiences*. Her work has also appeared in the *Journal of Performance Improvement*; *Training and Development* Magazine; *Chief Learning Officer* Magazine; and ASTD's *Learning Circuits* web-zine (www.learningcircuits.org).

In addition to working with learning and development organizations, Margaret teaches at Suffolk University in Boston and the Teachers College of Columbia University, in New York City, where she earned her Ed.D.

Saul Carliner is an assistant professor of educational technology at Concordia University in Montreal, where he teaches courses on human performance improvement, knowledge management, educational evaluation, and adult education. His research interests include emerging genres of online communication for the workplace, means of assessing the productivity, effectiveness, and business performance of workplace content, and informal learning in a variety of contexts.

Saul also has extensive industry experience. He has helped corporate management develop strategies for moving content online and taught numerous workshops. His clients include Berlitz, BellSouth, Georgia-Pacific, Guidant Corporation, IBM, Microsoft Corporation, ST Microelectronics, 3M, UPS, and several state and federal government agencies.

A popular conference speaker, Saul frequently hosts the Training Director's Forum and has given keynote presentations and workshops at training conferences, e-Learning Guild events, ASTD International Conference and Exposition, and the Society for Technical Communication Annual Conference.

The author of over sixty articles in publications such as *Performance Improvement Quarterly, Human Resource Development Quarterly, Training and Development*, and *Learning Circuits*, Saul has written other books including *Training Design Basics, Designing e-Learning*, and *An Overview of Online Learning*. He is a research fellow of the American Society for Training and Development, a certified training and development professional, and a fellow and past international president of the Society for Technical Communication. Saul holds a Ph.D. in instructional technology from Georgia State University.

Pfeiffer Publications Guide

This guide is designed to familiarize you with the various types of Pfeiffer publications. The formats section describes the various types of products that we publish; the methodologies section describes the many different ways that content might be provided within a product. We also provide a list of the topic areas in which we publish.

FORMATS

In addition to its extensive book-publishing program, Pfeiffer offers content in an array of formats, from fieldbooks for the practitioner to complete, ready-to-use training packages that support group learning.

FIELDBOOK Designed to provide information and guidance to practitioners in the midst of action. Most fieldbooks are companions to another, sometimes earlier, work, from which its ideas are derived; the fieldbook makes practical what was theoretical in the original text. Fieldbooks can certainly be read from cover to cover. More likely, though, you'll find yourself bouncing around following a particular theme, or dipping in as the mood, and the situation, dictate.

HANDBOOK A contributed volume of work on a single topic, comprising an eclectic mix of ideas, case studies, and best practices sourced by practitioners and experts in the field.

An editor or team of editors usually is appointed to seek out contributors and to evaluate content for relevance to the topic. Think of a handbook not as a ready-to-eat meal, but as a cookbook of ingredients that enables you to create the most fitting experience for the occasion.

RESOURCE Materials designed to support group learning. They come in many forms: a complete, ready-to-use exercise (such as a game); a comprehensive resource on one topic (such as conflict management) containing a variety of methods and approaches; or a collection of like-minded activities (such as icebreakers) on multiple subjects and situations.

TRAINING PACKAGE An entire, ready-to-use learning program that focuses on a particular topic or skill. All packages comprise a guide for the facilitator/trainer and a workbook for the participants. Some packages are supported with additional media—such as video—or learning aids, instruments, or other devices to help participants understand concepts or practice and develop skills.

- *Facilitator/trainer's guide* Contains an introduction to the program, advice on how to organize and facilitate the learning event, and step-by-step instructor notes. The guide also contains copies of presentation materials—handouts, presentations, and overhead designs, for example—used in the program.

- *Participant's workbook* Contains exercises and reading materials that support the learning goal and serves as a valuable reference and support guide for participants in the weeks and months that follow the learning event. Typically, each participant will require his or her own workbook.

ELECTRONIC CD-ROMs and web-based products transform static Pfeiffer content into dynamic, interactive experiences. Designed to take advantage of the searchability, automation, and ease-of-use that technology provides, our e-products bring convenience and immediate accessibility to your workspace.

METHODOLOGIES

CASE STUDY A presentation, in narrative form, of an actual event that has occurred inside an organization. Case studies are not prescriptive, nor are they used to prove a point; they are designed to develop critical analysis and decision-making skills. A case study has a specific time frame, specifies a sequence of events, is narrative in structure, and contains a plot structure—an issue (what should be/have been done?). Use case studies when the goal is to enable participants to apply previously learned theories to the circumstances in the case, decide what is pertinent, identify the real issues, decide what should have been done, and develop a plan of action.

ENERGIZER A short activity that develops readiness for the next session or learning event. Energizers are most commonly used after a break or lunch to stimulate or refocus the group. Many involve some form of physical activity, so they are a useful way to counter post-lunch lethargy. Other uses include transitioning from one topic to another, where "mental" distancing is important.

EXPERIENTIAL LEARNING ACTIVITY (ELA) A facilitator-led intervention that moves participants through the learning cycle from experience to application (also known as a Structured Experience). ELAs are carefully thought-out designs in which there is a definite learning purpose and intended outcome. Each step—everything that participants do during the activity—facilitates the accomplishment of the stated goal. Each ELA includes complete instructions for facilitating the intervention and a clear statement of goals, suggested group size and timing, materials required, an explanation of the process, and, where appropriate, possible variations to the activity. (For more detail on Experiential Learning Activities, see the Introduction to the *Reference Guide to Handbooks and Annuals*, 1999 edition, Pfeiffer, San Francisco.)

GAME A group activity that has the purpose of fostering team spirit and togetherness in addition to the achievement of a pre-stated goal. Usually contrived—undertaking a desert expedition, for example—this type of learning method offers an engaging means for participants to demonstrate and practice business and interpersonal skills. Games are effective for team building and personal development mainly because the goal is subordinate to the process—the means through which participants reach decisions, collaborate, communicate, and generate trust and understanding. Games often engage teams in "friendly" competition.

ICEBREAKER A (usually) short activity designed to help participants overcome initial anxiety in a training session and/or to acquaint the participants with one another. An icebreaker can be a fun activity or can be tied to specific topics or training goals. While a useful tool in itself, the icebreaker comes into its own in situations where tension or resistance exists within a group.

INSTRUMENT A device used to assess, appraise, evaluate, describe, classify, and summarize various aspects of human behavior. The term used to describe an instrument depends primarily on its format and purpose. These terms include survey, questionnaire, inventory, diagnostic, survey, and poll. Some uses of instruments include providing instrumental feedback to group members, studying here-and-now processes or functioning within a group, manipulating group composition, and evaluating outcomes of training and other interventions.

Instruments are popular in the training and HR field because, in general, more growth can occur if an individual is provided with a method for focusing specifically on his or her own behavior. Instruments also are used to obtain information that will serve as a basis for change and to assist in workforce planning efforts.

Paper-and-pencil tests still dominate the instrument landscape with a typical package comprising a facilitator's guide, which offers advice on administering the instrument and interpreting the collected data, and an initial set of instruments. Additional instruments are available separately. Pfeiffer, though, is investing heavily in e-instruments. Electronic instrumentation provides effortless distribution and, for larger groups particularly, offers advantages over paper-and-pencil tests in the time it takes to analyze data and provide feedback.

LECTURETTE A short talk that provides an explanation of a principle, model, or process that is pertinent to the participants' current learning needs. A lecturette is intended to establish a common language bond between the trainer and the participants by providing a mutual frame of reference. Use a lecturette as an introduction to a group activity or event, as an interjection during an event, or as a handout.

MODEL A graphic depiction of a system or process and the relationship among its elements. Models provide a frame of reference and something more tangible, and more easily remembered, than a verbal explanation. They also give participants something to "go on," enabling them to track their own progress as they experience the dynamics, processes, and relationships being depicted in the model.

ROLE PLAY A technique in which people assume a role in a situation/scenario: a customer service rep in an angry-customer exchange, for example. The way in which the role is approached is then discussed and feedback is offered. The role play is often repeated using a different approach and/or incorporating changes made based on feedback received. In other words, role playing is a spontaneous interaction involving realistic behavior under artificial (and safe) conditions.

SIMULATION A methodology for understanding the interrelationships among components of a system or process. Simulations differ from games in that they test or use a model that depicts or mirrors some aspect of reality in form, if not necessarily in content. Learning occurs by studying the effects of change on one or more factors of the model. Simulations are commonly used to test hypotheses about what happens in a system—often referred to as "what if?" analysis—or to examine best-case/worst-case scenarios.

THEORY A presentation of an idea from a conjectural perspective. Theories are useful because they encourage us to examine behavior and phenomena through a different lens.

TOPICS

The twin goals of providing effective and practical solutions for workforce training and organization development and meeting the educational needs of training and human resource professionals shape Pfeiffer's publishing program. Core topics include the following:

Leadership & Management

Communication & Presentation

Coaching & Mentoring

Training & Development

E-Learning

Teams & Collaboration

OD & Strategic Planning

Human Resources

Consulting

What will you find on pfeiffer.com?

• The best in workplace performance solutions for training and HR professionals

• Downloadable training tools, exercises, and content

• Web-exclusive offers

• Training tips, articles, and news

• Seamless on-line ordering

• Author guidelines, information on becoming a Pfeiffer Affiliate, and much more

Discover more at www.pfeiffer.com

Customer Care

Have a question, comment, or suggestion? Contact us! We value your feedback and we want to hear from you.

For questions about this or other Pfeiffer products, you may contact us by:

E-mail: **customer@wiley.com**

Mail: **Customer Care Wiley/Pfeiffer**
10475 Crosspoint Blvd.
Indianapolis, IN 46256

Phone: **(US) 800-274-4434** (Outside the US: 317-572-3985)

Fax: **(US) 800-569-0443** (Outside the US: 317-572-4002)

To order additional copies of this title or to browse other Pfeiffer products, visit us online at **www.pfeiffer.com**.

For **Technical Support** questions call **(800) 274-4434.**

For authors guidelines, log on to www.pfeiffer.com and click on "Resources for Authors."

If you are . . .

A **college bookstore, a professor, an instructor, or work in higher education** and you'd like to place an order or request an exam copy, please contact jbreview@wiley.com.

A **general retail bookseller** and you'd like to establish an account or speak to a local sales representative, contact Melissa Grecco at 201-748-6267 or mgrecco@wiley.com.

An **exclusively on-line bookseller**, contact Amy Blanchard at 530-756-9456 or ablanchard @wiley.com or Jennifer Johnson at 206-568-3883 or jjohnson@wiley.com, both of our Online Sales department.

A **librarian or library representative**, contact John Chambers in our Library Sales department at 201-748-6291 or jchamber@wiley.com.

A **reseller, training company/consultant, or corporate trainer**, contact Charles Regan in our Special Sales department at 201-748-6553 or cregan@wiley.com.

A **specialty retail distributor** (includes specialty gift stores, museum shops, and corporate bulk sales), contact Kim Hendrickson in our Special Sales department at 201-748-6037 or khendric@wiley.com.

Purchasing for the **Federal government**, contact Ron Cunningham in our Special Sales department at 317-572-3053 or rcunning@wiley.com.

Purchasing for a **State or Local government**, contact Charles Regan in our Special Sales department at 201-748-6553 or cregan@wiley.com.